Between Remembrance and Repair

Between Remembrance and Repair
Commemorating Racial Violence
in Philadelphia, Mississippi

....

CLAIRE WHITLINGER

The University of North Carolina Press Chapel Hill

This book was published with the assistance of the John Hope Franklin Fund of the University of North Carolina Press.

© 2020 The University of North Carolina Press
All rights reserved
Set in Charis by Westchester Publishing Services

Library of Congress Cataloging-in-Publication Data
Names: Whitlinger, Claire, author.
Title: Between remembrance and repair : commemorating racial violence in Philadelphia, Mississippi / Claire Whitlinger.
Description: Chapel Hill : The University of North Carolina Press, 2020. | Includes bibliographical references and index.
Identifiers: LCCN 2019046687 | ISBN 9781469656328 (cloth) | ISBN 9781469656335 (paperback) | ISBN 9781469656342 (ebook)
Subjects: LCSH: Memorialization—Mississippi—Philadelphia. | Civil rights movements—Mississippi—Philadelphia. | Philadelphia (Miss.)—History—20th century. | Philadelphia (Miss.)—History—21st century.
Classification: LCC F349.P47 W47 2020 | DDC 976.2/685—dc23
LC record available at https://lccn.loc.gov/2019046687

Cover illustration: June 21, 1965, marchers memorialize the deaths of three civil rights workers near Philadelphia, Mississippi. *Memorial March* © 1976 Matt Herron/Take Stock.

Portions of this book are derived from previously published material in *Sociological Forum* 30, no. SI (2015), © Wiley Online, DOI: 10.1111/socf.12182; *Race and Justice* 5, no. 2 (2015), © Sage Publications, DOI: 10.1177/2153368715573366; and *Mobilization: An International Quarterly* 24, no. 4 (2019), © Mobilization: An International Quarterly, doi: 10.17813/1086-671X-24-4-455.

For Jamila

Contents

Preface, xi

Acknowledgments, xv

Introduction, 1

1 A Philadelphia (Mississippi) Story, 16
  Remembering in Black and White

2 From Countermemory to Collective Memory, 36

3 Prosecuting Edgar Ray Killen, 60

4 Legislating Civil and Human Rights Education, 80

5 Commissioning Truth and Reconciliation, 109

6 The Transformative Capacity of Commemorating Racial Violence, 132
  Comparing the 1989 and 2004 Commemorations

7 Commemorating Racial Violence as Intergroup Contact, 152

8 Commemoration Is a Constant Struggle, 168

Epilogue, 185
Fifty Years Forward

Appendix A. On Methods, 197

Appendix B. Archival Collections, 207

Appendix C. List of Interviews, 209

Notes, 211

Bibliography, 243

Index, 271

Figures, Graphs, and Tables

Figures

G.1 FBI missing poster for Andrew Goodman, James Chaney, and Michael Schwerner, 99
G.2 Martin Luther King Jr., August 1964, 100
G.3 Mt. Zion United Methodist Church, 101
G.4 Early memory marker for the 1964 murders, 102
G.5 Mayor Rayburn Waddell and the Philadelphia Coalition, May 26, 2004, 103
G.6 Governor Haley Barbour, Congressman John Lewis, and the mother of Andrew Goodman, June 20, 2004, 104
G.7 Stanley Dearman and Rita Bender, June 15, 2015, 105
G.8 Children at fiftieth anniversary commemoration program, June 15, 2014, 105
G.9 Local residents and civil rights movements veterans, June 21, 2014, 106
G.10 Memorial march, June 21, 2014, 107
G.11 Susan Glisson and Summer Institute students, June 2014, 108
A.1 Example of event structure (the 2004 commemoration), 200

Graphs

2.1 Articles mentioning the murders in the *New York Times*, 1964–2009, 42
2.2 Articles mentioning the murders in the *New York Times*, 1989, 43

Tables

4.1 Mississippi state senators who sponsored the education bill (SB 2718), 93
6.1 Comparing the 1989 and 2004 commemorations, 136
6.2 Leadership in Philadelphia, by race and year, 141
A.1 Chronology of the 2004 commemoration, 199

Preface

People often ask if I'm from Mississippi. I'm not. I grew up in the San Francisco Bay Area, where—like many places in the United States—racial inequality was ever present and rarely discussed. Attending a majority-minority public high school investigated by the *Washington Post* in the early 2000s as an example of modern segregation reinforced my interest in race, but it was the location of my childhood home that first sparked my sociological imagination.[1] Adjacent to Highway 101, one of California's major thoroughfares, the modest home where I grew up was situated on a sociocultural fault line, one that separated the vast (mostly white dominated) wealth of Silicon Valley entrepreneurs to the west from communities of color with startling rates of poverty and crime to the east. A desire to understand how such separate spheres were created and maintained led me on a journey around the globe—to South Africa, the Netherlands, and ultimately Mississippi.

In the mid-2000s, I moved to South Africa, where the recent conclusion of the country's Truth and Reconciliation Commission inspired passionate debates about the utility of such commissions—conversations that remain unsettled in both South Africa and the scholarly literature on truth commissions.[2] I later moved to the Netherlands, where the International Criminal Court in The Hague presented an entirely different model for addressing historic patterns of violence, adopting a legal approach. The juxtaposition of these two models challenged me to think more deeply about how various collectivities—governments, schools, businesses, and local communities—confront histories of group-based violence. Moreover, I wanted to better understand the consequences of this memory work and the conditions that enabled these collective efforts to transform their social surroundings. These are the concerns that motivated me as I entered the doctoral program in sociology at the University of Michigan—several thousand miles away from my hometown, where I first became aware of racial inequality and its many ramifications, including those in the realm of memory.

When I returned to the Bay Area for a workshop on transitional justice at the Stanford Law School in 2009, a brief conversation with Lisa Magarrell, then head of the U.S. Accountability Project at the International Center for Transitional Justice, drew my attention to Mississippi. In Mississippi, Magarrell explained, a civil society organization was planning a statewide truth commission, which would be the first of its kind in the United States.³ Eager to learn more about efforts to address histories of racial violence in the United States following my international travels, I thought that Mississippi was an opportune place to visit. That summer, with the support of a generous research grant, I drove from Michigan to Mississippi. I crisscrossed the state, attending regional truth commission meetings and speaking with Mississippians about "racial reconciliation," a term that I would quickly abandon after learning that it provoked strong, sometimes negative, reactions among those Mississippians who equated reconciliation with pacification. Thus, as my research developed, so did the language I used to describe it—shifting from "reconciliation" to "reckoning," a term that appeared to be less politically, culturally, and emotionally laden.

While this initial research proved to be an important primer, it was my visit to Philadelphia, in Neshoba County, that left the most lasting impression. Days before I headed south from Michigan, a colleague had forwarded an H-Net listserve announcement of the forty-fourth annual commemoration service at the Mississippi Martyrs Memorial in Philadelphia, serendipitously scheduled for the day I was set to arrive in the state.⁴ I was eager (and a bit apprehensive) to visit the place I knew only from the film *Mississippi Burning*, which a faculty advisor had encouraged me to watch in preparation for my trip. When I look back, the recommendation to watch a fictionalized depiction of an iconic civil rights story seems peculiar given the robust historical literature on the case. Yet on further consideration, it also suggests the significance of the film to a generation of Americans, many of whom learned, or were reminded, of this chapter of the civil rights movement from Alan Parker's fictional telling in his 1988 Oscar-winning film.

Undoubtedly, the film influenced my initial experience of Neshoba County, when I arrived after nightfall the evening before the commemoration service. Driving into the city, I could not help but think of James Chaney, Andrew Goodman, and Michael Schwerner, who had traveled those same dark, winding roads. The next morning, I grabbed a copy of the local newspaper, the *Neshoba Democrat*, from the hotel's front desk, wrongly assuming that the local newspaper would advertise the service. When I did not see the event featured, I panicked. Had I somehow gotten the month wrong? Was the commemoration service being held in July, not June—as I had originally thought? An advertisement for a memorial service being held the following day added to my confusion. Had I gotten the day wrong, or was this an entirely different memorial service that also commemorated the 1964 murders?

The latter turned out to be true. I had stumbled upon a "fragmented commemoration" before I knew the term or the sociological literature on collective memory that supported such theoretical formulations.[5] A participant at the Mississippi Martyrs Memorial event would later explain to me in a hushed tone that the fortieth anniversary commemoration in 2004 had resulted in two commemoration services organized by different groups and targeting different (albeit somewhat overlapping) audiences—one considered more moderate in its approach to racial reckoning and the other considered more radical. Four years later, the animosity between the two groups was still apparent. Despite this local tension, it appeared that the fortieth anniversary event had improved the reputation of the city that some described as "Mississippi's Mississippi," the most maligned city in the most maligned state. As I traveled throughout the state in the summer of 2009, Philadelphia and its fortieth anniversary commemoration kept emerging in conversations. Over and over again, people I interacted with described the event as the beginning of hopeful, enduring change to the state's racial status quo. It seemed, then, that the commemoration in 2004 had been deeply meaningful, and that what had generated a rift among local agents of memory had also reverberated across Mississippi in ways that seemed significant if not yet fully determined.

Over the coming months, a more concrete project emerged from these initial inductive inquiries, one that focused more explicitly on the causes and consequences of commemorating racial violence and Philadelphia's fifty-year journey—a process that appeared to transform Neshoba County's reputation from the "worst of the worst in racial hatred" to a "model of racial reconciliation," as one historian described it.[6] The following pages synthesize what I learned over nearly ten years of research, a time during which I have come to appreciate Mississippi's complex history and to admire the dynamic, witty, generous, and courageous Mississippians I have had the pleasure of meeting along the way.

Acknowledgments

As I reflect on the many people who made this book possible, I am filled with gratitude. During the years I have worked on this project, my life has been touched by many generous, kind-spirited individuals without whom this book would not have been possible. My first and deepest thanks goes to the sixty-two men and women I interviewed for this study who related their experiences to me with incredible candor, and sometimes with painful pauses. I am honored that you shared your stories with me. Countless others welcomed me into their lives, especially the parishioners at Holy Cross and the Payne family. You made Mississippi a home away from home.

For those at the University of Michigan who helped shape this project from the beginning, thank you for believing in it—and me. Peggy Somers spent many, many hours working with me on this research, from its early conceptualization to its final chapters. She has read countless drafts of articles, fellowship proposals, and chapters, always providing feedback that is thorough, direct, and constructive. It was on a long walk with Peggy in Palo Alto, California, that this project was first conceived. As we rounded the Stanford foothills, Peggy helped direct me through one of those challenging moments in one's professional life when there are more questions than answers. She reminded me why I wanted to be a sociologist and redirected me on a path that would lead to years of fulfilling research. Peggy consistently challenged me to be a better researcher, writer, and scholar. Thank you, Peggy, for your mentorship and your friendship.

Kiyo Tsutsui provided me with an amazing example of professional citizenship. Between organizing international conferences, presenting his work across the globe, and collaborating with researchers at foreign universities, Kiyo has shown me that one can be both rooted and expansive. He continuously challenged me to be more precise in my research methods and my theorization and provided me with invaluable opportunities to grow as a scholar, including a summer at the Max Plank Institute for Religious and Ethnic Diversity in Göttingen, Germany, where my life expanded in immeasurable ways.

Al Young's interest in this project was an unexpected gift. He was a first-rate sounding board, always making time to meet with me despite a chaotic schedule as department chair and offering encouraging words during moments of uncertainty. Moreover, his work has continued to be a constant touchstone throughout this research by providing insights on race in the United States and qualitative methods more generally. His writing on interviewing and identity was especially helpful as I entered the field.

Rob Jansen's keen insights and practical disposition made him an incredible asset to this research. Whether I was pained by an analytical conundrum or befuddled by professional norms, Rob provided thoughtful guidance. I admire his always sharp analysis, even when outside his direct area of expertise. Perhaps one of Rob's greatest gifts was his ability to uncover relevant insights from my initial, jumbled thoughts. I have been tremendously fortunate to have worked with him.

Stephen Berrey was an invaluable resource regarding Mississippi history and introduced me to authors and arguments I might have otherwise overlooked. He coached me through my first presentation at a history conference (never had I felt more like a sociologist!) and offered frequent words of encouragement throughout the project's development. The book is far richer for his involvement.

Along the way, many others at the University of Michigan served as important mentors who gave me the tools and guidance to complete this project. Barbara Anderson was one of the first to support me and my academic interests; John Romani broadened my thinking on civil society during an independent study early in my graduate studies; Howard Kimeldorf provided invaluable guidance on comparative historical methods; Rob Mickey and Pam Brandwein expanded my thinking beyond sociology; and Michael Kennedy nurtured my interest in transitional justice. Futhermore, Elizabeth Armstrong, Müge Göçek, Greta Krippner, Karyn Lacy, Sandy Levistky, Mark Chesler, and Geneviève Zubrzycki have provided helpful feedback and encouragement during my time at Michigan.

None of this would have been possible without fantastic teachers and mentors at George Washington University. Ivy Ken, Daina Stukuls Eglitis, Andrew Zimmerman, Mike Wenger, and Samantha Friedman, you introduced me to a discipline and a career that continues to bring me more joy than I could have hoped for. As I continue my life as a professor, I draw great inspiration from my interactions with you.

While my mentors at George Washington and Michigan provided the foundation of support for this project, I am equally grateful to my colleagues at Furman University who have continued to support me as I further developed this work. Thanks especially to Laura Morris, who offered encouragement and shared commiseration at weekly writing sessions during the final stages of crafting this manuscript. Thanks also to Sally Morris Cote, Ken Kolb, and Amy Jonason, who read proposals and chapters at various stages, and to Kyle Longest, Kristy Maher, Joe Merry, Paul Kooistra, Jason Hansen, Brandon Inabinet, Steve O'Neil, Deborah Allen, Neil Jamerson, Stephanie Hesbacher, Erik Anderson, and Michelle Horhota, with whom I had conversations that enriched my thinking on issues related to history, memory, and methods.

Other friends, family members, and colleagues played key supporting roles in this journey. In no particular order, thanks to Jim Campbell, David Cunningham, Geoff Ward, Raj Ghoshal, Christina Simko, Nicole Fox, Hollie Nyseth Brehm, Kerri Nicoll, Chris Leyda, Emily Bosk, Ethan Schoolman, Alex Jakle, Alex Von Hagen Jamar, Betsy Bringewatt, John Bringewatt, Tova Walsh, Allison Dale-Riddle, Molly Reynolds, Joel Rhuter, Ariana Orozco, Kyra Mangrum, Ashley Jardina, Dave Cottrell, Alton Worthington, Atef Said, Erica Morrell, Dan Hirschman, Nicole High-Steskal, Mathieu Desan, David Smith, Charity Hoffman, Elizabeth Young, Kelly Russell, Jeff Swindle, Austin McCoy, Charles Behling, Susan Glisson, Charles Tucker, April Grayson, Von Gordon, Portia Espy, Neddie Winters, Richard Feit, Brian Habig, and Bill Moore.

Working with the University of North Carolina Press has been a delight. I'm grateful to Joe Parsons, who first approached me about publishing this work, and to Lucas Church, who shepherded this manuscript through the publication process. To others at the University of North Carolina Press who have supported this project's journey from manuscript to print, thank you. I could not ask for a better editorial team.

Social science research can be an expensive endeavor, and the work presented in these pages would not have been possible without generous financial support. The Rackham Graduate School and Department of Sociology at the University of Michigan funded several early research trips to Mississippi. Research trips to South Africa and Switzerland were made possible by the Weiser Center for Emerging Democracies and the Norm Bodine Fellowship Fund. I am also thankful to have received funding from the Max Planck Institute for Religious and Ethnic Diversity and Furman

University's Research and Professional Growth Program, which provided additional resources to continue this work.

My family has remained a source of unwavering support. From early on, they nurtured my sociological imagination by allowing me to explore people, places, and cultures, even when it took me far away from them. They were my biggest cheerleaders, even though there were no sidelines to sit on and academic "victories" sounded like jibberish ("That's fantastic! But what's an R&R?"). Mom, thanks for all the after-work calls and for being my most dependable proofreader. Dad, thank you for driving me to City Teens in East Menlo Park all those years ago and for never questioning how long this book was taking. J. J., Kat, Trey, and Rhys, I still can't believe we all ended up in Greenville!

To my "crazy love," Jean-Baptiste, what forces of the universe brought a blues- and barbeque-loving French-German storyteller into my life, I will never know—but I am forever grateful. In Mississippi, you challenged me to take risks I might not have taken on my own; in Germany, you nursed me back to health; and in South Carolina, you have made our home a refuge. When my turn comes to support you through an all-consuming, multiyear project (and it will soon, I expect), I look forward to showering you with the same love, respect, and enthusiasm.

Finally, to Jules Henry who grew alongside this manuscript, may the social world in all its complexity continue to be a source of wonder and joy.

Between Remembrance and Repair

Introduction

On June 21, 2004, a thousand onlookers gathered for what would be a remarkable event at the Neshoba County Coliseum in Philadelphia, Mississippi.[1] Normally the site of rodeos, car shows, and concerts, the coliseum on this early summer day was set for an event of more serious consequence. It had been exactly forty years since three young civil rights workers—James Chaney, Andrew Goodman, and Michael Schwerner—were murdered outside of town, their bodies hidden in a makeshift grave, and in commemoration of that tragedy, a thirty-member multiracial task force of local citizens had organized a formal, community-wide gathering to honor their lives and loss.

In the packed coliseum, members of the task force—known now as the Philadelphia Coalition—gathered on stage. Among them were members of Philadelphia's Community Development Partnership, the city council, and the Mississippi Band of Choctaw Indians, all organizations whose representatives had signed resolutions calling on legal authorities to use every available resource to seek justice in the case. The coalition was united in its call for action: after forty years of impunity, those responsible for the 1964 murders must at last be held to account.

Although the commemoration and its call for justice were striking departures from the community's prior resistance to public discussions about this discomforting past, for many observers, the event recounted a story they knew all too well. Chaney, Goodman, and Schwerner's fateful ride into Ku Klux Klan territory on June 21, 1964, has been described as "the most depressingly familiar story of the Mississippi movement," having been recounted in numerous books and immortalized in the Oscar-winning film *Mississippi Burning*.[2] Furthermore, the crime had been thoroughly investigated by the Federal Bureau of Investigation and the Department of Justice, revealing in excruciating detail (the former had amassed some 144,000 pages of documentation in the case) how eighteen Klansmen, including local law enforcement officers, had conspired to kill Chaney, Goodman, and Schwerner when the trio returned to Neshoba County to investigate the firebombing of a local church.

The disappearance of the three men had generated global media speculation, and while the national press had adopted and reinforced civil rights organizations' initial suspicions that Philadelphia's sheriff and deputy were somehow involved, most white Philadelphians had believed the disappearances were a "hoax" or a northern conspiracy.[3] By the time the bodies of the three civil rights workers were discovered six weeks after their disappearance, Philadelphia and surrounding Neshoba County had garnered a national reputation as a "strange, tight little town" due to its citizens' evasive—and sometimes hostile—treatment of federal agents and media representatives throughout the investigation.[4] Two years later, after leading a memorial march in Philadelphia, Martin Luther King Jr. famously described the city as "a terrible town . . . the worst I've seen," calling it one of the two places where he had feared for his life.[5] King's assessment further solidified Neshoba County's enduring reputation as a dangerous, hate-filled place, and for decades travelers avoided the county, fearful that they too might face violence, harassment, or worse.

Yet today, to the surprise of many, Philadelphia's efforts to confront the city's history of racial violence has been commended by academics and racial-reconciliation practitioners as a model for other cities hoping to do the same, having precipitated meaningful change in Philadelphia's race relations and catalyzing broader transformations within Mississippi's legal, educational, and civil spheres,[6] including a Neshoba County jury's conviction in 2005 of Edgar Ray Killen for orchestrating the killings; the 2006 enactment by the Mississippi legislature of a groundbreaking education bill that mandated civil and human rights education at every grade level; and the 2009 initiation by Mississippi citizens of the Mississippi Truth Project, initially modeled after South Africa's Truth and Reconciliation Commission.

How do we explain such a striking turnaround? And what role have local commemorations of the 1964 murders played in this process? The national and local press praised the fortieth anniversary commemoration in 2004 as "a remarkable racial reconciliation," "great for the community," and "a turning point," but these early assertions, made in the immediate aftermath of the commemoration, require further investigation. Whether—and, if so, how—the fortieth anniversary commemoration marked a turning point in Philadelphia's race relations, facilitating subsequent institutional transformations, remains an open question, one that needs to be assessed empirically and retrospectively. This is the task ahead: to explore how commemorations of racial violence work and whether they can transform the often contested and tragic conditions from which they emerge.

Although Philadelphia may be unique, given its distinct role in the history of the civil rights movement, many local communities are now confronting their racial and ethnic violence in the past and the present, altering their city's commemorative practices, enacting new rituals of remembrance, and removing monuments and memorials that represent painful pasts. But these commemorative activities are not merely about the past; they are also about transforming the future. In this sense, the process by which the people of Neshoba County have come to terms with their past over the course of fifty years offers insights into the perils and possibilities of local commemorative projects and raises larger questions about whether and how commemorations have consequences.

Remembering Difficult Pasts: Conflict and Cohesion

The events that have unfolded in Neshoba County and across the state of Mississippi since 2004 must be situated within a broader political and cultural landscape, most notably the "memory boom"—a phenomenon ignited after World War II and accelerated by the end of the Cold War—and the accompanying "memory industry" of museums, monuments, memorials, heritage tourism, and legal battles over violence long past that together have come to characterize the second half of the twentieth century.[7] And while scholars have speculated on the multiple origins of this recent passion for memory, many have suggested that the collective trauma of the Holocaust contributed to memory's newfound prominence by cultivating a new ethics of remembrance that values the collective recollection of traumatic pasts as an urgent necessity, best encapsulated by George Santayana's oft-quoted assertion, "Those who cannot remember the past are condemned to repeat it."[8] In this way, as a new relationship between memory and justice began to emerge in the mid-nineteenth century, one that associates public acknowledgment and atonement with moral righteousness and legitimate political action—a new set of "feeling rules" on a macro scale.[9] Consequently, nonacknowledgment has come to seem like a nonoption for many institutional actors, and as a result, the political and cultural landscape is now bedecked with performances of political regret.[10]

One need only scan the current political landscape to observe this seismic normative shift. In the United States alone, cities and states have begun to reckon with decades-old—sometimes centuries-old—racial violence in the form of truth commissions, legislative inquiries, political apologies, and community remembrance projects.[11] In the educational sector, over forty universities have initiated ad hoc committees to investigate the institutions' historic ties to slavery and its legacies.[12] The Equal Justice Initiative's newly erected National Memorial for Peace and Justice has heightened national discussions about historic lynching, raising the stakes for communities unwilling to claim their roles in that history.[13] And since 2015, when Dylann Roof killed churchgoers in Charleston, South Carolina, public battles about the meaning of Confederate iconography have intensified, resulting in the removal of Confederate flags and monuments from—or their contextualization in—a number of southern cities, sometimes with fatal consequences.[14] Although rooted in distinct institutional histories, these developments all share a common thread: in their efforts to address and atone for historic harms, they represent a "politics of regret."[15]

Scholars attuned to the cultural fascia underlying social interactions have long observed such memory work. Whether as objects (monuments, memorials, and museums) or rituals (naming practices, holiday celebrations, and annual observances), commemorations—the tangible representations of collective memory—are symbols that reflect current cultural and political concerns and a community's deepest and most cherished values. Commemoration can therefore be understood as a point on a community's moral compass that both designates the current location and points the way forward.[16]

It is not surprising, then, that scholars of collective memory have been interested in what a group collectively considers worthy of remembering from essentially unmarked stretches of history.[17] In this way, commemoration is a product of social construction: families, neighborhoods, organizations, nations, and other collectivities identify the people and events deserving of distinct recognition, a process that can become self-reinforcing once commemorative activities are institutionalized. Moreover, as Emile Durkheim and his student Maurice Halbwachs observed long ago, enacting such ritual remembrance reinforces membership in the group, or a sense of collective belonging.[18] Thus, scholars across a wide array of disciplines have found that commemorative practices offer rich insights into the deep structures with which a society is built.

This classical understanding of commemoration's social function, however, was cultivated before "trauma and atrocity . . . supplanted heroism and triumph as the linchpins of collective identity"—a development that challenged prevailing understandings of what commemorations are and what they do.[19] After all, the commemorations of triumphant wars and beloved political leaders are quite different from the commemorations of military defeats, contested public figures, and widespread systematic violence. Commemorations of disconcerting, divisive, or otherwise difficult pasts complicate the traditional relationship between ritual remembrance and collective solidarity, often highlighting a culture's sociocultural fault lines. Of course, as recent conflicts over Confederate iconography suggest, commemorations can have multiple meanings, connoting positive values for one social group and negative values for another.

Despite this proliferation of memory projects and practices illuminating difficult pasts, the social role of such collective remembrance remains hotly debated. Does the remembering of difficult pasts facilitate social cohesion and stability or perpetuate social conflict? Proponents of the "never forget" or "never again" position highlight memory's preventive capacity as well as its ethical and social psychological imperatives.[20] In Paul Ricoeur's estimation, remembering violent pasts is not only a moral duty but also a powerful form of redress. "We owe a debt to the victims," Ricoeur insists. "By remembering and telling, we . . . prevent forgetfulness from killing the victims twice."[21] Others, drawing on Freudian psychology, highlight how sites of remembrance enable societies to "work through" collective trauma in productive ways, restoring dignity to survivors and laying the foundation for reconciliation.[22] Still others note collective remembrance's relationship to political practicalities in the context of political transitions: as authoritarian regimes gave way to third-wave democracies in the late 1980s and early 1990s, states enacted memory practices such as truth commissions, trials, and reparations in hope of acknowledging the past, restoring trust in civic institutions, and legitimizing ascendant political regimes.[23]

In recent years, however, arguments in favor of forgetting have gained new resilience. In his highly publicized book *In Praise of Forgetting*, David Rieff takes on the prevailing pro-memory zeitgeist, arguing forcefully in defense of collective forgetting. Drawing on such intractable conflicts as those in the Balkans and Palestine, Rieff highlights how centuries-old resentments continue to foment rancor and revenge, perpetuating social conflict and division in the present. In this way, Rieff and others suggest, remembrance may contribute to the pursuit of justice but at the expense of peace.[24] Furthermore, proponents of this position note the paradoxical relationship between collective memory and collective identity. While collective memory has long been understood as the cornerstone of collective identity, collective memory also fosters in-group loyalties, often to the detriment of intergroup relations.[25] In this way, those who criticize the contemporary "surfeit of memory" bemoan a culture of victimhood and the tyranny of guilt whereby political energies congeal around cultural rather than civic identity, potentially sowing the seeds of future identity-based conflicts.[26] Indeed, philosophers have long noted the social significance of collective amnesia as the starting point from which to build a new society.[27] Undergirded by this logic, societies emerging from violent conflict have adopted public forgetting as state policy. This practice goes back to ancient Greece and occurred more recently in Spain, where some people view the *pacto del olvido* (pact of oblivion) of the era after the regime of General Francisco Franco as a critical agreement between political factions that made way for democracy immediately following the military dictator's death.[28]

It appears, then, that we are in a bind. The very memory practices that may enable justice, recognition, and conflict prevention may also intensify group-based division, foster conflict, and inhibit peace. But this binary debate—whether to remember or to forget—is too simplistic. As Michael Schudson reminds us, "memory is a distortion since memory is invariable and inevitably selective. A way of seeing is a way of not seeing, a way of remembering is a way of forgetting too."[29] What is at stake are multiple ways of remembering, battles over which memories come to be privileged in the public spheres as part of a collective narrative and which fade into oblivion. So rather than presenting commemorations of violent pasts as entirely beneficial or detrimental to social life, as popular and scholarly texts often do, this study sheds light on the complexity of commemorating racial violence, highlighting the conditions under which commemorations of racial violence facilitate social change. After all, we know little about what memory practices do in the communities where they take place, an empirical question that social scientific research is particularly well suited to investigate.

Memory Movements and Social Change

When most people think of social movements, large-scale movements come to mind—such as the civil rights movement, the women's movement, the environmental movement, and so on. But social movements—defined as sustained collective challenges to political and cultural authority—are not only global or national in scope. Social movements also take place on the local level, organized around grievances that are particular to a county, city, or neighborhood. These are exemplified by NIMBY (not in my back yard) movements, in which local actors seek to prevent changes to their immediate surroundings. Likewise, "memory movements," as sustained efforts to change or preserve particular representations of the past, occur on different scales, from efforts to honor Martin Luther King Jr. with a national holiday to designating historic preservation districts or erecting plaques to highlight the significance of a street corner.[30] Memory movements, large or small, resemble what some scholars call "new social movements," whose goals can be understood as more cultural than political and, given the causes' historic invisibility, whose very existence is a victory.

Regardless of whether they change others' perceptions or transform social structures, new social movements make headway by initiating silenced conversations that may well lead to structural change, given time and persistence.[31] Like new social movements, memory movements by virtue of their very existence raise awareness of marginalized pasts—or marginalized interpretations of the past—and thereby represent a success, regardless of whether they change opinions in the short term. This was certainly the case in Neshoba County, where the memory of the murders had long been suppressed in the public sphere. The fortieth anniversary commemorative observance thus represents a notable success for the Philadelphia Coalition, which sought to raise awareness about the 1964 killings. But the group wanted more. They understood that the commemorative event was the beginning of a process that could, if nurtured, facilitate broader social change.

Until recently, research on collective memory developed independently of that on social movements, despite multiple points of synergy. This is beginning to change. As several recent review articles demonstrate, sociologists have begun to explore how memory and movements interact.[32] Researchers have found, for instance, that the collective memory of traumatic events shapes public opinion and, in some cases, future activism.[33] In one particularly notable case, Fredrick Harris observes that the remembrance of Emmet Till's tragic murder in 1954 motivated political participation in the civil rights movement by younger cohorts. In Michael Dawson's words, "The collective memory of the African American community continued to transmit from generation to generation a sense that race was the defining interest in individuals' lives and that the well-being of blacks individually and as a group could be secured only by continued political and social agitation."[34]

Drawing on symbolic material from the past can also be a conscious strategy whereby social movement actors appropriate historical symbols, events, and figures to mobilize potential participants—examples include the revival of John Brown as a sympathetic character to spur abolitionist activism and the Tea Party movement's historically informed choice of name.[35] These examples demonstrate how social movements rely on memory to provide legitimacy, identity, and continuity. It is the memory of movements that generates the repertoires in which activists find inspirations for songs, slogans, and tactics.[36] A song such as "We Shall Overcome" is suffused with cultural meaning, summoning memories of the struggles of those who had previously used the refrain and forging a bridge from past to present. Ron Eyerman perhaps best captures the multivalent relationship between memory and movements: social movements, he says, are the "bearers and shapers of individual and collective memory."[37]

Because memory is malleable, fraught with moral significance, and often contested, collective memory (and, by consequence, commemoration) is often the result of activities that resemble social movements. Memory activists, sometimes referred to as "mnemonic entrepreneurs" or "memory choreographers," operate much like Howard Becker's "moral entrepreneurs"—enterprising leaders who, often with humanitarian motivations, draw the public's attention to "deviant" behavior and mobilize its energies for a cause they deeply believe in.[38] Notably, such memory activists (whether or not they would identify themselves as activists) negotiate meanings about the past in the context of present institutional constraints and often in competition with other agents of memory.[39] Thus, those who succeed in crafting commemorations that become deeply embedded within the collective memory of a nation, community, or other social group are those who are able to frame the commemoration in a way that appeals to powerful constituencies, mobilize sufficient financial and human resources, and take advantage of political opportunities as they arise.[40] Each of these social dynamics—framing, resource mobilization, and political opportunities—are pillars of contemporary social movement research and have begun to enter the lexicon of scholarship on collective memory, providing helpful analytical tools for making sense of collective efforts to commemorate violent pasts.

Current research on memory movements draws heavily on this well-established social movement theory to suggest that memory movements successfully alter representations of the past when political opportunities are advantageous, resources are plentiful, and frames resonate with target audiences.[41] For example, Timothy Kubal finds that memory movements succeed in institutionalizing their collective memory when demographic changes disrupt the political status quo, when movement organizations mobilize pan-ethnic constituents, and when the memory movements use resonant frames.⁴² Likewise, Raj Ghoshal emphasizes external factors when arguing that "mnemonic opportunity structures" powerfully affect the success of commemorative initiatives, suggesting that memory movements are most advantageous when the event being commemorated was considered important at the time it took place (ascribed significance); when the main "characters" were depicted as sympathetic victims or valiant heroes at the time of their death (moral valence); and when the present-day environment had high levels of commemorative capacity, referring to the number of institutions (libraries, archives, and universities) that support commemorative efforts.⁴³

Additionally, Elizabeth Armstrong and Suzanna Crage find that a particular event (that is, the Stonewall Riots) became central to gay collective memory due to a confluence of external and internal factors.⁴⁴ These include opportunities in the cultural and political environment, the resonance of the Stonewall narrative, the commemorative form, and the organizing capacity of local movement groups, what they refer to as "mnemonic capacity."⁴⁵ In its initial formulation, however, mnemonic capacity is conceptualized somewhat narrowly as the skills and resources required to enact a commemorative vehicle. To commemorate a difficult past that continues to be culturally and politically salient requires more, as such contexts that are particularly ripe for mnemonic battles about the nature and relevance of the past.⁴⁶ Commemorating difficult pasts demands that organizers engage in dual tasks: constructing commemorative vehicles and maintaining intergroup relations. After all, those who engage in the labor of memory work are not merely rational actors who deploy resources and strategies; they embody social group identities and are embedded within distinct—and sometimes overlapping—"communities of memory" that influence their experiences of the past, their willingness to participate in commemorative projects, and their hopes for the future.⁴⁷ Regardless of a group's skills and resources, intergroup conflict, which is often grounded in different perceptions of the past, can threaten the viability of commemorative projects and possibilities for continued mnemonic activism.

It is also important to note that current research often fails to distinguish memory movements from the commemorative work they pursue, instead conceptualizing commemorative projects as evidence of a priori memory movements. While commemorative projects may be the product of memory movements, commemorative initiatives may also cultivate memory movements that are analytically distinct from the conditions out of which they emerged. So while current scholarship focuses on commemorations as outcomes of collective action, this study reverses the causal arrow to explore the commemorative outcomes themselves, or when and how commemorative activities facilitate social change.

Skeptics will correctly note that most commemorations, including those of racial violence, are often banal in a broader social sense despite being meaningful to those involved. Many commemorative activities happen with modest fanfare and leave little in their wake other than the satisfaction or frustration of those who participated, and major social structures remain unchanged. But the fortieth anniversary commemoration in Philadelphia appeared to have significant reverberations across various spheres of social life, contradicting general patterns and allowing a more nuanced analysis of commemoration's causal consequences.[48] The question is, how?

Between Remembrance and Repair: Studying Commemorative Outcomes

To assess whether and how the fortieth anniversary commemoration in Philadelphia was, in fact, a turning point toward more stable and durable trajectories, I had to begin at the end, starting not with the commemoration and moving forward but with the outcomes that might reasonably be linked to it and working my way backward in time. Given the range of possible outcomes, I approached this process inductively, first probing archival materials for insights into the commemoration's aftermath and later conducting interviews. Interviews with key informants became an essential part of my research: the people closest to the commemoration planning process were deeply invested in the event's potential reverberations and provided rich insights into the sequence of events and the motivations underlying key decisions in the historical sequence. Their understanding of their work provided focus as I investigated whether these reported outcomes could be verified empirically and systematically.

The archival and interview data revealed numerous outcomes, ranging from the personal to the political and from the micro to the macro. New friendships were formed, new organizations were founded, new policies were written, and new fissures were opened. And despite notable institutional transformations in the wake of the fortieth anniversary commemoration, not all participants were pleased with the event. By 2005, a second group of memory activists had coalesced around a different memorial event, demanding more rigorous action than that proposed by the Philadelphia Coalition.

Given this panoply of outcomes, I focused the second stage of my research on four potential (or hypothesized) institutional outcomes, three of which appear in this book: the 2005 prosecution of Killen; the passage in 2006 of the civil and human rights education bill, Mississippi Senate Bill 2718; and the Mississippi Truth Project. The fourth, the 2009 election of James Young as Philadelphia's first black mayor, may be attributable to the commemoration (Young was a member of the Philadelphia Coalition), but my research did not yield enough concrete data to confirm the relationship between these two occurrences.[49] To assess whether and how these three key events were causally connected to the fortieth anniversary commemoration in 2004, I employed the tools of comparative historical sociology: counterfactual analysis and systematic comparison. Although counterfactual analysis has long been a part of the sociological tradition, going back to Max Weber, critics have often dismissed it as virtual history.[50] After all, how can we know with any certainty what would have happened? All history, including natural history, takes place in an open system. "Replaying the tape," according to Stephen Gould's depiction of paleontology in *A Wonderful Life*, would inevitably result in a different outcome. But this does not prevent us from making causal generalizations.[51] In fact, any attempt to make causal claims about historical phenomena involves counterfactual reasoning.[52] To claim that X caused Y is also to suggest that if X had not occurred, neither would Y. In Johannes Bulhof's words, "Counterfactuals, causes, and explanations are three sides of the same strange three-sided coin; you cannot have one without the other two."[53] Thus, after providing historical context for Philadelphia's commemorative practices, this book examines the following counterfactual question: Had the 2004 commemoration never happened, would these three outcomes still have occurred? To systematize this counterfactual analysis, I employed event structure analysis, a formal qualitative method that allowed me to trace the causal connections between acts of remembrance and subsequent episodes of social repair.[54]

After establishing that the Killen trial, the education bill, and the Mississippi Truth Project were causally connected to the fortieth anniversary commemoration, I set out to explain why, drawing analytical leverage from a structured comparison. Fifteen years earlier, an interracial coalition of local citizens had organized a remarkably similar commemoration to mark the twenty-fifth anniversary of the murders, which had failed to yield such transformative outcomes. The final section of this book explores the fortieth anniversary commemoration alongside this negative case, asking what factors were present in 2004—and missing in 1989—that enabled the fortieth anniversary commemoration to be transformative. Social scientists will recognize this comparative logic as inspired by John Stuart Mill's method of difference.[55]

To answer these questions, this study relies on a combination of archival, interview, and observational data. After familiarizing myself with the secondary historical literature on the civil rights movement, the Freedom Summer, and the 1964 Mississippi Burning murders, I conducted research at six archives that provided rich troves of historical documentation (newspaper clippings, speeches, meeting notes, and journal entries) related to the 1964 Mississippi Summer Project and the killings that came to define it, as well as some material related to early commemorative efforts.[56] Given the time, effort, and serendipity required for documents to be archived, these traditional archives had less information related to events after 1989 at the time this research was conducted. To fill in this gap in the textual data, I turned to local and regional news coverage, which proved to be especially rich. The *Neshoba Democrat*, *Meridian Star*, and *Clarion-Ledger* covered the commemorations of milestone anniversaries (the tenth, twentieth, twenty-fifth, and so on) and those that were held every year after 2004. For information about certain commemorations, however, national news coverage was more illuminating. I located national news articles using targeted word searches in the Access World News database.[57] Beyond media sources and traditional archives, I received access to the personal papers (meeting notes, journals, and emails) of several key informants. These were especially valuable, as they provided contemporaneous accounts of the historical events of interest.

In-depth interviews with sixty-two key informants complemented this archival data, providing nuance and context to the textual sources and shedding light on happenings that were not likely to appear in an official state-sanctioned archive. Interviews were open-ended and tailored to each informant, each of whom had a unique relationship to the history under investigation. The informants included members of the Philadelphia Coalition; members of the 1989 commemoration task force; staff members of the William Winter Institute for Racial Reconciliation; a range of government officials, including several from the Mississippi Department of Education and Governor Haley Barbour's administration; and racial reconciliation practitioners from Mississippi and beyond who at one point intersected with the historical trajectories of the fortieth anniversary commemoration. These informants were gracious, frank, and remarkably generous with their time (and their sweet tea!).

In an effort to protect the privacy of those interviewed in the relatively small social ecosystem that is Mississippi generally and Neshoba County in particular, I have refrained from attributing some quotations to specific individuals, choosing instead to specify an aspect of their identity (for example, their gender or race) or their relationship to the commemoration, the trial, the education bill, or the truth project as a way to provide some context for the quotation while also maintaining anonymity. However, I do use specific names when quoting from previously published texts or when the interviewee has explicitly granted me permission to do so. Interviews generally lasted from one to four hours and in most cases were recorded and transcribed in full.

Finally, participant observation also constitutes an important part of the data. Since 2009, when I first entered the field to attend the forty-fourth anniversary commemoration, I have participated in six consecutive commemoration services from 2009 to 2014, marching alongside memory activists—a harrowing task in Mississippi's oppressive June heat—and noting both the continuity and the change in the commemorations during that time. Over the course of ten years, I spent a total of thirteen months in Philadelphia and the surrounding area, including nearly half a year living in nearby Union, Mississippi, the town of two thousand from which Killen hailed. Residing in the county proved to be especially useful, as it allowed me to live as a local and gave me insight into the relationship between the city and the county that had until then remained obscure. On-the-ground interactions with residents of Neshoba County in myriad institutional settings and social circles—at family dinner tables, professional conferences, after-school clubs, political meetings, church services, and local festivals—inform my analyses of texts, interactions, and other happenings.

The Path Ahead

Previous research on Philadelphia and Neshoba County focuses overwhelmingly on the 1964 murders and subsequent legal trials (in 1967 and 2005), providing relatively little insight into the area's commemorative practices. Such research, for example, often depicts the twenty-five years following the murders as "the long silence," a description that is not entirely accurate.[58] It overlooks the annual commemoration services hosted by Mt. Zion United Methodist Church, the African American church that the three civil rights workers visited just before their deaths. In chapter 1, I recognize and reconstruct the commemorative activities of Philadelphia's African

American community, which reveal a different Philadelphia story. The chapter uncovers two distinct communities of memory: one characterized by Philadelphia's dominant white public sphere, the so-called official, government-sanctioned memory; the other representing a powerful and persistent countermemory embedded in Philadelphia's African American community.

Having established the dual trajectories of Philadelphia's communities of memory, in chapter 2 I consider how Philadelphia's long-silenced countermemory became part of the community's collective memory. Here I examine the community-wide commemoration services in 1989 and 2004, which can be understood as silence-breaking commemorations—that is, as commemorations that punctuated the silence in Philadelphia's dominant public sphere. By comparing these two commemorations, I suggest that commemorating silenced pasts is arguably more challenging than commemorating merely difficult pasts.

Chapters 3, 4, and 5 explore three racially significant transformations (the Killen trial, the civil and human rights education bill, and the Mississippi Truth Project) and whether they can be attributed to Philadelphia's fortieth anniversary commemoration in 2004. Chapter 3 investigates how Killen came to be prosecuted forty-one years after the fact, especially following several previous failed attempts to prosecute him. Chapter 4 examines the connection between the 2004 commemoration and another racially significant transformation: Senate Bill 2718, which mandated civil rights education across the state of Mississippi. This chapter provides new historical perspective on the legislation—the first of its kind in the country—by tracing the legislation's origins to the fortieth anniversary commemoration in Philadelphia. In chapter 5, I explore the relationship between the 2004 commemoration and the Mississippi Truth Project, which was initially modeled after South Africa's postapartheid Truth and Reconciliation Commission and later focused on oral history collection, among other community-based truth projects.

With the connections between the three racially significant transformations (the Killen trial, Senate Bill 2718, and the truth project) and the 2004 commemoration established, chapter 6 examines the differences between the 1989 and 2004 commemorations to identify the factors that were present in 2004—but not in 1989—that enabled the 2004 commemoration to have transformative outcomes. This chapter explores how the members of the fortieth anniversary commemoration task force, initially drafted to organize a onetime commemorative observance, came to understand themselves as the Philadelphia Coalition, an organizational structure and collective identity that cultivated deep commitment to broader mnemonic activism. Chapter 7 then examines the social psychological aspects of commemorating racial violence that made this level of commitment possible. This chapter extends insights from the social psychologist Gordon Allport's "contact theory" to commemorations of racial violence, suggesting that such commemorations can provide the foundation for broader social change when the commemoration planning process involves sustained informal interaction between members of racial groups that have experienced conflict; these groups engage equally in the task of planning the commemoration; and the commemoration is supported by relevant authorities, laws, or customs.[59]

Finally, while the bulk of the historical analysis focuses on events that occurred in the period between 2004 and 2014, much has happened since. The epilogue brings the Killen trial, the education bill, and the truth project up to the present, highlighting both progress and setbacks. In many ways, the three transformations unfolded at a peculiar time in Philadelphia's history, and in some respects, the progress of the 2000s have been rolled back. Since then, Mississippi has made national headlines when citizens organized a "Confederate heritage" ballot petition that would have required all public venues to play "Dixie" (a Confederate anthem) immediately following the "Star Spangled Banner."[60] And as states across the South abandoned Confederate emblems in the wake of the 2015 Charleston shootings, Mississippi stood firm: in February 2016, Governor Phil Bryant declared April "Confederate History Month"—just two weeks before nineteen bills seeking to remove the symbol of the Confederacy from Mississippi's flag died in committee.[61] Thus, when considered in its entirety, the story of Philadelphia does not reveal a continuous linear march toward mnemonic inclusivity. Rather, it reveals the challenges and complexity of commemorating racial violence over decades as various constituencies assert different, sometimes conflicting, interpretations of the past. Now having reviewed the path ahead, let us begin at the beginning.

1 A Philadelphia (Mississippi) Story

Remembering in Black and White

. . . .

The sheer number of aphorisms about remembrance can make the subject seem almost trite. They include: "The struggle of man against power is the struggle of memory against forgetting;"[1] "History is written by the victors;"[2] and "He who controls the past controls the future."[3] But encoded in these adages is an expression of a common experience and a general truth: that history and memory are embedded within systems of power—systems that privilege certain historical "facts" and relegate others to oblivion. The local memory of the 1964 murders of civil rights workers James Chaney, Andrew Goodman, and Michael Schwerner is no different, for while the contours of Philadelphia's story are known, key elements remain obscured—elements that illuminate how the residents (black, white, and Choctaw) of Philadelphia and its surrounding county have reckoned with their racially charged past.

Most histories of Neshoba County provide only a cursory account of its commemorative practices. In general, they depict the twenty-five years following the murders as "the long silence," a period during which the murders remained unacknowledged in any official capacity and local people maintained a conspiracy of silence even as the murders became memory.[4] Describing the twenty-five years following the murders as "silent," however, is not wholly accurate. It overlooks the vibrant commemorative landscape that was nurtured by Philadelphia's and Neshoba County's African American communities, sometimes putting them at great risk. As white residents largely avoided discussing what they often referred to as "the troubles" of 1964 in the decades following the murders, black churches erected monuments, hosted memorial services, and nourished protesters who marched in memory of the three civil rights activists. Philadelphia, then, was not silent about the murders. Rather, its long history of commemoration has been silenced by historical reconstructions that conflate the city's history with the history of its white citizenry, a phenomenon that has been common throughout much of southern historiography.[5]

This sort of erasure is not specific to professional historians. Rather, it stems from a long-standing tendency to treat white history as synonymous with southern identity. Florence Mars, a member of one of Neshoba County's most prominent white families, reflects on this in her 1977 memoir, *Witness in Philadelphia*: "As I was growing up, I learned how the South saw itself . . . *southerners were white; Negroes were Negroes.*"[6] Furthermore, Mars remembers having been inculcated with a sense of white superiority. "White civilization of the South," she recalled, "was one of the greatest in the history of the world. Negro culture," alternately, "was primitive and greatly inferior." Consequently, this prevailing metanarrative rendered invisible the contributions of African Americans to southern life and its recorded history.[7]

Acknowledging the commemorative activities of local African Americans thus casts new light on memory practices in Philadelphia and Neshoba County. It reveals two parallel mnemonic trajectories: one embedded within Philadelphia's dominant white public sphere, and the other enacted within Philadelphia's black counterpublic—a space where local African Americans and their allies preserved competing versions of the past. To understand these parallel mnemonic trajectories and their significance for Philadelphia's community-wide commemorations in 1989 and 2004, one must understand the history of Neshoba County itself, for as Mars observes, "In Neshoba County, Mississippi, the basement of the past is not very deep. All mysteries of the present seem to be entangled in the total history of the county."[8]

The Red-Clay Hills of Neshoba

The recorded history of Neshoba County begins in the 1830s, when white settlers from Georgia and the Carolinas descended on the red-clay hills that would become the twenty-four square miles that made up the county of Neshoba, the Choctaw word for wolf. Not far from Philadelphia lies a massive burial mound, Nanih Waiya, that contains the remains of some eighteen thousand Choctaw Indians who had long inhabited the sloping hills and swamps (called *bogues* in Choctaw) that would come to be dominated by white pioneers who sought to eke out a living in cotton after the U.S. government compelled the Choctaw to move to the Oklahoma Territory following the Treaty of Dancing Rabbit Creek in 1831. Not all the Choctaw submitted to this forced emigration, however. Some five thousand refused to relinquish their land, and these are the ancestors of the nearly four thousand Choctaw who reside in Neshoba County today and have been recognized as the Mississippi Band of Choctaw Indians.[9]

By 1860, some thirty years after the county's founding, there were roughly twenty-two white landowning families in the region, eighteen of which still had direct descendants there in 1960.[10] There was little migration to or from Neshoba County during its history, a product of its remote location and hostile conditions: the same thick red clay that failed to yield the rich cotton crops of the Mississippi Delta made it difficult to traverse the county. As late as the 1940s, Mars recalls her daily rides with "Poppaw" to visit his tenants. Prudent investments had allowed her grandfather to become the largest landowner in the county. But on rainy days, the slippery, clotted clay was unmoved by Poppaw's local status. "Except for a sprinkling of native gravel in the hillier sections of the county and the occasional sandy spot," remembers Mars, "the roads were pure red clay, which, when they were wet," caused wagons to slip or get bogged down. "The roads weren't made for automobiles in those days," Mars lamented, "though not many people had them anyway."[11]

Indeed, it wasn't until 1931 that the first road in the county was graveled, much later than was the case in counties whose seat stood between two major cities. Through the early twentieth century, transporting goods from Philadelphia, the Neshoba County seat since 1838, to Meridian, thirty-five miles to the east, could take up to three days, and receiving goods from Jackson via flatboat on the Pearl River could take upward of one month.[12] Local merchants perhaps should have been more civic-minded about Neshoba's isolation, but they benefited greatly from the limited outside competition and were instrumental in keeping the highways unpaved.[13] In 1909, the editor of the county newspaper, the *Neshoba Democrat*, described the county in the early twentieth century as being "classed as one of the most under-developed and backwoods counties in the state." "This impression," he wrote, "went out over the country not on account of the barrenness of the soil or the ignorance of the citizenship but on account of the fact that we were without telegraph and railroad communication with the outside world."[14]

The beginning of the twentieth century brought new hardships to the region but also new possibilities. The railroad, which finally arrived in Philadelphia in 1905, stimulated commerce. However, by then the boll weevil had destroyed much of the cotton crop, an additional blow to the land and its people—whose losses during the Civil War were still in living memory. As white farmers left for greener pastures, the racial demographics of the region shifted, and the already sparse population of the county became sparser still. In the 1940s, a white businessman sold small lots to black residents on credit. This further bolstered the population in the western portion of Philadelphia, which would come to be known as Independence Quarters,[15] but here—as in most Mississippi towns at the time—"the other side of the tracks bespoke another universe."[16] Unlike the white part of town, with picturesque homes on avenues with idyllic names like Poplar, Independence Quarters had no sidewalks, no running water, no sewer system, and until the 1950s no garbage pickup—as well as no mail delivery until much later.[17]

Though the county's whites prided themselves on having "good race relations," the county was no stranger to racial violence and intimidation. The regional resurgence of the Ku Klux Klan in the 1920s[18] led local Klansmen to burn crosses throughout the county. Residents of the county also seemed indifferent to due process. According to Willie Morris, during a four-year period there were thirty-three homicides, and only two culprits "paid their debt to society"—and they did it by hanging themselves in their jail cells.[19] But local white leaders spoke out against the Klan and the climate it cultivated. In an open letter published in the *Neshoba Democrat* that took up nearly one-third of the front page, Ab DeWeese, who owned a prominent lumber company in the area, admonished the Klan: "I take the position that [the Klan] is acting in opposition to constitutional government. It assumes to indict, to represent the jurors, and to judge, and then to execute, and this power and right should come through the constitutional government. And furthermore, it acts behind a mask and does not out in the open." Another white businessman regretted that "so many weak-kneed politicians and preachers had become intimidated to the point that they were afraid to express their honest convictions on the Klan issue."[20] Clayton Rand, the editor of the *Neshoba Democrat* since 1918, was equally dismayed. While viewing the Klan as having served a "good purpose" during Reconstruction, defending the South from "plunderers and brigands," Rand described the 1920s Klan in his newspaper as "an outlaw organization going about its work behind masks and in clown suits."[21] The vocal public resistance to the Klan that was evident in the 1920s was notably missing in the 1960s.

The "Long, Hot Summer"

In 1964, the Philadelphia Chamber of Commerce issued a promotional brochure describing Neshoba County as "a thriving community" of twenty-one thousand people—with six thousand residing in the county seat,

Philadelphia—located "in the East Central part of the beautiful Magnolia state."[22] "The most outstanding attraction," the brochure boasted, "is the friendly and hospitable people who make the area their home. A visitor to our community finds an old-fashioned welcome and a degree of friendliness that exists in no other place." In addition to a "diversified" industrial base—milk, motors, and lumber—the chamber advertised the county's new hospital, swimming pool, nine-hole golf course, and numerous lakes. "For the hunter," it claimed, "Neshoba County is a paradise."

This depiction of a cheerful, industrious county provides a stark contrast to the reputation it would have earned by the summer's end. The summer of 1964 is often referred to as the "long, hot summer," a phrase that describes not only Mississippi's stifling summer climate but also the racial tensions that came to a boiling point during those particularly contentious months. Over the previous decade, private citizens and state actors had buttressed their defenses against so-called civil righters who threatened to dismantle Jim Crow segregation, but these invaders seemed to be gaining ground. Not even the citizens' councils—local organizations founded in reaction to the Supreme Court's decision in *Brown v. Board of Education*, which mandated the desegregation of public schools at "all deliberate speed"—could stay the impending offensive planned by the Council of Federated Organizations.[23] COFO, as it was known, became the umbrella organization coordinating the efforts of civil rights organizations operating in the state, primarily the National Association for the Advancement of Colored People (NAACP), the Congress of Racial Equality (CORE), and the Student Nonviolent Coordinating Committee (SNCC). Such coordination became crucial when disagreements among the organizations threatened to destroy the fledgling Mississippi movement from within. Originally created before the 1961 Freedom Rides and revamped in 1962, COFO became the touchstone of civil rights activity in the state and a lightning rod for the animosity toward it.

Since 1954, the citizens' councils had been the state's self-appointed watchdogs, resisting educational content presented at public schools and universities that challenged segregation. A grassroots movement initiated by Robert Patterson in Indianola, Mississippi, and made up primarily of affluent white men, the councils sought to maintain school segregation without violence, earning them the moniker "Uptown Klan."[24] But they had other tools at their disposal. Within the first three months, the councils had twenty-five thousand dues-paying members, and they intimidated activists, people suspected of being activists, and those sympathetic to activists through a range of economic and political tactics such as boycotting businesses, firing employees, or revoking the leases of rental homes.[25]

Such treatment of civil rights activists and sympathizers was not limited to the private sphere. In 1956, the Mississippi Legislature created the Mississippi State Sovereignty Commission, a government body with a broad mandate to "do and perform any and all acts deemed necessary and proper to protect the sovereignty of the state of Mississippi and her sister states from encroachment thereon by the Federal Government."[26] Throughout its tenure (1956–77), the commission served a variety of functions, at first acting as the "eyes and ears" of Mississippi, engaging in a public relations campaign to counter negative depictions of the state, and obtaining information to maintain segregation, and later—following passage of the 1964 Civil Rights Act—finding ways to resist the possibility of public integration through discourse and suggestions for individual action.[27] But in 1964, the organization's investigative program was in full force, suppressing civil rights activities by cultivating a network of informants (white and black) to gather surveillance on tens of thousands of suspected activists and sympathizers. By 1967, according to the commission's former director, Earl Johnson Jr., the organization had dossiers on approximately 250 organizations and about ten thousand individuals alleged to "work for or represent subversive, militant, or revolutionary groups."[28] In addition to wiretapping, bugging, and influencing press coverage, the commission would cut credit, audit taxes, or cancel insurance of those who dared to support COFO. It was, in the words of the journalist Wilson F. Minor, "something akin to NKVD [Soviet Secret Police] among the cotton patches."[29]

The commission wasn't the only Mississippi organization shoring up the state's defenses.[30] The Ku Klux Klan, which had been dormant in Mississippi since the 1930s, began to mobilize alongside state actors. Sam Bowers, a former soldier in the U.S. Navy and the owner of a vending machine company in Laurel, Mississippi, started his own chapter of the organization—a Klavern he called "the White Knights"—appointing himself imperial wizard and protector of the realm. Like Bowers, other less affluent white Mississippians were anxious about the future and found his message appealing: "The purpose and function of this organization is to preserve Christian Civilization. . . . The Will and Capacity of the Liberals, Comsymps, Traitors, Atheists, and Communists to resist and subvert Christian, American Principles MUST BE DESTROYED. This is our Sacred Task."[31]

By the spring of 1964, more than five thousand sympathizers had joined the White Knights of the Ku Klux Klan. Some of them were firmly established in Neshoba County, and on April 5, 1964, they announced their presence with fire.[32] Crosses were burned in twelve spots across the county, including Philadelphia's courthouse lawn. The courthouse in Philadelphia, as in many southern towns, marked the physical center of the city and represented the symbolic touchstone of local political culture. Yet despite the fact that one cannot drive through Philadelphia without passing the courthouse, not a single local law enforcement officer would admit to having seen the crosses burned.[33] The *Neshoba Democrat* attributed the burning of the crosses to "outsiders," Klansmen who had crossed into the county.[34] A few weeks later, circulars were distributed to every white household in the community advertising the White Knights of the Ku Klux Klan, which was described as a "Christian, democratic, politically independent, pro-American organization dedicated to total segregation of the races and destruction of Communism."[35]

These measures by the Klan were a reaction to the impending Mississippi Summer Project, later known as Freedom Summer. Spearheaded by SNCC, the project was set to bring nearly a thousand wealthy, educated, and predominantly white students to Mississippi to register African Americans to vote and to organize freedom schools that would offer remediation for Mississippi children as well as civic education. Like their adversaries, SNCC activists used military analogies to describe their upcoming work. They spoke of "cracking Mississippi," establishing "beachheads," and working "behind enemy lines."[36] Indeed, Mississippi had proved immensely difficult for civil rights activists to crack. In 1963, shortly after Medgar Evers, a field secretary for the NAACP, was shot and killed outside his Jackson home, Roy Wilkins, head of the NAACP, lamented, "There is no state with a record that approaches that of Mississippi in inhumanity, murder, brutality, and racial hatred. It is absolutely at the bottom of the list."[37] Despite the efforts of civil rights activists who had toiled in Mississippi for years to build indigenous black leadership throughout the state, only 6.7 percent of Mississippi's eligible blacks had been registered to vote.[38]

The struggle took its toll. COFO staff members were exhausted and seemed to be making few gains. In John Dittmer's detailed account of the struggle for civil rights in Mississippi, he describes the political climate in 1963 and its impact on COFO strategy:

> It was clear that by the late summer of 1963 COFO was facing a dilemma: as long as white hoodlums and police could attack black organizers with impunity, it would be extremely difficult for the movement to make further substantive gains. Although the patient,

grassroots organizing pioneered by SNCC in McComb and in the Delta had politicized many local people, the combination of fear and inertia had left the vast majority of black Mississippians on the sidelines; these men and women were unlikely to enlist in the struggle without some degree of protection from retaliation. All previous efforts to persuade the Kennedy administration to safeguard human rights in Mississippi had failed.[39]

In response, SNCC leaders devised a different strategy based on new logic: they would shock the general public into demanding federal action. Throughout the so-called freedom vote campaign in November 1963, which featured a mock election that sought to demonstrate that Mississippi's African Americans would vote if given the chance to register, the media had focused overwhelmingly on the campaign's white volunteers. The Mississippi Summer Project of 1964 sought to exploit this tendency. In the words of Doug McAdam, "Perhaps the national media—and, in turn, the federal government—would take notice if those being shot at and beaten were the sons and daughters of privileged white America."[40] The idea was contentious among SNCC staff members, some of whom felt that it might divert resources away from their primary mission: organizing local communities and cultivating black leadership.[41] In addition, bringing white students to Mississippi would garner attention, but perhaps the wrong kind of attention. The students' naiveté might get them killed.

"A Strange, Tight Little Town"

Michael Schwerner, James Chaney, and Andrew Goodman were the summer's first casualties. Schwerner, known as Mickey, was a gregarious veterinary student turned social worker with a degree from Cornell University who had moved to Mississippi in January 1964 to work for CORE. He and his wife, Rita, an equally committed activist, had been assigned to Meridian in the eastern part of the state—the first white staff members to be stationed outside of Jackson. Their task was to establish a community center, and within months, the center was offering reading instruction, sewing classes, and a story hour for children, among other programming. The Schwerners became a fixture in Meridian's black community. They also became a fixture in the minds of local Klan members, who had been given orders to eliminate "Goatee." Schwerner's civil rights activities—and his facial hair—proved to be an affront that would have fatal consequences.

Twenty-one-year-old James Earl (J. E.) Chaney was one of the first locals from Meridian to befriend Schwerner, and the two quickly became inseparable. Owing to the encouragement of a local activist named Cornelius Steele, the Longdale community—a rural area inhabited by black farmers since the 1930s—became a frequent destination for Schwerner and Chaney, who made some thirty trips there from February through June 1964.[42] They hoped to establish a freedom school at the Mt. Zion United Methodist Church, and after some persuading, the church's leaders agreed. Longdale was some eight miles east of downtown Philadelphia, where a recently elected sheriff had initiated a new era of law enforcement.

Lawrence Rainey, described as a "beefy man of forty," had defeated nine other people running for sheriff—a position that came with considerable power in Neshoba County, where the sheriff was also the tax collector and where an underground moonshine industry could prove immeasurably profitable.[43] At the Neshoba County Fair, a weeklong festival featuring stump speeches from politicians across the state, Rainey had introduced himself with a simple promise: "I'm Lawrence Rainey and I want to be your next sheriff. Ya'll [sic] know me and if I'm elected, I take care of things for you."[44] "Taking care of things" during Rainey's tenure looked quite different from what had happened in previous administrations. For the first time in the county's history, the sheriff and deputy sheriff, Cecil Price, sported western-style outfits, with boots, cowboy hats, and six-shooters at their hips—perhaps a subtle nod toward the vigilante justice that would unfold under Rainey's watch. On June 16, the Klan attacked a group of Mt. Zion members who had gathered at the church, inflicting lifelong physical impairments on some and destroying the church with firebombs.

When Schwerner and Chaney returned from Ohio, where the summer project volunteer training was taking place, they went to Mt. Zion with Andrew Goodman, a twenty-year-old student at Queens College in New York City and a summer volunteer who was preparing to work as a canvasser. By nightfall, when the trio had failed to return or to call in with their whereabouts as was standard protocol, COFO staff members knew that something was amiss. Fearing that the trio had been beaten or worse, they contacted federal officials, reporters, and other prominent individuals who might convince the federal government to intervene.[45] Only after the civil rights workers' car was discovered at the bottom of a lake on nearby Choctaw tribal land did President Lyndon Johnson and Attorney General Robert Kennedy order more than two hundred sailors from the Meridian Naval

Air Station to dredge local swamps in search of the missing men. Though the effort failed to uncover the whereabouts of Chaney, Schwerner, and Goodman, it did unearth the corpses of three additional African American men, two of whom were later identified as Charles Eddie Moore and Henry Hezekiah Dee—both nineteen and from Franklin County.[46] The third, a boy younger than Moore and Dee and wearing a CORE T-shirt, was never identified.[47]

The disappearances quickly garnered global media coverage, which largely reinforced COFO's suspicions that Philadelphia's law enforcement officers were somehow involved. Locally, however, the narrative was quite different. Most white Philadelphians considered the disappearances to be a hoax or a northern conspiracy.[48] Even after the discovery of the civil rights workers' burned-out station wagon, many white Philadelphians still believed COFO was behind what they referred to as the prank. As more time passed, this theory became untenable. Many locals projected blame onto the civil rights workers themselves.[49] The journalist William Bradford Huie, who covered the story in 1964, captured this prevailing sentiment: "If the three were dead—well, what the hell? *They* were to blame! They had asked for it. *They* had come 'looking for trouble.'"[50]

If the civil rights workers had come "looking for trouble," so too had the nearly eighty journalists who descended on Philadelphia to cover the story for their rapt readers. Within days after the trio was reported missing, white Philadelphians felt besieged. As Howard Cole, a local radio station owner, recalled in 1973, many local whites "didn't expect the bodies to be discovered" and felt that the spectacle had "been forced on us" so "we had to fight back."[51] Much of this animosity grew from local whites' feeling that national news coverage was shaded, portraying Neshoba County in unflattering and, they believed, unjustified ways. According to Turner Catledge, the managing editor of the *New York Times* from 1952 to 1964 who was raised in Philadelphia, "Our reporters told me that my friends and my relatives, although greeting them politely, would rarely discuss the murders with them. They closed ranks against outsiders."[52] Clay Lee, a United Methodist minister, also recalled this cold treatment toward "outsiders": "If you came through Philadelphia, Mississippi, and your car had a tag on it other than a Neshoba County tag—even another Mississippi tag—I guarantee you, before much time passed [the Klan would] know who you were and what you were doing there. . . . The tenseness within the community was unbelievable."[53]

While most harassment of journalists and federal agents was not overtly violent, those who stayed worked under the constant threat of violence and in some cases faced acts of aggression. In one notable instance, an NBC cameraman was chased by a man with a knife after an altercation involving their cars. Later that week, while the same cameraman was shooting footage from a low-flying helicopter, he was shot at by a farmer with a rifle—after which he asked the network to transfer him.[54] "Some of this [violence and intimidation] is sheer bravado," observed a New York journalist who had witnessed arguments between citizens and reporters in Philadelphia, "but some of it is also very conscious and very controlled, and it is difficult to distinguish the one from the other, to know which situation is simply unpleasant and which may be fatal."[55]

Indeed, the Klan presence in Philadelphia posed a threat to people who sought to uncover the fate of the civil rights workers, but Klan intimidation was not limited to African Americans. "Everyone who fails to conform, white and black alike, learns to fear," observed the reporter David Nevin. "There may only be a few hundred Klansmen, but they reach the whole community. . . . To speak out against the Klan or even to question Lawrence Rainey's treatment of Negroes has come to be equated somehow with disloyalty to one's own."[56] Indeed, the Klan structure in Neshoba was pervasive, earning Philadelphia a national reputation as a "strange, tight, little town loath to admit complicity"—the title of Nevin's article in *Life* that introduced America to an otherwise obscure Mississippi hamlet. Joseph Sullivan, the lead agent on the case for the Federal Bureau of Investigation (FBI), described the Neshoba County Klavern as "one of the strongest Klan units ever gathered [in the state of Mississippi] and one of the best disciplined groups."[57] "In spirit," Sullivan reflected, "everyone in Neshoba County belonged to the Klan."[58]

Despite this seemingly iron grip, a paid informant ultimately led the FBI to the bodies buried deep beneath an earthen dam off Highway 19. After forty days of searching, the mystery was solved. For some, it had never been a mystery at all.

Silence and Denial in Philadelphia's Dominant Public Sphere

A month after the bodies were discovered, a Neshoba County grand jury, failing to bring indictments, issued a "scortching [sic]" report that admonished federal agents for failing to cooperate despite having been issued subpoenas. "It is common knowledge in and around Neshoba County," the report insisted, "that the Federal Agents have made numerous statements to the effect that they have the case 'wrapped up.' . . . If these be true, why hesitate to come before the Grand Jury, being the only Grand Jury with jurisdiction to bring 'Murder' indictments?" The grand jury leveled blame at other actors as well, notably "outside agitators" who "seek to divide the races, stir up friction, and breed hatred."[59]

The authors of the grand jury statement were clearly indignant and felt that their community has been mistreated, especially when the local murders were compared with egregious acts of violence elsewhere in the nation. "There is more crime and violence committed on the streets of New York City in one night," the authors reasoned, "than there has been in all of Neshoba County for the past one hundred years."[60] The grand jury may have been echoing the sentiments of Judge Barnett, who oversaw the case and used similar forms of evasion when confronted about impending indictments. "The citizens of Neshoba County," he said, "are no more responsible for these deaths than were the citizens of the City of Dallas, Texas, responsible for the death of the late president."[61] When indictments were issued against twenty-one men for their involvement in the crime, many white residents of Neshoba County were relieved: twelve of the twenty-one were from nearby Meridian, suggesting that the triple homicide had been a Meridian plot that "just happened" to involve some people from Neshoba.[62]

James Silver, a University of Mississippi historian and one of the state's harshest critics, described Mississippi in 1964 as a "closed society." "In such a society," Silver wrote, "a never-ceasing propagation of the 'true faith' must go on relentlessly, with a constantly reiterated demand for loyalty to the united front, requiring that non-conformists and dissenters from the code be silenced, or, in a crisis, driven from the community."[63] Some might think this an exaggeration. By painting such a stark picture, Silver seems to suggest that few if any white Mississippians challenged the prevailing status quo. But as Paul Hendrickson notes in *Sons of Mississippi*, almost every town in the state had "ordinary heroic white people doing ordinary jobs who tried to bear some kind of witness—quiet or otherwise—against what was going on, and who didn't leave, and who weren't murdered, and who, in some cases, are living today in the same houses on the same streets."[64]

Philadelphia was no exception. Two scions of the county's most highly esteemed families offer notable examples of white resistance. The reactions of their peers, however, suggest that if not entirely "closed," Neshoba County maintained a dominant culture of compliance to Jim Crow norms of segregation and white superiority. For instance, Buford Posey had been known as an iconoclast and was notorious for challenging the city's newspaper editor to a duel in 1958 and for being the first white member of the NAACP in

Mississippi. When Posey insinuated in a widely broadcast NBC interview that Neshoba County's sheriff was involved in the civil rights workers' disappearances, he had gone too far. Within hours, his car was being shadowed and his property defaced. Confronted with death threats, Posey fled the state, fearful even after crossing the Alabama line that Klansmen would apprehend him.[65] Florence Mars didn't fare any better. After she testified before a federal grand jury in Biloxi, many in Philadelphia, including those who regularly played bridge with her, believed that Mars was working for COFO. In addition to having her car tailed, those intent on intimidating Mars organized a boycott of her local stockyard, ultimately forcing her to sell her business.[66]

In the midst of the contention, Philadelphia's white religious leaders also presented a moderate view. Following the initial arrests, the white interdenominational ministerial association issued a statement that was broadcast on local radio, acknowledging the shame that came from being part of a community in which some members would be accused of such a crime. Nevertheless, the ministers expressed their desire for justice and their dedication to providing leadership so that through "this damaging and deteriorating experience of the past five months the result may be stronger character and deeper appreciation for those basic elements of democracy which made our nation great."[67]

According to Lee, the minister who read the statement on the radio, they "weren't accusing anyone" or "trying to intimidate anyone," but he was "marked" nonetheless.[68] The Sunday after the arrests, Lee delivered a sermon on King Herod and bigotry—largely a coincidence, according to Lee, but a poignant topic nonetheless. As it happened, some fifteen newspaper reporters attended Lee's church that day, and their accounts of his sermon propelled Lee into the spotlight. "I never saw myself as riding a white horse, blowing bugles, and waving flags," Lee contended, yet the minister who had taken up his post just three weeks before Chaney, Schwerner, and Goodman went missing came to be a prominent figure in the local white resistance.[69]

For nearly three years, those who had been issued federal indictments went about their lives as usual, going to church, buying groceries, and attending high school football games. But after extensive legal wrangling, a federal conspiracy trial in 1967 would reveal that the Neshoba County Klavern, including local law enforcement officials, had indeed conspired to take the lives of Chaney, Goodman, and Schwerner. As the defendants approached the courthouse in Meridian, they seemed remarkably at ease. No doubt they expected to be acquitted, as had been the case with everyone charged with killing a black man in Mississippi since Reconstruction. Testimony from two Klan informants, however, must have proved too compelling, for the jury returned a guilty verdict in seven instances. In the case of Edgar Ray Killen, the reputed mastermind of the abduction and "elimination," the jury was hung: one juror insisting that she "could not convict a preacher."[70] Perhaps no group was more surprised at the verdict than the black communities of Neshoba County, where there seemed to be an especially potent sense of vindication. Indeed, as Hazel Brannon Smith, a reform-minded white Mississippi newspaper editor, wrote, "For those who know not the American South and the place within it called Mississippi, it may be easy to underestimate the travail and the heart-searching which must have attended to the preparations of the case in Meridian, and above all, the deliberations of the jury in the courtroom."[71]

For all its potency, that victory for civil rights was short-lived. All the Klan conspirators were paroled before they had served their full sentences, and by the mid-1970s, most had returned to the region. Working as convenience store clerks, car salesmen, and mall security guards, the men were folded back into the fabric of local life. And life went on. Ten years after the trial, according to Mars, it was almost never discussed, and it was certainly not acknowledged by those who held positions in official institutions such as city government or the chamber of commerce. For the next twenty-five years, public discussion of the murders within Philadelphia's white community was largely concealed by what Eviatar Zerubavel has described as a "conspiracy of silence"—when "a group of people tacitly agree to outwardly ignore something of which they are all personally aware."[72]

Throughout the succeeding decades, the prevailing tendency of white residents of Neshoba County was to avoid the topic or distance themselves and their community from this peculiar past. Neshoba County "is where the lid blew off," reflected Cole when he was interviewed in 1973, but "it could have happened in any community in Mississippi at that time."[73] On the twentieth anniversary of the murders, Philadelphia's mayor, Charles McClain, expressed frustration and bewilderment. The events of 1964, he said, "almost pitched us as a city of murderers, whereas virtually all of the townspeople here were not even involved, did not even know that it did happen, and wondered, if it did happen, why did it happen to us? To me, it was sort of like a plane crash. It was just a part of history that happened near Philadelphia, and there's nothing we could do to erase it."[74]

By the late 1970s, Neshoba County had, with relief, turned its attention from the trials of the past: a talented high school running back named

Marcus Dupree had captured the attention of the nation and its most sought-after college recruiters. For once, Neshoba County was known for something other than the 1964 killings. By then, federally subsidized housing had come to Independence Quarters, along with a swimming pool and a sports facility—referred to as Westside Park—that attracted people from across the city. More importantly, by 1970, Philadelphia and Neshoba County schools had been desegregated without incident, and an entire generation, including Dupree, had grown up studying in integrated classrooms and playing on integrated teams. The past seemed less present, at least for some. When asked about his friendship with Cecil Price Jr., the son of one of the Klan conspirators, Dupree responded, "I like him and he likes me. . . . It's not hard to understand. I don't know his father. I only met him once or twice."[75] The younger Price could have attended one of the many segregated private academies established after *Brown v. Board of Education*, but his father, who had been released from federal prison after serving four years for his role in the murders, insisted that if society was going to be integrated, "it's better for him to be brought up in it."[76]

Resisting Silence in Philadelphia's Counterpublic

In December 1976, twelve years after that "long, hot summer," spectators gathered outside a small wooden church, covering their heads as best they could from the rain, and bore witness to a new memorial that their nickels and dimes had helped erect. The sloping marble structure resembled a gravestone, with three small cameo portraits inlaid above the names and date that marked that hallowed ground: "Andrew Goodman, James Earl Chaney, Michael H. Schwerner—June 21, 1964" (see figure G.4). The memorial was the product of a grassroots effort initiated by members of Mt. Nebo Baptist Church, which stood just blocks from COFO's former offices in Philadelphia's Independence Quarters and signified a triumph for local activists who, like Lillian Jones, believed that there should be a monument to the three civil rights workers at every church in Neshoba County. Lonnie Wheeler, a reporter for the Jackson *Clarion-Ledger*, recorded the scene in detail, including its emotional valence: "The fire that raged 12 years ago has calmed to a cinder here and there, and they burn gently in the souls of the Rev. Smileys and the Rev. Colliers and the Sister Jones. . . . But the bearers of that flame—of the memory of 1964, of the death of three workers for civil rights—want to make certain that it will still flicker, that it will still illuminate that era of progress for the black community, and the toll it took."[77]

These musings capture the significant role of local carrier groups, those who mediate the meaning of the past—cultural "specialists" such as politicians, intellectuals, journalists, social movement leaders, and other moral entrepreneurs who articulate to a wider public the understandings of the past and the interests and desires of those most affected by historic trauma.[78] In instances where remembrance of a particular past has been suppressed or silenced, carrier groups are those that keep the memory alive, periodically stirring its embers and illuminating the past's present significance— which may contradict official narratives. Such counterrepresentations can be understood as countermemories, memories that oppose or contradict understandings of the past that are most dominant within a given context. In *Recovered Roots*, Yael Zerubavel highlights countermemory's subversive potential when regimes prohibit minority groups from practicing their commemorative rituals. Demands to incorporate countermemories within a society's more widely accepted collective memory, for example, often require a redefinition of collective identity, an expansion of we-ness.[79] Thus, countermemories can be threatening to dominant regimes that are invested in maintaining the status quo, because changing cultural representations can have material consequences that challenge long-established constellations of power.

The meaning and memory of Chaney, Schwerner, and Goodman began to take shape in the days and months following their deaths as key figures interpreted those deaths in the public sphere—a process that Gary Alan Fine describes as "reputational entrepreneurship."[80] Robert Goodman, Andrew's father, was one of the first to present the event in the context of national politics. In a faltering voice, Goodman read a prepared statement for the press that had gathered in the Goodmans' home in New York City's Upper West Side: "Our grief, though personal, belongs to our nation. This tragedy is not private. It is part of the public conscience of our country. . . . The values our son expressed in his simple action of going to Mississippi are still the bonds that bind this nation together—its Constitution, its law, its Bill of Rights. . . . Throughout our history, countless Americans have died in the continuing struggling for equality. We shall continue to work for this goal and we fervently hope that Americans so engaged will be aided and protected in this noble mission."[81]

Days later, Ella Baker, the coordinator of the Washington office of Mississippi's Freedom Democratic Party and a longtime SNCC activist, echoed this sentiment while also highlighting inequality in the nation's response to the civil rights movement's casualties. Speaking at James

Chaney's funeral on August 8, 1964, Baker noted: "The tragedy has become a symbol. . . . The unfortunate thing is that it took this kind of symbol to make the rest of the country turn its eyes on the fact that there are other bodies lying under the swamps of Mississippi. Until the killing of a black mother's son becomes as important as the killing of a white mother's son, we who believe in freedom cannot rest."[82]

Baker was not alone in this assessment. Rita Schwerner, Michael Schwerner's widow, had been one of the first to admonish the federal government and the American public for their racially biased response. After learning of her husband's disappearance, she spoke to the press. "It's tragic," she said, "that white northerners have to be caught up into the machinery of injustice and indifference in the South before the American people register concern. I personally suspect that if Mr. Chaney, who is a [black] native Mississippian, had been alone at the time of the disappearance, that this case, like so many others, . . . would have gone completely unnoticed."[83] In conveying these messages, Goodman, Baker, and Schwerner constructed the civil rights workers' disappearance and deaths as a cultural trauma. In other words, they acted as Jeffrey Alexander described, "when members of a collectivity feel they have been subjected to a horrendous event that leaves indelible marks upon group consciousness, marking their memories . . . and changing their identity in fundamental and irreversible ways."[84] Therefore, the social process of constructing and representing collective cultural traumas most often involves struggles over meaning—the nature of the pain, the nature of the victim, and the attribution of responsibility.[85]

Indeed, as Mississippians grappled with their own understanding of the event, some perceiving the civil rights workers as "outside agitators," the artless portraits of Chaney, Schwerner, and Goodman in the FBI missing persons' poster became emblazoned on the American public's imagination, reproduced on countless newscasts that were broadcast across the nation and often characterizing Chaney, Schwerner, and Goodman as innocent victims (see figure G.1). Civil rights activists mediated this messaging by incorporating the names and faces of the three men into their protest repertoire and replicating the three men's visages on placards and leaflets. This was especially pronounced in late August 1964, when hundreds of protesters gathered at the Democratic convention in Atlantic City, New Jersey, and demanded that the Mississippi Freedom Party delegates be seated. An often-reproduced photograph shows Martin Luther King Jr. addressing protesters at the Atlantic City gathering with sketches of Chaney, Schwerner, and

Goodman's likeness positioned on placards behind him, a visible reminder of the summer's loss and the movement's stakes (see figure G.2).

As these images reiterated the national significance of the Mississippi Burning murders, as they came to be called, the local mnemonic landscape looked quite different. For many local whites, the three civil rights workers were not martyrs; rather, they were a menace that disrupted a social system that the whites had believed to be harmonious. Likewise, threats of Klan retaliation continued despite the ongoing federal investigation, further constraining early commemorative efforts. For this reason, there are few historic records of local commemorations in the years immediately following the killings. Those that do exist tend to come from national news outlets such as the *New York Times* and *Washington Post,* and in some cases from the Jackson *Clarion-Ledger.* However, these scarce archival resources do reveal that a local commemoration service took place at Mt. Zion two months after the Klan firebombed the church. With the church still in ruins, participants sat on wooden benches among the oak trees, some visibly scarred from the flames, and collectively remembered Chaney, Schwerner, and Goodman. As Sheriff Rainey and Deputy Sheriff Price looked on from a distance, Ben Chaney, James Chaney's eleven-year-old brother, spoke defiantly: "I want us all to stand up here together and say just one thing. I want the sheriff to hear this good. *We ain't scared no more of Sheriff Rainey!*"[86] Reverend Clinton Collier followed Chaney: "All the cops in Neshoba County will not be able to kill this cause. This Heaven which the white man has made for himself in Neshoba County, it's hell for us. Lord, give us the strength to make a Heaven for ourselves here too."[87]

On the first anniversary of the murders, some two hundred people gathered again at Mt. Zion (then in the early stages of being rebuilt), beginning what would become an annual tradition. The individuals, mostly local African Americans who had marched some ten miles from the Headquarters of the Mississippi Freedom Democratic party (previously COFO's office) in Independence Quarters to Mt. Zion, met a memorial motorcade carrying more than fifty civil rights workers. Assembling around the charred stone steps—all that was left of the church—they cleared the dust from their throats and sang: "There ain't gonna be no more killins, oh Lawdy. There ain't gonna be no more killins over me. Before I'd be a slave, I'd be curried in my grave and go home to my Lord and be free."[88] Again, Deputy Sheriff Price observed the event, this time from behind the wheel of his truck, with a gun rack behind his head cradling a submachine gun.[89]

The following year's commemoration service in 1966 would prove to be more explosive. Martin Luther King Jr. had arrived in Philadelphia to lead the memorial march from Independence Quarters to Mt. Zion when violence broke out near the courthouse. Stones, bottles, and firecrackers were thrown at King as he spoke from the curb, causing him to abort the march. Three days later, he returned to complete the march. With some three hundred marchers, he attempted to follow the same route and was again stymied by local law enforcement officials, who refused to let him proceed.

Trouble began as the march neared downtown. Having proceeded a dozen dusty blocks, the marchers, chanting civil rights slogans and singing freedom songs, paused at the county jail where Chaney, Schwerner, and Goodman had been incarcerated. Here, the marchers knelt to pray, as Deputy Sheriff Price and ten other men looked on, armed with pistols and nightsticks. Historians contend that King then whispered under his breath as he knelt to pray, "I believe the murderers are somewhere around me at this moment." "You damn right," Price responded. "They're right behind you."[90] By now, there were as many hostile onlookers as there were marchers. As the demonstrators prayed and listened to speakers, a young white man turned a hose on them. Within minutes, a car skidded near the crowd, fists hurled stones and bottles, clubs were swung, and a young African American man suffered a seizure and fell writhing to the pavement amid the growing chaos.

King would later describe these minutes as the most frightening of his life.[91] For local African Americans, the violence was at least as disturbing, if not more so. "It revealed Philadelphia to me," one elderly black woman remarked two years later. "I just couldn't believe it. We all lives here, was raised here, my parents stayed here all my days. It don't make me feel good walking up the streets now. Folks looking for us to trade with them even treats me nicer than before, but I'll never feel the same again."[92]

Since the turbulent 1960s, much has changed in Neshoba County. The county jail has been converted into an architecture firm and law offices, streets have been paved, and Mt. Zion has been rebuilt, this time in brick. But despite the march of time, one thing has remained constant. Every year, members of Mt. Zion have organized a commemoration service to honor the three civil rights workers who lost their lives on Neshoba soil (see figures G.3 and G.8). Come spring, congregants like Mabel Steele, who in 1964 had been beaten by the Klan and who took a special interest in honoring the civil rights workers, would gather in their community hall to organize a program.[93] Once Mabel and her generation had passed, their sons and daughters carried on the tradition, each year listening to keynote speakers call for the continued pursuit of justice; lighting three candles in remembrance; laying a wreath outside at the memorial to Chaney, Schwerner, and Goodman; and singing freedom songs in their memory. As Mars put it in the conclusion of her memoir, the people of Neshoba County—black, white, and Choctaw—who have gathered to commemorate the three civil rights workers, including those who met at Mt. Nebo Baptist Church on December 12, 1976, "are not mute. They spoke and the monument they erected . . . will continue to speak for them, with them, of them."[94]

· · · · · ·

Given this bifurcated mnemonic landscape, one where the dominant public sphere has remained largely silent on the murders once they became memory and where Philadelphia's counterpublic commemorated the event annually, when and how did this countermemory become collective memory? In the following chapter, we will explore this question by examining interracial efforts to coordinate community-wide commemorations in 1989 and 2004—events that were unique for incorporating Mt. Zion's annual commemorations, historic rituals of countermemory—in the dominant public sphere.

2 From Countermemory to Collective Memory

Visitors to Philadelphia today—of which there are many, the city's notoriety having been well established over the decades—are invariably directed to the Depot, a converted train station that serves as the city's welcome center. The single-story wood structure with cheery red trim, which is also a small city museum and the headquarters of the city's chamber of commerce, is wedged between Beacon Street and Main Street, the city's major east-west throughway. Whether arriving by car or bus, one simply can't drive through downtown Philadelphia without passing the Depot.

Once inside, a visitor will walk across the wide, weathered floorboards and be greeted by a volunteer at the front desk, most likely a retiree eager to interact and full of friendly chitchat and loads of information about notable nearby destinations—the Pearl River Resort and Casino, the centuries-old Williams Brothers General Store, and Peggy's Restaurant, a hometown favorite that has been serving up fried pork chops and sweet tea for more than forty years. She'll then point to a case brimming with glossy pamphlets, among them an African American heritage driving tour titled "Roots of Struggle: Rewards of Sacrifice," a sleek quarter fold that retraces Chaney, Schwerner, and Goodman's final hours. The pamphlet invites visitors to "join us on the journey toward freedom, . . . [a way] paved by sacrifice, pain, suffering, and even death."[1]

Not long ago, representatives of the city would have avoided any mention of 1964. The events of that summer were, for many Philadelphians, a history best forgotten. Yet since 2004, Philadelphia's Community Development Partnership and the Philadelphia-Neshoba Tourism Board has openly advertised this history and encouraged visitors to retrace the three civil rights workers' final steps. How did this violent past transition from a public secret to a point of pride? Or asked differently, how did this long-suppressed countermemory become Philadelphia's collective memory?

Only two large-scale public commemorations ruptured Philadelphia's dominant silence in the forty years following the murders: the twenty-fifth anniversary commemoration in 1989 and the fortieth in 2004. These two episodes represent notable instances of silence breaking, collective efforts to challenge the long-standing public silence about and denial of a discomforting past. Comparing these two silence-breaking commemorations that occurred at separate and unique historical moments therefore helps to clarify the conditions that make silence-breaking commemorations possible.

Acknowledging Silenced Pasts

Sociologists have long been interested in collective representations of the past,[2] as well as the challenges communities face when commemorating difficult pasts.[3] So in addition to conducting research on collective memory and the many commemorative vehicles through which that memory is represented (memorials, museums, marches, and so on), scholars have demonstrated a growing interest in memory's inverse: silence, denial, and collective forgetting.[4] Like two sides of the same coin, remembering and forgetting are intimately intertwined. It is important to recognize them as interrelated processes: remembering is a form of forgetting, too, for the people and occasions that come to be collectively remembered are only a fraction of those that could be remembered. Collective remembrance entails decisions about what should occupy pride of place within a collectivity's cultural life, and these decisions are rarely straightforward. Various communities of memory interpret the past differently, often resulting in mnemonic battles over what ought to be remembered and how. The American holiday of Thanksgiving is a prime example.[5] While public schools teach American children a particular version of the Thanksgiving story, one that privileges friendship, cooperation, and a bountiful harvest, Native American communities since the 1970s have recognized the holiday as a day of mourning—an annual protest against the treatment of native peoples, past and present. These perspectives represent cultural battles in which individuals and groups compete to define the meaning of the past.[6]

Given these contested and often competitive mnemonic landscapes, sociologists have identified several types of commemorations. In their groundbreaking work on commemorations of difficult pasts, Robin Wager-Pacifici and Barry Schwartz illuminate the task of representing contrasting interpretations of the Vietnam War within one monument, what they identify as a multivocal commemoration.[7] In contrast, Vered Vinitzky-Seroussi observes how various constituencies have come to remember the assassinated Israeli prime minister Yitzhak Rabin on different days and at separate locations, in what she has termed a fragmented commemoration.[8] Rather than accommodating multiple viewpoints within one commemorative space, fragmented commemorations reinforce particular narratives for particular audiences and are most likely to emerge when the political culture is conflictual, agents of memory are well resourced, and the past remains relevant to present-day political concerns. As Christina Steidl notes, however, these forms of commemorations represent "ideal types," for commemorative fields remain dynamic over time, sometimes including both multivocal and fragmented commemorations at different points in history.[9]

Thus, while current scholarship enhances our understanding of how difficult pasts come to be commemorated, it often obscures the different ways that pasts can be difficult. The case studies that animate this literature and its theoretical contributions—the Vietnam War, the assassination of Rabin, and the shootings at Kent State University—represent divisive or even dishonorable historical events. However, these events were never excluded from public discourse for a substantial period of time, a process that is characteristic of "conspiracies of silence."[10] As noted in chapter 1, such conspiracies occur "when a group of people tacitly agree to outwardly ignore something of which they are all personally aware."[11] Eviatar Zerubavel notes in his study of silence and denial in everyday life that this particularly pernicious form of silence engenders a number of social consequences. While maintaining the status quo, conspiracies of silence also undermine social solidarity by impeding open communication and the communal trust that forms the basis of democratic political culture.[12]

It would seem, then, that the challenges to commemorating silenced pasts are formidable and arguably more difficult to overcome than those to commemorating merely difficult pasts. Indeed, the two phenomena encompass several analytical distinctions that help explain their emergence and outcomes, including the nature of the mnemonic battles at hand. Whereas commemorations of difficult pasts often involve disputes over the nature of the past or its present-day relevance, commemorations of silenced pasts generally embody conflicts over the very existence of a past experience.[13] The mnemonic battles surrounding the Armenian genocide is an example of the latter conflicts, in which one mnemonic community insists on commemorating a past event while another mnemonic community refuses to concede that there is anything to commemorate. In this case, Armenian organizations argue that the World War I–era massacre was a deliberately organized genocide that resulted in as many as 1.5 million Armenian deaths, while the Turkish government insists that this massacre did not occur.[14] Memory movements that are engaged in battles over existence thus constitute a form of consciousness-raising, drawing attention to memories that have been suppressed or publicly silenced.

This highlights the second major difference between difficult and silenced pasts: the degree to which power is distributed between various mnemonic communities. A sociological perspective on silence and denial highlights the fact that collective memory is structured and maintained by asymmetrical social relations. Those who occupy powerful social positions are specially equipped to advance an "official" version of the past that is advantageous to their own interests. By controlling access to information, the means of its dissemination, and the very terms of discussion, those in positions of power have disproportionate influence over public representations of the past.[15] Those who construct official public memory advance their agendas by flooding public space with their version of the past, often at the expense of countermemories—a phenomenon well documented by historians of the American South who have demonstrated, for instance, the resilience of the "Lost Cause" narrative to the detriment of other explanations for the American Civil War.[16]

Considering the power asymmetry characteristic of southern history, the challenges facing advocates of alternative representations of Philadelphia's past were ample, given that the 1964 killings had been absent from public discourse. And while few if any Philadelphians would suggest that the 1964 killings never happened—there was simply too much historical documentation—most white Philadelphians did not consider the event worthy of commemoration. After all, why would the community choose to highlight a historical moment for which many believed the national media had wrongly cast the city and its citizens as villains? Since 1964, the conspiracy of silence that reinforced Ku Klux Klan rule and protected local assailants from prosecution had become transformed into something different, a sort of benign neglect. It was better to let sleeping dogs lie. And while conspiracies of silence become more difficult to dismantle as time passes, the progression of time also creates more opportunities to break the silence.[17] As Iwona Irwin-Zarecka reminds us, the state's control over the interpretation of history is never total, even in totalitarian societies.[18] Countermemory can survive—and even thrive—under powerful and seemingly all-encompassing regimes.[19] So, while the dominant or hegemonic collective memory often suppresses oppositional memory, subversive stories do emerge, and in some cases countermemories gain enough momentum to disrupt their oppositional status and become official memories.[20] But how does this happen?

Efforts to commemorate are both enabled and constrained by a number of factors. First, a particular person or event is more likely to be commemorated when a community has deemed it worthy of commemoration.[21] Events that are disruptive, violent, or large scale tend to be most readily perceived as commemorable, as are events in which the victims are particularly sympathetic.[22] The 1964 murders fulfill these criteria: the event was certainly violent, and its youthful victims were perceived sympathetically by a growing number of Philadelphians. But while a community may decide that an event is worthy of commemoration, enacting commemoration still requires financial, human, and organizational resources. For a commemoration—multivocal, fragmented, or silence breaking—to emerge, communities must have the ability to organize and enact commemorative vehicles such as marches, memorials, and other commemorative rituals. That is, they must have what the sociologists Elizabeth Armstrong and Suzanna Crage refer to as "mnemonic capacity."[23] While these factors may account for the commemoration of difficult pasts, they do not fully address situations where the resistance to a particular historical episode is so powerful and pervasive as to prevent public discussion of that event for decades. To investigate how silence-breaking commemorations emerge, we will consider two instances where long-suppressed and publicly silenced countermemories became prominent—at least temporarily—within Philadelphia's dominant public sphere.

The 1989 Commemoration

Philadelphia's conspiracy of silence began to be dismantled on the eve of the twenty-fifth anniversary. Alan Parker's film *Mississippi Burning*, which is based on the 1964 murders, had been released on December 9, 1988.[24] The film went on to receive critical acclaim and seven Academy Award nominations, but it is perhaps known best for having sparked a national debate on the responsibility of filmmakers to portray historical events accurately.[25] Critics charged that the film obscured the importance of blacks in the civil rights movement, incorrectly portrayed the intimidation tactics of the FBI, and depicted all white southerners as bigoted.

Others defended the filmmakers' creative freedom. Parker spoke candidly in defense of his film, arguing that he was "trying to reach an entire generation who knows nothing of that historical event."[26] According to Parker, he attempted to captivate a generation not likely to watch *Eyes on the Prize* or any of a number of documentaries that illuminated this particular story. "That's enough of a justification," he reasoned, "for the fictionalizing."[27] Regardless of the film's historical inaccuracies—or perhaps because of the national controversy those inaccuracies engendered—*Mississippi Burning* reignited national interest in the 1964 murders and turned the national spotlight on Philadelphia once again.[28]

The film's release did more than reinvigorate national awareness of the 1964 murders, however; it also renewed national interest in the case, which ultimately placed pressure on the local community to publicly acknowledge the murders. Stanley Dearman, the former owner and editor of the local weekly paper, the *Neshoba Democrat*, was keenly aware of the newly awakened national interest in the 1964 murders. Born in 1932 in the Whynot community in Lauderdale County, outside Meridian, Dearman had become editor of the *Neshoba Democrat* in 1966 after graduating from the University of Mississippi, where he had edited the student newspaper (see figure G.7). As editor of the *Neshoba Democrat*, he fielded questions from eager newspaper reporters interested in tracking Philadelphia's racial progress. Each anniversary, especially milestone anniversaries such as the twentieth or twenty-fifth, unearthed a new cohort of inquisitors. "I've talked to reporters from China, Sweden, France, England, Germany over the years," an elderly Dearman recalled, while sitting among the many stacks of books in his personal library. "I don't know how many—so many, just so many newsmen."[29]

The release of *Mississippi Burning* just months before the twenty-fifth anniversary intensified this effect. For decades, national media coverage of the murders had been virtually nonexistent. Outside of a single pro forma article on most anniversaries of the murders, reporters and their readers seemed to have moved on. After the debut of *Mississippi Burning*, however, the national news coverage skyrocketed. In 1989, the year of the movie's release, the *New York Times* referred to the 1964 killings in 170 separate instances (see graph 2.1). Forty-six of those mentions were in substantive articles about the upcoming twenty-fifth anniversary and the related film. In one instance, a brief article reported that Lulu Ellis, the owner of Philadelphia's only theater, was not planning to show the film, citing threats of boycotts from local church groups. "It's not worth it," said Ellis. "I just don't play controversial pictures."[30]

Examining the news coverage by year, however, obscures whether that coverage preceded or was a result of the 1989 commemoration. Breaking down the newspaper coverage by month, graph 2.2 demonstrates that the surge in coverage occurred in January through April, just after the film's

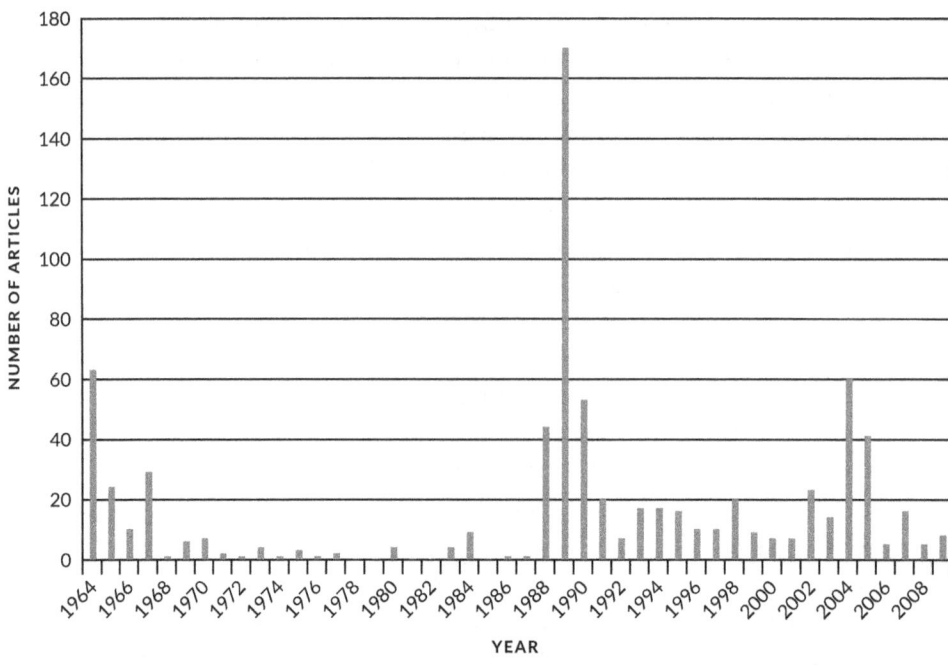

GRAPH 2.1 Articles mentioning the murders in the *New York Times*, 1964–2009

release but months before the June 21 anniversary, which supports Dearman's assertion that national media coverage precipitated the subsequent June commemoration.[31] On January 15, Bill Minor, a Jackson-based reporter known for his coverage of civil rights–era violence, covered *Mississippi Burning*'s Mississippi debut in a *New York Times* article titled "Image in Film Worries Mississippians." Minor noted that the film revived painful memories for its sold-out audience and raised concerns that the movie would negate the progressive image that the state had been trying to project. For Dick Molpus, a native Philadelphian who was then Mississippi's secretary of state who attended the screening, the film presented a moral obligation that might have influenced his public apology later that June: "It puts the onus on those of us who are part of a new philosophy and a new breed in Mississippi to carry the message that Mississippi is a remarkably different place now than it was then. Unfortunately, we can't undo what took place, but we must focus on the future and see that it never happens again."[32]

These reputational concerns were on the minds of many Neshoba County leaders who worried that the film would bring another flood of bad publicity. The Klan's selection of Philadelphia as a recruitment site because of its

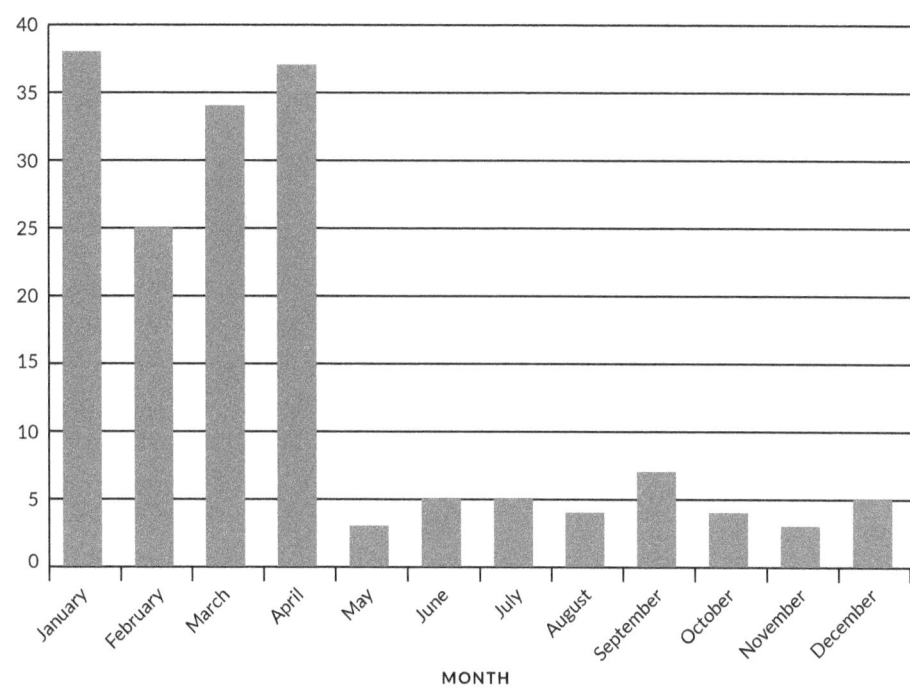

GRAPH 2.2 Articles mentioning the murders in the *New York Times*, 1989

portrayal in *Mississippi Burning* and the subsequent demonstration it held there in March 1989 certainly didn't help project an image of progress.[33] A staff reporter from the *Neshoba Democrat* in 1989 recalls Dearman's reaction to the movie's release: "*Mississippi Burning* was coming out, and [Dearman] knew all the media had come. And he knew with the movie and the twenty-fifth [anniversary] they were really going to come. So he got some people together and said, 'you know, we've really got to put our best foot forward.'"[34] Motivations of local citizens to acknowledge the murders were clearly complicated. Many people—at least those connected with the newspaper—were concerned that large crowds would descend on Philadelphia for the twenty-fifth anniversary and that the community would again be in the national spotlight.

Potential media scrutiny was not the only motivation for Philadelphians to publicly acknowledge the murders. For decades, tourists had been making the pilgrimage to Philadelphia on the June anniversary of the murders. But in 1989, Dearman received more phone calls than usual and sensed that the number of students and civil rights groups planning to visit for the twenty-fifth anniversary would be larger than the town had

From Countermemory to Collective Memory 43

ever experienced. This posed significant organizational challenges. With a population of roughly seven thousand, Philadelphia was not equipped to host potentially thousands of visitors. Housing, feeding, and transporting this many people could be a logistical nightmare. Philadelphia's previous experience with the national news media only intensified this concern, and Philadelphia leaders worried that without preparation, their town might be ridiculed.

But there would be opportunity here, too. With thousands of visitors and a large media presence, organizing some sort of public acknowledgment could be a public relations boon. Facilitating a community-wide commemoration would enable Philadelphians to challenge the *Mississippi Burning* narrative that had plagued the city's reputation for decades, a narrative that portrayed white residents of Neshoba County as villains and black residents as disempowered victims.[35] Members of Philadelphia's professional class—doctors, lawyers, and business owners—were particularly offended by this depiction of their community. Dearman remembered thinking in 1989 that "this would be a time to put a good face on things and let people know that we don't all think alike here." Furthermore, he reckoned, "It would be a great opportunity . . . to show ourselves for our own benefit . . . to start changing what's in here [teary-eyed, he placed his hand first on his head and then on his heart] and here."[36]

After Dearman passed away in 2017, many remarked on his internal moral compass that had driven his work as a journalist.[37] When Dearman received the Silver Elm Award from his alma mater, the University of Mississippi (the highest award in journalism offered by the university), the investigative journalist Jerry Mitchell told those gathered, "Stanley Dearman is a legend in journalism, and he will never be forgotten in Mississippi history because Stanley Dearman never forgot."[38] Dearman once told the *New York Times*: "I can say without exaggeration that in 40 years, not a single day has gone by that I don't think about those boys. . . . It's just something you can't wash off. People may not want to talk about it, but it will never go away. The thing won't let us forget."[39]

After *Mississippi Burning* reinvigorated national interest in the 1964 murders, local leaders like Dearman began to mobilize and organize local community members. As the editor and owner of a local rural weekly, Dearman possessed unrivaled control over local public discourse.[40] He single-handedly decided what was printed—and ultimately read—by the majority of Philadelphians, white, black, and Choctaw.

Dearman had taken over the *Neshoba Democrat* in 1966 from the previous editor, Jack Tannehill, who had been largely criticized for his coverage of the 1964 murders. In the first two decades of his tenure, Dearman began writing stories about, and including pictures of, local African Americans who had previously been excluded from the newspaper's content. In this subtle yet significant way, Dearman primed Philadelphia for change while also maintaining his stellar reputation. More importantly, Dearman's position as the newspaper's editor and owner afforded him control over essential silence-breaking technology. The local newspaper could—and would—be used to promote the 1989 commemoration, and it later reinforced the event's importance by reprinting a transcription of the event in the next week's issue. With a mix of pride and amusement, Jim Prince, an intern at the *Neshoba Democrat* in 1989, recalled recording the event and making the transcription: "We had to listen to those recordings so many times to get it right. I can still hear those voices."[41]

Despite his leadership, Dearman could not have organized a community-wide commemoration on his own. Although he had lived in Philadelphia for years, he was not born in Neshoba County and thus was not a native son. Dearman knew that he needed a strong local ally, and fortunately, he knew just the right person to enlist: Dick Molpus, who was as connected to the community as one could be. Born in Neshoba County and hailing from one of the county's most prominent families—which since 1905 had owned and operated a lumber company that would eventually become one of the largest independently owned lumber operations in the United States[42]—Molpus was serving as Mississippi's secretary of state when Dearman reached out for a collaborator.

Molpus had been fourteen in 1964 and recalls being deeply affected by his community that was "filled with good people . . . who were afraid to step up."[43] Despite the prevailing narrative that the civil rights workers were hiding up north, Molpus remembers that "many—even we kids—knew that wasn't true. We knew they were dead. We had even heard who was involved; we knew the names."

After attending the University of Mississippi, Molpus became a rising star in Mississippi politics. In the ten years preceding the twenty-fifth anniversary, Molpus served as an advisor to Governor William Winter, helping pass the 1982 education reform, and in 1984 he became secretary of state.

"There will be a lot of people in Philadelphia [for the twenty-fifth anniversary]," Dearman wrote to Molpus, "and we need to start thinking about what we can do about it."[44] Molpus agreed, and he offered to help organize a commemoration planning committee, despite stern warnings from his key advisors that such an act would be political suicide.[45]

Once Dearman and Molpus decided to organize a community-wide commemoration, they convened a planning committee made up of local leaders. Though efforts were made to engage African American members of the community, including those from Mt. Zion United Methodist Church, the planning committee was dominated by local white businessmen.

Then, as a local organizational infrastructure began to take shape, an unexpected ally emerged. After viewing *Mississippi Burning*, several prominent residents of Philadelphia's sister city—Philadelphia, Pennsylvania—envisioned a Philadelphia-to-Philadelphia project whereby citizens of the northern Philadelphia would assist with some sort of commemoration in the southern Philadelphia. They urged their mayor, Wilson Goode, to support the idea.[46]

Under most circumstances, it would be difficult to imagine a mayor from a large northern city allocating significant financial resources to commemorative efforts in a small southern town. But Goode had some reputation-management issues of his own, and his support for the initiative—his true motivations notwithstanding—was successful. Several months before the twenty-fifth anniversary, representatives from Goode's office reached out to Pete Talley, president of the Neshoba County branch of the NAACP, offering their services to support a citywide commemoration. While at first suspicious of the Pennsylvanians' motivations, Mississippi-based planning committee members came to find their institutional support—including a substantial financial investment—advantageous. "We were out of our league," one committee member remembered, but "we had the mayor's office from Philadelphia, Pennsylvania—from a major city in the United States [that] knew about public presentations and these kinds of things and had people on staff who were professionals doing that kind of stuff, particularly getting the word out." The Philadelphia-to-Philadelphia project was formalized, and as a result, two representatives from the northern Philadelphia made regular trips to Mississippi in preparation for the commemoration service.[47] Thus, with access to sufficient resources, an organizational infrastructure to channel those resources, and the motivation to acknowledge the town's violent history, the first community-wide commemoration of the 1964 commemoration came to fruition.

Commemoration and the Return to Public Silence

On June 21, 1989, more than a thousand people from around the country descended upon the southern Philadelphia, among them planeloads of VIPs from the northern Philadelphia and more than thirteen chartered busloads from New York City.[48] Countless others witnessed the first citywide commemoration service through a live feed streamed on "Good Morning America."

Meant to "commemorate the past, acknowledge the present, and celebrate the future," the three-part program began outside Mt. Zion, whose structure had been rebuilt to replace the building torched by the Klan in 1964.[49] Perched on a temporary stage, civil rights veterans, community members, and family members of the slain civil rights workers withstood the blistering Mississippi heat to deliver their remarks. The message from Michael Schwerner's widow, Rita, was simple and stern: "This is the very first time in my life a Mississippi highway patrolman waved at me."[50]

Of the many speeches delivered that day, the statement delivered by Molpus is particularly notable. Holding back tears, Molpus spoke directly to the victims' family members sitting in the audience. "We deeply regret what happened here twenty-five years ago," Molpus lamented. "We wish we could undo it. We are profoundly sorry that they are gone."[51] In light of decades of silence and denial in Philadelphia's public sphere, this acknowledgment was a radical act. Molpus was the first Mississippi elected official (and native Philadelphian) to publicly apologize for the murders.

For many locals, especially those with significant political or economic stature, the twenty-fifth anniversary commemoration presented an opportunity to articulate the city's positive change. This narrative is exemplified by Molpus's remarks at the commemoration service: "I mean it when I say it, that this is a new day in Philadelphia, this is a new day in Mississippi. No one is saying that this corner of the earth is perfect, and of course it isn't. There are shortcomings that we see every day, but we are working, we are struggling, we are trying to create the kind of community and state that can be a beacon to the nation and to the world. . . . We've come through a tough, a sad chapter in our state's history, but we've learned this lesson. We've learned that our real enemies are not each other."[52]

As the "commemoration of the past" gave way to a "celebration of the future," visitors gathered for an upbeat picnic on the football field of Neshoba Central High School, where the goal posts had been cut down to accommodate the crowd. Decades later, Molpus would describe the end of that extraordinary day: "B. B. King [was] playing. And when I left there was

David Goodman, who is Andy Goodman's brother, this Jewish guy with big mutton chop side burns, black hair. . . . He's out there dancing with some local Neshoba County girl and they're just dancing away and I was thinking 'this has been one hell of a day.'"[53] As members of the commemoration planning committee settled into bed that evening, they must have felt some sense of accomplishment. The event appeared to signal that the city had reached a turning point.

Despite this optimism, the reality of Philadelphia's moral redemption was challenged. When employees of the local newspaper arrived at work the day after the commemoration, they were confronted by an ominous message. The white columns flanking the entry to their downtown office had been defaced with red spray paint spelling "K-K-K," the lettering large and hurried.[54] Within three days of the event, Molpus received twenty-six death threats, "some of them very serious,"[55] and was compelled to retain a security detail to protect him and his family members, who had also been the target of threats. When he ran for governor five years later, he didn't even carry his hometown.[56]

Except for the dedication of a state-sponsored historical marker at Mt. Zion immediately following the 1989 commemoration, commemorative activity largely reverted to its previous habits. The Goodman family—and to a lesser extent, the families of Chaney and Schwerner—continued to serve as powerful agents of memory, organizing annual commemorations in New York City, calling for justice, and spearheading initiatives such as Freedom Summer '94, a project of the Andrew Goodman Foundation whose intent was to educate the wider public about issues facing young people.[57] Locally, African American churches continued to commemorate the event annually, but the memory of the murders remained generally absent from the city's dominant public sphere except for a perfunctory article in the local paper acknowledging the annual commemoration.

The 1989 commemoration also appeared to have left some residue in the hearts and minds of those who had been most connected to its planning. When Dearman retired as editor of the *Neshoba Democrat* in 2000, he wrote a final editorial headlined "June 21, 1964: It's Time for an Accounting." There, Dearman called on Mississippi's attorney general to pursue the case, encouraged by the recent prosecution of Byron De La Beckwith Jr. for the 1963 murder of Medgar Evers. Dearman spoke directly to his readership, a community that he had come to know well as the editor of the local paper for thirty-four years. "There are those in this community who will say that it's been too long," he wrote. "The trouble with that position is that they were saying it after five years, after ten years, after fifteen years. If it involved a member of their family or a friend, they would never say it's been too long. And if they claim that right for themselves, how can they in good conscience deny it anyone else?"[58]

The 2004 Commemoration

Fifteen years would pass before Philadelphia collectively confronted the 1964 murders once again. As in 1989, the approach of a milestone anniversary precipitated efforts to organize a citywide commemoration. This time, the city had a cohort of individuals who had previous experience with a citywide commemoration. Those involved in the twenty-fifth anniversary commemoration anticipated that the fortieth anniversary might also draw large crowds. That expectation was confirmed when Molpus received a phone call from an individual associated with Mt. Zion who claimed that forty busloads of visitors were planning to attend. Following the precedent established by the 1989 commemoration, Molpus convened a meeting of city leaders, many of whom had participated in the 1989 commemoration, to discuss the possibility of hosting a second community-wide commemoration.

While the 1989 commemoration influenced how organizers thought about the form and content of the 2004 commemoration, it was not determinative.[59] A lot had changed in the preceding years. Globally, human rights practitioners heralded a new era of truth-telling; nationally, President Bill Clinton had encouraged racial dialogue across the nation through his One America Initiative on race; regionally, civil rights–era crimes were being successfully prosecuted across the South;[60] and locally, communities across Mississippi were beginning to commemorate civil rights movement milestones. New issues and concerns had shaped the formative years of Mississippi's next generation of potential leaders.

On March 15, 2004, Molpus corralled Philadelphia's civic and business leaders to discuss the upcoming anniversary. At the meeting, recognizing the need for new leadership, the group appointed two members of the younger generation as cochairs of a newly formed commemoration task force. The proverbial torch had been passed. Leroy Clemons, a jovial African American and lifelong Philadelphian who had been recently elected president of the local branch of the NAACP, and Prince, a University of Mississippi graduate and successor to Dearman as the editor and owner of the *Neshoba Democrat*, graciously stepped into the role. Both Clemons and Prince had come of age during the so-called long silence,[61] the period between 1964 and 1989 when the city failed to acknowledge the murders in any official capacity. As a result, Philadelphians who grew up during this period had to discover this history on their own. Clemons uncovered this history at school. He knew little about the role of African Americans in the state's history until an enthusiastic American history teacher shared, to his surprise, the fact that Mississippi had had many African American legislators during Reconstruction. Clemons recalled wondering, "How many children just like me don't have a clue?"[62] In contrast, Prince did not discover this history until he was an adult. According to Prince, his parents were not the type to be "fanning the flames." His father was busy building his business, and his mother focused on maintaining their home. He did not recall ever speaking about the civil rights workers with his parents: "We didn't know to ask, and they didn't know to tell."[63]

Prince's first major exposure to the 1964 murders came just weeks before the twenty-fifth anniversary. In preparation for the 1989 commemoration, Dearman traveled to New York to interview Carolyn Goodman, an exchange that Dearman printed at length in the *Neshoba Democrat*.[64] Prince recalled reading the interview for the first time as a college student in 1989 and remembered the effect it had on him: "I sat down and read that and was just captivated because here was this doctor in New York talking about her then-eighteen-year-old son. . . . Whew, this could have been one of my friends. It could've been me. . . . There was the wanted poster, the missing [persons] poster. And that's all I ever knew of them. Nothing of their personal lives. If I knew anything about them, it was negative because they had come down here to stir up trouble."[65]

In many ways, these two stories of discovery exemplify Philadelphia's extremes. As coleaders of the fortieth anniversary commemoration task force, Clemons and Prince would have to traverse a deep cultural divide at a personal level. Only then could they lead their community into the trenches. And these young leaders knew the risk. "If we mess this up," Clemons would ponder, only partially in jest, "we're going to set race relations back by at least fifty years in this community." The two men used the analogy that it was like carrying a crate full of nitroglycerin through a minefield. "I mean, that's how delicate[ly] we had to move in this," Clemons recalls, "because we knew if we made one mistake we were going to destroy race relations in this community."[66]

These personal discoveries were an important first step toward a more public form of silence breaking, for any public reckoning requires that individuals recognize the existence of something that needs to be told.[67]

However, broader historical developments enabled Clemons and Prince to articulate and share these realizations with one another. In 1970, the U.S. Supreme Court compelled Mississippi to integrate its public schools, a process that had been successfully delayed by ardent segregationists since 1954. Philadelphians, like so many others across the state, feared that a violent reaction to desegregating the schools would confirm the prevailing national perception of Mississippi as brutish and backward. To their relief, Philadelphia schools were desegregated without incident. For the first time in the history of Mississippi, large numbers of white and African American children attended school together.

The desegregation of public schools enabled Prince and Clemons to interact not only in school but also at work. As high school students, the two had become friends while working for Dearman at the *Neshoba Democrat*. Without having established this relationship in their youth, it is unlikely that Clemons and Prince would have stopped to catch up with each other outside City Hall in the fall of 2003.[68] After the usual chitchat of longtime acquaintances, the conversation turned to the upcoming anniversary of the 1964 murders, and Clemons and Prince realized that they shared the sense that it was time for another community-wide commemoration. According to Clemons, he and Prince were "just having a general conversation about our vision for the city," and both noted their frustrations with previous commemorations of the murders:

> Local blacks didn't go. Local whites didn't go. It was just that small group of people out [at Mt. Zion] and the people that would come in on the buses. . . . And what we saw is people that were being interviewed were not people that lived here. . . . So they would be interviewed and talking as if they are residents of Philadelphia saying there ain't nothing changed about this place. It still is that same ole horrible place it was in the 1960s. The black folk are still scared of the white folks. . . . This is what they would be spouting out there on the platforms. And this is what the news media captured, and this is what they showed all over the country, and Jim and I was just talking like we're tired of other people speaking for us and telling our story.[69]

Clemons and Prince—both members of the post–civil rights generation—felt that the 1964 murders were continuing to affect their community. The commemoration, argued Clemons, "does not need to come from just the black community," referring to the annual commemoration held by African

Americans at Mt. Zion. "It needs to be a *community-wide* approach to doing something."[70] Prince agreed. "So here I am," recalled Prince. "It's 2004 and I know the fortieth is coming, and I'm right where Stanley Dearman was [in 1989]. I knew when I bought the paper I was inheriting that burden, . . . so it was kind of natural for me to say let's model this after what we did in '89."[71] As in 1989, two community leaders recognized a joint objective and joined forces to organize a citywide commemoration service.

After being anointed as the cochairs of the newly formed commemoration task force, Clemons and Prince began to recruit collaborators. They turned to key community stakeholders—those who were respected members of Philadelphia's white, African American, and Choctaw communities—as well as those who had unique connections to the civil rights movement and the 1964 killings. On April 28, an article appeared in the *Neshoba Democrat* announcing the "broad-based, tri-racial task force" and inviting others to participate in what would ultimately become a thirty-member multiracial coalition.[72]

Meanwhile, institutional support for local racial reconciliation efforts was growing. In 2002, Susan Glisson, a Georgia native who had received her master's degree in southern studies at the University of Mississippi, was appointed director of the newly created William Winter Institute for Racial Reconciliation at the University of Mississippi. The institute had been founded to sustain the work of William Winter, the former governor of Mississippi who had been responsible for bringing the only southern forum of President Clinton's One America Initiative to the University of Mississippi.[73] Just two years after the institute was founded, Molpus, who was serving on its board, asked Glisson to come to Philadelphia to advise Philadelphia's Community Development Partnership (CDP) on a new project: a brochure highlighting Philadelphia's African American heritage.[74]

This represented new terrain for Philadelphia's CDP. Never before had the business-minded organization sought to highlight local African American history. Like so many recent efforts to honor African American history across the South, the brochure's roots lay in the tourism industry. In 2000, the state of Mississippi granted Philadelphia's request to create a tourism council, a legal body empowered to collect a 3 percent bed tax at city hotels. This created a new source of revenue for promotional materials such as heritage brochures. The request to establish a tourism council had been a response to a recent surge in local casino tourism. In 1994, the Mississippi Band of Choctaw Indians had opened the Pearl River Resort and Casino, a Las Vegas–style complex offering slot machines and cocktails in an otherwise dry county. As a new source of revenue, the bed tax bolstered the city's capacity to organize and promote commemorative activities, without which the 2004 commemoration might not have occurred.

This new source of revenue coincided with broader efforts across the southeast to promote regional tourism. In 2003, Kaye Rowell, Philadelphia's director of tourism, and Clemons met for the first time at the Southeast Tourism Society Professional Marketing Institute in Dahlonega, Georgia. There, Rowell and Clemons connected with regional and state resources for local tourism. Alex Thomas was one such resource. As an African American teenager in Jackson, Mississippi, during the 1980s, Thomas had developed a deep interest in civil rights history. Years later, in December 2002, he was hired by the Mississippi Development Authority as the first director of heritage and cultural tourism. In the winter of 2004, Thomas was invited to Philadelphia, where the CDP was interested in attracting visitors other than casino tourists. Thomas encouraged the CDP to embrace the city's rich African American history and, more important, to "tell their own story." "If you don't tell your own story," Thomas warned, "someone else will."[75] This seemed to resonate with local participants, who had grown weary of being defined by the national media.

Already in Philadelphia supporting the African American heritage tourism efforts, Clemons and Prince, on the recommendation of Molpus, invited Glisson to consult with the newly formed group that had been tasked with organizing the fortieth anniversary commemoration. Bringing Glisson into the commemoration planning process at this early stage ultimately proved crucial, since her experience with programming on the University of Mississippi's racial past enabled her to assist the multiracial, multigenerational Philadelphia Coalition as they navigated sensitive conversations. The thoughts of one coalition member reflect a common sentiment regarding Glisson's involvement: "Well, you know, having Susan Glisson involved—it probably couldn't have happened without her help and expertise."[76]

Standing before a diverse group of Philadelphians on April 5, 2004, Glisson spoke about the University of Mississippi's 2002 Open Doors commemoration service, which represented the institution's first major effort to commemorate James Meredith's desegregation of the university. She explained that organizers began by deciding to present a unified story: all disagreements—and there had been many—had been worked out behind the scenes and not in front of the media.

Philadelphia's fortieth anniversary planning process would also be plagued with disagreements. Certain organizational issues—where to hold the commemoration and who should speak were prominent among them—were deeply symbolic, involving not merely logistics but also questions of representation and recognition. Complicating matters further, and unbeknown to members of the local commemoration task force, a national committee of civil rights activists from outside Mississippi had been separately organizing a commemoration, also to be held in Philadelphia, on the fortieth anniversary of the 1964 murders. The legitimacy of this national group was supported by the fact that it had the support of Ben Chaney, James Chaney's younger brother, and John Steele, a member of the Mt. Zion community who lived in California. For a time, it appeared that the fortieth anniversary in Philadelphia would include two rival commemorations: one organized by a group of national civil rights activists and the other by a group of local citizens of Philadelphia. Amid this competition and confusion, Glisson emerged as an important broker, ultimately orchestrating a compromise.

Glisson's access to the resources of the University of Mississippi also proved to be a critical asset. "We invited all the top officials," one coalition member recalls. "And that's the sort of thing . . . where Ole Miss helped us." Since the coalition was unequipped to handle media relations, the University of Mississippi's Public Relations Office provided assistance, inviting statewide officials to attend the commemoration and coordinating with the media. According to the coalition member, "we couldn't have done it without the Winter Institute."[77]

On Sunday, June 20, 2004, thousands of visitors once again came to Philadelphia, this time to mark the fortieth anniversary of the infamous 1964 murders. The program, titled "Recognition, Resolution, Redemption: Uniting for Justice," was more explicitly oriented toward social justice than the 1989 commemoration had been. While some were vocal about pursuing legal justice, others argued that the call for justice and commemoration would be good for business. Prince, then editor of the *Neshoba Democrat*, articulated this position in a June 9 editorial: "As an economic development issue, we could not be able to pay in a lifetime for the type of positive coverage for our county."[78] The commemoration offered an opportunity "to show the world this community has changed." And the editorial continued, "the world will be watching."[79]

The program began at 2:00 P.M. with an hour-long service at the Neshoba County Coliseum, the only venue large enough to accommodate the number of visitors who would attend. Here, a diverse set of speakers flanked the stage, perhaps best exemplified in an Associated Press photograph that captured Mississippi's conservative governor, Haley Barbour, shaking hands with Congressman John Lewis, a civil rights veteran and activist (see figure G.6). The CDP integrated itself into the commemoration by passing out various promotional materials, including circular cardboard fans that said "I'm a fan of Philadelphia Tourism" and civil rights tourism brochures that highlighted several civil rights–related sites. Driving tours of these sites ran at regular intervals from the coliseum, each narrated by a white and an African American Philadelphia native (who at times advanced competing perspectives).

As part of the compromise between the two commemoration planning committees, the day's events concluded with a smaller church service at Mt. Zion. Molpus returned to the stage, but this time he went further than he had in 1989—when he had been the first Mississippi elected official to publicly apologize for the murders. In 2004, Molpus delivered a thundering speech, reminding his fellow Philadelphians of their complicity in allowing impunity to reign and urging those with "local roots" to support the efforts of the state attorney general and local district attorney who sought to prosecute the case. Furthermore, Molpus called on local citizens to challenge the pervasive narrative that had cast them as villains: "Forty years from now I want our children and grandchildren to look back on us and what we did and say that we had the courage, the wisdom, and the strength to rise up, to take the responsibility to right historical wrongs."[80] Where the previous generation had failed, the new generation could be heroes.

Mnemonic Battles, Commemoration, and Silence Breaking

This brief history demonstrates that Philadelphia's journey toward silence breaking was neither straightforward nor inevitable. It required the confluence of several key processes, some of which unfolded over decades. First, for Philadelphia's commemorations to emerge, the previously silenced event—the 1964 killings—needed to be perceived by locals in positions of power and influence as worthy of commemoration. This required personal awakenings, with individuals becoming cognizant of the community's racial past—which was only possible because the past was not entirely suppressed, at least not in private or semiprivate settings. Teachers, parents, and other agents of socialization conveyed the history of the 1964 murders to individuals like Prince and Clemons, who came to believe that a public reckoning with this past was key to the community's future. These individuals then became memory activists, encouraging others to see the event as commemorable and the commemoration as necessary. Highlighting Neshoba County's long-standing negative reputation—believed to be a product of national news reporters who gravitated toward those with the most extreme positions—proved to be an effective rhetorical tool. The desire to defend the character of their community and articulate their own narrative compelled a diverse group of citizens to join the silence-breaking effort.

To enact community-wide commemoration, however, required more than rhetoric; it also demanded the financial and human resources necessary to enact a large-scale event. By 2004, resources to support racial reconciliation efforts had developed within Mississippi. In many ways, the Winter Institute, under Glisson's stewardship, served the same role as had the mayor's office of Philadelphia, Pennsylvania, fifteen years previously. Members of the fortieth anniversary commemoration task force—the Philadelphia Coalition—were all volunteers, most of whom held full-time jobs. The Winter Institute provided the coalition with a consultant who could essentially work full time on commemoration planning. Furthermore, Glisson's experience in mediating racial dialogues ultimately proved crucial, as divisions within the coalition and challenges from outside it threatened the group's viability and thus the commemoration's emergence. In both cases, it is important to note that the local ability to commemorate the murders was buttressed by institutional support from outside the local community. It appears, then, that external forces are critical not only for creating pressure on the local community (which provides incentives for the local community to hold a commemoration), but also for attracting essential financial, organizational, and political support—without which less well-resourced agents of memory might not be able to construct a commemorative vehicle.

These developments (commemorability and the capacity to commemorate) are characteristic of how commemorations of difficult pasts emerge, but they do not entirely explain how Philadelphia's silence-breaking commemorations came to be. Two other developments appeared to be essential: growing national pressure and the converging interests of those historically opposed to and in favor of commemorating the 1964 murders. In both 1989 and 2004, national developments placed pressure on the local community to acknowledge the 1964 murders just prior to the commemorations. The first and most significant of these developments was the national release of *Mississippi Burning*. The film reinvigorated national interest in the case and inspired a number of individuals, including representatives from the national media, to visit Philadelphia for the upcoming twenty-fifth anniversary. This interest preceded any local efforts to organize a community-wide commemoration and appears to have been the primary impetus for local agents of countermemory to mobilize. In other words, if the film had not drawn attention to the case—and, by extension, to Philadelphia—the national interest in the twenty-fifth anniversary would have been far less. Surely, major national news outlets would have covered the anniversary as they had the tenth, fifteenth, and twentieth, but it is unlikely that the story would have saturated the news cycle as it did. *Mississippi Burning* made the 1964 killings national news.

Likewise, in 2004, national interest pressured local citizens to plan a fortieth anniversary commemoration. And as in 1989, in the months preceding the anniversary in 2004, local leaders experienced a dramatic increase in the number of phone calls regarding the commemoration, alerting them to the potential arrival of thousands of visitors in Philadelphia for the event. This came after the fortieth anniversary celebrations commemorating several civil rights milestones, notable among them the Freedom Rides and the murder of Medgar Evers, the Jackson-based NAACP field secretary. In June 2004, members of the national civil rights community were prepared to travel to Philadelphia—whether the local community was prepared for them or not.

In 2004, locals also experienced national pressure through another mechanism—the memory of commemoration.[81] Despite the fifteen-year hiatus, the twenty-fifth anniversary commemoration in Philadelphia in 1989 had set a precedent for local memory activists to follow. Having witnessed the twenty-fifth anniversary commemoration as young adults, a new generation of memory activists felt compelled to hold another commemoration service. Some members of this younger generation saw the 1989 commemoration as a missed opportunity: it had not transformed their community as the 1989 organizers had hoped. Others believed that the fortieth anniversary offered another chance for them to right the wrongs of the past once and for all. The twenty-fifth anniversary commemoration provided a blueprint and clearly affected the form, content, and conditions of possibility for a fortieth anniversary commemoration. As a blueprint, the 1989 commemoration also provided a template on which the 2004 organizers could improve; and as a moral touchstone, it provided the rhetorical footing on which subsequent memory activists would cultivate a collective consciousness in favor of collective reckoning.

In addition to national pressure on the local community, the interests of those opposed to and those in favor of acknowledgment converged.[82] With the release of *Mississippi Burning* just six months before the twenty-fifth anniversary of the murders, the national spotlight was on the small community of Philadelphia. Aware that representatives of the national media would be in town covering the twenty-fifth anniversary, local leaders had seized the opportunity to challenge the *Mississippi Burning* narrative that portrayed Philadelphia's white community as ignorant and deeply racist. Although restoring Philadelphia's damaged reputation was motivation enough, many local business owners hoped that the commemoration would also stimulate the local economy. Consequently, those who had previously condoned the public silence, whether explicitly or implicitly, had sufficient motivation to publicly acknowledge the murders.

The same reputational and economic motivations for acknowledging the murders were present in 2004—arguably even more so. By the early 2000s, a number of political and economic developments on both the state and local levels had shifted the conditions of possibility for local community-wide commemoration. On the state level, the Mississippi Development Authority had developed an infrastructure to support African American heritage tourism statewide. This was part of broader regional efforts to cultivate African American tourism.[83] Locally, a burgeoning tourism industry had enabled Philadelphia's CDP to create a tourism council that could both provide support for commemorative activities and channel profits back into the city. Thus, in both 1989 and 2004, reputational concerns and economic opportunities reduced resistance from those who had previously opposed public acknowledgment.

While the circumstances surrounding each commemoration were unique, both represent similar moments of public acknowledgment in the trajectory of Philadelphia's official public memory that helps explain when and how conspiracies of silence are deconstructed. First, it appears that deconstructing conspiracies of silence takes time. While this point may seem simplistic, it has important theoretical and practical implications. The passage of time is not an explanatory factor in its own right: rather, it enables the necessary political, economic, and normative shifts to occur. Just as the accumulation of memory makes silence more difficult to dismantle over time, countermemory is characterized by that same cumulative effect. The passage of time can enable agents of countermemory to develop a robust oppositional infrastructure. Second, this analysis of the 1989 and 2004 commemorations indicates that singular episodes of silence breaking do not necessarily dismantle a conspiracy of silence. The 1989 commemoration, while notable as the first moment of acknowledgment within Philadelphia's dominant public sphere, could not sustain open public discourse regarding the 1964 murders. The second community-wide commemoration further transformed the official public narrative of 1964.

Furthermore, the shift in Philadelphia's public narrative was not the only outcome of the 2004 commemoration. In the months following the commemoration, a number of racially significant transformations began to unfold: Edgar Ray Killen was convicted for his role in the 1964 murders; the Mississippi legislature passed a bill mandating civil and human rights education at every grade level; and Mississippi citizens established the Mississippi Truth Project, among whose initiatives was the formation of a South African–style truth and reconciliation commission, which would have been the first statewide truth commission in the United States.[84] The next three chapters examine how these notable events can be attributed to the 2004 commemoration in Philadelphia and, in doing so, illuminate the processes connecting local commemoration with subsequent efforts for social repair.

3 Prosecuting Edgar Ray Killen

On June 21, 2005, hundreds of journalists and onlookers gathered outside the Neshoba County courthouse, a tiny brick building flanked by towering magnolias, where a momentous verdict had been reached: forty-one years after the crime, eighty-year-old Edgar Ray "Preacher" Killen had been convicted for his role in the 1964 Mississippi Burning murders of the civil rights workers James Chaney, Andrew Goodman, and Michael Schwerner. After hearing the verdict, many people who had gathered outside the courthouse embraced in cathartic release. Others stood still, stunned, as they contemplated its potential ramifications. This was the first time Mississippi's legal authorities had held anyone accountable for the murders, a charge that could only be brought by the state. Now, so long after the fact, the main instigator behind the killings had been tried and convicted in Philadelphia, the city notorious for its decades-long silence and denial surrounding the case. What could possibly explain this remarkable turn of events after so many decades of impunity?

The 2005 prosecution of Killen was not the first high-profile cold-case trial, nor was it the first Mississippi Burning trial.[1] In 1967, seven men from Neshoba County or nearby Lauderdale County had been convicted in federal court for conspiring "to deny the civil rights" of the three young activists.[2] None served more than six years. For Chaney's mother, Fannie Lee, the 1967 trial offered some consolation. After the trial, she told reporters, "They did better than I thought they would do."[3] Indeed, the outcome of the 1967 federal verdict against the men who killed her son was notable: nearly a century had passed since any white man in Mississippi had been convicted and sent to prison for a federal civil rights violation.[4] But while the outcome of the 1967 federal trial may have been better than expected, it did not satisfy the victims' families' desire for justice.

Between 1967 and 2005, the families continued to press Mississippi legal authorities to reopen the case, and in 1989, these demands finally gained traction. After seeing *Mississippi Burning*, Mike Moore, the state's attorney general, was moved to consider reopening the case. Those responsible could still be prosecuted, at least in theory, since murder is one of the few charges without a statute of limitations. The case's viability was therefore not a question of law but one of evidence. Whether there would be enough credible evidence after so many years remained to be seen.

After several months of preliminary investigation, the attorney general's office issued a confidential report concluding that enough vital evidence was still available to reopen the case.[5] The confidentiality of the report was short-lived. Despite efforts to protect the "Saladin Project"—the code name for the investigation and an homage to the main character from Salmon Rushdie's inflammatory novel, *The Satanic Verses*—sensitive information was leaked. Under public pressure, Moore equivocated: "What I'm doing is taking a preliminary look into this case . . . to make a determination if it is in the best interest of this state to prosecute. The first hurdle we have to jump is whether the evidence is enough to successfully prosecute." The second hurdle, Moore continued, was to decide whether "it is in the best interest of the people of this state."[6] Despite there being sufficient evidence to proceed, Moore's answer to that second question was negative. Shortly after the investigation became public, Moore abandoned the project.

Ten years passed before new information and growing public interest in civil rights–era crimes fueled a second major attempt to reopen the case. In 1999, Jerry Mitchell, a reporter for the Jackson *Clarion-Ledger*, acquired and published a transcript of a previously sealed interview with Sam Bowers, the former imperial wizard of the White Knights of the Ku Klux Klan. Without regret or remorse, Bowers boasted that he had "obstructed justice" in the probe of the Neshoba County murders by the FBI and was "quite delighted to be convicted [in the 1967 trial] and have the main instigator of the entire affair walk out of the courtroom a free man."[7] Even though Bowers did not name the "main instigator," the 1964 FBI investigation pointed to one man: Killen, the Klan's kleagle (main recruiter and organizer), who had received the "number 4" order to eliminate Michael Schwerner. Following Bowers's orders, Killen bought rubber gloves, gassed up the cars, gathered the guns, and ensured that the burial site was prepared and the bulldozer ready.[8] Killen narrowly escaped justice in the 1967 federal trial when one member of the all-white jury refused to convict him on the grounds that she "could never convict a preacher."[9]

When Mitchell published Bowers's interview, the families of Chaney, Schwerner, and Goodman again demanded that the state reopen the case, and on February 25, 1999, Moore, together with Ken Turner, the Neshoba County district attorney, answered the call.[10] Moving quickly to enrich the case, Moore and Turner found two witnesses who reluctantly agreed to testify: Cecil Price, the former deputy sheriff who had been convicted in the 1967 trial, and Bob Stringer, who as a teenager had worked for Bowers in the 1960s. The investigation seemed to be gaining momentum.

Then, in 2001, a seemingly fatal blow struck the prosecution's case. At the age of sixty-three, Price fell from a cherry picker at his workplace and died. Price's death felt eerily reminiscent of an era in the not so distant past when dissenters were disappeared by the Klan, leading some locals to speculate that the fatal fall had been the result of foul play. Within days of Price's death, Moore signaled that his office was winding down the investigation. "We've still got the zeal to do it," said Moore, "but there's no sense in doing it if you can't make a strong case."[11] "If [Price] had been a defendant," Moore told the *New York Times*, "he would have been a principal defendant. . . . If he had been a witness, he would have been our best witness. . . . His death is a tragic blow to our case."[12] In 2002, Moore indicated that there was only a "slim chance" of murder charges being brought by the state. The case was effectively closed.

Yet in 2005, after forty years of failed attempts and without having uncovered any additional evidence, Jim Hood (Mississippi's newly elected attorney general), along with Marc Duncan (then Neshoba County's district attorney), presented the case before a grand jury in the county, which ultimately issued an indictment. Less than a year later, local jurors found Killen guilty of the crime. The fact that this seemingly intractable case moved forward in 2005 without any new evidence and after so many failed attempts presents a historical puzzle. How did Killen come to be prosecuted for murder forty-one years after the fact? Furthermore, what role might local commemoration have played in this process? Might the Philadelphia Coalition's community-wide commemoration and its call for justice—made only a year before the indictment—be the missing piece of the puzzle? And if so, how did a local commemorative event help cultivate the conditions that would bring about a legal outcome where previous efforts by family members and investigative reporters had failed?

How Do Civil Rights Cold Cases Emerge?

While the prosecution of Killen is a unique historical event, it also represents a broader social phenomenon—efforts to seek legal redress for crimes long past. Following World War II, the Nuremberg trials, which prosecuted prominent members of the Nazi regime, set a new precedent for international jurisprudence. Indeed, the Nuremberg trials not only created new categories of crime (crimes against humanity, genocide, and so on), but they also cultivated the expectation that the perpetrators of widespread human rights violations would be held to account, even as their crimes became distant memories.[13] As recently as 2018, the United States extradited Jakiw Palij, a ninety-five-year-old alleged former Nazi, to face criminal proceedings.[14] Palij joined at least twenty-three other alleged Nazi criminals who were facing charges in Germany and Austria.

Prior to 2009, when the Munich trial of John Demjanjuk determined that the "mere support of the whole system of a [death] camp is punishable," such trials would have been rare.[15] Similar dynamics have played out elsewhere, as the post-Nuremberg legal infrastructure enabled actors outside of Germany to seek legal redress for human rights violations. For example, since 2008, individuals and collectivities have pursued legal actions for crimes committed during the civil war in Spain, a county previously known for its state-sponsored "forgetting"—when political parties negotiated the *pacto del olvido* and the subsequent amnesty law that freed political prisoners and permitted those who had been exiled to return.[16] In recent years, victims' groups have become more vocal, calling on authorities to investigate the Franco regime and leading some observers to ask if Spain is recovering its memory after all.[17] Likewise, mnemonic battles have raged in Japan and South Korea as representatives of the remaining Korean comfort women continue to seek legal recognition of their forced sexual slavery by the Japanese Imperial Army during World War II. Yet as this recent resurgence of legal redress for distant crimes reveals, the prosecution of systematic violence is neither steady nor certain.

In the United States, recent efforts to adjudicate racially motivated killings that took place during the 1950s and 1960s indicate similar dynamics. Since 1989, authorities across the country have reopened and investigated more than a hundred of these civil rights cold cases that have remained unsolved or insufficiently prosecuted, leading to twenty-four convictions.[18] This includes Byron de la Beckwith's 1994 conviction for the 1963 murder of Medgar Evers and his 1998 conviction for the 1966 killing of Vernon Dahmer, both important precursors to the Killen trial.[19] Despite this notable trend, social scientists have yet to systematically explore the underlying factors that precipitate such cases.[20] However, the detailed work of journalists and historians illuminates several sociological factors that help explain the multiple pathways through which these cases emerged.

First and foremost, victims' family members have played an essential role by keeping the memory of their lost loved ones alive. Without their caring stewardship, the memory and meaning of civil rights–era murders would have grown more distant with each generation. Without the memory of these murders, prosecuting those responsible would be impossible. As the legal analyst Joseph Gill notes, family members "give the victims of decades old crimes a fresh 'face' for prosecutors to visualize rather than faded black and white photographs from the 1960s."[21] Who better to humanize these long-gone victims than those who knew them best? Victims' families not only keep the memory alive, they also curate public acts of remembrance through annual commemoration services and institutionalize this commemorative work through foundations and charities—and in some cases, they provide new evidence that can lead to a conviction.[22]

Journalists and documentary filmmakers have also played an important role in bringing these cases to fruition, having been especially adept at securing previously undiscovered documents and compelling potential witnesses to provide testimony. In the history of Mississippi's civil rights cold cases, Mitchell's role is particularly notable. Beginning with his first civil rights story in 1989, in which he revealed how the state of Mississippi had secretly provided legal assistance to Byron De La Beckwith Jr., the man who murdered Medgar Evers, a field secretary for the NAACP, in 1963, Mitchell has uncovered information that helped convict at least four other former Klansmen, a track record that earned him a reputation as a "Klan-busting journalist" and the recognition of a MacArthur Foundation "genius" grant in 2009 for his groundbreaking investigative work.[23]

These initial convictions paved the way for subsequent cases, and in their wake, institutional structures emerged to organize and support similar legal efforts. The university-initiated Cold Case Justice Initiative at Syracuse University Law School and the Civil Rights Restorative Justice Project at Northeastern University routinely send students to assist families seeking legal redress in civil rights cases. The journalist-driven Civil Rights Cold Case Project, established in 2008, coordinates the efforts of journalists and others working on these cases. And the Emmett Till Unsolved Civil Rights Crime Act of 2008 (known as the Till Bill) provided the Justice Department with the mandate and funds to investigate civil rights–era crimes.[24] The organization and institutionalization of civil rights cold-case investigations not only expanded efforts that had only been pursued by private individuals until that point, but it also signified a broader political and cultural shift.

Indeed, cold-case investigations were by and large enabled by the historical developments taking place across the South. In Mississippi, the political environment had been greatly transformed in the decades following the civil rights movement, most notably by the ascendance of black political power.[25] Legislative redistricting and nondiscriminatory single-member districts enabled the number of black lawmakers to grow. And as the terrain of racial politics began to change, so did public sentiment. By the 1990s, attitudes toward civil rights–era cold cases had become more favorable. Although the public opinion data on civil rights cold cases are limited, two polls provide some insight. In 1994, a Mississippi State University poll probed public opinion about Beckwith's trial. After being informed that all-white, all-male juries had been unable to agree on Beckwith's guilt or innocence in previous trials, roughly 45 percent of the respondents felt that it was fair to try him again, 41 percent felt that it was unfair, and 14 percent offered no opinion.[26] Ten years later, a 2005 poll of Neshoba County residents found that only 35 percent opposed the Killen trial.[27] While still divided, Mississippians seemed to be more open to the civil rights prosecutions than they had been in previous years.[28]

Finally, as political opinion began to shift, so did the political impetus to support civil rights–era cold cases. For decades, southern cities and states had competed to attract industrial development, often emphasizing their supply of cheap nonunion labor. By the second half of the twentieth century, these efforts extended to a community's social image. In an effort to downplay the prospects of racial tensions, cities like Atlanta adopted slogans such as "too busy to hate."[29] Civil rights–era cold cases thus represented an opportunity for southern sunbelt states to demonstrate that they had moved past the Jim Crow era to embrace a postracial future—a veiled selling point directed at global firms looking to relocate. As exemplars of this postracial narrative, cold-case trials provided an opportunity to pin the history of southern racism on a few old men, relics of a bygone era. When the barriers to prosecuting civil rights cold cases are viewed through the lens of economic opportunity, it is not surprising that they were reduced as the economic climate of southern states began to flourish.

While all these factors—the persistent advocacy of family members; the tireless efforts of local journalists; and the transformation of the political, cultural, and economic landscape—certainly shaped the conditions of possibility surrounding the Killen trial, they do not fully explain why Killen was finally brought before a grand jury in 2005, less than three years after the Mississippi attorney general had abandoned the case in 2002 and in the absence of new witnesses or evidence. Family members of the 1964 victims had been pressuring state and local authorities since the 1960s, and thus the mobilization of victims' families after 2002 was neither new nor particularly notable. Furthermore, in the years between 2002 and 2005, the political, cultural, and economic environment remained relatively unchanged. And finally, the federal resources provided by the Till Bill were not available until several years after the Killen trial. If none of these factors sufficiently explain the Killen trial, what could have occurred between 2002 and 2005 to propel this case forward? The answer to that question lies within the 2004 commemoration in Philadelphia. In many ways, that signal event served the same social functions as family activism, investigative journalism, and broader cultural change, and alongside those developments, the commemoration offers an alternative pathway to cold-case revivals.

Forging the Philadelphia Coalition: Creating a Collective Identity and Organizational Infrastructure

By April 2004, the fortieth anniversary commemoration task force had been meeting for several weeks in preparation for the upcoming June 21 event. It hadn't taken long for the group to recognize the futility of organizing a commemoration without acknowledging the deeper issues at hand, and on April 20, as they considered themes for the upcoming commemoration, the task force's white cochair, Jim Prince, paused the discussion. Scanning the diverse faces before him, he asked each member to share one word that the event should communicate. One after the other, each member shared his or her hopes: unity, togetherness, redemption, truth, and resolution. Of all the aspirations uttered, one stood out as especially potent: justice. On this point, two members of the task force found rare common ground. Don Kilgore, a white lawyer, and James Young, an African American county supervisor, were unified in their insistence that without seeking justice, the event would be meaningless. The group agreed.

Stanley Dearman, the former editor of the local *Neshoba Democrat*, echoed these sentiments. "We aren't party planners here," he reminded those present. "There is a soul and heart issue that needs to be dealt with. . . . Before we go any further, we need to have a call for justice."[30] But the discussion about what form a "call for justice" should take broke down along racial lines. When black participants recommended a march, whites in the room visibly shrank in their seats. When white participants suggested a community declaration, black participants decried a resolution as merely words on a page. The debate itself was not surprising. At its heart, it was a debate about tactics, how best to achieve the group's ultimate goal of transforming the narrative of Philadelphia and Neshoba County. Moreover, the impact of race on public opinion, collective memory, and numerous other behaviors is well documented.[31] It was to be expected that disagreements about tactics would be racially patterned. But what happened next was surprising: the task force recognized and acknowledged the racial divide among the members, and they began sharing stories about their own experiences during the civil rights era. For most participants, this was the first time that they had spoken about this time period in interracial company. For the people around that table, it was an eye-opening and deeply emotional experience.

Transforming racially rooted disagreements into productive discourse is not a simple task. Often, despite the most unassailable intentions of the participants, achieving constructive outcomes of such potentially charged interactions can be elusive without skilled facilitation. Although the task force had not planned to have a facilitator attend their meeting, Susan Glisson, the soft-spoken Georgia native working for the William Winter Institute for Racial Reconciliation, had taken on that role. Reflecting on the task force's early conversation, Glisson noted her initial concern: "It was clear that one of [the group's] difficulties would be communication. . . . Without a common language, which could only come with a common understanding of past events, [they] would not be able to move forward together."[32]

Mediating the debate about what form a call for justice should take was just one of the many times Glisson would be called on to facilitate difficult conversations among task force members. But as it turned out, the more difficult conversations were not within the task force but between it and the national planning committee that had claimed ownership of the fortieth anniversary commemoration service and maintained its own ideas about when the service should take place, where it should be held, and who should be given the right to speak. For the committee, the efforts of the Philadelphia Coalition were too little, too late. The committee had been working on a fortieth anniversary commemoration since 2003, and its members were suspicious of local commemorative efforts. The relationship between the two groups was further complicated by miscommunication, misinformation, and a long history of distrust between locals and those whom they perceived as being outsiders.

The location of the commemoration became a particularly contentious point. The Philadelphia Coalition had decided that the commemoration would be more inclusive if it were held at the Neshoba County Coliseum, a venue that could accommodate a larger group and would better represent the various African American communities that had supported the movement for civil rights. For coalition members Eva Tisdale and Nettie Cox Moore, who had been on the front lines of Neshoba County's civil rights movement, the historic focus on Mt. Zion had overshadowed the important contributions of other nearby African American communities. The national committee, in contrast, insisted that the commemoration be held at Mt. Zion as it had been every year since 1964. Not doing so, they argued, would be an insult to the Mt. Zion community and the sacred ground on which the church stood.

Again, Glisson was thrust into the role of mediator, and as a result of her careful arbitration, a fragile compromise was reached. Preceding a smaller ceremony at Mt. Zion, the Philadelphia Coalition would host a larger event at the coliseum and provide a live broadcast of the Mt. Zion ceremony for the overflow crowd remaining at the coliseum. Glisson became caught in the cross fire of accusatory emails from the national organizers, but she still found some comfort: "If the [Philadelphia Coalition] is unified on nothing else, it's unified against [members of the national planning committee], which seems to help cement the group."[33] The perceived threat from outside organizers thus had an unintended consequence: it muted divisions within the local task force and helped the group forge a collective identity. What began as a local commemoration planning committee became an organization with goals that extended far beyond the local event. The alchemy of common cause and collaborative reflection had transformed a committee into a coalition.

And the coalition wanted justice. With this core goal defined, the group divided its efforts. Some members served on administrative subcommittees (related to hospitality, finance, transportation, and security), while others focused on the commemoration program (the program committee) and considered a more permanent memorial (the memorial committee). Two additional committees focused on the pursuit of legal justice. As local lawyers examined the legal minutiae surrounding the Killen case to map a path forward (the justice committee), others drafted a resolution calling for justice (the resolution committee). These committees formed the organizational infrastructure of the newly named Philadelphia Coalition, and with this structure in place, they could begin the hard work of planning a large-scale commemoration service in the pursuit of justice.

Collaborating with the Winter Institute: Leveraging Statewide Resources

One of the first major tasks for the Philadelphia Coalition was to draft a resolution. The resolution committee, cochaired by the former and current editors of the *Neshoba Democrat*, drafted the document and presented it to the rest of the coalition. After some discussion and several drafts, the coalition passed the resolution unanimously on May 3, just seven weeks before the fortieth anniversary. The resolution, which called on Mississippi legal authorities "to use every available resource and do all things necessary to bring about a just resolution to this case," represented the coalition's first official public statement.

Before introducing the resolution to the general community, however, the Philadelphia Coalition sought support from the city, county, and Choctaw tribe as part of a strategy to bolster the legitimacy of its demands. But while the task force's cochairs had recruited representatives from each of these governmental units to participate in the Philadelphia Coalition, none of these representatives could ensure that the resolution would be endorsed. Young, who served on the county commission, was cautiously hopeful. Presenting the resolution to these governmental bodies, he said, "would be a good test of leadership."[34]

As anticipated, city, county, and Choctaw leaders were tested. Initially, Philadelphia's mayor resisted signing the resolution, and speculations arose about why he resisted. Some wondered if the city's attorney had discouraged the mayor from signing the document, since doing so could make the city liable. Others speculated that the mayor was beholden to the defunct White Citizens' Council—or worse yet, to the Klan. Philadelphia's city council members were also reluctant to sign when they first considered the resolution at one of their sessions, and the councilors exhibited a number of common responses to difficult pasts: denial, evasion, projection, and ultimately tepid acceptance.[35] As the session came to a close, a soft-spoken white member of the council offered his view: murder is wrong, whenever it's done. If his children were harmed, he would want their killers brought to justice.[36] No one disagreed, and by the end of the session, the Philadelphia City Council voted unanimously to support the coalition's resolution.

Outside the city on the nearby Choctaw reservation, the tribe's leaders were not so easily convinced. According to one Philadelphian, "the tribe doesn't explore the past"—an interesting stance given that the Mississippi Band of Choctaw Indians are descendants of those who evaded the Trail of

Tears.[37] To remember the Jim Crow era, in the tribe's estimation, risked teaching the next generation to hate. Forgetting was safer.

Throughout the process of securing endorsements, Glisson worried that the Philadelphia Coalition would get scooped by reporters in the state capital. Since the coalition's legitimacy came from its local grassroots origins, if the community learned about these efforts from Jackson-based news outlets, the commemoration and its call for justice could be at risk. To ensure that the community understood the grassroots origin of the project, the Winter Institute staff worked diligently to arrange a local press conference. Simultaneously, staff members carried out other administrative tasks: they secured endorsements, spoke with reporters from state and national news outlets, developed talking points for potential questions from the press, and wrote speeches for city officials to present at the press conference. For the Winter Institute staff in the weeks leading up to the press conference and the commemoration, supporting the Philadelphia Coalition was a full-time job.

On May 26, 2004, the morning of the press conference, members of the Philadelphia Coalition arrived at City Hall dressed in their Sunday best (see figure G.5). The letter of support from the tribal council had not yet arrived, and the county board of supervisors had yet to vote on the resolution. The coalition would have to adjust its statement to say that it expected support from all local government entities. Amid a multitude of reporters and flashing cameras, Philadelphia Coalition cochairs Leroy Clemons and Prince invited members of the coalition to come forward. One by one they filed in behind the podium, some searching the crowd for their children, whom they had brought to witness the historic occasion. After an opening prayer, Clemons read from a prepared statement: "With firm resolve and strong belief in the rule of law, we call on the Neshoba County District Attorney, the state Attorney General and the U.S. Department of Justice to make every effort to seek justice in this case. We deplore the possibility that history will record that the state of Mississippi, and this community in particular, did not make a good faith effort to do its duty." Prince continued: "We state candidly and with deep regret that some of our own citizens, including local and state law enforcement officers, were involved in the planning and execution of these murders. We are also cognizant of the shameful involvement and interference of state government, including actions of the State Sovereignty Commission, in thwarting justice in this case." And finally, Mayor Rayburn Waddell, who had decided to support the coalition's efforts, read the resolution that the city council had voted to support just the night before.

White-haired and speaking in a thick southern drawl, Waddell addressed the press:

> Forty years ago, on June 21st, 1964, three young men, James Chaney, Andrew Goodman, and Michael Schwerner were murdered in Neshoba County. The state of Mississippi has never brought criminal indictment against anybody for these murders. There is for good and obvious reason no statute of limitations on murder. This principle of law holds that anyone who takes the life of another person for any reason not provided by law is never immune to prosecution however remote the time. With firm resolve and strong belief in the rule of law, we call on the appropriate authorities to make every effort to seek justice in this case.[38]

By all accounts, the press conference was a success, and it could not have been achieved without the resources of the Winter Institute, which had assigned multiple staff members to supporting the Philadelphia Coalition. As a result of the press conference, major newspapers—including the *New York Times, Washington Post,* and *Atlanta Journal-Constitution*—decided to send reporters to cover the fortieth anniversary commemoration. Local television stations in Mississippi also began to develop programming on what was happening in Philadelphia. And while this additional media coverage would bring more attention to its cause, the Philadelphia Coalition had a particular audience in mind: its members hoped the press conference would spur Mississippi legal authorities to action. Just two days after the press conference, that hope was realized. On May 28, 2004, Mississippi's new attorney general, Jim Hood, asked the U.S. Department of Justice for help investigating the 1964 murders. The case, which had been effectively closed since 2002, when Moore had abandoned it, was suddenly open again.

Governor Barbour Attends the Commemoration: Broadening Political Opportunities

While the positive response to the press conference had bolstered the Philadelphia Coalition, the fortieth anniversary commemoration service still lay ahead, and major logistical details remained unclear. Most notably, the coalition was deeply divided on whether to invite Haley Barbour, then Mississippi's governor, to the June 21 commemoration. For decades, the Yazoo City native had been one of the Republican Party's most successful foot soldiers, long before Mississippi Republicans were commonplace. After returning to

Mississippi to run for governor in 2003, Barbour was accused of pandering to the most racist elements of the state. In the fall of 2003, just months before the Philadelphia Coalition began planning the commemoration, Barbour became embroiled in a racially charged media scandal. His picture was featured on the website of the Council of Conservative Citizens, an offshoot of the White Citizens' Councils that had defended segregation during the civil rights era through economic boycotts and other forms of intimidation. Barbour refused to ask that his picture be removed, despite mounting public demands that he do so.[39] Needless to say, this event must have been in the minds of Philadelphia Coalition members as they considered whether to invite the governor to the commemoration.

Before coming to a clear consensus on whether Barbour would be a welcome guest, the Philadelphia Coalition received word: Barbour would be attending. The revelation received mixed reviews. The more liberal factions of the coalition felt that Barbour's participation was not only hypocritical, it was insulting. The governor's penchant for wearing a lapel pin showing the Mississippi flag worried some people, who anticipated that the state's flag—which incorporates the Confederate battle flag in its top-left corner—would be mistaken for the Confederate flag, a particularly contentious symbol among civil rights veterans who would be in attendance. Other Mississippians, like Donna Ladd, a Philadelphia native and editor of the progressive *Jackson Free Press*, interpreted Barbour's appearance as a "chink," however small, in the "armor" of the "Southern Strategy," referring to Republicans' historical efforts to use thinly veiled racial references to win southern votes.[40] Whatever the case, Barbour's appearance signaled the governor's tolerance of, if not support for, efforts to confront civil rights–era violence.

Barbour's political stance was signaled and sealed with a handshake. As he entered the stage at the commemoration service, he reached out to shake hands with congressman and civil rights activist John Lewis—a civil gesture that had deep impact (see figure G.6). The photograph of the event, with members of the Philadelphia Coalition representing Philadelphia's triracial heritage in the background, was reprinted in hundreds of newspapers across the country, indicating the shifting political tenor in the state and creating conditions of possibility for the attorney general and district attorney to move forward with the case. One member of the Philadelphia Coalition summarized the significance of the photograph this way. "We knew [the Philadelphia Coalition] had opposition in the state down in Jackson against what we were trying to do. We knew that [Attorney General]

Jim Hood had opposition, people against him reopening the case. After that memorial service, and the governor, and that picture [with John Lewis] surfaced all over the place, that went away. . . . At that point Jim Hood was able to move on freely without getting those calls late at night saying, 'What you doing? Politically you need to leave this alone.' . . . When that opposition went away, [Hood] was able to move freely."[41]

On September 14, 2004, Hood arrived in Philadelphia to meet with the Philadelphia Coalition and members of the victims' families—most notably Andrew Goodman's mother, Carolyn, who was approaching her nineties. Over a meal of pulled pork and corn, she and members of the Philadelphia Coalition asked Hood to pursue the case. The Philadelphia Coalition had organized the meeting to demonstrate how the unresolved case continued to affect the victims' families and the Philadelphia community more broadly. For the first time in the history of the case, a diverse cross section of that very community implored Mississippi legal authorities to pursue justice. If the victims' families could not compel the attorney general to action, perhaps the community could.

While Hood may have felt inclined to prosecute the case after the September 14 meeting, he did not have the sole legal authority to bring the case before a grand jury.[42] The Neshoba County district attorney, Mark Duncan, also had to be convinced, and efforts to mobilize Duncan had been under way for several months. In early March 2004, Clemons and Prince, the newly appointed commemoration task force cochairs, had met with Duncan to gauge his feelings on the case. Like the leaders of the Philadelphia Coalition, the district attorney was frustrated by his hometown's dubious reputation. Duncan had lived in Philadelphia his entire life, and his children attended public school there. Because of Duncan's deep embeddedness in the local community, he could not take prosecuting the 1964 case lightly. Duncan risked not only his job—an elected position—but potentially the safety and well-being of his family as well.

Despite these risks, Duncan approached his position as district attorney with a no-nonsense attitude, which is reflected in his thoughts after the trial. "I am just a prosecutor," Duncan insisted. "My job in this case was to hold a man accountable for his role in these killings. That is the only reason the case was pursued. It was not done for any social cause."[43] Yet other comments reveal that Duncan was also motivated to present a more positive image of Philadelphia: "I knew from having lived here for so long, that the rest of the world had a negative view of Neshoba County and Mississippi. I just did not know how bad it was. [The trial] gave me a chance to say something good about us."⁴⁴ Thus, though the prosecutorial basis of the case remained essentially unchanged since its original, failed consideration in 1999, in 2005, state and local legal authorities were compelled to act. On January 6, just six months after the fortieth anniversary commemoration, Hood and Duncan stood before a grand jury made up of Philadelphia and Neshoba County citizens.

Priming the Jury Pool: Transforming the Local Political Culture

Convincing legal authorities to bring the case before a grand jury was a significant step, especially after the prime eyewitness, Price, had fallen from the cherry picker in 2001. While convincing legal authorities was necessary, it was not sufficient to secure an indictment: the twenty-one citizens who made up the Neshoba County grand jury had to be compelled to issue one. In other words, a small group of Neshoba County citizens—long portrayed by the national press as the meanest, most unforgiving folks in the state— stood between impunity and the pursuit of legal justice.

Serving on this particular grand jury was not a civic duty that most Philadelphia citizens were enthusiastic about fulfilling. The close-knit nature of this small community made this service especially complicated. Few people in the town could claim that they were not somehow connected to the case. After the names of those serving on the grand jury were published in the local newspaper, tensions mounted. A longtime resident of Neshoba County and member of the grand jury, Sally Beam, recalled her trepidation after the jurors' names were published: "It alarmed me because . . . there were a lot of people related to Edgar Ray Killen. . . . He was not an isolated person, and there were a lot of people who worked with him or had connections with him over the years. . . . Those names [of the jurors] were not supposed to be made public, and I didn't really expect anything, but I knew that once my name was known, [harassment] was a possibility."⁴⁵

More than forty years after the Klan dominated east central Mississippi, the collective memory of Klan retaliation remained tangible. And while some people continued to fear the Klan, others from Neshoba County remained unconvinced that prosecuting an elderly man for a crime committed so long ago would offer any real benefits to the community. Given the concerns for safety, the skepticism about the social utility of the case, and the absence of new evidence, something significant must have occurred to convince the grand jurors to indict Killen. While it is certainly possible that the legal arguments presented by Hood and Duncan were enough to convince jurors to act other factors appear to have been more significant. According to one grand juror, "the conversation [between jurors] actually surprised me because there were some in there [that said] . . . he was an old man, that it shouldn't go any further, that there was no true evidence, that we had no witnesses, that it was going to be a waste of taxpayer money. . . . But a good many people felt like this is our opportunity, not to wipe the slate clean, but to give Philadelphia a chance to start over and then rebuild their race relations in a healthier way, and take this festering sore and, you know, expose it for what it was and move on."[46]

Thus, in addition to the legal merits of the evidence presented, the grand jurors considered the broader social impact of their decision. They were not immune to the surrounding cultural landscape and appeared to be deeply affected by the stigma associated with their hometown.

For decades, Dearman, in his role as owner and editor of the *Neshoba Democrat*, had attempted to humanize the civil rights workers, first by publishing a lengthy interview with Carolyn Goodman in 1989 and finally with his farewell editorial in 2000 on the need "for an accounting" in the case.[47] Following Dearman's lead, in the months leading up to the fortieth anniversary commemoration, Prince published a series titled "44 Days," referring to the number of days Chaney, Schwerner, and Goodman had been missing before their bodies were discovered. In this series, Prince reprinted articles from 1964, hoping to provide Philadelphia residents, especially young ones, with the historical context for understanding the 2004 commemoration and its call for justice.

These intentional editorial efforts did affect their readers, including members of the local jury who would consider Killen's case. "The people on that grand jury are a product of forty years of reading the *Neshoba Democrat* and certainly all the stuff Stan [Dearman] had done," noted a long-time Philadelphia resident and coalition member. "All these little things . . . over time began to become a part of the psyche of Neshoba Countians. . . . It was this preparation. None of us probably knew it, but we were preparing a jury pool."[48]

This "preparation" may have been unintentional in 1989, but leading up to the 2004 commemoration service, it became a purposeful strategy. The Philadelphia Coalition's resolution had been part of a media campaign to transform the mindsets of the local community. When asked why the coalition presented the resolution calling for justice at a press conference before the 2004 commemoration service, Glisson revealed this plan: "We knew that if there was going to be a trial, it was unlikely that there would be a change of venue. Only the defendant can request a change of venue and we didn't believe that Edgar Ray Killen was going to ask to have the trial moved somewhere else, because why would he? He had been protected in that community for forty years. So there was a strategy to have a press conference to first really educate the people in the community and then . . . begin to change the narrative nationally and internationally of what Philadelphia's story is."[49]

The Philadelphia press conference was an effort to educate the broader community about the long-silenced history surrounding 1964, which involved serious acts of state collusion and neglect. The press conference also framed the coalition's pursuit of justice as a legal, moral, and reputational issue. After reminding the public that there is not a statute of limitation "for good and obvious reasons," the resolution highlighted the responsibilities of the local community. "We deplore the possibility that history will record that the state of Mississippi, and this community in particular, did not make a good faith effort to do its duty," the resolution charged, "and we are mindful of our responsibility as citizens to call on the authorities to make an effort to work for justice in this case. Continued failure to do so will only further compound the wrong."[50]

These efforts to infuse the collective memory of the 1964 murders with a different moral valence and a sense of urgency were successful.[51] This transformation of Philadelphia's political culture was the final factor that enabled the Killen trial to come to fruition. On January 5, 2005, a grand jury composed of Neshoba County citizens issued an indictment against Killen for the murders of Chaney, Goodman, and Schwerner. Six months later, on June 21—exactly forty-one years after the murders—another set of Neshoba County jurors issued their final verdict: guilty.

From Commemoration to Conviction

The prosecution and conviction of Killen represents a remarkable transformation of the status quo in Philadelphia. For decades, members of the lynch mob who, according to the 1967 trial, had "denied the civil rights" of Chaney, Schwerner, and Goodman had lived out their lives in Neshoba County.[52] No one had been tried for murder—a state charge—and by all accounts, it appeared that no one ever would be. For this civil rights–era cold case to be prosecuted, several conditions had to be met: the murders had to be publicly acknowledged, which was a daunting task; Mississippi legal authorities had to be persuaded to pursue the case; and a grand jury of Neshoba County citizens had to be convinced to issue an indictment.

From this thicket of historical contingencies, we can discern what is characteristic of successful social movement mobilization. Like social movement activists, a new generation of local leaders became memory activists in Philadelphia when they mobilized around a common grievance: the stigma their community continued to suffer as a result of the 1964 murders. These memory activists then mobilized in response to a precipitating event (the fortieth anniversary); they developed a list of demands (including justice); and they debated tactics (holding a march versus issuing a resolution). The activists then cultivated their capacity to organize a commemorative event by drawing on outside resources (the Winter Institute) and developing a community-level organizational infrastructure with a distinct collective identity (the Philadelphia Coalition). Notably, these developments occurred before the fortieth anniversary commemoration, which suggests that the outcomes of a commemoration are affected by the circumstances under which it is put together.

Building on the decades-long advocacy of the victims' families and local journalists, the fortieth anniversary commemoration shifted the conditions of possibility surrounding the case. By providing a platform for powerful political and cultural actors to engage, the commemoration facilitated unique interactions that might not have otherwise occurred. We can see this in the photograph of Lewis and Barbour shaking hands, which became a representation of a shifting political climate. The presence of Barbour, however contentious that might have been for members of the Philadelphia Coalition, signaled the governor's tolerance for discussions of civil rights–era crimes. In other words, it created a political opening for the attorney general and the district attorney to move forward with the case.

Finally, efforts to promote the commemoration and call for justice reinforced longtime efforts to transform Philadelphia's political culture from one that tolerates impunity to one that demands legal accountability for wrongdoing. The local newspaper played a crucial role in this transformation. Beginning with Dearman's conscientious editorials and continuing with Prince's "44 Days" series, the jury pool was primed. The Philadelphia Coalition's press conference in 2005 supported and enhanced this media strategy. For older residents, this news coverage reminded them of the past and gave efforts to confront the past a new moral valence. By highlighting their community's decades-long denial, local news coverage also generated a "memory of commemoration." In other words, "the past includes not only the history being commemorated," according the sociologist and memory scholar Jeffrey Olick, "but also the accumulated succession of commemorations, as well as what has occurred between those powerful moments."[53] This memory of commemoration thus empowered a new generation of memory activists to change the narrative about Philadelphia once and for all.

But this is not merely a social-movements story. The history of the Killen trial suggests several important insights concerning the relationship between collective action, commemoration, and the law, as well as several processes through which commemorations may contribute to belated legal justice. First, commemorations are moments when history and memory are particularly dense. "By carving socially marked events out of essentially unmarked stretches of history," Eviatar Zerubavel notes, commemoration "helps to articulate what groups collectively consider eventful."[54] In other words, commemorations demarcate the sacred from the profane and the cherished from the ordinary. In doing so, commemorations provide unique opportunities for mobilizing memory activists, cultivating resources, and framing legal claims.

Second, by consolidating resources, commemorations may further strengthen a community's capacity to translate legal claims into tangible outcomes. This occurred in Philadelphia with the assistance of the Winter Institute. As a neutral broker, Glisson mediated conflicts within the task force and between the task force and outside groups. While not without challenges, this facilitation solidified relationships among task force members and helped them cultivate their identity as the Philadelphia Coalition in the process. Presenting a united front, the coalition was able to draw media attention and legal resources to the case that would have been difficult, if not impossible, had the group been fragmented.

Commemorations' periodicity may contribute to their cumulative effect. Each year, anniversaries of commemorable events—especially milestone anniversaries—present opportunities for mobilization and reflection. When coupled with other cultural and political developments, commemorative events may catalyze further social transformations. The annual nature of commemorations also generates path dependency, the process by which prior commemorations shape future commemorations in both form and function.[55] Prior commemorations influence not only the discourse of future commemorations but also the capacity of memory activists to advocate for future social change. The path-dependent and cumulative nature of commemorations may create a repository of expertise within communities, thus strengthening the capacity to commemorate as years pass.[56]

In these ways, community-based commemorations may reinforce some of the same social processes initiated by family advocacy, investigative journalism, and shifting cultural norms, enhancing possibilities for cold-case revivals. Like families, communities (cities, counties, churches, and so on) can serve as powerful carrier groups and mnemonic entrepreneurs, helping sustain the collective memory of particular people or events and at times advocating for the inclusion of that memory within broader institutional spaces—in this case, the legal domain. Additionally, commemoration planners sometimes become intimately familiar with the history they are helping commemorate, possibly serving as local experts helping guide investigators toward new evidence and brokering introductions with potential witnesses. And finally, commemorative activities can serve an educational function, exposing the broader public to information about the past and potentially shifting public opinion in favor of legal action. Thus, in the absence of family advocates and investigative journalists, community-based commemorations may be a viable option for those seeking to revive long abandoned legal cases.

That said, the prosecution of Killen and other civil rights–era cold-case trials is not without limitations—and certainly not without critics. These trials, according to the historian Renee Romano, have become "a key site of contestation between those who wanted to harness them to the project of declaring and celebrating the end of racism in a 'post-racial' nation and those who saw in them the potential to challenge the denial of the significance of race that was at the foundation of the new racial order."[57] Many people who hoped these trials would transform the current racial order have grown disillusioned. The trials portrayed racism as a distinctly southern phenomenon, confined to individual acts of overtly racist men. Furthermore, critics argue that these trials not only confined racism to the past but also obscured the widespread collusion of southern states in these historic acts of racial violence. In other words, the Killen trial represented both acknowledgment and denial. On the one hand, the state of Mississippi had for the first time held an individual accountable for the murders of Chaney, Goodman, and Schwerner. On the other hand, the state of Mississippi had gotten off scot-free. In the next chapter, we will explore how this paradox propelled an emerging group of memory activists in Philadelphia and across the state of Mississippi to continue mobilizing around memory issues, this time in the realm of education.

4   Legislating Civil and Human Rights Education

Reviewing a new textbook on Mississippi history in 1975, the historian James Silver, a former University of Mississippi professor, observed that the "recorded history of Mississippi has changed more slowly than the state itself."[1] From someone who had been ostracized a decade earlier for publicly admonishing Mississippi's institutions and citizens for keeping the state's doors and shutters closed to outsiders,[2] this was a noteworthy statement indeed. In his 1964 work *Mississippi: The Closed Society*, Silver argued that efforts to suppress the rights of African Americans had generated negative consequences for the state, including "a relative lack of industry, vastly inferior and censor-hounded schools, a politics of racist gibberish, a consistent loss of the state's brightest young people, and an atmosphere which can be likened to that of the Iberian Inquisition."[3] Ten years after his forceful critique, Silver conceded that although "the closed society" might have changed, its recorded history had remained stubbornly fixed.

Although groundbreaking civil rights legislation and Supreme Court decisions had transformed public life in the Magnolia State, in the decades after *Brown v. Board of Education* (1954), defiant citizens and state officials worked diligently to preserve the status quo separation of learning environments for white and black children. Moreover, alongside the battle over where students learned was the battle over what they learned—and for good reason. Textbooks, curricula, and state-issued learning objectives are about far more than reading, writing, and arithmetic. As objects of collective memory, they are expressions of a community's values and identity,[4] and schools, by extension, are sites of mnemonic socialization, where children learn to be productive members of a society through instruction in a community's most valued traditions and ideals.

Given the social significance of the education system for cultivating functioning members of a society, decisions about what to include in history and social science curricula often ignite passionate debate among educators, parents, and politicians. This process can be especially contentious in societies beset by histories of racial and ethnic conflict. Mississippi is just such a case, where de jure racial segregation has given way to a de facto segregation that continues to affect the lives of its citizens. In the decades after Mississippi reluctantly desegregated its schools, dominant political forces in the state worked to stymie efforts to incorporate into the statewide curriculum any formal recognition of the historical elements that generated and sustained segregation in the first place—slavery, the civil rights movement, and other aspects of Mississippi's racial past.[5]

In 2006, all that changed. With Governor Haley Barbour's signature on Senate Bill (SB) 2718, Mississippi became the first state to mandate civil and human rights education at every grade level.[6] This unprecedented piece of legislation authorized the Mississippi State Board of Education to include civil rights and human rights as part of the K–12 education system and to develop appropriate guidelines for grade-level classroom learning in those subjects. To anchor those efforts, the board of education was further authorized to establish a Mississippi civil rights education commission to coordinate civil rights awareness and education in public schools. Most significantly, the bill affirmed "the important role the Civil Rights Movement had on the State of Mississippi" and the need to teach "Mississippi's central role in the civil rights struggle . . . as a beacon of hope for all of our citizens."[7]

After so many decades of resistance, the enactment of SB 2718 was a remarkable achievement. But what explains this sudden and uncharacteristic state-level support for civil and human rights education in 2006? To answer this question, we must look more locally—once again, to the city of Philadelphia.

Desegregating Mississippi Schools

Prior to 1870, Mississippi's white leaders eschewed the idea that the state was responsible for educating its children. But emancipation revived the issue of public education in Mississippi, and in 1870, the Republican-led legislature, whose ranks included both white and black lawmakers, created a system of free public schools through which "all children between the ages of 5 and 21 shall have equal advantages.[8] However, a climate of white racial superiority and inadequate statewide funding conspired to produce a profoundly unequal two-tiered school system. Through a combination of factors including paternalism, self-interest, and fear that northerners would take the lead in the endeavor and corrupt freed slaves, some white Mississippians began to advocate for the establishment of black schools. Still, by the 1940s, the startling disparity between black and white education in

Mississippi was beyond deniability. Black citizens demanded improvements, and the state, anticipating federal intervention, began to pursue a largely unsuccessful program of "equalization."[9]

For white Mississippians, maintaining separate schools for black and white children was central to maintaining a segregated social system. This meant that losing the battle to preserve single-race schools "was tantamount to losing the war over the continuation of racial separation," as the historian Charles Bolton observed.[10] If students learned together, they might learn to like each other, and it did not take much to imagine that social equality and—even more threatening—interracial relationships would be very close behind.

By 1954, the federal government had intervened and seemingly ended segregated school systems across the South in the landmark *Brown v. Board of Education* Supreme Court decision, which overturned the 1890s ruling in *Plessy v. Ferguson* that had allowed southern states to establish "separate but equal" education for black and white children. Immediately following the 1954 court ruling, Mississippi lawmakers contrived ways to resist or circumvent the desegregation order (including threats to abolish the entire public school system if forced to integrate it, a plan that never came to fruition). Ultimately, lawmakers pursued a policy of "voluntary segregation" alongside "equalization" in the decade following *Brown*, urging black educators to disavow any desire to press for integrated schools. "Before the state moved to expend large sums of money to improve black schools," Bolton explains, "they needed firm assurance from blacks that they favored the status quo of segregated schools."[11] Meanwhile, thousands of white Mississippians joined newly formed White Citizens' Councils in their efforts to maintain a dual education system through threats of violence, economic sanctions, and later the establishment of private academies.[12]

These strategies were remarkably effective, and in the decade after *Brown*, they helped maintain nearly complete segregation of elementary and secondary public schools. Even after the Civil Rights Act of 1964 engendered "freedom of choice" policies that allowed black families to send their children to white schools ten years after the landmark case, only 5 percent of the Jackson school district participated.[13] While the "freedom of choice" program implied that black families had the freedom to choose, it had been designed to keep students separate, rather than to enable segregation. In reality, intimidation and harassment prevented many black families from "choosing" to send their children to white schools. As of 1967, only 3 percent of the state's black children attended school with white children, and from

1966 to 1970, the number of private academies nearly doubled—from 121 to 236—as the number of students attending them more than tripled.[14]

The vast majority of this growth in private academies occurred in 1969 and 1970, as a direct consequence of another Supreme Court intervention. In the final months of 1969, the court mandated the immediate desegregation of public schools in *Alexander v. Holmes County Board of Education*. Following their winter break and with little preparation, Mississippi students completed their second semester in desegregated schools. But the Supreme Court ruling had a secondary effect: white students continued to exit the public school system in record numbers to enroll in hastily organized segregated private academies that in effect re-created a dual school system. Private education became a proxy for white-only education, a trend that largely persists today. Examining the racial enrollment patterns in 239 of the largest U.S. school districts, Erica Frankenberg and Chungmei Lee found that virtually all of the districts showed lower levels of interracial exposure after 1986, suggesting a trend toward resegregation. While resegregation is a national trend, the racial demographics of Mississippi's schools remain particularly striking. In 2000, the Jackson school district was only 5.6 percent white.[15]

As the legal justification for a dual school system began to erode in the wake of *Brown*, state officials turned to the curriculum as the next line of defense. In 1958, the state expanded the required curriculum to include a course on Mississippi history for all ninth graders in the state, thereby creating a mechanism "to reinforce not only the existence of a segregated society," according to the historian Rebecca Davis, "but [also] the belief in it."[16] If Mississippi could not control where students learned, it could control what they learned, and the state proceeded to furnish the classroom with texts that presented a narrative of harmonious race relations that carefully skirted any mention of "disruptive or contentious issues, including slavery, white supremacy, violence, secession, poverty, [and] disenfranchisement."[17]

Selecting an "appropriate" textbook for the new course thus became paramount in maintaining the status quo, and in 1960, the power to authorize textbooks for use in Mississippi history classes fell to one man: Governor Ross Barnett. Responding to protests from Mississippi's Society of the Daughters of the American Revolution about so-called subversive texts promoting progressive causes such as integration, the Mississippi Senate passed a bill giving Barnett full control over textbook selection, an unprecedented legislative move even in the Deep South. True to his anti-integrationist stance,

Barnett approved only one text: John K. Bettersworth's *Mississippi: A History*, which historians later described as "stuck in the . . . Old South and Lost Cause mentality."[18] Indeed, Barnett had publicly expressed his objection to "textbooks that would teach subversion and integration," arguing that Mississippi children ought to be "properly informed about the Southern and true American way of life."[19]

Twenty years would pass before Mississippi schools were permitted to select a state-authorized Mississippi history textbook that covered the civil rights movement in any depth—and that change occurred only as a result of a court order.[20] James Loewen and Charles Sallis (from Tougaloo College and Millsaps College, respectively) had edited the text, *Mississippi: Conflict and Change*—which was then swiftly rejected by Mississippi's textbook selection committee in 1974.[21] Loewen and Sallis appealed the decision, and five years after their suit was filed, a federal district judge ruled that there was no justifiable reason to reject their text and approved it for statewide use.[22] Despite this victory, fewer than five thousand copies of the text sold in the six years it was on the approved list, and the publisher never issued a second edition.[23] Nevertheless, the text precipitated a vigorous debate about the portrayal of Mississippi's history, and subsequent texts began covering issues related to slavery and civil rights in greater depth. Throughout the 1990s and into the 2000s, Mississippi history textbooks continued to expand their coverage of civil rights, including civil rights–era violence.[24]

This brief history reveals a striking pattern of avoidance and aversion, first to integrated schools and then to revisionist texts, in which Mississippi delayed action on both counts until forced to comply by federal court orders. Given this context, Mississippi's 2006 civil and human rights education bill seems startlingly out of place. What compelled Mississippi legislators to mandate civil and human rights education—and to do so of their own volition?

Teaching Difficult Pasts in Mississippi and Beyond

The idea for an education bill that required Mississippi educators to teach students about a difficult past was not without precedent in the state. In 2004, two years before encountering SB 2718, the Mississippi Legislature passed a Holocaust education bill that created a commission to survey, design, and promote the implementation of Holocaust education programs throughout Mississippi.[25] The bill denounced the Holocaust and affirmed remembrance as a key component of democratic citizenship by articulating that "all people should remember the horrible atrocities [in 1945] and other times in human history as the result of bigotry and tyranny, and therefore should continually rededicate themselves to the principles of human rights and equal protection under the laws of a democratic society."[26] Given the state's failure to confront its history of racially motivated violence, however, the language of the bill struck some African American lawmakers as ironic if not troubling, "Before we deal with issues that occurred in Europe," argued Senator John Horhn, an African American legislator representing Hinds and Madison Counties, "I think it's unconscionable that we don't try to get our own house together first."[27]

On the day that Barbour was set to sign the Holocaust education bill, Horhn and other lawmakers submitted two amendments. The first would expand the conception of genocide to include systematic violence against African Americans and Native Americans, and the second would establish a South African–style truth commission in Mississippi, which Horhn had proposed unsuccessfully every year for a decade (see chapter 5). According to Horhn, the amendments faced a "firestorm of opposition"—not only from his conservative colleagues but also from Mississippi's Jewish community, which accused him of minimizing the violence against Jews and, worse, of being anti-Semitic.[28] In light of this criticism, Horhn and his collaborators withdrew the amendments, after being promised that the amendments would be considered the following year as an independent bill. The Holocaust education bill passed both houses with relative ease.

The Holocaust education legislation in Mississippi reflects a decades-long national curricular movement. Beginning in the 1970s, U.S.-based educators developed curricula on the Holocaust in response to rising interest in it, students' demands for more inclusive pedagogy, and the "affective revolution" animated by Lawrence Kolberg's newly articulated stages of moral development.[29] By the 1980s, organizations such as Facing History and Ourselves had begun to formalize their support of educators teaching the Holocaust, and states had begun to institutionalize this grassroots curricular movement though statewide initiatives that included legislatively mandated curricula. As of 2004, when Mississippi joined this effort, seventeen states had Holocaust education statutes, a number that continues to grow as nonprofit organizations such as the Butterfly Project continue to push for adoption.[30]

However, this legislative precedent does not fully explain how Mississippi's civil and human rights education bill emerged in 2006. Given the historic alliance between Jewish Americans and African Americans during the civil rights movement, it would be reasonable to assume, for instance, that the same actors who had advocated for the Holocaust education bill in Mississippi would have also been proponents of a bill that encompassed civil and human rights more generally. But this was not the case. The authors of the Holocaust bill and the civil and human rights education bill did not overlap, and none of Mississippi's Jewish civil-society organizations lobbied on behalf of SB 2718.[31] Furthermore, if the civil and human rights education bill was a natural outgrowth of the Holocaust education bill, we would expect to see similar civil or human rights education bills in at least some of the states that passed Holocaust education bills—but as of 2019, Mississippi remains the only state to have enacted such legislation.

Furthermore, while the Mississippi education bill's focus on the civil rights movement may be unique, its emphasis on human rights is not. Since World War II, human rights have become an orienting frame around which politicians and human rights activists support their claims, including those in the realm of education. In 1995, the United Nations Decade for Human Rights Education reinforced and catalyzed the global diffusion of human rights education as legitimate knowledge. As human rights education gained traction as a global norm, so have efforts to enforce it. Since 1989, European institutions have made their commitment to human rights education clear by formalizing Holocaust remembrance and education for both member states and potential member states. Between 1989 and 2014, the European Parliament adopted twelve documents—nine resolutions and three declarations—meant to combat racism, xenophobia, and anti-Semitism through a variety of memory practices, such as preserving Nazi concentration camps as historical monuments and designating Holocaust remembrance days. In 2002, the Council of Europe's forty-four member countries—including all Eastern European states that had historically resisted Holocaust education initiatives—adopted a declaration stating that each country would observe a "Day of Remembrance of the Holocaust and for the Prevention of Crimes against Humanity" in schools.[32] The United States has not been immune to the normative transformation evident in the global proliferation of human rights education, but international bodies have not compelled the U.S. Department of Education and its equivalents at the state level to adjust their curricular standards.

Historically, curricular changes in the United States have come about not by top-down mandate but by bottom-up negotiated compromises between dominant and marginalized groups over what truths would be taught and whose knowledge would be privileged. The rise of multicultural education practices since the 1960s, for example, can be understood as a response to the movements for civil rights and women's rights that sought representation and inclusion across all spheres of public life.[33] Of course, not all states have embraced multicultural education principles to the same degree or on the same timeline. Some states were already implementing multicultural educational curricula in the 1970s when Mississippi, still in the early throes of desegregation, was expressing vehement opposition to revisionist history textbooks. This would change, but the change would come gradually and not as a result of an organized grassroots social movement.

Thus, while these broader cultural transformations, legislative precedents, and oppositional campaigns helped lay the foundation for Mississippi's civil and human rights education bill in a broad sense, they do not fully explain how Mississippi—a state notorious for its resistance to integrated classrooms and later its aversion to inclusive textbooks—came to mandate civil rights and human rights education. Again, Philadelphia holds the key.

Broadening Commemorative Capacity: The Philadelphia Coalition Turns to Education

Among all the outcomes of the fortieth anniversary commemoration of the 1964 murders—the silence breaking, mobilization of a new generation of memory activists, building of an organizational infrastructure, and new cultural legitimacy—perhaps the most significant was the strengthening of Philadelphia's commemorative capacity. The sociologist Raj Ghoshal describes this as the extent to which "institutions or groups that can be readily mobilized in commemorative efforts," including the pursuit of legal justice (see chapter 2).[34] And while the Philadelphia Coalition had achieved some legal justice through the conviction of Edgar Ray Killen, for many members of the coalition, it was an insufficient remedy for what they perceived as decades of impunity. "If all they ever did was get a trial," recalled Susan Glisson, "they would have considered it a failure."[35] The Philadelphia Coalition wanted to institutionalize the memory of the 1964 murders in local schools, an ambition that emerged through the process of planning the fortieth anniversary commemoration.

As coalition members gathered to plan the commemoration, they came to know each other by sharing stories, and in the process they discovered that many of their narratives involved striking similarities despite never having been voiced in public. Many of the narratives that members shared coalesced around education or the lack thereof, for many members felt that local civil rights history had been lacking in their formal schooling. Most members had not learned about the 1964 civil rights murders in school, and those who wanted more information were forced to seek it on their own. These stories and subsequent discussions that emerged from these early meetings motivated further reflection on the degree to which local schools were teaching the history of civil rights struggles for both African Americans and the Mississippi Band of Choctaw Indians, whose tribal center is in the Philadelphia area. "We don't feel like young people are getting that taught to them," noted Steve Wilkerson—owner of Steve's on the Square, a local clothing shop, and a member of the Philadelphia Coalition—to a reporter in 2004.[36] "We're mindful," added Fenton DeWeese, another coalition member and an attorney for the Mississippi Band of Choctaw Indians, "that if you don't put what happened in front of people, there's a likelihood that it could repeat itself."[37] Harnessing this "never again" mantra, the Philadelphia Coalition reasoned that if their efforts were to have a lasting impact, education had to be a priority.

But in 2004, local educators had kept their distance from the commemorative efforts. None of the members of the Philadelphia Coalition was an educator, a fact that did not go unnoticed by Deborah Owens, a local middle school teacher, when she attended the fortieth anniversary commemoration service in June of that year. "It was as if the education community had not embraced [the commemoration]," she observed.[38] Although she had lived in Philadelphia for fourteen years, Owens still felt like an outsider, and she had been hesitant to join the coalition prior to the anniversary commemoration. She recalled that the first people to join the Philadelphia Coalition, whose identities had been publicized in the local newspaper, were from "old Mississippi families," and she worried that there "wouldn't be a place" for her as a relative newcomer.[39] Furthermore, she worried about being ostracized by her fellow teachers, many of whom had family members or students with family members who might be implicated by unearthing the community's discomforting past.

Still, resolved that the education community needed to be represented in the Philadelphia Coalition and encouraged by what she had seen at the 2004 commemoration, Owens attended the next coalition meeting to offer her insight as a local educator. "You know, one thing I've noticed since I've been [in Philadelphia]," Owens shared with the group, "is that none of the kids know anything about this history. They know [the film] *Mississippi Burning,* but it's not talked about. . . . I think the best way you can memorialize their legacy is by ensuring that kids in Mississippi know their history."⁴⁰ This reinforced impressions from other coalition members that the history of the 1964 murders and their impact on the community remained largely excluded from Philadelphia's schools. "I mean, I'm telling you," insisted one African American coalition member, "if you came to Philadelphia you could have gone into any of the public schools and you could have taken a thousand dollars into that school and said, 'I'll give this thousand dollars to the five kids that can name all three of the civil rights workers.'" As he spoke, he pointed to the invisible cash in his hand, and he continued: "You would have left that school with your money intact. Most of them probably couldn't name one."⁴¹

With a local teacher now involved, the coalition was better equipped to consider how to transform the local curriculum. Its next step was to appoint Owens the chair of a committee to explore possible educational initiatives. After investigating several options, Owens suggested that the coalition go beyond its local context, proposing that Philadelphia host a conference that would bring together teachers and civil rights activists from across the state to discuss teaching civil rights history. The William Winter Institute for Racial Reconciliation had facilitated similar interactions through its Welcome Table program and was able to provide the necessary institutional and personal connections to make the conference a reality. While the idea of a conference was generally well received, it faced some resistance both from outside and within the coalition. Outside the coalition, local educators expressed concern for the safety and well-being of their students, many of whom had family ties to the eighteen men implicated in the 1964 murders. However, the strongest opposition came from within the coalition: Jim Prince, its cochair, was skeptical of the planned education summit, describing it in the local newspaper as "sensitivity training" partially funded by the United Nations, a reaction that befuddled more liberal-leaning coalition members.⁴² Despite this contention, with an educator on board and the institutional resources of the Winter Institute made available to the coalition, it was able to expand its educational efforts, and in doing so, coalition members demonstrated the strength of their organization in the face of opposition.

On the morning of June 21, 2005—the forty-first anniversary of the murders—more than a hundred educators, public historians, and civil rights activists gathered at the public high school in Philadelphia for the three-day "Chaney, Schwerner, and Goodman Living Memorial Civil Rights Education Summit," an event cosponsored by the Philadelphia Coalition, Neshoba Education Foundation, Philadelphia High School, and the Winter Institute and supported by a small grant from the United Nations Educational, Scientific, and Cultural Organization. It included a variety of sessions ranging from "Using Archived Media to Teach Civil Rights" to "Strategies for Teaching Civil Rights in Junior High and Middle School," many of which were moderated by members of the Philadelphia Coalition.

The final plenary session, "Building a Regional Network," was particularly significant. During this session, as Mississippi educators discussed challenges to teaching civil rights history in their own state, the idea for a civil rights education bill began to take root. Two challenges emerged as discussions progressed. First, many teachers felt unprepared to teach about the civil rights movement, which was only natural given Mississippi's contentious racial past and the continuing salience of race. The solution to this challenge seemed clear: civil-society organizations such as Teaching for Change were already providing support to school districts interested in giving their teachers resources and training on civil rights education and could continue to do so on an expanded scale.[43] Second, teachers felt constrained in what they could teach, a challenge that proved more difficult to address. In 2000, under State Board of Education Policy IHF-1, completing the Subject Area Testing Program (SATP) had become a requirement for high school graduation, and the SATP included an exam on U.S. history. If students did not pass the exam, they could not graduate. As a result, teachers felt constrained to "teach to the test," and there was simply no curricular space for non-SATP material.[44] In an educational climate in which testing formed the basis of state assessment of the success of schools, only a state mandate authorizing civil rights education would create the conditions under which teachers could integrate civil rights into their lesson plans.

Owens recalls conversations at the education summit in 2005: "The big thing [teachers] wanted to see happen was something more momentous and more institutionalized, like a curriculum in the state."[45] What began as an effort by the Philadelphia Coalition to build upon the 2004 commemoration and facilitate a discussion about civil rights education had transformed into an idea for a more ambitious statewide program.

Priming the Political Environment: The Commemoration and the Killen Trial

No one could have foreseen the confluence of events that would occur in Philadelphia during the week of June 21, 2005. Killen, the first person to be held accountable for the 1964 murders in a Mississippi courtroom, was set to be tried, and as a result of delays, his trial took place in Philadelphia the week before the education summit. To the surprise and delight of Philadelphia Coalition members, whose declaration calling for justice in the case had prompted Mississippi's legal authorities to act, Killen was convicted—just as educators and activists arrived in Philadelphia for the scheduled educational summit, held only a block from the county courthouse where the momentous verdict had been reached.

Coalition members had hoped that the summit would inspire more dialogue on race around the state. In this they were not disappointed: the timing could not have been more advantageous. According to one observer, the trial imbued the education summit with "a contagious buzz" that circulated through the large gathering of Mississippi educators, who arrived poised to discuss the trial and its implications for civil rights education throughout the state.[46] "When history comes alive in the form of an internationally publicized civil rights trial in a small Mississippi town," observed Donna Ladd, editor of the *Jackson Free Press*, "the time is ripe to tackle the dearth of civil rights curriculum available in America's schools."[47] The fact that the education summit coincided with the verdict in the Killen trial created a unique political opening for the coalition and the Winter Institute to leverage the experience in Philadelphia to pursue institutional change at the state level.

Following the Killen trial, state and national media used Neshoba County as a metonym for Mississippi as a whole. If Neshoba County's failings were Mississippi's failings, this comparison suggested, Neshoba County's redemption could be Mississippi's. After the verdict, an interview with Robert Clark, the former speaker pro tem of the Mississippi House of Representatives and the first African American to serve in that body since Reconstruction, revealed the symbolic significance of the trial within the state. "This is the kind of Mississippi I have been living to see," he said. "[The verdict in the Killen trial] will make people look at us and realize we are real people. . . . This is a new day in Mississippi."[48] Reflecting Clark's enthusiasm, the Jackson *Clarion-Ledger* wrote: "Whatever anyone thinks, the people of Neshoba County spoke clearly through the judge and jury. *They also spoke for the state.*"[49] The education summit in Philadelphia may have highlighted the institutional challenges to civil rights education, but it was the Killen trial that generated the opportunity to discuss curricular reform statewide.[50]

If the Killen trial threw open the door of political possibility, the fortieth anniversary commemoration unlocked it. When asked if the Philadelphia Coalition would have pursued an educational initiative without the relative success of the 2004 commemoration, the answer of the coalition cochair Leroy Clemons was a definitive "no."[51] The fact that the commemoration was successful—or at least was perceived that way—was essential for enabling future efforts to institutionalize civil rights memory within the state education system. Without such a commemoration, the coalition would not have continued to meet, nor would the education summit in Philadelphia have been planned.

But the fortieth anniversary commemoration had done more than create a local organizational infrastructure; it also signaled a change in Mississippi's moral code. To deny, obscure, or otherwise discount civil rights–era violence and the state's role in it—at least in a public political context—became a liability, and the state's political actors had to navigate a shifting and sometimes treacherous political terrain.

Mobilizing Resources at the State Level: The Winter Institute Lobbies the Legislature

With the idea of a statewide mandate for civil rights education in place and the political opening created by the Killen trial and the fortieth anniversary commemoration, the Winter Institute enlisted the help of a master's student in southern studies at the University of Mississippi who had been conducting research on similar curricular efforts. In just three days, the student drafted what would become SB 2718, a bill authorizing the State Board of Education to make civil rights a part of the K–12 curriculum and affirming the need to teach Mississippi's children "all of our history . . . as a beacon of hope for all of our citizens."[52] Mississippi's 2004 Holocaust education bill served as a model for both what to do and what not to do. The Holocaust education bill had empowered the governor to appoint the members of the Holocaust Education Commission, but a year after the bill was signed, Barbour had yet to appoint a single commissioner. If the civil rights education bill were to be effective, the Winter Institute knew that more autonomy would be required, and it crafted the bill's language accordingly. The proposed civil rights education commission would have four permanent members selected from four institutions—the Winter Institute at the University of Mississippi, Tougaloo College, the Oral History Project at the University of Southern Mississippi, and Jackson State University—thus reducing the control of the governor and inoculating the commission against potential political manipulation. Despite these safeguards, however, implementation difficulties would plague the education bill.

TABLE 4.1 Mississippi state senators who sponsored the education bill (SB 2718)

Senator	District Office Location	Winter Institute Active in District	Member of Black Caucus
Gray Tollison	Oxford	✓	
John Horhn	Jackson	✓	✓
Gloria Williamson	Philadelphia	✓	
Alice Harden	Jackson	✓	✓
David Jordan	Greenwood	✓	✓
Hillman Frazier	Jackson	✓	✓
Sampson Jackson	Preston		✓
Kelvin Butler	McComb	✓	✓

With the language for a civil rights education bill under way, the Winter Institute began seeking a Mississippi legislator willing to sponsor it. Glisson, the institute's director, approached her local senator, Gray Tollison, just days before the legislative deadline with a sense of renewed urgency—for if they missed the deadline, the bill would not be considered until the next legislative session, and the momentum generated by the Killen trial might be lost. Tollison agreed without hesitation to introduce the bill, knowing that Glisson and the Winter Institute were well-respected constituents in the Oxford community, a reputation supported by the institute's involvement in the 2004 commemoration in Philadelphia and the 2005 Killen trial.[53]

Tollison was not the only politician to support the bill, and an examination of the other senators who cosponsored the bill reveals the true extent of the Winter Institute's significance in the process.[54] Of the bill's original eight cosponsors, all but one represented districts where the Winter Institute was active, and all but two were members of Mississippi's Legislative Black Caucus, a significant political force within the state (table 4.1).[55] The only other white cosponsor besides Tollison was Gloria Williamson, a longtime resident of Philadelphia and its representative in the Mississippi Senate.

At the start of the legislative session in January 2006, Tollison introduced SB 2718. Although Barbour's signature on the bill came quickly—a mere eight weeks after the bill's introduction—the bill Barbour signed into law had been altered from the original in two important ways. After going through the Senate Education Committee, the bill authorized civil rights and human rights education, but whether the committee added human rights to expand the mandate or to dilute the focus on civil rights remains unclear. Regardless of the motivation, adding human rights to the curricular change might have broadened the curriculum at the expense of civil rights by sidelining aspects of Mississippi's civil rights story. The sociologists Vered Vinitzky-Seroussi and Chana Teeger define this sort of covert silence in the domain of memory as "bland commemoration," which generally involves a compromise that seeks to "make an account of the past palatable to all tastes—hence bland and uncontroversial."[56]

The language in section 2 of the final bill was also made nonobligatory. Whereas the earlier text had stated that "the State Board of Education *shall* make civil rights part of the K–12 curriculum," the final text declared that "the State Board of Education *may* make civil rights and human rights education a part of the K–12 curriculum" (my emphasis). Seemingly, the transition from "shall" to "may" made the bill unenforceable, and the bill passed with near unanimous support in both houses of the state legislature.

Despite these changes, the law authorized the Mississippi State Board of Education to incorporate civil rights and human rights education into the K–12 curriculum framework, which made a strong statement about the shared common knowledge considered essential for residents of the state. According to the Southern Poverty Law Center's 2011 report on civil rights education, "Just as teachers set expectations for their students, states set expectations for their education system—their largest expenditure as well as their best investment in future prosperity."[57] In this way, state curriculum frameworks for history and social studies provide a guide, however broad, for how the history of Mississippi should be taught. Prior to passage of the bill, the civil rights movement had not been part of the Mississippi Department of Education's curricular framework, but that does not mean that civil rights history was entirely excluded from schools. Any number of individual teachers may have covered the movement to varying degrees—especially since 1980, when the state textbook committee approved Loewen and Sallis's *Mississippi: Conflict and Change*. However, in a state like Mississippi with a decentralized education system, including a topic on a statewide subject area test is the only way to ensure that it is taught, which first requires that the topic be included in the curricular framework.

Additionally, SB 2718 established a civil rights education commission that was granted relative autonomy, as the bill's designers had hoped. Members did not have to be appointed by the governor, which created a structure that circumvented political obstacles from the state's highest office. As noted above, representatives from the Winter Institute, Tougaloo College, the Oral History Project at the University of Southern Mississippi, and Jackson State

University were made permanent members of the commission to serve as the driving force behind all of the commission's activities, including assisting, coordinating, and modifying courses or programs that included the civil rights movement and acting as a liaison between the legislature and organizations that support civil rights education—responsibilities that the commission has continued to uphold since 2006.

In this way, SB 2718 effectively mandated civil rights and human rights education in Mississippi schools even though the language of the bill was nonobligatory. Given Mississippi's historical resistance to history texts that address the state's racially divisive past, both adding civil and human rights to the state curricular framework and creating an oversight committee dominated by professional historians represents a notable transformation in the domain of education.

From Commemoration to Curriculum

By reconstructing the journey of Mississippi's civil and human rights education bill, we can see that the impetus for the state mandate that would become SB 2718 emerged in part out of the 2004 commemoration in Philadelphia. That commemoration mobilized a new generation of local memory activists in Philadelphia, which helped establish a local organizational infrastructure (the Philadelphia Coalition) that when joined with institutional resources (the Winter Institute), generated the commemorative capacity to organize the 2004 commemoration and also the "Chaney, Schwerner, and Goodman Living Memorial Civil Rights Education Summit," a commemorative vehicle in its own right. Hosting an education summit to discuss civil rights education at this site was an attempt to leverage the energy created by the 2004 commemoration to institutionalize civil rights memory in a more systematic way.

Without the 2004 commemoration, this summit—and subsequent education bill—might not have occurred. The commemoration helped further strengthen Philadelphia's commemorative capacity by attracting new members to the coalition, including a local teacher. With a member of the target audience among their ranks, the Philadelphia Coalition and Winter Institute were able to create a space for educators across the state to identify challenges to civil rights education and plan appropriate next steps—specifically, a state mandate. And in this way, the commemoration helped launch a broader movement to reform how Mississippi educators bring the history of the civil rights movement into their classrooms.

However, this grassroots organizing around civil rights education coincided with the murder trial of Killen—an event that further transformed the matrix of political possibilities across the state. The trial created a political opening in which these local organizing efforts could be broadened to the state level. The conviction of a perpetrator in a high-profile civil rights–era cold case suggested that the behavior and opinions of Mississippi citizens and state actors were not intractable. Additionally, the trial demonstrated to Mississippi lawmakers that their constituents might be more open to efforts to confront Mississippi's racially charged past. In this way, the Killen trial primed the political environment in which the civil rights education bill was introduced, thereby making that environment more sympathetic than it had been even a year before—when state senators had attempted to amend a Holocaust education bill to include Mississippi's history of slavery and racism. Finally, both the commemoration and the trial provided the Winter Institute with new legitimacy at the state level. Prior to 2004, the institute was a relatively unknown entity in Mississippi. As a result of the 2004 commemoration, and even more so after the 2005 trial, the Winter Institute had become a well-recognized and well-respected civil-society organization in the state. This legitimacy enabled it to leverage the political opening created by the Killen trial and cultivate the necessary political support for SB 2718.

This origin story differs notably from those of other multicultural or human rights education mandates that have been the outgrowth of large-scale progressive social movements or the diffusion of global norms. Indeed, scholars and human rights practitioners working in societies beset by histories of racial or ethnic conflict have come to view educational curricula as a key component of transitional justice—alongside criminal trials, truth commissions, and other mechanisms designed to restore trust in civic institutions after violent conflict. Based on the premise that teaching respect for human rights and civic responsibility will prevent future atrocities, interest in both Holocaust and human rights education has soared since the 1990s, along with legal mandates that have hastened curricular change in states and nation-states less inclined to pursue these curricular objectives on their own. Alongside these legal mandates, civil-society organizations such as Teaching for Change and Facing History and Ourselves have made related educational materials more readily available. However, to fixate on the role of nonprofit organizations, educators, and activists obscures the conditions that brought them together—in this case, the fortieth anniversary commemoration. And to focus solely on these broader cultural changes overlooks how local memory practices created the conditions possible for broader curricular change.

Whether or not change in the official curriculum has engendered change in the classroom is also a worthy question, for law and society scholars have long noted the disconnect between law in books and law in action. In the ten years since its passage, the implementation of Mississippi's civil and human rights curricular mandate has faced notable challenges. In the only scholarly study on the topic to date, the sociologists David Cunningham and Ashley Rondini found that as of 2011, only two Mississippi communities—McComb and Philadelphia—had integrated civil and human rights education into formal school curricula (McComb) or durable civic structures (Philadelphia), an outcome the authors attribute to structural constraints.[58] The decentralized nature of Mississippi's public education system meant that early implementation relied almost exclusively on "civic energies of *local* youth development efforts."[59] More specifically, Cunningham and Rondini found that the successful implementation of civil and human rights education occurs only in the presence of long-standing civil rights organizing efforts, which is conditioned by the degree of historical white resistance to civil rights initiatives and the extent of white participation in local public schools. In this way, the authors' findings demonstrate how the histories of past contention shape possibilities for future civic action.

It turns out that uneven implementation is a common dilemma for decentralized education systems worldwide. Studies of curricular change in South Africa, Rwanda, Colombia, and Israel also note the challenges of teaching racially or ethnically charged topics in contexts where individual schools or teachers have full control over their lesson plans. Under such circumstances, an official state mandate can go only so far, thus blurring the lines between the official curriculum, the intended one, and the actually implemented one.[60] Since 2011, however, and for the first time in Mississippi's history, the State Board of Education has included civil rights history questions in the U.S. history test, a requirement for high school graduation.[61] Whether and how these most recent changes will function as enforcement mechanisms remains to be seen.

If teachers hesitate to engage contentious histories, whether out of fear or lack of knowledge, they may reinforce the structure out of which these histories emerged. Yet these challenges also suggest that as critical as classroom learning is to transforming the collective memory of the past, the learning that occurs outside the classroom—in the broader civil sphere—is as least as significant, and perhaps even more so. Engaging the state's citizenry outside of formal classrooms is just what Mississippians set out to do by attempting to establish a South African–style truth commission, as we will see in the next chapter.

FIGURE G.1 On the first day of the Freedom Summer Project, the sudden disappearance of (left to right) Andrew Goodman, James Chaney, and Michael Schwerner shocked the nation and provoked an FBI investigation that brought hundreds of federal agents and National Guardsmen to Neshoba County in search of the three civil rights workers. Courtesy of the Archives and Records Services Division, Mississippi Department of Archives and History.

FIGURE G.2 In August 1964, Martin Luther King Jr. speaks to Freedom Democrats and their supporters at the Democratic national convention in Atlantic City, New Jersey, the portraits of (*left to right*) Andrew Goodman, James Chaney, and Michael Schwerner appearing as symbols of the movement's stakes. George Ballis/TakeStock.

FIGURE G.3 A family walks toward Mt. Zion, the United Methodist Church that local Ku Klux Klansmen firebombed in 1964, luring James Chaney, Michael Schwerner, and Andrew Goodman back to Neshoba County, and the site of annual services in their memory since 1965. Courtesy of Jean-Baptiste Chuat.

FIGURE G.4 One of the first sites of memory marking the 1964 murders locally, this private monument was erected in 1976 outside of Mt. Nebo in Independence Quarters to the west of downtown Philadelphia, thanks to small private donations from church members and other local residents. Courtesy of Jean-Baptiste Chuat.

FIGURE G.5 Philadelphia's mayor, Rayburn Waddell, reads a proclamation calling for justice in the 1964 slaying of the three civil rights workers in Neshoba County, during a news conference on Wednesday, May 26, 2004, in Philadelphia. Members of the Philadelphia Coalition, a multiracial task force charged with planning the fortieth anniversary commemoration of the event, surround the mayor. The coalition's cochairs, Leroy Clemons and Jim Prince, stand to the left and right of the mayor, respectively. *Neshoba Democrat,* Steven G. Watson/Associated Press Images.

FIGURE G.6 Governor Haley Barbour (*left*) greets Congressman John Lewis, who represented Georgia's fifth district, upon his arrival as the mother of slain civil rights worker Andrew Goodman, Carolyn (*center*), looks on. This image from the fortieth anniversary commemoration of the slayings of three civil rights workers on June 20, 2004, was circulated widely and transformed the conditions of possibility surrounding future commemorative efforts. Charles Smith/Associated Press Images.

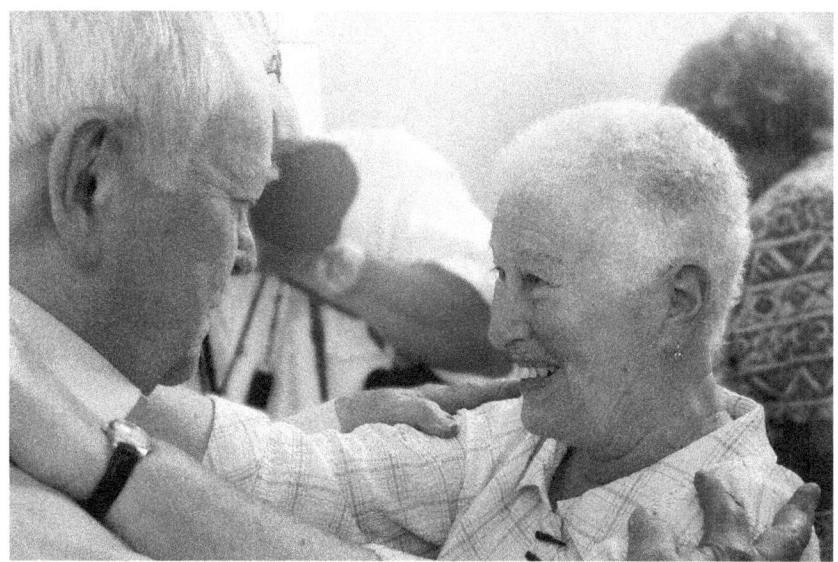

FIGURE G.7 Stanley Dearman (*left*), a Philadelphia Coalition member and former *Neshoba Democrat* editor, greets Michael Schwerner's widow, Rita Bender (*right*), at the fiftieth anniversary commemoration at Mt. Zion on June 15, 2014. Courtesy of Jean-Baptiste Chuat.

FIGURE G.8 Two children reading the fiftieth anniversary commemoration program at Mt. Zion United Methodist Church on June 15, 2014. Courtesy of Jean-Baptiste Chuat.

FIGURE G.9 Local residents and civil rights movement veterans, including Diane Nash (*fourth from right*) gather outside the ruins of the Longdale community center for the fiftieth annual Mississippi Civil Rights Martyrs Memorial Service on June 21, 2014. Courtesy of Jean-Baptiste Chuat.

FIGURE G.10 Local residents and activists march to the Neshoba County Courthouse in downtown Philadelphia on June 21, 2014, marking the fiftieth anniversary of the Mississippi Burning murders. Courtesy of Jean-Baptiste Chuat.

FIGURE G.11 Susan Glisson (*second from right*), then director of the William Winter Institute for Racial Reconciliation, discusses the 1964 killing of Andrew Goodman, James Chaney, and Michael Schwerner with Summer Institute students at the memorial erected in the civil rights workers' honor at Mt. Zion United Methodist Church in Neshoba County in June 2014. Courtesy of Jean-Baptiste Chuat.

5 Commissioning Truth and Reconciliation

In 2009, Archbishop Desmond Tutu recorded a message for Mississippians. Sitting before a video crew in his native South Africa and wearing a dark blazer and clerical collar, the graying anti-apartheid leader and former chairman of the South African Truth and Reconciliation Commission (TRC) looked straight into the camera. "It is never easy for a people to talk about painful things," he said in a slow, measured tone. "That is why I am so heartened to hear that people in Mississippi had the courage to take up such a difficult process." He was speaking of the recently launched Mississippi Truth Project that was being modeled after South Africa's postapartheid truth-seeking process. Between 1996 and 1998, the new democratic government in South Africa deployed the largest and most public truth commission to date. Hundreds of victims and perpetrators of apartheid-era violence delivered televised testimony in the hopes that truth would lead to reconciliation and that their collective storytelling would serve as a social catharsis, enabling forgiveness and restoring people's trust in civic institutions and their fellow citizens. Since then, truth commissions have become an accepted, if not expected, mechanism to facilitate transitions from authoritarianism to democracy or from violence to peace. And as they have grown in popularity, states and civil-society organizations have adopted truth commissions in a variety of contexts, including those where the violence being investigated was long past.[1]

In 2005, Mississippi joined the truth commission bandwagon when private citizens began work to establish a statewide truth commission that would investigate racial violence and discrimination in the state in the period 1945–75 and recommend appropriate remedies.[2] After years of planning—and an unplanned hiatus at the start of the commission's efforts, forced upon it by Hurricane Katrina—the Mississippi Truth Project launched its public phase at a ceremony in Jackson on January 30, 2009, as several hundred people gathered in the state's capital to sign the declaration of intent endorsing the creation of a statewide truth commission.[3]

This was not the first time that efforts had been made to create a truth commission in Mississippi. The idea had first occurred to John Horhn, a stylish silver-haired Democrat who represented the Jackson metropolitan area in the Mississippi Senate and now hosts his own community-based radio show, *Tell John*. Beginning in 2001, Horhn introduced a bill every year to create a state-sponsored truth commission that would "advise and assist the governor and the legislature in developing politics, plans and programs to increase racial diversity and enhance racial harmony in the state." Tutu's leadership had inspired Horhn long before Tutu recorded his message for Mississippians. And Horhn credits South Africa's TRC with "helping that country get through its racist past." While many scholars would disagree with Horhn's interpretation of the South African case, that was of little consequence for the senator, who continued to view the TRC as enviable. In his estimation, a Mississippi truth commission would not hold anyone legally accountable, but it would "get things out in the open so wounds could heal." However, each time he introduced the bill, it met the same fate: left to languish in the Rules Committee, the bill, according to Horhn, "died a slow, torturous death." Years later, he reflected on those failed attempts: "No one had the stones to do it."[4]

Yet in 2005, four years after Horhn first introduced his truth commission bill, a group of Mississippians initiated a statewide truth commission that received strong civil-society support, a development that requires further explanation. How did a Mississippi truth commission finally gain traction? What can the Mississippi Truth Project tell us about rituals of remembrance in Mississippi's civil sphere? And what if any connection did this have to the fortieth anniversary commemoration in Philadelphia?

The Truth Commission Bandwagon

Defining "truth commission" can be surprisingly tricky, since many people apply the term to their truth-seeking endeavors because of the term's cultural salience and despite the fact that their projects do not resemble the temporary, state-sanctioned, investigative bodies to which the term "truth commission" was originally applied. Still, scholars generally agree with Priscilla Hayner's widely cited definition, which specifies that a truth commission "(1) is focused on the past, rather than ongoing, events; (2) investigates a pattern of events that took place over a period of time; (3) engages directly and broadly with the affected population, gathering information on their experiences; (4) is a temporary body, with the aim of concluding with a final report; and (5) is officially authorized or empowered by the state under review."[5]

Truth commissions are thus distinguished from permanent investigative bodies such as parliamentary human rights commissions and truth-seeking efforts not sponsored by the state, or what Louis Bickford refers to as "unofficial truth projects."[6] As national, state-sponsored entities, truth commissions "indexed a unique moment in Latin American history," according to the historian Greg Grandin, "as the decline of socialist movements crossed paths with ascendant efforts to consolidate liberal constitutional rule," therefore emerging as a distinct institutional form in Argentina and later Chile and El Salvador.[7] Depending on the definition and the database, researchers have identified anywhere between thirty and forty national truth commissions, which proliferated only after South Africa's highly publicized TRC drew global attention and praise in the mid-1990s.[8] And while truth commissions were initially designed as alternatives to criminal trials—especially in transitional or postconflict contexts, where prosecutions were impractical because of the number of individuals involved or unlikely because the judiciary lacked the capacity to adjudicate fairly—they now represent one item on a menu of transitional justice offerings that include criminal trials, reparations, and political vetting and are often implemented alongside these other mechanisms, albeit with a specific purpose in mind. "The raison d'être of a truth commission," observes Onur Bakiner, "is to establish an honest and impartial account of past events and reconstruct historical memory where conventional state institutions, such as courts and parliamentary committees, have failed to do so."[9]

Thus, truth commissions have come to serve a number of social functions, albeit with varying degrees of emphasis. They create a comprehensive factual record on the basis of sound evidence; establish the causes, patterns, and consequences related to the violence in question; strengthen respect for human rights and democracy; cultivate a new collective identity that bridges historic animosity; and encourage forgiveness and reconciliation between social groups that have historically been in conflict.[10] In this way, truth commissions engage in a variety of forensic, historiographic, and cultural tasks. Whether and to what extent the commissions have succeeded along these dimensions remains a topic of debate, but the cultural salience of seeking truth and performing reconciliation operates nonetheless.[11] Invoking the rhetoric of truth and reconciliation commissions has become a powerful discursive tool, imbuing truth projects with authority in the context of a growing international transitional justice community.

Given this cultural salience, truth commission mandates have expanded. In recent years, both state and nonstate actors have initiated truth commissions in consolidated democracies where the systematic violence under investigation is long past and for which a transitional justice framework may not apply.[12] In this sense, truth commissions are retrospective in nature, revisiting distant periods of systemic violence that remain politically and socially salient in the present. The Canadian government, for example, established a truth and reconciliation commission in 2006 in response to the staggering number of lawsuits related to damage inflicted on indigenous children who were taken from their families and forcibly enrolled in the Indian resident school system—a state institution that operated for most of the twentieth century with the purpose of assimilating school-age children into the dominant Canadian culture (the final school closed in 1996).[13] Likewise, one of South Korea's truth commissions, established in 2000, investigated the large-scale massacres of civilians in 1947 and resulted in the first public apology of a South Korean president for the historic abuse of state power.[14]

Truth commission initiatives in the United States have been notably less fruitful, despite more than a century of truth-seeking efforts. For example, throughout the 1890s, Ida B. Wells conducted extensive research on and kept records of lynching in the United States, publishing her findings in *The Red Record*, a hundred-page report that detailed the history and scope of racial violence since emancipation.[15] Such early efforts to systematically document racial violence in the United States are important and often overlooked precursors to modern truth commissions. By aggregating disparate data on seemingly isolated episodes of racial violence, Wells and others drew attention to the alarmingly high rates of lynching throughout the South and, in doing so, established a significant counternarrative. Nearly a century later, in the 1980s, motivated by a shifting relationship between history, politics, and ethics—what Jeffrey Olick has called "the politics of regret"[16]—truth-seeking efforts in the United States moved from the margins to the center of political life as governmental and nongovernmental organizations (NGOs) created bodies to inquire into past episodes of racial violence that resemble truth commissions in both form and function. The Commission on Wartime Relocation and Internment of Civilians, established by the U.S. Congress, is one example. Having conducted public hearings across the country to collect testimony from Japanese Americans affected by the World War II internment, the commission's final report concluded that the relocation and internment was a "grave injustice" and recommended compensation for survivors. By 1992, the U.S. government had paid more than $1.2 billion in reparations to Japanese Americans affected by the internment.[17]

Several states have also provided material and symbolic reparations for historic racial violence. In 1993, the Florida Legislature commissioned a report on the 1923 race riot in Rosewood, where white vigilantes attacked members of an African American community after hearing allegations that a white woman had been raped by a black man from Rosewood. The following year, Florida became the first state to compensate victims for racial violence when it passed the Rosewood Compensation Bill, which provided more than $2 million to surviving victims.[18] Likewise, in 1996 the Oklahoma Legislature commissioned a report on the 1921 Tulsa Race Riot, an event that left an estimated ten thousand black residents homeless. In 2001, the legislature passed the Tulsa Race Riot Reconciliation Act, which established scholarships for the descendants of survivors, provided economic development for the neighborhoods affected, and created a memorial park for the victims. Following suit, the North Carolina legislature authorized a commission in 2000 to investigate the 1898 Wilmington Race Riots, during which a white mob violently overthrew a democratically elected black government. In 2007, the North Carolina Senate passed a resolution expressing "profound regret" for the riot.[19] Despite this precedent, the Mississippi Legislature showed no interest in investigating the state's racial past, as Horhn discovered year after year when he submitted his truth commission bill.

In instances where national governments resist demands for official reckonings, collective truth-seeking efforts tend to be unofficial in nature, emerging from civil society.[20] This was the case in Uruguay, for example, when civil society pressured the government to investigate human rights violations after the country's return to democracy in 1985. When those demands went unmet, civil-society actors published a report on human rights violations that resembled the work of a truth commission. Similar dynamics unfolded in Brazil and Paraguay, as human rights organizations and the Catholic church conducted their own investigations into political violence when the government failed to do so.

In the early 2000s, the United States followed this trend. At this time, the idea of a truth commission had great normative appeal and mobilization potential, shaping the values, rhetoric, and strategies of civil-society actors. In Greensboro, North Carolina, for instance, local organizations partnered with NGO consultants and philanthropic funding agencies in 1999 to reinvestigate a decades-old shooting that had come to be known as the Greensboro Massacre. Members of the Ku Klux Klan and the American Nazi Party had opened fire at a racially mixed crowd of union activists during a demonstration in 1979, leaving ten people injured and five dead.[21] Despite having been videotaped in broad daylight, the accused perpetrators were acquitted by all-white juries in two separate trials. In 2004, inspired by the South African TRC, local organizations launched the Greensboro Truth and Reconciliation Commission to examine the causes and consequences of that shooting, and in 2006, the commission issued its final report. Other U.S.-based truth commissions soon followed, including ones in Detroit, Michigan; Maine; and, as we will see below, Mississippi.[22]

As of the early 2000s, Mississippi's civil society had not mobilized around any major memory projects. It was not until 2005 that efforts to establish a statewide truth commission began in earnest. But how did this project come to be? With the exception of the Greensboro Truth and Reconciliation Commission, whose history has been fairly well documented, few researchers have examined instances of civil-society–based truth commissions in the United States.[23]

Creating Conditions for Truth Telling: The Fortieth Anniversary Commemoration and the Killen Trial

When an interracial group of Neshoba County citizens began to organize the fortieth anniversary commemoration of the 1964 Mississippi Burning murders, most had never heard of a truth commission, let alone transitional justice. They wanted to transform the local memory landscape on their own terms—a process, as we saw in previous chapters, that focused on both curricular reform and legal recourse. For the group whose efforts had brought Edgar Ray Killen to justice for his role in the 1964 murders, his 2005 conviction was only a partial victory. The legal system's narrow focus on the misdeeds of a single individual masked the broader social and structural context that had enabled the crime to take place, a sentiment that is evident in the Philadelphia Coalition's statement to the press immediately following the guilty verdict. "These three brave young men were not murdered by a lone individual," the statement contended. "While a vigilante group may have fired the gun, *the State of Mississippi loaded and aimed the weapon.* The Mississippi State Sovereignty Commission monitored and intimidated civil rights activists to prevent black voter registration. The White Citizens' Council enforced white supremacy through economic oppression. And decent people remained silent while evil was done in their name. These shameful actions have been little understood by Mississippi citizens."[24]

The people who prepared the Philadelphia Coalition's press statement must have been aware of its potential impact. Representatives of dozens of local and national news outlets were in Philadelphia to cover the trial, and now their cameras were turned on the coalition. The neatly crafted prose seems intended to educate the public about the past by offering a brief primer on Mississippi's Jim Crow–era institutions. But it also represents a narrative recasting of these events that challenged the dominant narrative of the state's past. In the coalition's retelling, the three civil rights workers are depicted as brave compatriots rather than outside invaders, and the state actors (the Mississippi State Sovereignty Commission and the White Citizens' Council) are portrayed as antidemocratic institutions rather than democracy's defenders. In other words, historic villains were now heroes, and historic heroes were now villains. Furthermore, having problematized the past, the coalition also provided a recommended remedy: truth seeking. "We must now seek the truth," the coalition members told their fellow citizens. "We call on the State of Mississippi, all of its citizens in every county, to begin an honest investigation in our history."[25]

The state's highest elected official, Governor Barbour, felt differently, as did many people across the state. From their perspective, the trial was not a beginning but an end to a long story in which the state, victorious in its efforts, had finally held the primary villain (Killen) to account. Within a week of the conviction, Barbour had declared closure for Mississippi's racial past.

For Rita Bender, Michael Schwerner's widow, who had worked in Meridian alongside Schwerner in the months leading up to his death, Barbour's declaration was a provocation. A Seattle attorney, remarried with grown children, the petite but powerful Bender had returned to Neshoba County for Killen's trial, her first visit there since her husband's murder (see figure G.7). Throughout the trial, she refused to answer questions about her feelings and instead took the press to task: "You're interested in this trial as the most important trial in the Civil Rights Movement because two of the [victims] were white." For her, the trial itself was not paramount; her concerns were more far reaching. "The discussion about racism in this country has to continue," Bender asserted in 2005. "If this is the way to that, then this trial has some meaning."[26]

So when Barbour's remarks suggested that Killen's conviction marked the end of Jim Crow injustice, Bender drafted an open letter to him that was published in the Jackson *Clarion-Ledger*. After detailing the systematic abuses committed by the Mississippi State Sovereignty Commission during the 1960s—as well as more recent instances in which, in her opinion, Mississippi's elected officials had increased racial tensions—Bender encouraged further truth-seeking efforts. "Restorative justice," she wrote, "can only come with recognition of the past, acknowledgment of wrongdoing, and acceptance of responsibility in the present by government and individuals to ameliorate the harm done. . . . Only with such acknowledgment will the present generation understand how these many terrible crimes occurred, and the responsibility which present officials, voters, and indeed, all citizens, have to each other to move forward."[27]

Like the statement from the Philadelphia Coalition, Bender's letter positioned truth as a precondition for justice and broadened the responsibility for seeking truth or justice to include not only elected officials but all citizens. Taken together, these were powerful public pleas that constructed Killen's trial as a catalyst for subsequent transformations to Mississippi's memory landscape. In a state that had long nurtured a culture of impunity surrounding civil rights–era violence, the Killen trial had created a political opening, however small, that enabled memory activists to reinterpret the story of Mississippi's past, present, and future within the civil sphere.

Surviving the Storm: A Truth Project in Abeyance

When confronted with inhospitable political and social climates, social movements sometimes pause to weather the storm, in what Verta Taylor has described as "abeyance."[28] If a movement is sustained by a cadre of committed activists, it will continue when a more advantageous context presents itself, sometimes decades later. In Mississippi, the storm was not metaphorical. In August 2005, Hurricane Katrina ravaged Mississippi's Gulf Coast, diverting both attention and resources to recovery efforts and effectively pausing the positive momentum created by the Killen trial in June.

Inspired by the conviction and Bender's open letter, William Winter (a former Mississippi governor) and Susan Glisson (director of the William Winter Institute for Racial Reconciliation) convened the Mississippi Coalition for Racial Justice (MCRJ), a group of civil rights veterans, progressive activists, and religious leaders who were brought together to explore how best to leverage the positive momentum created by the justice process undertaken by citizens in Neshoba County.[29] The MCRJ had been meeting for only a matter of months before Hurricane Katrina hit Mississippi. In the end, the storm did more than temporarily suspend the group's deliberations. By exposing the stark racial divide in who was most affected by the storm and who was most likely to receive aid, Katrina underscored the need for a truth commission.[30] As a result, according to one MCRJ participant, Katrina "became a very important condition of possibility for thinking through the stakes of systemic injustice as a historical phenomenon that still has historical effects."[31]

In January 2006, the MCRJ published a statement on Hurricane Katrina in the Winter Institute's newsletter, the *Wellspring*, expressing its hopes for recovery in the Gulf Coast but also using Philadelphia as a touchstone for its own efforts to build a more equitable and inclusive Mississippi:

> In June 2004, the community of Philadelphia, Mississippi, witnessed a rebirth. That positive renewal grew from a courageous commitment on the part of a multiracial group of community leaders to honestly appraise their past and its legacy of racism. They showed us that such explorations, however painful, can be positive and productive and can establish a more inclusive, sustainable foundation for community development. . . . Hurricane Katrina has now laid bare for many of us the illusion that we have always cared adequately for others. . . . We hope that the Governor's Commission for Recovery, Rebuilding, and Renewal and its subcommittees will reflect these concerns in their personnel and operations.[32]

In many ways, the state's approach to recovery fell short of this idealized vision. But the perceived failures of the recovery fueled frustrations about racial inequity in the state—frustrations that sustained nascent efforts to develop a truth commission while the hurricane had forced those efforts into abeyance.[33] And more than two years after the fortieth anniversary commemoration in Philadelphia, the MCRJ invoked the Philadelphia Coalition as a model for interracial collaboration across the state, keeping the memory of the coalition alive in the minds of Mississippi citizens.

Two years after the storm, in the winter of 2007, the Winter Institute and the MCRJ resumed their focus on truth telling by hosting a series of meetings at Millsaps College, in Jackson, to initiate discussions about "The Welcome Table: A Year of Dialogue on Race," a project inspired by the events in Philadelphia. According to Patrick Weems, a Winter Institute staff member, the Philadelphia Coalition's call for justice had "showed that a multiracial and multicultural group could work together for progress."[34] The Winter Institute thus sought to replicate Philadelphia's experience through the Welcome Table, which would inform a more comprehensive and longterm truth-telling project. If Philadelphia had taught the Winter Institute anything, recalled one institute employee, it was that "you can't put a diverse group of Mississippians in a room until you build some trust."[35]

To further connect this pilot year of dialogue with the success in Philadelphia in an effort to legitimize the project, the Winter Institute officially launched the Welcome Table on June 21, 2007, the forty-third anniversary of the Neshoba murders, in a public ceremony that attracted more than three hundred Mississippians.[36] Choir members; interfaith religious leaders; former and current elected officials; and students from high schools, colleges, and universities came together at the state capitol for both "a celebration and a challenge to help make [Mississippi] a better place for all its citizens," according the Winter Institute.[37] With calls to prayer from Christian, Jewish, and Muslim clerics, the ceremony linked race, dialogue, and religion in its call for participation as speakers like Winter encouraged attendees to be courageous leaders.

Around the same time, the Winter Institute began to develop a Mississippi truth commission in earnest after meeting with civil rights veterans, scholars, and others who were engaged in examining Mississippi's racial past. By and large, members of these early conversations endorsed the idea of such a commission and began to leverage their professional networks for support. Through these efforts, the Winter Institute was introduced to the Andrus Family Fund, a key supporter of the civil society–sponsored truth commission in Greensboro, North Carolina. Based on Greensboro's perceived success, Andrus was open to supporting subsequent truth-seeking projects.

With seed money from Andrus, the Winter Institute hired part-time organizers who held exploratory meetings across the state to gauge interest in a possible truth commission.[38] These meetings were also educational, as each began with a brief history of truth commissions (including the South African case) and a synopsis of how the idea for a Mississippi truth commission had emerged after the Killen conviction when Barbour declared closure on Mississippi's racial past. Facilitators from the Winter Institute then gathered opinions about a Mississippi truth commission, which ranged from total enthusiasm ("Truth transcends time. We must keep digging.") to outright skepticism ("What is the purpose?"). For the most part, the conversations at these initial meetings considered broad logistical concerns, such as amnesty for perpetrators, possibilities for reparations, potential future criminal trials, and whether to seek state sponsorship. In this regard, these meetings were already beginning to incorporate the international discourse of transitional justice within a local setting. And despite some concern about the effectiveness of a truth commission, all five exploratory meetings generated significant support for the project.[39]

Leveraging Global Norms and Resources: Learning from Greensboro

On April 4, 2008, the Winter Institute invited community partners from the exploratory meetings to attend a statewide gathering later that month at Wells Memorial United Methodist Church, in Jackson, to further explore parameters for a Mississippi truth commission and meet with representatives from the recently concluded Greensboro Truth Commission and the International Center for Transitional Justice (ICTJ)—which had provided technical support in Greensboro. At this point, the idea of a statewide truth commission in Mississippi had been circulating for several years, so this meeting, while not officially a public event, was an important step in bringing together truth commission supporters from across the state to solidify their vision.

Because of widespread mistrust of state leadership, the MCRJ and the Winter Institute decided not to pursue state sponsorship and sought other models for their truth-seeking initiative. In this regard, the Greensboro Truth and Reconciliation Commission was ideal. As the first truth commission in the United States, it spearheaded a new approach to truth commissions rooted in civil society. When the Winter Institute came into contact with representatives from the Greensboro Truth Commission at a regional conference in 2006, the commission was about to release its final report.[40] Hosted by the Winter Institute at the University of Mississippi, the conference—"Southern Exposure: A Regional Summit on Racial Violence and Reconciliation"—provided a rare opportunity for nonprofit organizations, grassroots groups, and scholars interested in legacies of racial violence to interact; share experiences; and forge a regional network, the Alliance for Truth and Racial Reconciliation.[41] While the alliance was relatively short-lived and its founding members ultimately focused on more local concerns, the meeting in Oxford brought together key stakeholders and facilitated the regional diffusion of civil-society–sponsored truth projects.

The initial response to the Greensboro Truth Commission from those in the transitional justice community had been resoundingly optimistic, with transitional justice practitioners describing the commission in 2006 as "a towering achievement" and its work "a remarkable set of best practices."[42] Social scientists' assessments of the commission have also been generally positive, with research suggesting that the commission generated a more complex public narrative of the killings that took place on November 3, 1979, and opened up new spaces for local political engagement.[43] Subsequent research has demonstrated that victims of the shootings, including those who lost family members and close friends in 1979, were generally satisfied with the truth that came out of the commission.[44] And perhaps most telling, an analysis of the results of a survey of more than eight hundred North Carolina citizens found that respondents who had heard of the commission were significantly more likely than those who had not to blame the Klan and police for the killings—actors the commission report had found most responsible.[45]

In 2008 the impact of the Greensboro Truth Commission was not yet known, but it offered a powerful touchstone for the Winter Institute and the MCRJ nonetheless. "We had learned from the Greensboro model," reflected Glisson, "that collective community could potentially create the authority to call for a commission. By outlining our intentions and then inviting Mississippians to endorse the document, we could try to legitimize ourselves through grassroots endorsement."[46] These observations mirrored insights from Paul van Zyl, who served as the executive secretary of South Africa's TRC and who watched the development of Greensboro's Truth Commission with interest and concern. "It's going to have to rely on its moral credibility to get people to cooperate with it," said van Zyl during the early stages of Greensboro's Truth Commission. "It can't just be a body which is seen as dealing with black people's grievances."[47] Mississippi's truth commission project faced the same risks, and the people initiating the Mississippi process eagerly sought lessons learned from Greensboro.

By seeking guidance from representatives of the Greensboro Truth Commission, the MCRJ and the Winter Institute became connected with an international network of truth commission practitioners, most notably the ICTJ, a global NGO that assists countries and groups pursuing accountability for mass atrocities or widespread human rights abuse. Founded in 2000, the ICTJ was one of the first organizations to explicitly focus on transitional justice, still a relatively new concept at the time. Consequently, the ICTJ helped constitute the field of transitional justice while becoming one of its major players. When the citizens of Greensboro forged ahead with their plans for a civil-society–based truth commission in 2003, Andrus, their funder, put them in contact with the ICTJ.[48] Given its prominence in the field, the ICTJ not only provides legitimacy to emerging efforts to establish truth commissions but also serves as the gatekeeper to the essential resources necessary to create a truth commission (such as financial resources and field-specific expertise). This was evident in 2003, when the ICTJ invited representatives from Greensboro to Peru for a meeting of the Managing Truth Commissions affinity group, a gathering where representatives of past, existing, and future truth commissions exchange ideas and strategies.[49]

When representatives of the Winter Institute and the MCRJ met with those of the Greensboro Truth Commission and the ICTJ in Jackson on April 26, 2008, they gained access to the collective wisdom of this international network. Based on the guidance its members received during that meeting, the MCRJ established two committees: a declaration committee responsible for drafting a declaration of intent, a document outlining the reasons to establish a statewide truth commission; and a temporary steering committee charged with calling future meetings, expanding the base of support for the project, setting a time frame for the establishment of a permanent steering committee, and recruiting and hiring three part-time organizers.

The organizers, who were hired with financial support from Andrus, set to work immediately. They were an eclectic bunch—a retired teacher, a social worker, and a former labor organizer—but they were all committed to their collective task: mobilizing support and building capacity for the hoped-for truth commission. As Howard Turberville put it, "When you're doing a project like that, you're not doing it for the money."[50] Throughout the summer and fall of 2009, these community organizers traveled to every corner of the state, holding meetings in school classrooms, community centers, and church halls to find people interested in the project. "We would just talk about . . . where they would like to see a truth commission go," recalls Tomeka Harbin, one of the community organizers. "That was pretty much my job—to organize and get the people to come out and then kind of let them stir in a way that they wanted it to go."[51]

On one such occasion, Harbin and her husband facilitated a meeting in the Delta town of Drew (just a few minutes down Highway 49 from the infamous state penitentiary known as Parchman Farm), where a local minister was "on fire for change."[52] In a single-room church with dark wood paneling and a modest gold cross marking the altar, Harbin explained to an audience of fifteen how the truth commission was being modeled after the commission in Greensboro, but as a statewide truth commission that could serve as a model for other states. Like people in other locations where the community organizers had held meetings, the citizens of Drew seemed interested in sharing their stories. One told a gruesome tale in which the severed fingers of a slave who had cursed his master were put on display in city hall. Recalling similar stories that he encountered when traveling throughout the state, Turberville reflected: "There are many times when I walked away and asked how the hell did they live through that. And it makes you wonder what human being can be so mean."[53]

With stories of racial violence circulating more openly, people began to wonder whether the commission could provide protection for those who came forward, both white and black. Understandably, those who had been targets of racially motivated violence and their descendants were concerned that speaking out would provoke retribution from those who continued to hold power in the state. But descendants of the perpetrators of civil rights–era violence were also concerned about negative repercussions if the community discovered that their family members had been part of a heinous act. The part-time community organizers did their best to allay these concerns, and such stories, factual or not, provided valuable information about the types of collective memories circulating in these communities as the organizers continued to think through what a Mississippi truth commission might look like.

Drafting the Declaration of Intent

As the organizers cultivated support across the state, a committee was drafting a declaration of intent that would outline the justification for a truth commission as well as the scope of the project. This was a precursor to an official mandate, which would be drafted later in the process and would serve a different function. While a mandate provides the legal and organizational frameworks for a truth commission as a series of bylaws or policies, a declaration of intent is an organizing tool used to mobilize support for the project. In this way, the process of writing the declaration of intent resembled what social movement scholars refer to as framing—that is, when social movement actors "assign meaning to and interpret relevant events and conditions in ways that are intended to mobilize potential adherents and constituents, to garner bystander support, and to demobilize antagonists."[54] Like governments, the media, and other collective actors, social movements are involved in the politics of signification, which—along with resources and political opportunities—can affect the movement's chance of success. A social movement is therefore most likely to succeed when a movement's frames resonate with their target audience.

The people charged with crafting the Mississippi declaration were keenly aware of their target audience as they drafted and redrafted a document that sought to challenge dominant perceptions of the past and mobilize support for a statewide truth commission. In the document's early iterations, they relied heavily on Greensboro's example, even using the perceived success in Greensboro to justify their efforts.[55] Later, however, the reference to Greensboro was dropped from the declaration, as was a reference to a proposed national advisory committee when committee members grew concerned that the focus on outsiders would be off-putting to those Mississippians who tend to be skeptical of meddling from external actors.

The declaration committee was not only attuned to language that might dissuade participation, but they also sought to craft a document that would encourage the participation—or at least the endorsement—of a broad spectrum of Mississippians. The authors of the final draft that was widely circulated throughout the state abandoned the dense essay format of previous iterations in favor of clear, bolded statements with supporting paragraphs. The result was more accessible and more like a story, articulating a connection between past and present and situating a truth commission as the key to a hoped-for future. Perhaps unknowingly, the authors of the declaration also engaged in three primary framing tasks, what David Snow and Robert Benford have identified as diagnostic framing, prognostic framing, and motivational framing.[56] Animated by a social constructivist perspective, framing theory asserts that social problems, like medical conditions, are not inherent and must be defined or diagnosed. Those seeking to achieve change must therefore articulate the problem (diagnostic framing), propose a solution (prognostic framing), and provide a reason to support the cause (motivational framing). The declaration of intent attempted to do just that.

Since the primary motivation of drafting the declaration was to convey why there should be a truth commission, most of the statement centered on constructing the problem: Mississippi's failure to reckon with its Jim Crow past. Taken together, the first three bolded statements make that argument:

From 1945 to 1975, racism cast a shadow over the experiences of all Mississippians.

. . .

We still feel the effects of that dark time.

. . .

The courageous struggles of many have yielded progress, but a full and accurate measure of our state's history and its lasting impact has been obscured.[57]

The declaration then further specifies who and what is to blame by correcting dominant interpretations of the past: "Too often stories are told of this time focusing on individuals and not institutions. While it is true that vigilantes terrorized the night, it is also true that public officials and community leaders shaped the daily experience of oppression. Moreover, the white establishment enabled the violence that occurred. The failure to understand this connection has allowed the premature declaration of closure following instances of individual justice that have happened."[58] Like the Philadelphia Coalition's press statement following Killen's conviction, this text highlights the state's culpability and the need to explore institutional (as opposed to individual) explanations underlying civil rights–era violence. It also makes a not-so-subtle indictment of Barbour by noting the "premature declaration of closure," thus further connecting the justification of the truth commission to preceding events in Philadelphia.

The next two bolded statements offer the solution to this problematized past in the form of a truth commission:

A just and inclusive future can only be ensured by a comprehensive inquiry of this unjust and segregated past.

. . .

The establishment of a Mississippi Truth and Reconciliation Project will allow us to develop appropriate remedies and to create a culture of equity, harmony, and prosperity.[59]

In constructing this story, the declaration authors engaged in causal emplotment, constructing a causal narrative of contingent progress.[60] In other words, they presented a narrative showing how Mississippi could transition from its negative Jim Crow past to a positive, more inclusive future—if Mississippians engaged in truth telling. The truth commission was therefore articulated as the linchpin in Mississippi's moral reckoning.

Identifying social problems and solutions is one thing; motivating constituents to act is quite another. The declaration authors appear to engage in this motivational framing by cultivating a sense of urgency. They stress not only the importance of engaging Mississippi's past, but also of doing it while there are "still living witnesses." "This is a unique moment," the declaration states, "wherein we have attained a measure of distance and insight into this period while still having living participants and observers of this time." And if temporal urgency wasn't enough, the declaration appealed to the sensibility of Mississippi's predominantly Christian population: "Acknowledging and working to understand our deliberate, insidious and systematic racism can *set us free* to understand our past and to create opportunities to *heal our wounds*."[61]

Having drafted the declaration of intent and circulated it throughout the state, the Winter Institute and the MCRJ then had to wait and see if this was a document around which Mississippi citizens would rally.

Legitimizing the Truth Commission: The Mississippi Truth Commission Enters Its Public Stage

Efforts to mobilize Mississippians in support of the truth commission culminated with a statewide meeting in Jackson on January 31, 2009, at which the organizers sought grassroots endorsement. Until that point, the truth commission project had operated under the radar, since the organizers wanted to cultivate a broad base of support before more powerful political forces in the state could squash the emerging project. This changed when the Mississippi Truth Project launched its public phase and officially announced its intention to create a statewide truth commission.

On January 31, several hundred people gathered in the Family Life Center at Central United Method Church for the daylong gathering that included both plenary sessions on the history of the truth commission initiative and truth commissions in general and breakout sessions where participants discussed topics such as the ideal qualifications for future commissioners. But the day was centered on an hour-long signing ceremony that involved a series of civil and religious rituals. Standing on a raised stage in the church gymnasium, Bishop Hope Morgan Ward opened the ceremony: "Let us open our hearts and minds to a place of quiet attention. Let us make ourselves ready for the soft, gentle coming of the light."[62] A candle lighting followed, along with an invocation of the names of "those who lend strength in our lives." After singing "Lift Every Voice and Sing" and listening to a reading of the declaration of intent, audience members were invited to sign the document, copies of which were displayed on metal folding tables. Over

130 people signed it, including Harbin and her two small children. For her, the declaration represented a once-in-a-lifetime opportunity for the three of them. She later recalled her thinking at the time: "So my husband and I were like, you know, this is a part of history and you can look back at this and say, 'Hey, I may not have fully understood what was going on, but my little name is scribbled on that piece of paper.'"[63]

After the signing ceremony, truth commission planning began in earnest, with a five-region structure (the Gulf Coast, central Mississippi, the Delta, the Pine Belt, and the Hills). Each region would elect representatives to serve on a permanent statewide steering committee that would direct the next phase of the project. By the summer of 2009, three of the five regions had elected representatives, and planning for a Mississippi truth commission appeared to be well on its way—at least for the time being.[64]

Mississippi's Truth Commission Transitions

Some people who were closely involved with the Mississippi truth commission project have described the declaration of intent signing ceremony as the beginning of the end. "It was kind of just a nose dive after that . . . the fire that had been lit just burned out."[65] By the following summer, the Winter Institute announced that the Mississippi Truth Project was entering "a new phase."[66] The project was beset by a number of local challenges as public interest failed to translate into sustained momentum. For some people, the idea of a truth commission was not easily comprehensible. Regional organizers found that most meetings required a basic introduction to transitional justice concepts and logic—what one organizer described as "Transitional Justice 101."[67] In this regard, each meeting was like starting from scratch. Then in December 2009, key staff members of the Winter Institute attended a conference titled "Beyond Reconciliation: Dealing with the Aftermath of Mass Trauma and Political Violence" in Cape Town, South Africa, and brought together transitional justice scholars and practitioners to assess the impact of the South African TRC and the growing field of truth commissions worldwide.[68] As representatives from the Winter Institute engaged in critical dialogue about truth commissions' possibilities and limitations, a conversation with Peter Storey, a South African religious leader and former member of the South African Truth and Reconciliation Commission, proved to be especially meaningful. Storey cautioned the Mississippians against getting "distracted by the super event," which he suggested "misses the microaggressions, the bystanderism, and the activities of everyday people to create the lived experience of a society organized around the oppression of others."[69]

The cautionary warning caused the Winter Institute staff members to pause, and they returned to Mississippi with a more cautious and critical approach to their truth project. Therefore, when the Mississippi truth commission steering committee had difficulty agreeing on substantive issues surrounding the mandate in the fall of 2009, the Winter Institute approached the project's key stakeholders to reassess matters. Many people who had been invested in the project up until that point were wary that a onetime truth commission would come and go without making substantive change.[70] Rather, they were interested in developing programming that could be sustained for years to come if and when Mississippi communities were ready to engage their histories of past racial violence. As the motivation to initiate a South African–style truth commission tapered off, the Welcome Table emerged as the cornerstone of the Winter Institute's programmatic lineup. Inspired by the work of the Philadelphia Coalition, the institute had designed a series of three-day Welcome Table retreats with community leaders to provide a foundation for participants to organize racial justice efforts in their own communities. What the institute had previously described as a "year of dialogue" on race was now being billed as an "era of dialogue."[71]

Efforts to organize a truth commission had also highlighted the social significance of storytelling. One community organizer recalls how her truth commission meetings quickly became forums for storytelling: "After asking questions about how Mississippi might benefit from a truth commission or what Mississippi needs to move forward, you would have some people say, 'Child, sit down,' and they would just tell you their story, and it was enough to bring tears to your eyes because they hadn't had an opportunity to talk about it."[72]

In 2009, stories of the civil rights movement were not yet a major part of Mississippi's public sphere. Unlike the neighboring states of Alabama, Georgia, and Tennessee, which had museums dedicated to the civil rights movement, Mississippi at that time had no major repository for civil rights–era artifacts and oral histories. Thus, the desire to collect oral histories about the era became paramount for its cathartic potential and historical significance.

Many people hoped that conducting oral histories and systematic research might help justify the need for a truth commission. Around this time, the Winter Institute began collaborating with academics and students, including those from Brandeis University, to establish a database tracking the impact of various institutions (schools, banks, hospitals, police, and so on) in an effort to connect past discrimination with present inequality.[73] Meanwhile, the University of Southern Mississippi's Center for Oral History and Cultural Heritage partnered with the Winter Institute to provide trainings on how to conduct oral histories across the state.

Taken together, the Welcome Table and the oral history initiative, both outgrowths of the Mississippi truth commission initiative, were reconceptualized as components of a Mississippi Truth Project—a broader effort to facilitate a culture of accountability and truth telling across the state. As Glisson most clearly articulates in a 2015 article, the Winter Institute came to understand its work as a "deconstructed" truth commission.[74] In other words, while Mississippians did not implement a singular truth commission, the institute found that the Mississippi Truth Project encompassed the various ingredients that make up a truth commission: public rituals of atonement (memorials and commemorations), academic investigations into patterns and legacies of abuse, institutional reforms (scholarly articles, reports, and curricular development), and legal accountability (criminal trials). In this way, the institute suggested that it could provide a more decentralized and multifaceted approach to truth seeking than the sort of all-encompassing truth commission that may be more effective in certain contexts, like the United States as a whole. However, Glisson concedes that a more typical "official" truth commission might have had its own advantages: "While we might have moved at a quicker pace if we had been able to take advantage of the political moment offered by public hearings hosted by an official commission, in the end, we hope that the various interrelated strategies are building a solid and sustainable grassroots foundation for substantive, positive social change."[75]

From Commemoration to Commission

Did the Mississippi truth commission fail or merely transform itself? The answer depends on one's point of view. After all, it can be difficult to establish when and how the idea of a truth commission becomes a truth commission in practice, especially when considering civil-society–based truth commissions like the one proposed in Mississippi. For hard-liners, a truth commission only counts if it succeeds in issuing a final report, and by this measure, the Mississippi truth commission failed. Shortly after the commission entered its public stage, it changed direction: instead of seating commissioners and drafting an official mandate, as the declaration of intent had called for, the organizers turned to collecting oral histories across the state and building the capacity of local communities through Welcome Table retreats. In this regard, the Mississippi truth commission is better understood as an incomplete truth commission, with the idea of a truth commission having considerable social appeal but falling short of realization.[76]

While efforts to establish a South African–style truth commission were ultimately abandoned, Mississippi's truth commission-turned-project still represents a significant transformation in the state's civil sphere. Sitting down for coffee outside the hip Jackson-based Lemuria bookstore in 2010, Glisson and Charles Tucker, both intimately involved in the Mississippi Truth Project and the truth commission initiative, reflected on what the initiative had accomplished. In their estimation, it had begun to "expand the range of permissive truth that can be told and open the ranks of who gets to tell it,"[77] a play on Michael Ignatieff's frequently quoted, if cynical, observation that all "a truth commission can achieve is to reduce the number of lies that can be circulated unchallenged in public discourse."[78] Glisson and Tucker's more positive outlook is echoed by Patryk Labuda, a legal scholar who has studied the proposal to establish a truth commission in Mississippi. It is "perhaps noteworthy," Labuda suggests, "that the [Mississippi truth commission] has even gotten this far," a sentiment that points to Mississippi's historic resistance to racial reckoning.[79] Thus, taken together, the efforts to establish a Mississippi truth commission and its subsequent manifestations as an oral history initiative and Welcome Table program signify a shifting mnemonic landscape within Mississippi's civil sphere.

Whether and how this transformation can be traced to the fortieth anniversary commemoration in Philadelphia is a separate question, and one on which this chapter bears. Despite previous efforts to establish a statewide truth commission in Mississippi, the idea did not gain widespread support until after a local jury convicted Killen of being the mastermind behind the 1964 murders of the civil rights workers James Chaney, Andrew Goodman, and Michael Schwerner in Neshoba County, an event that "had even country music stations in the state calling for honest investigations into the past."[80] Thus, the conviction of a Klan leader forty-one years after the crime brought renewed attention to the case and generated a political opportunity that, given Neshoba County's cultural salience, was unique.

Political opportunities, however, can easily be squandered, and leveraging a political opening for sustained transformation requires leadership and organizational infrastructure—two components that the fortieth anniversary commemoration in Philadelphia had helped cultivate at the local and state levels. Locally, having formed to organize the commemoration, the Philadelphia Coalition was poised to reinterpret Mississippi's racial past and present, ultimately drawing attention to the state's culpability. That message was reinforced by Rita Bender, who had returned to Mississippi to witness the trial. The commemoration and later trial also helped further legitimize the Winter Institute, which—along with the support of its namesake, the former governor—enabled the organization to mobilize civil rights and memory activists across the state in the form of the MCRJ. In effect, this enhanced the mnemonic capacity of the state by coordinating efforts, resources, and expertise, enabling the Winter Institute to serve as an anchor organization for funders (most prominently, Andrus) and international content experts (the International Center for Transitional Justice).

This explains the emergence of a statewide memory movement following the Killen verdict, but it does not explain what form that movement would take. For that, Mississippians looked to available cultural scripts, which they found in Greensboro. This supports prior truth commission research on neighborhood effects, which finds that states are more likely to adopt a truth commission when a neighboring state has already done so.[81] The Greensboro Truth Commission offered a model that prescribed certain norms and processes but also allowed Mississippians to envision themselves as leaders in the field for undertaking the first statewide truth commission in the United States. In some ways, however, the Mississippi case confounds previous understandings about the global proliferation of truth commissions. Much of this research suggests that a state is more likely to adopt a truth commission when connected to the international field of transitional justice practitioners, what some world society scholars refer to as global "epistemic communities."[82] In Mississippi, the opposite occurred: the more globally connected participants became, the more the idea of a Mississippi truth commission began to unravel. More research needs to be done on why truth commissions like Mississippi's do not come to fruition, but several issues seem to have played a role in Mississippi. In addition to the issues with funding, leadership, and legitimacy that plague nearly all truth commissions, the more the Mississippians learned, the less convinced they seemed to be that their situation was analogous to other postconflict contexts like South Africa.

As the Mississippi case demonstrates, however, a failed or incomplete truth commission may not always be a total failure. The process of coordinating a large-scale memory project like a truth commission may illuminate other social needs that correspond with different, perhaps smaller-scale, memory projects. Likewise, this chapter has shown how local memory projects can be leveraged to initiate broader memory movements. To better understand when and how commemorations have transformative consequences, in the next chapter I will compare the processes leading up to the Killen trial, the education bill, and the Mississippi Truth Project to draw more general conclusions and explore how the fortieth anniversary had such transformative consequences when the similar twenty-fifth anniversary commemoration did not.

6 The Transformative Capacity of Commemorating Racial Violence

Comparing the 1989 and 2004 Commemorations

• •

The day after the fortieth anniversary commemoration, members of the Philadelphia Coalition gathered in a cinder-block church basement to reflect on the event they had helped organize. Ta'Shia Shannon, an African American lawyer and one of the group's youngest members, affirmed the work of the coalition. The commemoration was "really, really good," she said, her voice cracking with emotion. "It will resonate not only through the state of Mississippi, but throughout America that a group of common people came together for justice, and that makes me proud."[1] Deborah Posey, a white working-class woman whose brother-in-law participated in the 1964 killings, was also deeply touched by the work of the coalition: "I never thought that there was a group of people in the town that I love that cared so much about it that they wanted to see a difference."[2] For Rayburn Waddell, Philadelphia's long-serving mayor, the highlight of the day came from his interaction with a black woman from southern Mississippi. Having seen his name tag, which identified him as the mayor, the woman had approached and said, only partially joking, "Where's the dark cloud? . . . I've seen nothing but sunshine in Philadelphia, Mississippi."[3]

The story seemed to resonate with members of the Philadelphia Coalition, who laughed knowingly, relieved that visitors had come to see their hometown in a new light. For decades, travelers had avoided Neshoba County, fearful that they might face harassment in the county infamous for its ill treatment of outsiders. Yet to the nearly thousand visitors who gathered on June 21, 2004, to honor James Chaney, Andrew Goodman, and Michael Schwerner, Neshoba County seemed changed. The national press reinforced this perception in its coverage, which was overwhelmingly positive, and in some cases the press identified the county as a new model for truth and reconciliation in the United States.[4] It seemed that the proverbial cloud had been lifted.

Whether the fortieth anniversary commemoration would mark a turning point in the county's commemorative practices or resonate across the state as Shannon and others hoped was not yet certain—and skeptics had good reason to doubt the commemoration's transformative potential. This was not the first time a local commemorative project had been characterized as a turning point. Fifteen years earlier, an interracial coalition had hosted a remarkably similar community-wide commemoration to mark the twenty-fifth anniversary. As in 2004, local leaders who had been motivated by reputational, economic, and moral concerns had emerged as memory activists, hoping to end the county's dominant silence on the murders once and for all. In both instances, the victims' family members—along with notable civil rights movement veterans, major state politicians, and representatives of national media outlets—attended a picnic and memorial service where speakers claimed, albeit in different words, that change had finally come to Philadelphia and that the "momentum of [the day's] activities would not be lost."[5]

Despite commonalities in form and content, the twenty-fifth and fortieth anniversary commemorations had notably different outcomes. The 1989 commemoration generated few substantive transformations. Outside the dedication of a state-sponsored historical marker at Mt. Zion immediately following it, commemorative activity was limited to the county's African American communities, which continued to commemorate the murders annually. In contrast, the fortieth anniversary commemoration in Philadelphia sparked significant transformations in Mississippi's legal, educational, and civil spheres. As discussed in the previous three chapters, the 2004 commemoration precipitated the successful prosecution of Edgar Ray "Preacher" Killen, the mastermind behind the murders (chapter 3); catalyzed an education bill that mandated civil and human rights education at every grade level (chapter 4); and engendered the ongoing Mississippi Truth Project and the truth commission initiative (chapter 5). The trial, the bill, and the truth commission project can therefore be understood as outcomes of the local commemoration in 2004. Certainly, the fortieth anniversary commemoration was not the only cause of these three outcomes. On the contrary, each outcome was undoubtedly the result of a confluence of factors, including the resurgence of civil rights cold cases, the global proliferation of human rights education curricula, and the emergence of transitional justice as a field of scholarship and practice. Yet without the 2004 commemoration, these developments might not have congealed as significant institutional transformations at that particular time and place. The 2004 commemoration can thus be understood as a necessary, albeit insufficient, cause of the Killen trial, education bill, and truth commission initiative. And while the previous three chapters uncovered what the fortieth anniversary commemoration did in Mississippi's legal, educational, and civil spheres, this chapter begins to explain how this happened, with the 1989 commemoration as a point of comparison to examine what factors were present in 2004 but not in 1989 that enabled the fortieth anniversary commemoration to be transformative.[6]

A Framework for Commemorative Success

At the heart of this inquiry is an examination of the relative success of commemorations. Why do some commemorative events transform collective memory and corresponding institutional practices while others do not—or at least not to the same degree? This presumes that commemorative events can cultivate social change with processes and prerogatives similar to those of social movements. Indeed, in recent years, scholars have begun to interrogate the multiple points of connection between memory and movements, finding that collective memory and its related rituals help generate collective identity and social solidarity—which are crucial for social movement survival and success.[7] Research has also found that memory activism sustains and shapes collective memories, which are often politically and culturally contentious, given their close relationship to collective identity and cherished values.[8] Still, few studies have addressed the issue of commemorative success explicitly, focusing instead on commemorative activities as consequences of memory movements rather than their cause.

There are several notable exceptions.[9] In their research on the 1969 Stonewall Riots, during which gay activists rose up to protest a police raid in a series of spontaneous, violent demonstrations, Elizabeth Armstrong and Suzanna Crage examine two separate but related questions: How did Stonewall come to be commemorated (which positions the commemoration as an outcome), and why did it become central to gay collective memory (which explores an outcome of the commemoration)? Drawing insights from collective memory scholarship and resource mobilization theory, Armstrong and Crage find that Stonewall was commemorated for two primary reasons. First, activists viewed the event as historically significant, a phenomenon referred to as commemorability. Without being perceived as worthy of commemoration, which tends to be more likely in cases with extreme violence and where targets of that violence are sympathetic characters, an event may not be commemorated.[10] Second, in the case of Stonewall, activists had the necessary skills and resources—the mnemonic capacity—to organize a commemorative vehicle. Without the raw materials and technical knowledge about how to organize a large-scale public event, such a commemoration would not have been possible.

However, the conditions that enable a commemoration's emergence do not ensure its success. In other words, commemorating the Stonewall uprising is necessary, but cannot fully explain how the event came to be understood as the most important event leading to the gay liberation movement, when similar events in the 1960s did not. Looking more closely at Stonewall's commemorative outcomes, Armstrong and Crage discern two additional conditions that make sense of the event's significance to gay culture and memory. First, the commemorative vehicle—an annual gay pride parade—resonated with target audiences in New York City and beyond. In other words, activists outside the initial context were convinced that Stonewall was commemorable and that, given the history of the movement, a public parade was an appropriate and viable commemorative form. Additionally, the commemorative vehicle had the potential for institutionalization, whereby other gay activist communities could replicate the experience—thereby enabling the commemorative form, and consequently the memory of Stonewall, to survive and to proliferate geographically. Given this, the authors reiterate Stonewall's commemorative consequences when concluding that the Stonewall story is "better viewed as an *achievement* of gay liberation rather than a literal account of its origins."[11]

Extending this work on commemorative outcomes, Raj Ghoshal investigated variations in the success of social movements whose central concern is transforming how the past is remembered—namely, the memory of lynchings between 1877 and 1954. For Ghoshal, success is synonymous with scope: the more successful a memory project is, the more it will have achieved physical commemorations, public participation, and government support.[12] Importantly, this comparative research reveals a number of commonalities among successful commemorative projects, including several historical factors. Ghoshal finds, for instance, that the historic perceptions of lynching structure its future commemorative impact. More specifically, racial violence is more likely to be commemorated successfully when it meets two criteria: groups considered it important at the time it took place (what Ghoshal and others refer to as ascribed significance),[13] and historical victims of racial violence had a positive moral valence at the time of their death that depicts them as innocent victims or valiant heroes.

TABLE 6.1 Comparing the 1989 and 2004 commemorations

	1989	2004
Explanations for commemorative success		
1. Ascribed significance of key characters (historical)	✓	✓
2. Moral valence of key characters (historical)	✓	✓
3. Potential for institutionalization of the commemorative form	✓	✓
4. Commemorative capacity of the environment		✓
5. Resonance with target audience(s)		✓
Outcome	Silence or denial	Racially rooted institutional transformations

In additional to these historical factors, Ghoshal finds that present-day factors influence the conditions of possibility for commemorative outcomes. Like an individual, group, or organization, an environment can vary in its commemorative capacity—which includes, among other things, variation in the number of historic and educational institutions such as libraries, archives, and universities and helps explain why some commemorative projects are successful while others are not. In other words, according to Ghoshal, environments with "more institutions dedicated to marking the past and more individuals habituated to seeing history as important are more conducive to commemorative efforts."[14] For example, commemorations of the 1908 race riots in Springfield, Illinois, were supported by long-standing institutions with a well-developed commemorative capacity, including the Illinois State Library, Illinois State Museum, and Lincoln Presidential Library. Thus, Springfield, as the state capital and the hometown of an iconic U.S. president, was well situated to become one of the first northern cities to commemorate a race riot from the early twentieth century.[15]

While this research does not fully explain how commemorative projects facilitate social change beyond the direct realm of collective memory, it offers a helpful framework to explore what enabled the 2004 Mississippi Burning murders' commemoration to be transformative. Taken together, this research presents five factors relevant to commemorative outcomes: the ascribed significance of the historical event, moral valence of the historical characters, potential institutionalization of the commemorative form, commemorative capacity of the surrounding environment, and resonance with target audiences (see table 6.1).

In the following section, I use this framework as a starting point to compare the 1989 and 2004 commemorations and identify what was present in 2004—but not in 1989—that enabled the later commemoration to have such significant consequences. This comparative logic is inspired by John Stuart Mill's method of difference, where two instances being compared have similar attributes on all but one critical factor.[16] However, this is not a strict application of Mill's method, given that the two commemorations are not independent and vary on more than one factor.[17] Instead, I use Mill's method of difference as a helpful heuristic to untangle critical differences between the two commemorations while also taking these complexities into consideration.

Historical Content and Commemorative Form

The twenty-fifth and fortieth anniversary commemorations were remarkably similar in content and form: both were community-wide commemorations for James Chaney, Andrew Goodman, and Michael Schwerner presented through two-day events that incorporated memorial services at Mt. Zion Church, with future-oriented celebrations held at large public venues nearby. Because these and many other factors of the events were held constant, we must look elsewhere to explain the events' difference in commemorative outcomes. More specifically, the factors related to historical context—ascribed significance and moral valence—were the same in both cases and thus have limited utility in explaining these cases' divergences. While the 1964 murders have come to be understood as one of the few events that shaped the trajectory of the civil rights movement by precipitating the 1965 Voting Rights Act, the disappearances and deaths of the three young civil rights workers were also perceived as historically significant at the time they took place. The Student Nonviolent Coordinating Committee understood this, and it cautiously anticipated that the violence against white activists might generate much-needed media attention and pressure on government actors. Within days of the disappearances, the story had ricocheted across the national and international media, creating widespread interest in the case. Even the residents of Neshoba County who resented the media attention could not deny that the event had a significant impact on their local community.

Chaney, Schwerner, and Goodman's moral valence was more complicated. Beyond Neshoba County, the three were constructed as martyrs, their faces appearing on protest posters throughout the movement (see figure G.2).

For civil rights activists and sympathetic onlookers, they were perceived as innocent victims, idealistic twenty-somethings who had lost their lives "fighting for others to be free."[18] The perception among most white residents of Neshoba County was quite different. Before the bodies were discovered, the three men were referred to as "commies," "hippies," "tricksters," and the masterminds of an elaborate hoax.[19] These sentiments remained fairly engrained even after the bodies were discovered, with some locals suggesting that they had it coming.

Regardless of these divergent perceptions, the historical context did not change between 1989 and 2004, nor did the commemorative form or its potential for institutionalization. However, the two remaining factors—the environment's commemorative capacity and the commemorations' ability to resonate with target audiences—did vary between 1989 and 2004 and require additional consideration.

The Environmental Capacity to Commemorate

In both 1989 and 2004, local leaders recruited representatives to serve on a task force to organize the respective commemorations, and in both cases, the task forces were able to acquire the necessary knowledge, skills, and resources to bring a commemorative vehicle to fruition. This mnemonic capacity is crucial for an event to be commemorated, but it is not sufficient to alter memory practices in a way that is sustained. For that, the environment itself must have ample capacity to commemorate. As Ghoshal suggests, social environments with a robust institutional infrastructure to support memory work are more likely to enact commemorative projects with enduring consequences.

While both commemoration task forces relied on external actors for critical knowledge and financial resources, the nature of that external support differed. In 1989, external support came from outside the state, when representatives from the mayor's office in Philadelphia, Pennsylvania, offered their services. Those representatives traveled to Mississippi several times throughout the planning process, even chartering a plane for the Pennsylvania contingent to attend the commemoration. After the commemoration, however, they disappeared, returning to Pennsylvania along with their institutional capacity and ending the Philadelphia-to-Philadelphia project. In addition, the 1989 commemoration planning committee disbanded after its goal—hosting the twenty-fifth anniversary commemoration—was achieved. "There was no residual," recalled Steve Wilkerson, a member of the committee. "It wasn't like we met after and people were talking about what a good thing [the commemoration] was.... I think people thought there would be more."[20] Despite ambitions for the 1989 commemoration to provoke additional reconciliatory efforts, the organizational structure and resources that had enabled the commemoration collapsed almost immediately.

In the succeeding years, a number of developments occurred that enhanced the state's and Philadelphia's capacity to commemorate. In 1997, President Bill Clinton launched his One America Initiative that encouraged racial dialogue across the country, and in 1999, William Winter helped bring the initiative to the University of Mississippi, which hosted the only public forum in the Deep South.[21] In an effort to sustain the momentum generated by that forum, the university founded the William Winter Institute for Racial Reconciliation to promote community development, public service, and educational advancement through collaborations with civic leaders and community residents of all races and cultures. Meanwhile, the state government had begun to expand its efforts to include African American heritage tourism, hiring Alex Thomas to spearhead the program. When Philadelphia's Community Development Partnership decided to explore its own African American heritage tourism, it relied on the state's tourism office and the Winter Institute to provide guidance—setting the stage for what would be a longer collaboration that ultimately included the fortieth anniversary commemoration. Consequently, the establishment of these state-level institutions enhanced the commemorative capacity of local communities across Mississippi.

However, these institutional developments must be situated within the broader political climate across the state. The literature on social movements has long demonstrated that political environments enable and constrain possibilities for social change. Social movements, including memory movements, are more likely to achieve their goal when sympathizers are in positions of political power, when they gain access to other elites who can help advance their goals, and when state actors are less able or willing to repress dissent about the status quo.[22] While one might expect that the political environment in 2004 would be more amenable to commemorations of the 1964 murders than the political environment in 1989 was, data suggest that the opposite is true. Between 1989 and 2004, the political environment at the local level remained relatively stable, while the political environment at the state and national levels became more conservative.

Despite the fifteen-year gap between the community-wide commemorations, the political environment in Philadelphia remained remarkably unchanged. In both 1989 and 2004, Philadelphia's mayor was a conservative white Democrat, a legacy of the one-party South, and the racial composition of the city's and county's elected officials remained relatively stable, despite a growing black electorate (see table 6.2).[23] In 1989, African Americans constituted 28.5 percent of Philadelphia's total population, but by 2004, this percentage had increased to 39.5 percent. The citywide racial distribution of voters is less significant for voting outcomes than the racial distribution within voting districts. Neshoba County had no majority-black voting districts until after the 1989 commemoration, which accounts for the one additional African American elected official on the County Board of Supervisors in 2004.

The perception of risk for participating in certain political activities is another way to evaluate the political environment. In the absence of systematic attitudinal data from 1989 and 2004, anecdotal reflections of Philadelphian citizens demonstrate a pervasive fear of retaliation in both years:

Wilkerson: Back to . . .'89. . . . I know there's a lot of people that didn't go [to the commemoration] because . . . they didn't want to get involved where there might be some fights or shootings. 'Cause you get that many people in a small confined area. . . .

Author: So people in '89 thought violence could happen?

Wilkerson: Yeah. . . . I mean, you know it was the first time the white community had come out and said we're going to in a more open way recognize 1964. . . . There were people saying, "Y'all are crazy. Why do you all want to do that," you know?[24]

This same fear characterized the 2004 context. The night before the fortieth anniversary commemoration in 2004, police swept the Neshoba County Coliseum with bomb-sniffing dogs, ostensibly to ensure the safety of those participating in the commemoration. Again, according to Steve Wilkerson, "A lot of people were nervous, so they just stayed away."[25] Months after the 2004 commemoration, threats of violence in Philadelphia continued. And a member of the Philadelphia Coalition received credible death threats in 2004—as Dick Molpus had in 1989, when he became the first elected official to publicly apologize for the murders.

During the same time period, the political environment throughout the state grew even less sympathetic toward commemorative efforts of civil rights–era violence. In 1989, the state government had been awash with young, idealistic, reform-minded politicians who had been elected to Mississippi's most powerful political offices (state auditor, secretary of state,

TABLE 6.2 Leadership in Philadelphia, by race and year[a]

	1964	1989	2004
City population			
Black			
Number	1,596	1,832	2,930
Percent	31.8	28.5	39.5
White			
Number	3,406	4,447	4,056
Percent	67.9	69.2	54.7
Other			
Number	15	155[b]	427[b]
Percent	0.3	2.3	5.8
City governing board			
Black	0	1	1
White	6	5	5
Other	0	0	0
County supervisors			
Black	0	0	1
White	5	5	4
Other	0	0	0
Chamber of Commerce			
Black	—[c]	1	1
White	—[c]	16	16
Other	—[c]	1	1
School board			
Black	0	1	1
White	5	4	4
Other	0	0	0

[a] Data for 1964 and 1989 come from page 2H of a June 18, 1989, article, "25 Years Later: Opening the Closed Society?" in the Jackson *Clarion-Ledger*, while data for population in 2004 come from the 2000 census. The remainder of the data from 2004 were compiled from various archival documents.

[b] Includes American Indians.

[c] Not available.

state treasurer, and governor). Referred to as the "Boys of Spring" or "Mississippi's Camelot," these young politicians had come of age during the civil rights movement, spent a significant amount of time outside of Mississippi, and promised to "unravel the status quo."[26] In 1987, thirty-nine-year-old Ray Mabus, a Harvard-educated lawyer intent on reform, had been elected governor of Mississippi on a platform of "basic, drastic change."[27] He promised Mississippi voters that he would replace the Mississippi constitution—which had not been altered since 1890—and institute immediate pay raises for Mississippi's teachers. "There's a real spirit of change this time," the Mississippi author Eudora Welty wrote of her home state in a 1988 *New York Times Magazine* cover article titled "The Yuppies of Mississippi." She added: "It's so different from [when] I was growing up, when they said, 'We'll change, but only because we're being forced to.' This is change that is real, and intended."[28]

Demonstrating his commitment to racial reconciliation efforts, Governor Mabus cancelled a trip to Paris to ensure that he would be present at the twenty-fifth anniversary commemoration, where he delivered a passionate speech honoring the lives and sacrifice of Chaney, Goodman, and Schwerner. The speech drew on the lyrics of "Lift Every Voice and Sing," a classic civil rights movement ballad, for inspiration: "Fueled by our faith, sustained by our hope, our struggle has just begun. Facing the rising sun of a new day just begun. Let us march on, march on until victory is won."[29]

The commemoration organizers received Mabus more warmly than their peers welcomed Governor Haley Barbour in 2004. Many civil rights veterans and some members of the Philadelphia Coalition were suspicious of Barbour's participation, given his dubious record on civil rights and race-related issues.[30] Thus, if the state-level political environment had any direct bearing on a local commemoration's transformative potential, 1989 would have been more favorable to reform than 2004. The same is true for the national political environment. The commemoration of the 1964 murders in 1989 received more attention from national political actors than the one in 2004 did. Most notably, in 1989 President George H. W. Bush released a statement calling Chaney, Goodman, and Schwerner "heroes" and describing their sacrifice as an effort "to guarantee one of democracy's most basic civil rights—the right to vote—for all Americans." "We can erect no greater monument to their memory," Bush continued, "than to ensure that the arrogance and bigotry that took their lives never again exists in America."[31] Yet a meeting between Bush and the three civil rights workers' family members became contentious when Schwerner's widow, Rita Bender, challenged the president to provide stronger federal support for voter registration efforts and new laws to restore affirmative action politics that had been struck down by the Supreme Court.[32] Also in 1989, Mike Espy, a congressman from Mississippi, introduced a bill in the House of Representatives that declared that "the lives and resultant deaths of James Chaney, Andrew Goodman, and Michael Schwerner have come to symbolize the dream of brotherhood and sisterhood among citizens of this nation from all races, religions, and ethnic backgrounds" and designated June 21 as "Chaney, Goodman and Schwerner Day."[33] The bill easily passed the House and the Senate, although both of Mississippi's senators—Thad Cochran and Trent Lott—declined to endorse it.[34]

Commemorative Resonance

Regardless of resources or political opportunities, to achieve social change activists must present a message that is compelling to their target audience.[35] How an issue is presented or framed thus matters for movement outcomes. This holds true for memory movements, which employ a variety of frames—often in combination.[36] Since the 1990s, the discourse of memory movements seeking to address difficult pasts has coalesced around three major framing categories, with legal frames highlighting the pursuit of justice, fair representation, and "the right to truth";[37] therapeutic frames adopting a trauma framework and focusing on the need to heal collective "wounds";[38] and religious frames in the Christian tradition employing the language of atonement, forgiveness, and reconciliation.[39] However, framing goes only so far. As Holly McCammon notes, the source of frame resonance "lies in the *conjunction* of the content of framing" and the "ideational elements in the wider cultural milieu."[40]

In 1989, neither content nor culture enabled the commemoration to strike a responsive chord. Dick Molpus's now famous public apology was met with apprehension. "I mean, we heard the apology," recalled a member of Philadelphia's African American community, "but it didn't resonate as being that big of a deal because, you know, he was a white man standing up and saying it, but he's the only one. . . . People didn't feel like they trusted it, even though today history has shown that he was sincere, but at that particular moment people in the community on both sides didn't believe it was sincere."[41] This first attempt to puncture the long-standing conspiracy of silence was therefore significant, but at the time it was not ultimately transformative. This is further reflected in the observations of Rev. Clint Collier, a local African American leader who found the 1989 event inauthentic. "It's sort of like the movie *Mississippi Burning*," he said. "It's a fakish act designed to make people believe that not much happened."[42] Nettie Moore, a longtime resident of Philadelphia and former vice president of the local branch of the NAACP, was also critical of the organizers' intentions in 1989. "I think they are trying to put on a front. They want to get a positive image from the press," she said. "You've got some who wholeheartedly feel that something like this is long past due, but there are a lot who are saying, 'Let's just get this over with.'"[43] These quotations are indicative of the feelings of many local African Americans in 1989 who believed that the African Americans on the commemoration planning committee were merely token members. As a result, the 1989 commemoration never had the support of key members of Philadelphia's African American counterpublic.[44]

Fifteen years later, the 2004 commemoration seemed to better appeal to its target audience. While some people remained skeptical, many—like Nettie Cox (previously Nettie Moore)—had a change of heart. After participating in the fortieth anniversary commemoration, Cox admitted to other members of the Philadelphia Coalition that "I haven't always been really positive when it came to Philadelphia because of the experiences I had received. . . . But I think, in some respect, I have to change my attitude."[45] A group of older white woman who frequented a downtown coffee shop also expressed positive perceptions of the commemoration as well. As Jim Prince recalls, the day after the event, "I was going to get a sandwich and some old ladies called me over and I'm like, 'oh crap, I'm about to get told off.' But you know what everybody was saying? . . . 'We appreciate what y'all are doing.' That's what they were saying. 'We feel good about this. It was a good thing.'"[46]

The stronger resonance in 2004 may have been related to the framing content, which focused more explicitly on justice. In 1989, the discourse had moralistic undertones, presenting the silence-breaking commemoration as the right thing to do, but few of the 1989 organizers embraced an explicit call for justice. In contrast, the pursuit of justice was central to the 2004 commemoration from the beginning, when members of the task force first met to discuss what they hoped to get out of the project. Not long afterward, the task force issued a formal call for justice at a well-attended press conference and later reissued the call at the commemoration itself.

This framing may have been effective for several reasons. First, as researchers have found, legal discourse is especially fertile ground for resonant frames in a democratic context.[47] Because "law may be the source of new expectations for existing relations" and given the ascendance of a global human rights discourse, activists can sustain successful challenges by reframing their grievances with legal symbols and terminology.[48] Similarly, in his study of the commemoration of Northern Ireland's Bloody Sunday, Brian Conway finds that a justice frame was particularly resonant after the mid-1990s by connecting the Bloody Sunday events to the plight of peoples in other national contexts.[49] While members of the 2004 task force and their target audience appeared to be compelled by quasi-legal framing, the concept of justice was broad enough to allow for multiple interpretations. Indeed, multivalent symbols—including language—can bridge gulfs between social groups that would otherwise be in conflict.[50] Robin Wagner-Pacifici and Barry Schwartz find this to be true for commemorative projects, noting how the ambiguous design of the Vietnam Veterans Memorial allowed it to assimilate contrasting and conflictual interpretations of the war.[51]

When the task force called for justice in 2004, the language was ambivalent enough for its members with diverse identities and opinions to show their support. For some of the members, the call for justice was undoubtedly related to legal justice. They demanded that the state's legal authorities use everything in their power to finally prosecute the case of the murders. Other members of the task force distanced themselves from this legal interpretation. As one member insisted, "We didn't call for Edgar Ray [Killen]'s indictment. We simply said justice."[52] For another task force member, "justice" was not legal, but cultural and educational: "We knew that was not our purpose . . . to get somebody brought to justice. Our purpose was, first, the memorial service to acknowledge what happened there. . . . Then we wanted to educate our children."[53]

In addition to this multivalent content, the broader cultural norms around truth telling, which shifted dramatically beginning in the early 1990s, likely influenced the degree of resonance. Victims of systematic violence and discrimination have long demanded contrition, accountability, and acknowledgment for past wrongdoing, but the degree to which perpetrators have addressed these demands as morally valid claims changed. This new international morality is evident in the global proliferation of official apologies; truth commissions; and use of the "right to truth" as a legal concept at the national, regional, and international levels.[54] Since the early 1990s, the proliferation of these truth-seeking mechanisms has crystalized as the field of transitional justice—an international field of inquiry, analysis, and practice.[55] Transitional justice was originally conceptualized to "account for the self-conscious constructing of a distinctive conception of justice associated with periods of racial political change following past oppressive rule." By the late 1990s, it constituted a global epistemic community, largely as a result of the enthusiasm surrounding the South African Truth and Reconciliation Commission.[56] In 2000, the International Center for Transitional Justice (ICTJ) opened its doors in New York City, creating an epicenter for transitional justice work worldwide and helping generate a global network of truth-seeking experts. In this way, organizations like the ICTJ represented a global normative shift and an emerging professional infrastructure that would influence the commemorative capacities of local environments.

The United States was not immune to this shifting moral and political landscape. By the late 1990s, President Clinton enacted a politics of apology as he initiated efforts to reckon with the country's history of slavery and racism. In 1997, he issued an official apology for the Tuskegee syphilis experiments on African American men and initiated a nationwide "conversation on race" through his One America Initiative. The following year in Africa, he apologized for the slave trade, although the apology had a mixed reception. Some people found it disingenuous, believing that it was subordinate to broader political interests.[57] Still, as the first U.S. president to recognize slavery as worthy of apology, Clinton's gesture represents a notable moment in the country's official memory practices. State legislatures also began to engage in a politics of regret around this time, investigating decades-old race riots and, in some cases, issuing monetary reparations to surviving victims.[58]

In addition to these state-sponsored initiatives, other historical transformations may have influenced the reception of the commemorations through cohort effects. Notably, the Supreme Court's 1969 decision in *Alexander v. Holmes County Board of Education* had compelled Mississippi's public schools to desegregate, which meant that Mississippi's adult population in 2004 included the first generation in the state's history to attend integrated public schools for their entire primary education. Like race, class, and gender, generational cohorts have come to be understood by social scientists as social facts that shape individuals' experiences, outcomes, and even memories. Applying Karl Mannheim's theories of generational effects to collective memories, Amy Corning and Howard Schuman have found that individuals' memories of the past are most affected by the national and world events that they experience during their critical years, the period from late childhood to early adolescence.[59] We can therefore expect Neshoba County's memory activists in 1989 and 2004 (and their target audiences) to have distinct collective memories,[60] racial attitudes,[61] and political behaviors.[62]

Scholars have explained shifting racial attitudes in the American South as a consequence of generational imprinting, as later-born, less-conservative cohorts replace earlier-born, more-conservative ones, resulting in a society that is less conservative overall.[63] Yet the rapid change in southern racial attitudes that occurred around 1970 cannot be entirely explained by cohort replacement. Legal changes that took place in the 1960s undoubtedly altered patterns of social interaction and, consequently, racial attitudes in the region, and according to Larry Griffin and Peggy Hargis, this suggests that "stateways can indeed change folkways."[64] Despite the multitude of factors contributing to changing attitudes on race, many participants in and observers of the 2004 commemoration explained its success with cohort replacement arguments. For example, Philadelphia's local newspaper, the *Neshoba Democrat*, argued in 2004 that "the reconciliation movement required leadership of a new generation, those unencumbered by denial and the other residual effects of being raised in a once segregationist society."[65] Similarly, Stanley Dearman, the paper's longtime editor, observed in 2004, "Many of the younger members [of the Philadelphia Coalition] are part of a different generation from that of 1964. These young people are very socially aware and feel strongly about what they are doing to observe the anniversary and honor the lives of Chaney, Schwerner and Goodman. And furthermore, they don't care who knows it."[66]

Certainly, a large percentage of the Philadelphia Coalition participants were members of a distinct cohort that came of age after integration. But it is also important to note that journalists made cohort replacement arguments in 1989 as well. The success of young, liberal politicians in Mississippi throughout the 1980s—Mabus and Molpus among them—was understood as the result of "a maturing baby boom generation, which came of age during and immediately after the civil rights movement and witnessed close at hand the integration crisis."[67] According to one Mississippi baby boomer, "The lessons that were learned in the 60's, we learned a little better than most people."[68] So while cohort replacement and changing norms might partially explain why the racial attitudes of Mississippians in 2004 were more amenable to institutional change, a cohort replacement explanation—which was also applicable in 1989—cannot entirely explain how that process took place or why it unfolded when and how it did. To address this, we must consider levels of commitment and community infrastructure.

Commitment and Collective Identity

To launch protest campaigns, organizations require substantial contributions from participants, especially in local contexts where the organization does not have a professional staff.[69] To sustain a movement requires even more, including a deep commitment to the cause and one's fellow activists.[70] This is especially salient in contexts where a movement has achieved success, which can hasten the movement's decline. In such circumstances, having achieved the movement's ultimate goal, activists and organizations effectively work themselves out of a job.

For many small-scale memory movements, a commemorative event marks the culmination of their work. This was the case in 1989, when local memory activists in Neshoba County conceptualized the twenty-fifth anniversary commemoration as their target outcome. In this context, enacting the commemoration was a success in its own right, representing a fundamental change in how the past was publicly remembered. And while some organizers hoped that the 1989 commemoration would transform the county's memory practices, in the immediate aftermath of the event, commitment to further memory activism waned. In 2004, in contrast, the task force continued to work together after the commemoration, demonstrating a deeper commitment to continued activism. This is evident in Leroy Clemons's recollection of the time immediately after the fortieth anniversary commemoration: "Everybody was really pleased with how well it had gone. We just really never expected it to go that smoothly. And . . . the question that we were grappling with was, 'What's next?'"[71]

Research on social movement commitment can help illuminate why the 2004 organizers were motivated to continue their work together. The Dutch sociologist Bert Klandermans identifies three main categories of factors that influence levels of commitment to social movements, which he describes as the continuance, normative, and affective components.[72] The continuance component refers to the potential cost of leaving the movement, especially if an individual has made a personal sacrifice—material or nonmaterial—that would have been in vain should the movement fail. Thus, a substantial personal investment ties participants to a movement and increases their commitment with each contribution. Many of the 2004 task force members invested a significant amount of time in the planning process, which inevitably took them away from their families. In the months leading up to the commemoration, Elsie Kirksey's daughter would occasionally ask, "When am I going to get [my] mother back?" But before her mother could answer, she would interject the oft-repeated response: "Coalition meeting, coalition meeting, coalition meeting!"[73] Kirsky remembers this time proudly. "We were dedicated workers," she recalls. "Everybody that was there was a dedicated worker." For others, the investment was primarily monetary or reputational. Wilkerson—who, as noted in chapter 4, owned Steve's on the Square, a high-end clothing store in Philadelphia's central business district—recognized the risk involved for the business owners on the task force: "It could hurt your business, and it probably did." Although his business didn't show a deficit, he conceded years later that some people probably stopped shopping at his store, a consequence that for Wilkerson paled in comparison to the moral issue at stake: "I realize that there is a lot more to this than just how many shirts I can sell."[74]

This sentiment also reflects Klandermans's second category, the normative component, which refers to the moral obligation to continue fighting for the cause. An individual's previous socialization is likely to affect his or her level of commitment by influencing how much a cause resonates with his or her ideological or religious frameworks. For many residents of Neshoba County, their Christianity played a central role in how they made sense of the world and how they interpreted the fortieth anniversary commemoration and its aftermath as having biblical significance. As Deborah Posey explained in 2014, "The Israelites had to wait forty years to cross over into the promised land." Reflecting on Neshoba County's forty-year journey, Posey chuckled, "God has a sense of humor."[75] Alternatively, Jim Prince and others have noted the incremental and cumulative nature when people in Neshoba County came to understand their efforts as a moral imperative. As one resident said, "You can't go around and have conferences and just hold hands and sing kumbaya and walk out and do anything. It's got to be real genuine heart change, and it's happened here over forty years, in part because of the *Neshoba Democrat*, in part because of the teenagers who witnessed Martin Luther King coming to town. They witnessed it. They lived it."[76]

Out of these experiences came a commitment to justice, at least for the residents of Neshoba County who helped plan the fortieth anniversary commemoration. Despite differences among the organizers' social backgrounds, Kirksey recalled a prevailing commonality: "Everybody [the coalition] dealt with felt that it was something that needed to be done."[77] Prior socialization therefore influenced the normative commitments of task force participants, although it does not fully explain how the task force, as a particular group of county residents, came to be so deeply committed to transforming their community's memory practices.

Klandermans's third and final category, the affective component of commitment, recognizes the significance of culture and emotion in social movements.[78] Numerous studies have observed how shared rituals, narratives, and consciousness-raising activities can produce material and cultural rewards for participants, often strengthening ties of friendship to other activists in the process.[79] Such personal connections enhance the likelihood that an individual will not only participate in a movement but will stay committed to it. For example, in her study of the survival of the feminist movement, Verta Taylor found that close friendship ties, along with strong cultural practices, enabled a small cadre of activists to remain committed to the movement even as it retreated into abeyance.[80] Strong affective ties are evident in the 2004 commemoration planning process as participants came to know each other as individuals. Kirksey remembered her excitement about the group's work but also a sense of disconnect from the broader population: "Sometimes I would go home, and I would think maybe we're in our own little world up there, and Neshoba County is not really like this."[81] Despite these hesitations, the coalition pushed on. According to Posey, "The ones that truly wanted to see the difference came, and we began to grow."[82]

This sense of personal growth and newfound solidarity is evident in the quotation Susan Glisson chose to share at the coalition's after party the day following the commemoration. Adapting a quotation from Wendell Berry's *The Wild Birds*, Glisson stood and faced the Philadelphia Coalition members she had come to know over the past several months: "I'm not saying we ought not to know where we've been and where we ought to be. I'm just saying we shouldn't let it stand between us, because what we are, are members of each other. All of us. Everything. *And the difference is not in who is a member and who isn't but who knows it and who doesn't.*"[83]

Commemoration and Social Change

Comparing the 1989 and 2004 commemorations in light of current research on commemorative outcomes reveals notable differences that enabled the 2004 commemoration to be transformative. Between 1989 and 2004, several cultural and structural developments occurred at the global, national, and state levels that influenced local possibilities for commemoration. An emerging politics of regret altered expectations for state actors' interaction with historical violence, largely within a therapeutic framework where nations needed to heal.[84] In turn, institutional structures emerged to support this shifting global morality—including the ICTJ, which provided organizational support for national and local efforts to confront difficult pasts.

These structural and environmental developments are only part of the story. For a commemoration to resonate with target audiences, the content of the commemoration's framing must correspond with the broader cultural context and individuals' worldviews. By and large, residents of Neshoba County appeared to find more compelling the message presented in 2004, which largely focused on justice—a concept broad enough to allow for multiple interpretations, largely unifying potential divergent perspectives. The audience in 2004 had also been primed to receive the commemoration's content through prior commemorations and personal experiences attending integrated public schools, factors that contributed to the commemoration's more positive reception across the county and state.

That said, prior scholarly work on commemorative outcomes explores social change within the realm of collective memory, focusing on the degree to which particular pasts are remembered. I therefore suggest that the mnemonic capacity to enact commemorative vehicles (Armstrong and Crage's focus) is different from the capacity to leverage commemorations for broader institutional change. The latter requires a deep commitment and collective identity development on the part of memory activists to sustain collective action in the long run. In 2004, the Philadelphia Coalition was both a distinct collective identity and a community-based infrastructure, as we see above. Considering Neshoba County's long history of silence and denial surrounding the murders and the considerable challenges associated with interracial collaborations, this is a remarkable feat in its own right. Still, the question remains: How did a group of ordinary citizens cultivate a collective identity across racial lines, a development that cultivated a commitment to continued memory activism in a city previously known for its silence and denial surrounding its racial history? In the next chapter, we will explore this question, drawing insights from the social psychology of intergroup contact.

7 Commemorating Racial Violence as Intergroup Contact

Planning a large-scale commemorative event is a complicated undertaking. Architects of commemoration must pivot between the sacred and the profane, attending to potent cultural representations of the past—its symbols, songs, and artistic renderings—while managing such mundane organizational details as securing sound equipment and setting up chairs. This may help explain why organizers of commemorative events so often overlook the social-psychological dimensions of the planning process, an omission that is especially consequential when commemorating racial violence and other emotionally laden pasts when intergroup conflict could threaten the viability of commemorative projects.

When members of the 2004 commemoration task force first gathered in Philadelphia, few of them had engaged in public discussions of the 1964 murders, and those who had rarely did so within an interracial group setting. For residents of Neshoba County, like many other people in the United States, race was a topic to be avoided, a potential minefield of divisive topics and reactions.[1] These discursive challenges were further exacerbated by residential segregation, which provided few opportunities for interracial interactions: county residents tend to live, work, worship, and play in racially homogeneous settings.[2] In turn, these geospatial realities influence cognitive understandings and worldviews about the past, present, and future.[3]

Survey research has been especially adept at illuminating connections between race, place, and memory in the United States. National surveys in 1985, 1993, and 2000–2001 reveal that half of all African Americans in the country considered the civil rights movement an important event, compared to one-fifth of white southerners who came of age during the movement.[4] When survey respondents were asked to spontaneously recall the most important event of the past fifty years, the racial cleavages were even more extreme. Roughly half of the black Americans surveyed recalled the civil rights movement as important, whereas no more than 9 percent of the whites did so in any given year.[5] Furthermore, the likelihood of identifying the civil rights movement as historically important has been linked to contemporary racial attitudes and policy preferences, demonstrating the relevance of past recollections to present-day orientations.[6] This poses challenges to interracial collective action, including memory projects, as past events must be understood in a generally consensual way for a group to connect past experiences with present problems.[7]

Thus, when the interracial commemoration task forces began their work in Neshoba County in 1989 and again in 2004, their members' interactions can be understood as instances of intergroup contact, in which people from one or more social groups (in this case, racial groups with distinct mnemonic traditions) engage with each other for a sustained period of time. But it would appear that intergroup contact is not sufficient to spark sustained memory activism. While both cases involved intergroup contact, only one—that of the fortieth anniversary commemoration—transformed local memory practices. Drawing insights from the social-psychological literature on intergroup contact when comparing the 1989 and 2004 commemorations demonstrates how the 2004 campaign was more successful because it fulfilled all the conditions for positive intergroup contact. These intergroup processes, including storytelling, transformed the relationship between participants and helped to generate a distinct collective identity, developments that encouraged local mnemonic activism beyond the commemoration itself.

Social Psychology and Structural Change: A Paradox?

For decades, sociologists studying social movements avoided engaging with the psychological and emotional aspects of mobilization, instead focusing on structural factors such as resources and political opportunities—and for good reason. Nineteenth-century images of protest depicted otherwise rational individuals as having been transformed into members of angry, impressionable, and often violent mobs. Consequently, early perspectives pathologized emotions and other psychological phenomena in the context of collective actions, viewing crowds as impulsive and irrational, driven by anxiety and fear. They thus promoted what many scholars would now consider a false dichotomy between reason and emotion. As Jeff Goodwin, James Jasper, and Francesca Polletta observe, emotions, once at the center of the study of the protest, "have led a shadow existence for the last three decades, with no place in the rationalistic, structural, and organizational models that dominate academic political analysis."[8]

More recently, a growing number of movement sociologists have been revisiting the social-psychological elements of protest and their complementary emotional processes, noting, for instance, the social-psychological dimensions underlying social movement participation. Strong emotional reactions such as anger and grief can spur activism in the absence of preexisting social ties with other activists. Jasper refers to visceral unease as a "moral shock," an unexpected event or piece of information triggered by a personal or public event that evokes such outrage that individuals feel compelled to take political action.[9] For many, Emmett Till's 1955 nationally publicized funeral functioned in this way because Till's mother insisted on having an open casket. The fourteen-year-old boy had been lynched and thrown into a river near Money, Mississippi, and his body was bloated and mutilated—an image that stunned the American public when it was reproduced in *Jet* magazine.[10] In addition to moral shocks, intimate networks of activists in high-risk movements engage in "emotion management," providing encouragement and moral support in the face of danger or disappointment.[11] An emotional affinity with other activists not only spurs movement participation but also helps maintain commitment to the cause when political contexts become unfavorable.[12] Despite this effort to bring psychology and emotion back to the center of the sociological study of social movements, few studies have explicitly addressed how psychological and emotional processes cultivate collective identity across significant social divides such as race in the United States.

This represents a tension between the psychological literature on prejudice and the sociological literature on collective action and social movements. These two areas of research present remarkably different, seemingly paradoxical, strategies for achieving social change. While the scholarship on prejudice reduction emphasizes the significance of intergroup harmony and social cohesion, scholars who embrace a more structural collective-action perspective identify conflict as key. Social conflict, they suggest, exposes inequality, and social movement actors can mobilize challenges to that inequality. These two perspectives also tend to focus on different targets. Whereas people focused on prejudice reduction seek to change hearts and minds (that is, interpersonal attitudes), those interested in collective action generally seek to alter large-scale institutions, policies, and norms (that is, structures). Given these significant differences, it is not surprising that the perspectives have developed in relative isolation.[13] Yet in the Philadelphia case, social-psychological processes and structural change appear to be inextricably linked.

Commitment, Collective Identity, and Intergroup Contact

To understand how the micro and macro intersect in this case requires that we more closely examine the interactional dynamics involved in commemorating difficult pasts. Following the publication of Gordan Allport's seminal *Nature of Prejudice* in 1954, social psychologists have examined the consequences of intergroup contact as well as its ideal conditions for more than fifty years. While Allport noted that superficial intergroup contact could do more harm than good, by reinforcing adverse associations and implicit bias, a substantial body of research confirms that intergroup contact reduces intergroup prejudices provided that certain conditions are met.[14] These conditions include: equal status within the situation, so that each group can fully participate in the relationship; cooperation toward a common "superordinate" goal or task that requires groups to work together; support of relevant authorities, laws, or customs, which helps normalize the interaction between groups; and possibilities for intimate, informal contact, or what Thomas Pettigrew calls "friendship potential."[15] The research supporting Allport's initial findings has been resounding. A recent meta-analysis synthesizing more than five hundred studies finds that "there is a fundamental, robust, and positive impact of contact on intergroup attitudes regardless of target group, age group, geographical area, or contact setting."[16]

Having established that intergroup contact reduces prejudice under certain conditions, social psychologists have identified a number of mechanisms connecting contact to more positive intergroup relations.[17] They have found, for instance, that repeated intergroup encounters reduce fear and anxiety, functioning similarly to cognitive behavioral therapy by encouraging behavior modifications that enables future intergroup encounters to feel comfortable and right. For example, in a study of middle-class whites' reactions to the Watts race riot in Los Angeles, Vincent Jeffries and Edward Ransford found that those whites who had had contact with the black community were significantly less fearful of blacks, less punitive, and less likely to view the riot as caused by outside agitators—an outcome the authors attribute, in part, to better knowledge of problems in the black community and black grievances as a result of intergroup contact.

Additionally, researchers have observed that well-planned intergroup contact often involves a cognitive component: the interaction helps educate individuals about the experiences and perceptions of people from different social groups.[18] Furthermore, scholars have found that emotions such as comfort, appreciation, and most notably empathy are critical in intergroup contact, generating a shared sense of humanity or an increased overlap between the self and the other.[19] Self-disclosure is key to this process. By revealing meaningful aspects about themselves, often through storytelling, participants challenge stereotypes by adding complexity and nuance.[20] Such self-disclosure constitutes a form of intimate contact, a necessary condition for friendship—including that forged across racial groups.[21] For example, the South African researchers James Gibson and Christopher Claasen found that intimate contact was a more salient explanation for individual white, colored, and Indian prejudice toward blacks and black prejudice toward whites than the strength or importance of in-group identities. Taken together, these affective and cognitive processes can encourage participants to question unexamined assumptions about their own social experiences or develop new perspectives on their social group, a process that social psychologists refer to as "ingroup reappraisal."[22]

This may come as no surprise to social movement scholars, for in some ways, the mechanisms that generate positive intergroup contact mirror the conditions for collective identity building, a key component for social movement commitment and continued activism.[23] Enacting boundary setting rituals can highlight participants' awareness of commonalities and frame interactions between a newly constructed in-group and out-group;[24] developing shared goals or frames can heighten political consciousness or oppositional consciousness;[25] and intimate contact can cultivate emotional affinity and relational ties.[26] Social scientists have also identified how storytelling plays a role in the development of action-mobilizing collective identity, as recent research suggests.[27] Storytelling can generate empathy by highlighting areas of unanticipated agreement; it can be equalizing by engaging each participants' experience as valid regardless of their social status; and perhaps most importantly, it can link particular experiences with more general normative concerns, transforming individual troubles into social problems with possibilities for collective redress. As Francesca Polletta powerfully argues in her study of storytelling in protest and politics, "Narratives may be employed strategically to strengthen a collective identity, but they also may precede and make possible the development of a coherent community or collective actor."[28]

Indeed, the scholarship on social movements overwhelmingly finds that strong identification with a collectivity makes participation on behalf of that collectivity more likely, as well as a deep and enduring commitment to continued activism.[29] Yet despite these findings, collective identity, according to James Jasper, remains "a necessary fiction. . . . All groups face the same challenge: the individuals who compose them may share some tastes, feelings, and goals, but never all."[30] This challenge is especially potent when groups that have historically been in conflict come together to commemorate a difficult past, as such contexts are particularly ripe for mnemonic battles about the nature and relevance of the past.[31] Maintaining constructive intergroup relations despite these potential cleavages is therefore a central concern for cultivating and sustaining mnemonic capacity across significant social divides such as race in the United States.

To examine how the 2004 commemoration cultivated subsequent mnemonic activism when the remarkably similar 1989 commemoration did not, the next four sections of the chapter will revisit and compare these two events in light of the four conditions for positive intergroup contact: equal status in the situation; cooperation on common goals; support of relevant authorities; and friendship potential through informal, intimate interactions. In doing so, they will demonstrate how all four conditions were met in 2004 but not in 1989, enabling the 2004 task force to develop a distinct collective identity as the Philadelphia Coalition and thus strengthening participants' commitment to continued activism.[32]

Equal Status: Task Force Composition and Interracial Cochairs

In 1989, Stanley Dearman and Dick Molpus, both white men in prominent leadership positions—the local newspaper editor and Mississippi's secretary of state, respectively—recruited individuals to serve on the commemoration task force. Although the leaders attempted to engage the local African American community by enlisting Pete Talley, president of the Neshoba County branch of the NAACP, and by coordinating with Mt. Zion United Methodist Church, African American involvement was largely tokenistic. When asked how members of Mt. Zion felt about the 1989 commemoration, Jennifer Hawthorne, a longtime member of the church, recalled, "They were excited about it, but [they] didn't do anything that was really significant."[33]

The absence of solid interracial collaboration in the project was not its only defining characteristic. Perhaps just as significantly, the commemoration established itself around a distinctly nonlocal initiative—the Philadelphia-to-Philadelphia project, an initiative developed by Wilson Goode, the mayor of Philadelphia, Pennsylvania, in support of the commemorative efforts of its sister city. With the Pennsylvania connection, the bulk of the organizational and economic support for the 1989 commemoration would come from outside of Mississippi. This outside involvement ruffled some Mississippi locals, who were skeptical of the Pennsylvanians' intentions (the fact that Goode saw the collaboration as an opportunity to rehabilitate his reputation in the wake of a deadly police encounter with the black liberation group MOVE would not have been lost on the local community), and as a result, the commemoration itself fell under a widespread cloud of suspicion.[34] The 1989 commemoration, then, took shape with a task force dominated by white businessmen and other white male professionals, some whom had little if any meaningful connection to Mississippi.

The 2004 commemoration planning committee, in contrast, was entirely local and prioritized racial inclusivity from the start, including the selection of the task force cochairs. Again, Molpus and Dearman initiated discussions about the upcoming anniversary, but they quickly passed the proverbial baton to a new generation of local leaders who represented Neshoba County's two largest racial groups. Both Leroy Clemons (African American) and Jim Prince (white) had grown up in Philadelphia, attended its newly integrated public schools, and worked for Dearman at the local newspaper, so they were familiar with each other and had each independently developed an interest in revisiting Philadelphia's past. In the spring of 2004, both men occupied notable leadership positions in the city—Clemons as the new president of the local branch of the NAACP and Prince as the new editor of the local newspaper—and were well positioned to accept Molpus's invitation to serve as cochairs of the fortieth anniversary commemoration task force.

From the beginning of the planning process, both men conceptualized the commemoration as an interracial project that depended on diverse representation. This is evident in their first conversations about the project, when they agreed, in Clemons's words, to "do a memorial service . . . [but] make it a *communitywide* memorial service."[35] Consequently, Clemons and Prince were intentional about the composition of the task force, reaching beyond their immediate social networks to ensure that various stakeholder groups were represented. Clemons recalls early conversations with Prince about the task force's composition: "We talked about who we needed to have at the table to plan this thing. . . . Mt. Zion [had] been carrying on this service for thirty-nine years by themselves. We need them at the table first. Then we reached out to the people that were from California, from New York that had been coming together every year and asked them if they would be a part of it, and then we went about the city asking and recruiting people from different areas of the city, different parts, different positions in the city saying, 'We would like you to be a part of helping us to plan this.'"[36]

As they began to assemble the members of the task force, Clemons and Prince also consulted with Susan Glisson, director of the William Winter Institute for Racial Reconciliation, who had become something of a racial reconciliation expert in the state after helping bring President Bill Clinton's One America Initiative to the University of Mississippi in 1998 and later convincing the university's reluctant chancellor to commemorate the fortieth anniversary of the university's desegregation in 2002.[37] Glisson happened to be in Philadelphia, assisting in the creation of an African American history brochure for the city's Community Development Partnership, when Prince and Clemons invited her to an early task force meeting. Quickly, she assumed the role of neutral facilitator, at times moderating emotionally charged conversations during meetings and behind the scenes. As Steve Wilkerson, a task force member, reported, "It probably couldn't have happened without [Glisson's] help."[38]

As they planned the commemoration, the cochairs' unique perspectives, friendly rapport, and personal respect proved to be assets. As cochairs and with the assistance of Glisson, Clemons and Prince were able to navigate racially charged conversations, first at an interpersonal level and later with the task force as a whole. When decisions about how to call for justice fell along racial lines, Clemons and Prince first expressed their own thoughts to each other. Prince recalled: "I was like, 'Leroy, I don't think we need to do a march. That's not going to go over.' And he says, 'Well you know how black people see proclamations, don't you?' And I say, 'No.' And he says, 'They just think it's white people trying to dismiss it.'"[39] For Prince, this "honest dialogue" was crucial to their effectiveness as cochairs: "There were so many times that Leroy and I both looked at each other and said, 'This is too much. We just can't do this.' And then we'd sort of slap each other and say, 'We've got to forge ahead for the good.'"[40]

For the two men—indeed, the entire task force—much was at stake, and they feared the fortieth anniversary might fail. Only when it was over could Prince and Clemons at last breathe a sigh of relief. While the event had not been without conflict, neither had it imploded race relations in Neshoba County, an outcome that Prince and Clemons had joked about when contemplating the repercussions of a potential failure in their work together. On the contrary, the commemoration seemed to have sparked a commitment to racial justice in Philadelphia and beyond—at least among a committed group of task force members. When Dearman rose to address the other members of the task force at the commemoration after party, he made a point to acknowledge the cochairs. "Before we go any further, I want to say a good word about those two gentlemen," Dearman said, pointing at Clemons and Prince standing side by side at a podium. "They did a fine job at bringing a lot of diverse points together. And that's no easy task, as you know. We want to thank you very much for your great work, and we'll remember that for a long time."[41]

Cooperation on Common Goals: Commemoration and Calling for Justice

In 1989, the commemoration planning committee's mandate had been fairly circumscribed: to plan the twenty-fifth anniversary commemoration. Its process flowed from the top down, and its agenda—implicit and explicit—did not embrace developing a shared common goal from the bottom up. Fenton DeWeese, a Philadelphia resident who participated in both commemoration services, described the 1989 mandate as confined only to the commemoration's planning: "I would say that people who got together to plan [the 1989 commemoration] . . . were there for that purpose. That was their purpose and nothing else."[42] Likewise, Steve Wilkerson insisted that in 1989, "we were planning an event. . . . It could have been a festival."[43] Although the 1989 commemoration did have a shared goal (event planning), it was not a goal that required interracial cooperation and collaboration in a meaningful sense.

Participants like Wilkerson, a white business owner who had been involved in both commemorations, felt that the fortieth anniversary had been better planned. "It had all three cultures'—white, Choctaw, and African American—involvement," he recalled. "Not just being on the committee but *involvement*. I don't think we had much of that [in 1989]."[44] Prince jokingly described the first task force meeting in 2004 as "kind of like an AA [Alcoholics Anonymous] meeting," with participants introducing themselves following the classic self-help formula: "Hi, my name is so-and-so, and I'm here because . . ."[45] As each participant read from small slips of paper, one thing became clear: regardless of race, all shared an affection for their community. For them, Neshoba County was not the cold, unfeeling place depicted in the film *Mississippi Burning*. And it certainly was not a place to be feared or avoided—feelings that were still held by many outside the county. Underlying this impulse for impression management was also a desire to seek justice for the three civil rights workers who had lost their lives. This was the shared goal that united members of the 2004 commemoration task force and the one that had emerged organically when each participant was asked to share what brought her or him to the meeting. "It's just so interesting," observed a local white business owner, "that most of us, being from different backgrounds racially and generationally, how we felt so much of the same thing."[46] In 2004, not every meeting went smoothly. But when tempers flared, the group's common commitment kept the core group united. According to Deborah Posey, the group did "not necessarily agree on every step that is taken," but they put their "differences down to come together for that one purpose"—their shared goal.[47]

The process by which the 2004 task force determined its collective goal appeared to have generated deep commitment to the project, as did the group's reliance on shared resources. Before the group could consider the cultural significance of the program, its members had to consider its more mundane practicalities, including finding a location for the event other than Mt. Zion—a rural church that could only accommodate several hundred people. Yet with each logistical challenge, the group discovered the breadth of their shared community assets. Clemons elaborated:

> We needed the coliseum, and the problem was the coliseum had been booked by a rodeo that weekend, so we weren't going to be able to get it. Somebody stood up in the room and said, "I know the guy over at the rodeo, and I'll call him and see if he's willing to change the date." Next, . . . we wanted to do a live feed from the church to the coliseum, . . . and we didn't know how we were going to be able to do this. . . . And someone says, "Well, I know a guy in Jackson that I think we can borrow those screens from." OK, got that. Then someone else says, "Well I know someone who works at the TV station at the cable company. We'll talk to him and see if he's willing to run the wires." Got that. Now we need an actual broadcast station to do it. Someone in the tribe said, "You know, we've got a TV station at the reservation. I'll ask the chief to see if . . . they will come record it." Got that done. We moved onto security. We had a security issue. How are we gonna secure these places with all these people coming in? Somebody stood up and said, "Well, I'm a police officer. I'll talk to the chief and some of the other officers and see if they're willing to volunteer their time to come do it." Got that done.[48]

This quotation reveals the remarkable willingness of the task force participants to pool their resources for a common cause. Social movement scholars have long noted the importance of local resources that are provided by social movement constituents. Not only can they bind participants more closely together through collective and shared giving, but they also tend to be more sustainable. Outside resources—whether economic, organizational, or moral—can be short-lived and often come with strings attached. The Philadelphia-to-Philadelphia project in 1989 was a case in point. When the commemorative event was over, the resources that had been provided by Mayor Goode's office to support it left town with the Pennsylvanians who had brought them, and Philadelphia, Mississippi, was left with neither an institutional nor an organizational infrastructure to build from.[49]

Support from Authorities: City, County, and State

Intuiting that the success of the commemoration would depend in part on how it was perceived by political authorities, the 2004 task force sought—and ultimately received—endorsements and financial contributions from the city, county, and tribe as part of a concerted public relations strategy to bolster the legitimacy of the commemoration and the group's call for justice.[50] The political environments in 1989 and 2004 were not entirely sympathetic to commemorating racial violence, but neither project faced substantial repression. On the contrary, in both 1989 and 2004, the city, county, and tribe made some monetary contributions. Furthermore, the donations had a symbolic dimension: they signified the tactical support of authorities, thereby establishing the norm of acceptance. Anyone opposing the commemoration would also be resisting the will of the city, county, and tribe.

Given the cultural significance of the 1964 killings, the 1989 and 2004 commemorations attracted attention from the state's highest official. In both cases, the governor delivered a speech at the commemoration service. In 1989, Ray Mabus was committed to "basic, drastic, change," including acknowledging Mississippi's dubious civil rights record.[51] Mabus's presence at the twenty-fifth anniversary commemoration was therefore not particularly notable or newsworthy. If anything, his participation in the commemoration reaffirmed the general perception of his liberal leanings and as a result did not shift political opportunities within the state.

When Governor Haley Barbour attended the fortieth anniversary in 2004, on the other hand, the media took note. A conservative Republican known for his illustrious lobbying career in Washington, D.C., and for wearing a pin in his lapel showing the Mississippi flag (one of a handful of state flags that use Confederate symbols), Barbour had become embroiled in racial controversies before the commemorative event. Progressives in the state accused Barbour of race-baiting during the campaign and refusing to ask the Council of Conservative Citizens to remove a picture of the governor posing with some of their leaders. The council had been formed using the mailing lists of the White Citizens' Council, an organization known for using economic intimidation and harassment to preserve segregation.[52]

Given these recent events, some commemoration participants—including civil rights movement veterans and members of the Philadelphia Coalition—were outraged when the governor walked on stage. However, the leaders of the Philadelphia Coalition thought strategically about what Barbour's presence might convey symbolically. "We had a bigger picture in mind," reflected Clemons. "We knew that the picture of [Barbour] being there sent a message all across the state that this was okay."[53] Sure enough, as Barbour appeared on the stage on the day of the commemoration, the press captured him shaking hands with John Lewis, a civil rights activist and U.S. congressman, as Andrew Goodman's mother, Carolyn, looked up at them from behind (see figure G.6). The photograph of the two men shaking hands was the most reproduced photograph from the day and appeared in hundreds of news outlets across the country. Clemons recalls how the photograph helped diminish opposition in the state: "After the picture that ran in the papers, all the opposition in the papers just collapsed to what we were doing. We were facing a lot of opposition from conservatives. The older conservatives who were like, 'Y'all don't need to bring this up. You gotta leave this alone because it's going to tear the state apart.' They saw the picture of the governor . . . [and] it was like everything evaporated overnight. There was no more opposition from the state, from the legislature, anyone that was basically in a position to stop us."[54]

By the time Barbour and Lewis were photographed, the Philadelphia Coalition had already released a statement to the press calling for justice in the case of the 1964 murders. Political opposition to the coalition was thus not only about the commemoration, it was also about the pursuit of legal justice in the case. As it turned out, Barbour's participation in the commemoration diminished opposition across the state, opening up space for a number of racially rooted transformations to take place. The support of the conservative governor was a crucial factor in enabling such transformations to take place. Structural factors, such as the political climate, could have been consequential only if the task force called for broader institutional change. Otherwise, the 2004 commemoration might well have been a one-time event without notable reverberations.

Intimate Contact: Storytelling and Dialogue across Difference

The group that became the Philadelphia Coalition "didn't gel right away," recalled DeWeese.[55] "We were . . . a real diverse group of folks. Everybody from Mt. Zion to dentists, lawyers, businesspeople, economic development people, a police woman, . . . and their motivations were different. We had to muddle through that." From the beginning, emotions on the task force ran high, as was to be expected. Conversations about race in the United States, especially among an interracial group, tend to be fraught with emotional tension, rhetorical incoherence, and defensive posturing.[56] The task force was no exception. For most of the participants, even those who had helped organize the 1989 commemoration, it was the first time they had openly discussed personal experiences of racism in an interracial setting.

So, while the 1989 task force had begun with the fundamental tasks of event planning, focusing on funding and other organizational concerns, the 2004 task force began with stories. When the 2004 task force moved its meetings from the Chamber of Commerce to the Fellowship Hall of the First United Methodist Church, the change in setting seemed to influence the emotional tenor of the meetings. Participants began to engage in ritual storytelling, revealing their personal connections to race and violence in Neshoba County. "The stories that tumbled out were powerful and moving," Glisson recalled. For instance, Jewel Rush McDonald—daughter of Georgia Rush and sister of John Thomas Rush, who were beaten at Mt. Zion by Ku Klux Klansmen the night the Mt. Zion was burned in 1964—"wept as she spoke of her family's fear that summer 'that Klansmen would return to "finish the job"' to keep them from identifying their assailants.'"[57] McDonald "told of hiding clothes in the chicken coop in case the house was burned and they needed to make a quick escape."[58] She had returned to Mississippi after living out of state for decades, always wanting justice for the three civil rights workers but also for her family. Posey, a white working-class woman who had married into the family of one of the murderers, had long believed her husband's family that James Chaney, Michael Schwerner, and Andrew Goodman were "dirty, communist infiltrators" until she saw a picture of them. After years of prayer, she hoped that faith would bring redemption to her community.[59] Task force members spent the majority of their time in the early meetings listening to each other's stories, many of which were being shared for the first time, and Glisson believed that it was these stories "that made the path to unity apparent."[60]

This facilitated dialogue served as a form of consciousness-raising, linking personal experiences to structural forces while also deepening and complicating participants' understandings of their own pasts and the racial experiences of others. This is evident in the recollections of Jim Prince who was especially moved after hearing a story from an African American woman he deeply respected and had known all his life. "She began talking about . . . when she was a little girl and going to the Moore Clinic," he recalled. "Well, I went to the Moore Clinic, and she talked about having to go in the other side. . . . I've never known what it felt like to be excluded, but to hear [her] get emotional about that. . . . I was moved by the fact . . . I had never thought in those terms."[61] This quotation reveals how storytelling enhanced the emotional affinity between participants who, in some cases, had known each other for decades without ever discussing these events. Learning more about out-groups also generated in-group reassessment. Some participants in 2004 were astounded to learn that there were other people, especially white residents, who felt ashamed of the community's actions in 1964 and wanted justice in the case. For example, Posey said: "I never thought that there was a group of people in the town that I love that cared so much about it that they wanted to see a difference."[62] It appears, then, that the storytelling served both cognitive and affective functions. It provided new information about others' racial experiences, while also illuminating points of commonality across and within racial groups.

Additionally, this growing emotional affinity began to transform the boundaries of in-groups and out-groups, as participants of the task force began to identify themselves as members of the Philadelphia Coalition. Elsie Kirskey, an African American coalition member, vocalized what others on the task force reported feeling: that "we were enjoying the coalition and sort of . . . not forgetting why we were there, but it was just . . . we were family."[63] As this statement reveals, members of the 2004 task force began to understand themselves as a particular group (a "family"), one that would quickly cultivate a distinct collective identity, a shared sense of "we-ness." This is most evident when, while planning the commemoration, members of the 2004 task force began to refer to themselves by a new name: the Philadelphia Coalition. One could downplay this change in terminology as merely rhetorical or, more cynically, as an effort at better branding. But the name change seemed to signify something more: it provided its members with a common identity that came to represent their shared experience that set them apart from other residents of Neshoba County.

When representatives from a national civil rights organization challenged the motivations of the group, a perceived external threat further reinforced this growing solidarity. After years of silence and denial, those who had been deeply involved in the civil rights movement were understandably skeptical, and the concurrent project to develop a local African American tourism brochure only validated the impression that the task force was motivated by the potential for profit as opposed to a sincere desire to seek justice. When one of these skeptics accused several white coalition members of harboring racial prejudice and being members of the Klan, the group "literally sat with their arms around each other as they responded to the charges in unity."[64] Having established mutual trust and respect among its members through a process of self-disclosure and storytelling, the task force did not facture under the weight of these accusations. Instead, the external threat appeared to enhance their commitment to mnemonic activism and their capacity to enact memory projects beyond the fortieth anniversary commemoration.

Commemoration, Contact, and Social Change

As social scientists have begun to consider the consequences of commemorating difficult pasts, research has illuminated a number of factors that explain why some commemorative projects transform mnemonic practices while others do not. In addition to political opportunities, ample resources, and effective framing, research shows that mnemonic capacity—the "skills and resources needed to build commemorative vehicles"—is especially consequential for a memory movement's emergence and success.[65] Indeed, it is well established that generating social movements—including memory movements—requires substantial contributions from participants, especially in local contexts where the movement organization does not have a professional staff.[66] Sustaining movements requires more, including a deep commitment to the cause and one's fellow activists.[67] This is especially salient in contexts where memory movements address difficult, divisive, or otherwise contested pasts in which the organizational task is twofold: to enact a commemorative vehicle and to maintain intergroup relations.

The social-psychological literature on intergroup contact thus illuminates why the fortieth anniversary commemoration in Philadelphia sparked subsequent mnemonic activism when the remarkably similar twenty-fifth anniversary commemoration in 1989 failed to stimulate such transformative aftereffects. More specifically, this research identifies four conditions that enable positive intergroup contact—the support of authorities, collaboration on common goals, equal status within the situation, and intimate, informal contact—only two of which were present in the 1989 case (i.e., support of authorities and collaboration on common goals).[68] In contrast, the 2004 event fulfilled all four conditions, by securing political endorsements from key leaders, cultivating common goals from the ground up, maintaining equal representation of racial groups within the composition of the task force, and providing ample opportunities for informal, intimate contact through storytelling. Taken together, these processes created the foundation for subsequent activism by managing intergroup relations more effectively and facilitating the formation of a collective identity across significant social divides including race, gender, age, and occupation.

Personal storytelling was especially salient to intergroup relations and collective identity formation in 2004. Sharing narratives about personal experiences of race and racism generated an emotional affinity among participants and functioned as a form of consciousness-raising for participants who had had few prior opportunities to interact with members of other racial groups. Furthermore, this storytelling enabled participants to identify common concerns both within and across social groups, strengthening their shared resolve to pursue justice in the case beyond the commemorative event that had initiated the group's formation. In this way, the four conditions for positive intergroup contact appear to be self-reinforcing. By addressing issues of power within the task force, the equal status among participants and cochairs enabled storytelling as a form of intimate contact—which, in turn, clarified the group's collective goals and cultivated their shared identity as the Philadelphia Coalition, an identity that helped establish their legitimacy for local and state political actors. This attention to intergroup processes enhanced the 2004 task force's mnemonic capacity to both enact a commemorative vehicle and sustain mnemonic activism beyond the commemoration. As communities continue to commemorate racial violence and other difficult pasts, they may draw insights from the experience of Philadelphia. It would appear that the process of planning a commemoration is critical to commemorative success, and by managing intergroup relations effectively, communities can strengthen a commemoration's transformative potential.

8   Commemoration Is a Constant Struggle

In 2005, the syndicated columnist William Raspberry described Mississippi as a "state of confusion." "The symbol of racism and backwardness," he observed, "is arguably the state that is trying hardest to repair the damage wrought by racism."[1] A Mississippi native, Raspberry had been left both hopeful and despairing by recent visits to the state. At the same time that Mississippi's legal authorities were at long last—forty-one years after the fact—moving to prosecute the Mississippi Burning murders by bringing Edgar Ray Killen to trial, Mississippi's representatives in the U.S. Senate, Trent Lott and Thad Cochran, were unapologetically declining to endorse a Senate resolution of apology for the body's failure to enact antilynching legislation. Noting this incongruence, Raspberry offered a tempered assessment of Mississippi's contemporary politics and culture: "Even now, it is well not to overestimate what is happening in the state. School segregation is widespread, thousands of whites having fled desegregated school systems for the so-called 'seg academies.' Racial fairness is still a dream. But there is movement. What was 'Mississippi Burning' is, surprisingly often, Mississippi yearning."[2]

What, then, accounts for the movement that lies at the center of Raspberry's guarded optimism? Was it merely the product of time, as an older, less tolerant, generation faded into the past? Or is there more to the story? How did Mississippi become a leader in racial reconciliation efforts while also remaining stubbornly resistant to change? In the mid-2000s, contemporary observers were quick to identify Philadelphia as ground zero of a nascent memory movement. An interracial coalition of citizens from Philadelphia and the surrounding county had coalesced in 2004 around the fortieth anniversary of the 1964 killings, ultimately calling for justice in the case. Such a group—let alone such a demand—would have been unthinkable just decades before, when the mere suggestion would likely have provoked the retaliation of night riders. Given the history of racial violence in the county and the state, which led the nation in the number of lynchings between 1882 and 1968, the Philadelphia Coalition was an extraordinary development.[3] However, it remained to be seen whether the fortieth anniversary commemoration would mark a turning point in the long period of public silence, as many observers projected.

Just fifteen years before, in 1989, a similar, albeit more loosely organized, interracial coalition of residents of Neshoba County had rallied to host a large-scale community-wide commemoration of the twenty-fifth anniversary of the murders. They too identified the event as a critical juncture in its immediate aftermath, a pivot point between past denial and present atonement. But these projections were not realized. While not without some reverberations, the 1989 commemoration largely failed to transform local memory practices or race relations. The 2004 commemoration, in contrast, provoked notable transformations in Neshoba County and across Mississippi's legal, educational, and civil spheres.

This historical trajectory raised a number of questions that guided this sociological inquiry on the relationship between commemoration and social change. Given Philadelphia's long public silence on the 1964 killings, how did large-scale, community-wide commemorations come to punctuate the mnemonic landscape in 1989 and 2004? Could the Killen trial, the civil rights education bill, and the Mississippi Truth Project reasonably be attributed to the fortieth anniversary commemoration in Neshoba County, as some suggested—and if so, how? And finally, if these three transformations could be traced back to the fortieth anniversary commemoration, what factors were present in 2004 and not in 1989 that enabled the 2004 commemoration to be transformative?

To answer these questions required deep sociohistorical research—involving trips to half a dozen archives, sixty-two in-depth interviews, and over a year of participant observation—for no scholar had yet written a comprehensive history of these more recent events. To be sure, previous historical works on the civil rights movement, Mississippi, and Neshoba County, some authored by fellow sociologists equally inspired by the state's rich legacy, guided my research and informed my understanding of this complex story.[4] As David Crew, a longtime Oxford native, has observed, "Mississippi, a fiercely complex land, is both mesmerizing and baffling. Our country's most impoverished state is undeniably our richest when it comes to writing, lyrics, and stories"—and perhaps also in commemoration.[5] But a sociologist's ultimate task is to identify patterns and more general social processes. It is important, then, to take stock of what this research reveals about Philadelphia, as well as the causes and consequences of commemorating racial violence more generally.

Commemorating Racial Violence: Cause and Consequence

Over the past thirty years, commemorations of so-called difficult pasts have become a staple of collective memory research, and out of this scholarship has emerged a rich body of knowledge about the causes and composition of such commemorative projects. However, research on commemorative consequences has remained less developed, perhaps because of its complexity. A commemorative project's possible reverberations are seemingly infinite, ranging from the political to the cultural, the macro to the micro, and the intended to the unintended. In social science parlance, the dependent variable can seem elusive. For this reason, I found it advantageous to begin with hypothesized outcomes and work my way back to their origins, a process that entailed counterfactual logic and systematic comparison. Yet before I could explore the consequences of Philadelphia's commemorations, I had to investigate how these commemorations came to be, for as this research has found, the context of a commemoration's emergence matters for its outcomes.

Chapter 2 positioned the twenty-fifth and fortieth anniversary commemorations within their historical context, uncovering the mnemonic landscape that preceded the emergence of these two community-wide commemoration services. It revealed two parallel mnemonic trajectories that operated simultaneously in the decades following the murders, one characterized by silence and denial and another that embraced ritual commemoration year after year. As civil rights legislation dismantled legalized segregation across the American South in the mid- to late 1960s, Neshoba County's memory practices remained largely segregated by race. While conversations about the murders occurred on occasion in the privacy of white households, the murders remained unacknowledged within Philadelphia's dominant public sphere and its corresponding structures in the county.

To describe this period as the "long silence," however, as some scholars have done, overlooks the rich mnemonic practices emanating from Neshoba County's African American communities.[6] Local African American churches like Mt. Zion in Longdale and Mt. Nebo in Independence Quarters hosted annual commemorations in the decades following the murders. These events usually went almost entirely unrecognized by the local and national media, except when the commemorative activities erupted in violence—as they did in 1966, when Martin Luther King Jr. led a march in Philadelphia. African American churches served as local movement centers throughout the civil rights movement, cultivating and sustaining the movement by providing spaces where black leaders could meet, exchange information, recruit new talent, and formulate strategy. But after the civil rights movement, African American churches like those in Neshoba County served as memory centers, where community leaders could tend to the memories of civil rights–era violence, keeping them alive during long periods of repression.[7] The stewardship of these countermemories was a necessary component of the subsequent silence breaking, for if neglected, the memory of past racial violence would fade into oblivion.

Given these parallel mnemonic trajectories, the twenty-fifth and fortieth anniversary commemorations in Neshoba County represent notable instances of silence breaking. In both instances, interracial coalitions of local citizens organized to commemorate the 1964 murders in the dominant public sphere, which, up until that point, had been characterized by silence and denial. Here, I suggest that commemorations of silenced pasts are more difficult to enact than commemorations of merely difficult pasts that have not been publicly suppressed. The former commemorations generally entail mnemonic battles over the existence of the past rather than debates over the interpretation or relevance of a past that has already been deemed worthy of commemoration. If commemorations of difficult pasts require that an event be understood as commemorable and that agents of memory have the capacity—the organization and the resources—to enact a commemorative vehicle, this research suggests that to be viable, commemorations of silenced pasts require additional developments.

In both 1989 and 2004, two additional factors seemed to enable countermemory to become collective memory, at least for a time: external pressure and interest convergence. In 1989, the release of the film *Mississippi Burning* stimulated national interest in the case and drew attention to Philadelphia and its engagement with the past. In 2004, the impending fortieth anniversary operated in much the same way, cultivating national interest in the case as a result of mnemonic entrepreneurship on the part of civil rights veterans who had by then become powerful and revered agents of memory within the national cultural landscape. Moreover, in both cases, the impending arrival of potentially thousands of visitors enabled the interests of people who had been against commemoration to converge with the interests of those who were in support of it. The potential for a commemoration to transform the city's reputation and improve its economic climate led to a tenuous alliance between some members of the white business community and African American agents of memory who had been commemorating the 1964 murders all along. Again, this mirrors dynamics that played out during the civil rights movement, where, as the critical race scholar Derrick Bell suggests, civil rights victories such as the Supreme Court's ruling in *Brown v. Board of Education* were made possible only when the outcome was advantageous to white Americans.[8]

Chapters 4, 5, and 6 focused on commemorative outcomes more explicitly, examining whether and how the Killen trial, the civil and human rights education bill, and the Mississippi Truth Project are causally related to the commemorations in Philadelphia. These chapters, while tracing the unique empirical pathways connecting rituals of remembrance to subsequent issues of social repair across Mississippi's legal, educational, and civil spheres, also highlight what commemorations do—or better yet, what commemorations can do. Looking across these cases of legal, educational, and civil repair, we can see that the local commemorations mobilized mnemonic activists; concentrated local, state, and global resources; broadened political opportunities; and shifted the political culture of the state. More specifically, the twenty-fifth and fortieth anniversaries provided opportunities for people interested in changing the city's representation of the past to coalesce around a common cause regardless of their individual motivations. While time is mathematically homogeneous, with each minute essentially identical to the previous one, not all minutes, days, or years are experienced in the same way.[9] Furthermore, this collective mobilization around the commemorative event required that organizers activate community resources and, when necessary, cultivate connections with external allies who could bolster the organizers' mnemonic capacity. After the commemorative event, however, this mnemonic capacity had a lingering impact, since the relationship between the local community and external support institutions like the William Winter Institute for Racial Reconciliation had already been forged.

A theoretically informed comparison proved to be a helpful tool in chapter 6, where I again compared the twenty-fifth and fortieth anniversaries—this time focusing on their differences to uncover the conditions that enabled the fortieth anniversary to be transformative. This structured comparison revealed several notable differences between seemingly similar events. The surrounding environment's capacity to commemorate was more developed in 2004 than in 1989, as a number of historic, educational, and civil-society organizations (most notably, the Winter Institute) had developed.[10] This enhanced potential commemorators' ability to organize a commemoration and pursue additional reparative efforts related to the state's racial history. The 2004 commemoration resonated more deeply with target audiences as a genuine effort to right the wrongs of the past, although some skeptics remained. And finally, the 2004 commemoration generated a deep commitment among those organizers who stayed involved throughout. As with any collective project, attrition occurred, but the diverse group's identification as the Philadelphia Coalition established an organizational structure and identity that lasted well beyond the commemoration itself.

The final empirical chapter then explained how the fortieth anniversary was able to generate a collective identity and deep commitment to memory activism across such a diverse group of citizens, most of whom had not been engaged in activism before that point. Drawing insights from the social-psychological scholarship on intergroup contact, I suggested that commemorating racial violence is most effective when certain conditions are met: the commemoration organizers collaborate on a common goal; the status of racial groups is equal within the commemorative planning process; the project has the support of relevant political and cultural authorities; and the commemoration planning process provides opportunities for informal interactions that enable participants to challenge preexisting stereotypes and develop new understandings of their own experiences and the experiences of others. The Philadelphia Coalition achieved some of these conditions through storytelling—an element that is often left out of commemoration planning processes—which helped the group develop empathy and identify shared goals: to encourage the pursuit of justice in the case and transform the prevailing narrative that had depicted members of their community as either victims or villains. The significance of storytelling to the fortieth anniversary commemoration in Philadelphia cannot be understated. It played a decisive role in the formation of the coalition's collective identity, which reinforced its members' commitment to their common cause. Most importantly, the significance of storytelling in this case suggests that the power of commemoration is in its process.

The Power of Commemoration

Commemoration would seem to be a powerful thing. At the very least, people act as if it is. In the United States, visitors continue to flock to the Tomb of the Unknown Soldier in Arlington National Cemetery to honor the lives of lost veterans and witness the ritual changing of the guard; official presidential portraits evoke cultural commentary as stylized depictions of outgoing presidents enter the National Portrait Gallery, where they will remain in perpetuity; and families venture to Revolutionary War reenactments, experiencing in vivid detail times long past. Aside from their cognitive and cultural impact, commemorations provoke powerful social conflicts, memory battles over the meaning of the past. In the recent past, state legislatures debated whether to make Martin Luther King Day an official holiday, with the last state (South Carolina) acquiescing in 2000;[11] civil-society organizations wrangled over the construction of a mosque near the 9/11 memorial, with one group calling it "a gross insult to the memory of those who were killed on that terrible day";[12] and since 2015, government institutions have grappled with demands for the removal of Confederate statues, flags, and names, igniting national debates about the meaning of the Confederacy and its contemporary relevance. These mnemonic battles suggest that commemoration matters, at the very least for what it says about the collectivities these commemorations represent.

Despite the apparent significance of commemoration, and even with the increasing number of cities, civic organizations, and other subnational actors engaging in commemorative projects that purportedly serve some social good, we know very little about what commemorations do in the communities where they take place. Still, mourners and community activists continue to gather in the wake of racial violence to remember the lives and loss of their loved ones, perhaps out of a human desire to connect or from a steadfast belief that remembering past violence can transform the context that brought about the violence. Understanding whether and how commemorations of violent pasts transform the contexts out of which they emerge is therefore an essential concern for scholars and activists interested in the relationship between collective memory and social change.

This research has been an attempt to more fully engage such questions about commemorations' causal consequences, concerns that until now have remained on the periphery of collective memory scholarship. Recent efforts to bridge scholarly thinking on memory and social movements have made important headway, highlighting the multiple points of synergy between two areas of research that have developed independently. This research, however, overwhelmingly conceptualizes commemorations (memorials, marches, and the like) as products of memory movements, the outcomes of collective memory mobilization. Undoubtedly, this is an important insight. Commemorative vehicles, like the twenty-fifth and fortieth anniversary commemoration services examined in this book, have many of the components characteristic of a successful social movement mobilization. They must acquire sufficient resources, seize advantageous political opportunities, and frame their projects in ways that their target audiences find compelling. Yet as I suggest throughout the book, commemorations may also promote memory movements, helping solidify commitment to memory activism and building the commemorative capacity of those communities undertaking such projects. Rather than conceptualizing the relationship between memory movements and commemorations as unidirectional, it is more advantageous to understand it as iterative, a feedback loop in which movements produce commemorations and commemorations produce movements.

Of course, one could reasonably ask: Do all commemorations of violent pasts cultivate memory movements? In this case, the answer would be no. People who participate in commemorative projects are quick to note that few commemorations reverberate beyond their immediate context. However, do all commemorations of violent pasts have the possibility to cultivate memory movements? Possibly. As Philadelphia demonstrates, commemorative projects that appear insignificant may in fact lay the foundation for subsequent social change. The annual commemorations enacted by African American church communities in the years before and between the 1989 and 2004 events may have seemed perfunctory, but they served an important social function: they kept the memory of the 1964 murders alive, without which the legal, educational, and civil transformations discussed in this book would not have been possible. In her study of commemorations in the years following the assassination of Israeli Prime Minister Yitzhak Rabin, Vered Vinitzky-Seroussi notes the significance of "banal" commemorations like renaming streets or photographs, which become a part of the routine daily rhythms of social life. "It seems to me," Vinitzky-Seroussi writes, "that agents of memory would prefer banal commemoration over nothing at all since the mere existence of such symbols may trigger future questions and awareness. In some ways, banal commemoration is like a time bomb, waiting to be uncovered."[13] This quotation captures the commemorations' subversive possibilities: those memories that appear static or even suppressed may be—and often are—mobilized by future agents of memory.[14] This should be encouraging news to memory activists who feel that their efforts have not yielded the desired outcomes, for perhaps the consequences have not yet been observed.

Likewise, although the twenty-fifth anniversary commemoration in 1989 did not appear to transform local racial relations, decades later, members of the Philadelphia Coalition attributed their involvement to the earlier community-wide commemoration. For some, the event's perceived failure was motivation enough to do things right once and for all. For others, the 1989 commemoration had demonstrated the possibility that citizens in

Neshoba County could reshape the narrative of the past and possibly that of their future. Still others found the 1989 commemoration and its surrounding press coverage informative, educating them on aspects of Philadelphia's history that had remained obscure. This suggests the cumulative impact of commemoration, with each commemoration enhancing a community's capacity to commemorate and leverage that memory work for broader social change.[15] Since commemorative observances tend to be cyclical, usually occurring on an annual basis, once commemoration gets under way, as Michael Schudson notes, "it picks up steam; it operates by a logic and force of its own."[16] And by occurring annually, commemorations generate residual knowledge about the how-to of commemoration among those who have been involved in the commemorative planning process. This extends previous thinking on the "memory of commemoration," as Jeffrey Olick has convincingly argued that "part of the context for any new commemoration is the residue of earlier commemorations."[17]

Furthermore, the possibilities for commemorative consequences are enabled and constrained not only by prior commemorative projects but also by the contemporary "mnemonic opportunity structure," what Raj Ghoshal defines as the "long-term stable features of particular environments, along with features of the past, that shape the memory movements' prospects."[18] However, while features of the past, like the ascribed significance of an event or the moral valence of key characters at the time the event took place, remain consistent across time and can explain variation across cases, examining commemorations of one event over the course of fifty years reveals that an environment's commemorative capacity can change remarkably. That is, the historic, educational, and civic institutions that support memory work ebb and flow with changing political contexts and shifting cultural norms. That is part of the reason why the fortieth anniversary commemoration in Philadelphia was able to be transformative: it benefited from a more advantageous mnemonic opportunity structure because of the number of supportive institutions that had emerged since 1989 on the global, national, and state levels. This book also suggests that a local community's capacity to commemorate is influenced by the mnemonic opportunity structure at all three of those levels. So municipalities vary in the number of institutions they have that can support commemorative projects (for example, nonprofit organizations such as libraries, museums, and universities), and municipalities in states that are rich in these resources may be better positioned to leverage local commemoration for broader social change. Likewise, nations rich in these mnemonic resources may better support state and local memory initiatives—what could be described as nested mnemonic capacity.

Taken together, these findings suggest that commemorations are powerful, albeit often in ways that are not intended or immediately observable. For memory activists hoping to coordinate commemorative projects that spark subsequent activism, Philadelphia's journey offers many lessons. Perhaps most profoundly, it reveals that the process of commemorating is essential to its product—an insight that has largely gone unrecognized by scholars and practitioners engaged in memory work.

The Process of Commemorating

Collective memories are embodied in a variety of commemorative forms (for example, books, statues, memorials, and marches) that vary within and across societies and that have different implications for the process of commemorating. This is evident in Elizabeth Armstrong and Suzanna Crage's study of the Stonewall "myth," in which they suggest that commemorative forms that are familiar to an audience are more likely to resonate, and that this resonance impacts commemorative outcomes. The fact that the Stonewall Riots were commemorated with a parade, a commemorative form familiar to gay activists and perceived as particularly fitting for the occasion, helped seal its fate as a defining event in the history and memory of gay liberation. After all, the form and content of cultural objects convey meaning, and "not all content fits with all forms."[19]

The form of a particular commemoration influences not only its potential for resonance, but also the types of skills required to enact it and the types of conflicts it is likely to provoke. Whereas state-sponsored historical markers make steep demands for their completion—knowledge of government processes and protocols (sometimes obscured in legalese), access to elite allies in instances where such markers require legislative approval, and the financial resources to fund an official marker that meets certain aesthetic specifications—monuments that are not sanctioned by the state or are unofficial tend to face fewer obstacles.[20] While unofficial monuments that are meant to be permanent, such as the one erected by Mt. Nebo Baptist Church in 1976, require substantial planning and resources, like their state-sponsored counterparts, they do not require knowledge of governmental processes. Furthermore, because the primary constituents are more likely to come from a single mnemonic community with shared experiences and interpretations, such monuments are less likely to face fierce mnemonic battles about the existence or interpretation of the past.

Such monuments, whether or not they are sponsored by the state, represent the culmination of months or years of diligent mnemonic activism, but once erected, they remain relatively static—normalized within the surrounding physical landscape—at least until they become problematized by future agents of memory. In contrast, commemorative events (sometimes referred to as memorial services) like those marking the twenty-fifth and fortieth anniversaries in Philadelphia represent a different commemorative form that ignites a different set of concerns and processes. Like marches, parades, and protests, annual commemorative events require that mnemonic activists mobilize individuals and groups at a particular time and place, where the collectivity then engages in rituals of remembrance (singing songs, lighting candles, delivering speeches, and so on). In this way, commemorative events like the twenty-fifth and fortieth anniversary commemorations in Neshoba County invoke the collective effervescence observed by Emile Durkheim when members of a community come together simultaneously to participate in the same action, creating and releasing emotional energy.[21] These collective kinetic rituals can, as Durkheim argues, unify the group, but they may also highlight social divisions fostering future conflict and dissension among those whose perspectives are not represented by the collective action.[22] Commemorative events can thus be understood as dramatic performances that embed and reproduce cultural systems when audience members accept the actions and gestures enacted through the commemorative ritual as plausible and compelling.[23]

If the commemorative form influences the process of commemorating, so too does the commemorative content. Commemorative events centered on contested pasts may be especially conflict ridden if the commemorated past remains politically salient in the present.[24] In the United States, commemorations of racial violence represent one such example. Because race continues to be a polarizing sociocultural fault line in the United States, influencing experiences, attitudes, and outcomes in a variety of social spheres, commemorations of racial violence cannot be disentangled from the systems of power and inequality in which they occur. Yet despite the significance of race in the United States and its apparent influence on commemorative possibilities, people who orchestrate commemorations of racial violence often underestimate the role of race in the planning process. When memory activists enact commemorations in racially homogeneous social spaces, those events—while meaningful—may lack the capacity to transform surrounding social structures, given their social isolation. In contrast, engaging multiple social groups that have historically been in conflict in the commemoration planning process involves intergroup dynamics that can be difficult to manage and, in some cases, threaten the viability of the commemoration. We must therefore understand commemorations of racial violence that engage members of different racial communities as instances of intergroup contact, where members of different social groups interact. In this regard, the robust social-psychological literature on the conditions that facilitate positive intergroup contact are instructive.

Commemoration planners may want to consider the composition of their leadership and their group as a whole. Ideally, the social groups that have historically been in conflict will have roughly even numbers and equal representation on the leadership team. This helps ensure that power is shared equally—an important condition for successful intergroup contact. Additionally, commemoration planners may want to seek out endorsements from relevant authority figures to ensure their support and signal that support to the broader public. This can help facilitate a more advantageous political climate in which to enact a potentially conflictual commemoration. Finally, commemoration planners should provide ample opportunities for participants to engage in both structured and unstructured activities to cultivate meaningful intergroup friendships, challenge persistent stereotypes, and revise understandings of the self and the other.[25] These micro-level interactions can have macro-level consequences. The process of planning and enacting commemorations of racial violence can, under certain circumstances, connect interpersonal dynamics to broader structural change.

Whether Philadelphia's experience can become a replicable model remains an important question. Once the Killen trial was over, community leaders across Mississippi began to wonder if they could have their own Philadelphia story.[26] Jim Prince, the former Philadelphia Coalition cochair and editor of the *Neshoba Democrat*, also noted this impulse to replicate Philadelphia's experience, albeit with skepticism: "I think there is a hunger, especially in some of the Delta communities. . . . They see the success of Philadelphia and they want to replicate it. But . . . you can't just turn on the switch and replicate. I mean, it takes decades. It's not an overnight."[27] For Prince, the decades-long preparation, which he attributes to thoughtful news coverage of the 1964 killings in the intervening years, laid the foundation for a successful community reckoning. Susan Glisson would agree, but she and others at the Winter Institute have come to view structured community dialogues as key to community-based social change.

Contrary to other intergroup dialogue practitioners, who believe that an element of magic or some sort of unpredictable contingent synergy is the key ingredient to a good dialogue, Glisson insists that "magic takes a lot of planning."[28]

In 2006, residents of Tallahatchie County began their own commemorative planning, which both mirrored and diverged from Philadelphia's.[29] As in Philadelphia, efforts to commemorate racial violence sparked significant conversations about the community's silenced past—in this case, the lynching of Emmett Till in 1955. For more than fifty years, local residents did not openly discuss the lynching and subsequent trial, where J. W. Milam and Roy Bryant were acquitted by an all-white jury (the men later confessed to the crime).[30] According to longtime Sumner resident Betty Pearson, it was not until the Emmett Till Memorial Commission of Tallahatchie County was formed and began putting up signs that it became possible to have a dialogue about this past.[31] Since then, Tallahatchie County has become the epicenter of Till memory, erecting even more memorial sites than Neshoba County has. Supported by federal earmarks secured by Senator Thad Cochran and Representative Bennie Thompson; grants from the National Park Service, the U.S. Department of Agriculture, and the Mississippi Department of Archives and History; and a generous donation from the actor Morgan Freeman, a Delta resident, Tallahatchie County maintains the largest collection of Till memorials in the world. This includes more than twenty historical signs, a museum, a park, an interpretive center, and a multimillion-dollar renovation to the county courthouse designed to return the building to its 1955 appearance.

The path toward commemoration in Tallahatchie County has been fraught from the beginning and continues to face substantial backlash. In the words of Dave Tell, the author of *Remembering Emmett Till*, memorial signs "have been stolen, thrown in the river, replaced, shot, replaced again, shot again and defaced with acid."[32] The vandalism, he notes, has been targeted and persistent, "revealing the currents of controversy, patronage, and racism lurking just behind the placid facades of historical markers."[33] The latest sign is bulletproof, and unlike the first three signs, it addresses the history of the vandalism in its language, suggesting that the bullet holes are an important part of Till's legacy. Thus, the memorial subverts future efforts to desecrate the site while also drawing attention to the continuing story of racial violence across the region, a rhetorical strategy that memory activists may wish to replicate in the future.[34]

Future Directions

I began this book with a seeming paradox: do commemorations of violent pasts facilitate social cohesion or conflict? This study suggests that commemorations do both: they hold the possibility of transforming their social surroundings and cultivating more inclusive communities, while also constituting the fodder for future contestations over the meaning of the past. Philadelphia's story reveals how in this case, a local commemoration cultivated a broader memory movement that transformed elements of the state's legal, educational, and civil spheres, at the same time sowing dissention that resulted in two competing annual commemorations. Rather than resolving this seeming contradiction, I embrace it, encouraging future scholars to explore the conditions under which commemorations facilitate social change.

This, of course, raises a number of questions regarding the nature of both commemoration and social change. The catchphrase "commemoration of difficult pasts" has made an important analytical distinction between memory projects related to inglorious events and those honoring triumphant victories or deeply respected public figures, but the concept's analytical utility may have reached its peak. The bulk of sociological research on commemoration now addresses so-called difficult pasts, which demands that future scholars provide additional clarification by better distinguishing between different types of difficult pasts and how historic content might impact present commemorative dynamics. For instance, commemorations of difficult pasts vary in their emphasis on the experience of victimhood or perpetration, their temporal distance from the episode of violence, and the degree to which the memory of violence has been suppressed in the public sphere. These variables may very well impact a commemoration's emergence and outcomes and require further specificity. More frequent comparative studies will therefore enhance a burgeoning discussion about the relationship between commemoration and social change.

Likewise, future researchers interested in commemorative outcomes should be careful to clearly define the commemorative outcomes of interest. To date, sociological research on commemorative outcomes has focused on the degree to which commemorative projects embed the memory of a particular past within the broader collective memory. This is an important first step. Others may wish to explore attitudinal outcomes. Do commemorations shift attitudes in noticeable ways? There is some research to suggest that it does. James Gibson's assessment of the impact of the South African Truth and Reconciliation Commission (TRC) on reconciliation finds only slight differences across racial groups' understandings of the country's apartheid past, and those who are more accepting of the TRC's truth are more likely to be reconciled. Still, given his survey's methodology, determining causality remains a challenge. At the very least, Gibson asserts, accepting the TRC's truth does not contribute to "irreconciliation," as so many feared."[35] Research on the truth commission in Greensboro, North Carolina, is similarly optimistic. Researchers have found that changing demography and institutional contexts have led to a decrease in the polarization of competing narratives, modestly stimulating support for the redress of historic injustice.[36] Still, much remains to be determined about whether and how commemorations impact the hearts and minds of participants. And examining the connections between memory projects and structural change, as I have done in this study, requires innovative methodologies to disentangle what, at its heart, is a counterfactual question: would these structural transformations have occurred if not for the commemoration?

The sociological literature on social movements, which has a more developed body of research on the political and cultural outcomes of collective action, will be a helpful resource for those interested in commemorative outcomes.[37] Despite a growing body of literature that bridges the gap between the study of collective memory and that of social movements, this memory-movement nexus could be explored further. For example, studies that examine commemorations over decades might draw insights from social movement theories of abeyance or protest cycles. Future studies might also explore how commemorations cultivate collective identities, experience attrition, or undergo co-optation. After all, Philadelphia's commemorative outcomes faced significant challenges related to implementation, reinforcing the notion that laws on the books are not laws in action. Whether and how such commemorative outcomes are sustained remains to be seen.

Finally, this study's research design, which follows the trajectory of commemorations in one municipality over the course of fifty years, has some advantages. It allowed for multiple within-case comparisons while holding a number of variables constant. It also raises questions about the applicability of its findings in other contexts. For instance, would interest convergence be as consequential for the emergence of silence-breaking commemorations in societies with less social inequality or in contexts where the community has been less maligned? Can nested mnemonic capacity go in the other direction with local commemorations, helping build a state's capacity to commemorate? Do the consequences of commemorations related to other salient identities (gender, sexuality, religion, and so on) rely on building intergroup empathy? The analysis of Philadelphia's commemorative planning process challenges researchers to consider agents of memory, mnemonic entrepreneurs, or memory activists—the people who engage in the labor of memory work—not only as rational actors who deploy resources and strategies but also as complex individuals with social group identities that have influenced their experiences of the past, willingness to participate in commemorative projects, and hopes for the future.[38]

· · · · · ·

At times, it is easy to believe that history repeats itself. The same conflicts seem to play out again and again. But as Mark Twain is believed to have quipped, "History doesn't repeat itself . . . it rhymes." In "rhyming," the past and present, while clearly distinct, are also similar—evoking, in Eviatar Zerubavel's words, "a déjà vu sense of 'there we go *again*.'"[39]

Observers of the Mississippi Civil Rights Museum's grand opening on December 9, 2017, may very well have felt that history was repeating itself.[40] After President Donald Trump announced his intention to attend the museum's opening and the state's bicentennial celebration, a handful of state leaders resolved to protest the ceremony, arguing that Trump's policies were insulting to the people portrayed in the museum.[41] This was not unlike the initial response to Governor Haley Barbour's participation in the fortieth anniversary commemoration in Neshoba County, which provoked similar ire from civil rights movement veterans. Although Trump was initially scheduled to attend the ribbon-cutting ceremony, he ultimately delivered remarks to a smaller crowd inside the museum before the larger event.

Since that day, the Mississippi Civil Rights Museum and its counterpart, the Mississippi History Museum, have exceeded expectations. In their first year, the joint museums are set to surpass attendance projections and could have as many as 300,000 visitors and annual revenue of $17 million.[42] But not everyone is excited by the prospect. Some Mississippians and civil rights movement veterans will not enter the building, vexed that their admission fees are channeled back to the state of Mississippi—an entity they believe should not profit from their struggles. For others, the state-sponsored museums represent the recognition of the past, an act of symbolic redress. Many who visit the museums find themselves overwhelmed with emotions and sometimes at a loss for words. Pamela Junior, the museums' director, recalled one particularly poignant interaction with a white man from Nebraska whom she found standing in the central gallery, pointing at the names circling above him and struggling to find his voice. "He was in tears,"

Junior remembered, "and he brought me to tears. . . . But I swallowed a couple of times and explained to him that the circle of names were people who were killed violently, and I started naming people: Emmett Till . . . Vernon Dahmer . . . Medgar Evers . . . Roman Ducksworth." When Junior was finished, the man looked at her a little longer and then walked away. She couldn't blame him. "Because of the emotions," she reasoned, "he couldn't talk."[43]

Several years earlier, and nearly fifty years after the long, hot summer that captured the attention of the American public and helped push forward some of the civil rights movement's most notable achievements, key elements of that legal infrastructure had been dismantled. In 2013, the U.S. Supreme Court effectively struck down key sections of the 1965 Voting Rights Act, freeing nine states—including Mississippi—to change their election laws without federal approval. When this occurred, reporters from national news outlets turned to Philadelphians for their opinions. Prince said that he "would submit that the pre-approval . . . is out of date. "It was needed at one time," Prince said, but now "we've got a lot more problems to worry about than having the Justice Department come in and approve lines." The more liberal-leaning Stanley Dearman, who has since passed away, offered a different perspective: "We've seen Philadelphia go from a racially divided, bitter, ugly town to a place with a black mayor." Still, he continued, racism among older residents "is so ingrained, it's almost genetic in its depth."[44]

So the story continues. For better or worse, more than fifty years after the 1964 murders that first drew the eyes of the nation to a small town in the eastern hills of Mississippi, Philadelphia remains a bellwether of racial change in the United States, an example of remarkable strides alongside continued conflict. Philadelphia's lesson is that commemorating the violent struggle against racial inequality has both peril and possibility. Its revelation is that commemoration itself is a part of that very struggle.

Epilogue
Fifty Years Forward

Much changed in Philadelphia in the ten years after the fortieth anniversary commemoration in 2004, but some things remained very much the same. Several new historical markers appeared in Neshoba County, including one marking the 1964 murder site on Rock Cut Road that has been pockmarked by the bullets of unsympathetic visitors.[1] And as with most social movement organizations that achieve some success, participation in the Philadelphia Coalition dwindled over time as its members returned to their daily lives, lost interest, or passed away. Still, several members of the group continued to attend Mt. Zion's commemoration year after year, showing their support and catching up with old friends. Jim Prince continued to serve as the editor of the *Neshoba Democrat*, which advertises the memorial service each year. Leroy Clemons went on to work for the William Winter Institute for Racial Reconciliation, assisting other communities who sought to recreate Philadelphia's experience. And more recently, his attentions have centered on running for local office and on the Neshoba Youth Coalition, a local program he created to empower young people to be agents of change through a focus on local history, education, race relations, and peer mentoring.[2] Most significantly, in 2009, Philadelphia elected its first black mayor, James Young—a notable feat in a majority-white and predominantly Republican municipality.[3]

Having been elected for a second term in 2013, Young addressed the nearly six hundred people in attendance at Mt. Zion's fiftieth anniversary commemoration. "You don't have to worry about being put in jail," he jested ironically, pausing for good effect. "I can get you out." Once the laughter subsided, he continued in earnest. "We hope you feel safe when you cross that county line. We have changed, are changing, and have changing to do. I hope you recognize the magnitude of change that has taken place in Mississippi."[4] John Lewis, a civil rights activist and member of the U.S. House of Representatives who had also been at the fiftieth anniversary event, further emphasized the degree of transformation: "If someone would have told me that I would come to Philadelphia and be greeted by a black mayor and that there would be an interracial audience, I would have thought they were drinking!"⁵

These are heartening and encouraging signs. But if these anecdotes and the preceding chapters suggest a steady march toward progress and racial inclusion, this epilogue should stand as a corrective. Progressive victories are often followed by backlashes, and the fortieth anniversary commemoration in Philadelphia and its subsequent institutional transformations were no different.⁶ In each case, reactive agents of memory have worked to challenge, subvert, or deny efforts to transform Mississippi's mnemonic landscape.

An Update on Three Transformations

From his 2005 conviction to his death in 2018, Edgar Ray Killen worked tirelessly to secure his freedom. Shortly after his incarceration, Killen was released on a $600,000 bond after claiming that the Mississippi Department of Corrections had denied him medical care for residual pain related to a recent logging accident that had left him confined to a wheelchair. The court sympathized. Yet just weeks after his medical release, it ordered Killen back to prison after a local deputy saw him walking around town.⁷ Undaunted, Killen pursued further legal challenges, arguing that his defense team had not represented him well in the 2005 trial and that his constitutional rights had been violated by the decades-long delay between the murders and his indictment; the variances between the charges in the indictment and the jury's verdict; and the prosecutor's alleged failure to turn over evidence that, Killen asserted, could have proven his innocence.⁸ The U.S. Supreme Court brought the matter to a close in 2013 when it declined to review lower-court rulings that found no violations of Killen's constitutional rights during the 2005 trial.⁹ To the dismay of the victims' families and a group of civil rights activists who have continued to call for additional prosecutions in the case, Killen remains the only individual to have been tried for the murders.

On June 21, 2016—fifty-one years after the crime—Mississippi's attorney general, Jim Hood, announced that the case was officially closed, this time for good. There were too few living witnesses to support any additional investigation. People who had been following the case had much to say about the announcement—including David Goodman, the chair of the Andrew Goodman Foundation that had been established in his brother's memory. "This case will never be closed until it heals the wounds that have divided our county," he insisted. "You can't move past a wound while it's open, even if you cover it up with a bandage."[10] Two years later and a week shy of his ninety-third birthday, Killen died at Mississippi's Parchman Farm state penitentiary, insisting to the very end that he was "not a criminal convict, but a political prisoner."[11]

Janis McDonald, the codirector of Syracuse University's Cold Case Justice Initiative, was also frustrated by the attorney general's failure to pursue additional prosecutions in the Neshoba County case. But her dissatisfaction ran deeper: "I'm angry at the Justice Department, not just for this case but for all of the cases that they are supposedly doing thorough investigations [of] under the Emmett Till Unsolved Civil Crimes Act. This doesn't have anybody's priority."[12] The federal act to which McDonald referred was signed into law in 2007. Named for the Chicago teen who was murdered in Mississippi in 1955, the act authorized $135 million for state and federal law enforcement agencies to investigate suspicious murders from the civil rights era (defined as having occurred before 1970). Many observers view the Till Bill as a failure. According to Richard Cohen, the president of the Southern Poverty Law Center in Montgomery, Alabama, "a pittance of that [$135 million] has been authorized,"[13] and in the first eight years after the law's enactment, the FBI, citing lack of evidence, had closed all but 8 of the 126 cases it had investigated.[14]

Despite these challenges, the U.S. Congress reauthorized the Till Act in December 2016 with bipartisan support. Often referred to as "Till Bill 2," the new law not only reauthorizes the original legislation but attempts to strengthen the collaboration between the Justice Department, the FBI, state and local law enforcement agencies, and civil-society organizations working on these cold cases. The reauthorization also expands the law's mandate from crimes committed before 1970 to those committed before 1980 and eliminates the sunset provision in the original bill. Whether this reauthorization will lead to a more robust public record of racially motivated violence remains to be seen, but as the historian Renee Romano cautions, "there is a limit to the kind of historical truth that can be expected out of even this expanded Till Bill."[15] As Romano explains in *Racial Reckoning*, a criminal justice framing rarely inspires the kind of historical investigations that illuminate the role of institutions in the practice of systemic racism that continues to have lasting consequences.

Mississippi's civil and human rights education bill has faced similar obstacles to implementation. When Governor Haley Barbour signed Senate Bill 2718 into law in 2006, the Mississippi Department of Education embarked on a complicated process of implementation that has been fraught with challenges, including outright resistance. Mississippi State Representative John Moore, from Brandon, Mississippi, sought to have the law repealed in each of the first five years after its enactment. "I want schools to be teaching my grandchildren to read, write a complete sentence and do math," said Moore in 2013. "I just want to make sure [the curriculum is] teaching the truth and facts and not being accusatory of one group of people or the other. I don't want it to be somebody's philosophical idea of what civil rights are."[16]

The education bill has also faced more subtle and systematic barriers. Initially, the nonobligatory language of the law ("may" instead of "must") made the new provisions difficult, if not impossible, to enforce—a barrier that was lifted only when the Mississippi Department of Education incorporated civil rights education into its new social studies framework in 2011. Until then, adoption of the civil rights curriculum was strictly voluntary for school districts, and as the sociologists David Cunningham and Ashley Rondini observed in their comparative study of the bill, this led to uneven implementation.[17] "Despite the de jure intention that these pilot reforms be applied in districts across the state," Cunningham and Rondini noted, the program lacked "mandate power, resources, oversight, and accountability."[18]

When the Department of Education incorporated civil and human rights into its revised social studies framework, many people were hopeful that teachers would be more likely to engage with those topics in the classroom. But Mississippi remains a "local control" state, where the state's educational frameworks and curricular recommendations can easily be disregarded at the local level.[19] To address the resistance of local teachers to teaching civil and human rights, the Department of Education enacted another policy change in 2012, this time adding civil or human rights questions to the U.S. history exam—one of four state exams students must pass to graduate. In its first iteration, the test received the lowest pass rate of any state exam in history, sparking concerns among the education community and discussions about removing the civil rights questions.[20] As of 2014, questions on civil and human rights constituted 15 percent of the seventy-question exam. Thus, though the Department of Education might not have a concrete mechanism of enforcement at its disposal, it has made its expectation quite clear: in Mississippi, educators should teach students about civil and human rights.[21]

Many Mississippi educators, however, feel inadequately prepared to teach a civil and human rights curriculum, in no small part as a result of Mississippi's outdated textbooks. An analysis of the state's school textbooks by *Hechinger Report* and *Reveal* from the Center for Investigative Reporting uncovered that for at least some grades, all of the state's 148 school districts rely on textbooks published before the new social studies framework was adopted in 2011.[22] Yet even if the textbooks' coverage of civil rights were more robust, teachers' comfort about teaching the topic would still vary widely. In 2014 a recent graduate of Philadelphia High School explained to a busload of high school students participating in the Winter Institute's Summer Youth Institute—a nine-day experiential learning program for young leaders—why Philadelphia's civil rights history continues to remain absent from classrooms (see figure G.11). "Teachers are iffy about discussing [the murders]," she said. "We still have Poseys. We still have Prices. We still have Killens"—referring to current students in the school system who share last names with those known to have participated in the 1964 killings. "Even if someone doesn't have one of those names, they could still be related."[23] Lee Ann Fulton, Neshoba County's curriculum coordinator, echoes this concern: "We have to be real careful to make sure that the children have the capacity to understand. . . . It's a sensitive topic and you have to be very careful how you handle it."[24]

In 2014, the Southern Poverty Law Center released its second report on the status of civil rights education in the United States. Its findings were discouraging.[25] Mississippi earned a C for including less than 40 percent of the recommended content and "covering the movement in patches rather than systematically."[26] Still, Mississippi fared better than most states in the report, which found that twenty states required little, if any, instruction on the civil rights movements, earning these states an F in the report's ranking system. Summarizing the 2011 version of the report, Henry Louis Gates Jr. highlighted some notable trends: "Going behind the numbers, we learn that, as of 2011–2012, only 19 states specifically require teaching *Brown v. Board of Education*, while 18 states require coverage of MLK [Martin Luther King Jr.]; 12, Rosa Parks; 11, the March on Washington; and 6, Jim Crow segregation policies."[27] The research also showed that states farther away from the South and with smaller African American populations paid less attention to civil rights in school educational standards and curriculum frameworks, making southern states leaders in the field.[28] Thus, while Mississippi may be in the vanguard of civil rights education, having been the only state to adopt such a comprehensive civil and human rights education mandate, substantial challenges remain.

The life of the Mississippi Truth Project (MTP) as a South Africa–inspired truth commission was also short. By 2009, after significant delays due to Hurricane Katrina, MTP organizers decided to move the project in a different direction. Interactions with Peter Storey, a South African religious leader and former member of the South African Truth and Reconciliation Commission, who critiqued the South African process and noted significant differences between South Africa and Mississippi, had been instrumental in the decision. As April Grayson, now the Winter Institute's director of community and capacity building, recalled in 2016, the Winter Institute didn't "want a one-time sort of truth commission that meets, does this thing, and then dissolves." Rather, it aimed for a "sustainable effort" that would be ongoing: "We wanted it to be more programmatic. . . . You know, longitudinal rather than a sort of moment in time."[29]

This new focus resulted in a new framing of the MTP, abandoning the commissionlike structure for a multipronged approach. First, the MTP partnered with the University of Southern Mississippi's Center for Oral History and Cultural Heritage and launched a statewide effort to collect oral histories in an effort to increase local engagement and to archive materials to be used by a future truth commission, should one arise.[30] Next, the Winter Institute enhanced its Welcome Table programming, which consisted of community-based dialogues designed to "create a safe space for diverse community stakeholders to form healthy relationships via open, honest communication."[31] With programs launched in more than eighteen communities in Mississippi, including Greenwood, Jackson, McComb, Meridian, Oxford, Pike County, Tupelo, and West Point, the Welcome Table that had been designed to be a pilot "year of dialogue" in 2008 was now being described by the institute as an "era of dialogue."[32]

In many ways, the Winter Institute's Welcome Table has been the most robust aftereffect of the aborted Mississippi truth commission initiative and warrants further consideration. The institute cites its experience in Philadelphia as having inspired the Welcome Table model. According to former Winter Institute employee Patrick Weems, the Philadelphia Coalition's call for justice diverse Mississippians citizens could work together for change.[33] This inspired a group of citizens to come together, Weems later recalled, "to see if the same kind of work that was done in Philadelphia could be replicated all over the state."[34] In 2013, a former Winter Institute employee reflected on the significance of Philadelphia to the work of the institute. He said simply, "Philadelphia *was* the work."[35] "It was the one unqualified success in what the Winter Institute wanted to do that kind of overshadowed all the other work." He explained further, "I think Philadelphia became the implicit model or the sort of archetype of what type of work the Winter Institute wanted to do. It involved multiracial cooperation. It involved the community itself sort of already building this conversation and then reaching out to the Winter Institute to support it. It involved a legal end, a ceremonial end, and an educational end. It had all the pieces of the puzzle that the Winter Institute wanted to have in one place."[36]

While the Welcome Table communities across Mississippi have had varied success, the model has generated significant interest well beyond Mississippi. In 2014, the Winter Institute began working with the city of New Orleans after the city received a $1.2 million grant from the W. K. Kellogg Foundation to launch a three-year initiative focused on race, reconciliation, and community building.[37] The Winter Institute faced hearty skepticism from locals wary of an outside group's taking on such important and sensitive work, but the desire to work with an impartial organization from outside the state prevailed.[38] Major state-level actors in neighboring states have begun to look to Mississippi as a model, envisioning their own versions of the Winter Institute.

South Carolina is a notable example, with the University of South Carolina (USC) having established the South Carolina Collaborative on Race and Reconciliation in consultation with Sustainable Equity, the Mississippi-based consulting firm founded by Susan Glisson and Charles Tucker when they left the Winter Institute in 2015. The collaborative's signature program is Welcome Table SC, which has trained local facilitators who will lead dialogues on the USC campus and which hopes to expand to communities across the state.[39] USC's chief diversity officer, John Dozier, was originally skeptical of the Welcome Table model but found himself proven wrong as "a trusting, motivated community was formed."[40] "I get a lot of pushback from some members of the community that we need to *do* something," Dozier reflected. "But it is my belief that it is indeed the talking, and intentionally creating spaces to have difficult dialogue across society's entrenched racial boundaries, that's able to educate and change people's hearts. That's the action we should be taking, because I believe that it's the only action that has lasting impact." Furthermore, Dozier notes, "Policies and laws are absolutely needed but are often ineffective if they don't reflect cultural norms. The work of the Welcome Table is an effort to help each participant to think differently about the members of our communities. It's shifting our cultural paradigm one Welcome Table at a time."[41]

More than ten years after the fortieth anniversary commemoration in Philadelphia, the Winter Institute conceptualizes Senate Bill 2718, the civil and human rights education bill, and community-based programs like the Welcome Table, as integral to the MTP.[42] In this way, the Winter Institute has come to refashion the MTP as an integrative process through which the organization and its collaborators help prepare the state for a more systematic accounting. Some still hope to see a South African–style truth commission in Mississippi, believing that a centralized project could concentrate truth-seeking energies within the state and perhaps generate political momentum for substantive change.[43] This seems unlikely to happen in Mississippi in the near future, but other communities in the United States have taken up the truth commission mantle. According to the Pennsylvania State University geographer Joshua Inwood, who studies U.S.-based truth commissions, at least six communities have initiated local-level truth commissions, and given recent political and social developments, the demand for truth commissions in the United States is as insistent as ever.[44] In 2018, 52 percent of white Americans reported that racism is a "big problem," according to a report by the Pew Research Center—up from 22 percent in 2009.[45] Furthermore, the Southern Poverty Law Center has found that the number of hate groups has grown for the second year in a row, from 892 in 2015 to 900 in 2017.[46] The recent national attention on police violence and the Black Lives Matter movement have thus renewed interest in a national-level truth commission.[47] One of the most vocal advocates for a national truth commission is Fania Davis, the founding director of Restorative Justice for Oakland Youth and the Truth Telling Project, who recognizes the many smaller-scale memory movements that have emerged across the United States. "These movements have started to fill in the gaps around truth-telling," Davis asserts, "but we still need a Truth and Reconciliation Commission . . . to bring together all of these disparate initiatives to coalesce in a more coordinated process that will result not only in truth-telling, but also in racial healing and transformative reparation."[48]

Since 2016, initiatives like the Truth Telling Project and the W. K. Kellogg Foundation's Truth, Racial Healing, and Transformation initiative have begun to coordinate different racial reconciliation efforts to connect groups, concentrate resources, and build capacity in an effort to cultivate a broader national memory movement.[49] So while Mississippi's truth commission has been abandoned for the time being, the state's truth project, including the Winter Institute's Welcome Table programming, may very well prove to be a critical node in the organizational, sociopolitical, and interpersonal framework necessary to create a national-level truth commission, should one be developed in the future.

Commemoration and Fragmentation in Neshoba County

To acknowledge that the fortieth anniversary commemoration precipitated notable changes in Mississippi's legal, educational, and civil spheres does not suggest that these were the only outcomes of that watershed event. The commemoration was also marked by conflict and controversy that resulted in a dramatic fissure between memory activists. Tensions ran high from the beginning of the planning process as two groups—the Philadelphia Coalition, whose members were local residents, and a national commemoration task force, whose supporters included iconic civil rights movement veterans as well as agents of memory with local connections—vied for the endorsement of Mt. Zion and control of the commemoration. Each group sought to articulate its role as the rightful commemoration caretaker, and each had reasonable claims. As a grassroots organization representing the county's three largest racial groups (black, white, and Choctaw) and the city's major institutional sectors (the chamber of commerce, local government, and so on), the Philadelphia Coalition claimed to represent the local community. But the national group questioned the coalition's intentions. Many of the national participants, including Diane Nash, Curtis Mohammed, George Roberts, and C. T. Vivian, had faced violence and harassment during their time as civil rights activists in Mississippi and nearby states, and they believed that the Philadelphia Coalition (or at least some of its members) was disingenuous, showing interest in the commemoration because of its potential for economic profit. The national group's claim on primacy was further anchored by the fact that John Steele—a native of the Longdale community, a childhood member of Mt. Zion when the church was firebombed in 1964, and the presumptive (at least to himself) heir apparent to the Mt. Zion's commemorations that his mother, Mable Steele, had spearheaded for decades, long before white Philadelphians took interest—had allied himself with the national task force.

After the groups struck a reluctant truce and vowed to collaborate, disagreements continued, centering on the program's location and list of speakers. Frustration and resentment continued before, during, and after the commemoration, sometimes playing out in the media. According to an article in the *Neshoba Democrat*—owned and edited by Prince, the Philadelphia Coalition's cochair—on the day of the commemoration, Ben Chaney launched into a "five-minute tirade before television cameras" in which he "claimed that the [Philadelphia] coalition 'used Negroes to do their bidding' to pull off the event."[50] In a separate *Neshoba Democrat* article, Clemons defended the work of the coalition and its positive economic impact: "We've had a major impact on that so far because we are the ones that are speaking now. In the past, we've had these guys coming in from California, from New York [referring to John Steele, who had moved to California]. They want to come in and portray Neshoba County the way they saw it forty years ago."[51] "The sad irony," observed the anthropologist Ronald Loewe, who attended the commemorations from 2003 to 2005, "is that the 'radicals' Prince and Clemons are referring to include the brother of James Chaney . . . , and the reference to 'outside agitators' matches both in tone and substance the rhetoric that helped fuel animus toward civil right workers in 1964."[52]

The trial of Killen only exacerbated this divide, with some people claiming that the Philadelphia Coalition had become complacent with a legal victory that critics viewed as meager.

By 2006, the stances of these two factions had solidified, and every year since, they have articulated their positions in two separate, nearly simultaneous commemoration services. In the sanctuary of Mt. Zion, speakers call on young people to honor James Chaney, Michael Schwerner, and Andrew Goodman by voting, while at the former Longdale community center, now in ruins, remnants of the 2004 national planning committee continue to question the state's legal and political authorities and demand additional prosecutions (see figure G.9). Few people participate in both commemorations, with one notable exception: in 2011, Young—Philadelphia's recently elected black mayor, the first in the county's history—attended both services. He also attended a third commemorative event initiated by Keith Parker, a sociologist and Neshoba County native: the National Civil Rights Conference.

Speaking about the new conference, Young, who attended grade school with Parker, was quick to dispel any suggestion that they were encroaching on the other events in 2011: "This conference was not designed to interfere with or take anything away from the other sponsoring groups. We tried to include those who were there at the time and knew these guys who were in the fight."[53] Rather, Young spoke with the future in mind: "We want to make it an annual event. We're building it as a place to come and talk. Our standpoint is, why have this national conference take place outside the most volatile historical area in our country? We must avoid any kind of stigmatized separation. . . . That's why I participate in all of it."[54] Other people have also attempted to broker a truce between the groups, but as of 2018, each group seems intent on continuing to organize separate events, even as the possibility of pursuing another prosecution dwindles.

This conflict over the memory of the civil rights movement is not unique to Philadelphia. As each anniversary of a civil rights–era milestone approaches, debates rage among civil rights movement veterans over how to depict the past and who has the right to do so. Recalling Barbour's efforts to commemorate the Freedom Rides in 2011, Nash shared her opinion with a group of students and activists in Meridian: "I consider this theft. Mississippi is the worst element to be in control of the memory of the civil rights movement.... The descendants of those who supported racial oppression will profit from the civil rights movement while the descendants of movement veterans will remain poor and in prison."[55] In contrast, Mississippi's director of tourism, Malcolm White, revealed the state's stance on civil rights memory in a brief address at the National Civil Rights Conference in Meridian, Mississippi, in 2014. "Mississippi's greatest asset is our story," he said. "Tourism is big industry. The state wants civil rights tourists just as they want golfers and blues enthusiasts." Furthermore, he suggested, "efforts to remember the civil rights movement do three things: they tell stories, they build economic development, and they build civic pride."[56] These two perspectives encapsulate one of the major fault lines in mnemonic battles over the memory of the civil rights movement: the commodification of memory. As evident in Neshoba County, battles over who profits from civil rights memory will likely remain a salient point of contestation in the years to come.

Appendix A
On Methods

I have come to understand that sociological research depends on thorough planning, serendipity, and the generosity of others. This book is the product of all three. Throughout nearly ten years of research and countless interactions with Mississippians, this research emerged from initial inductive inquiries guided by a deep interest in the causes and consequences of commemorating racial violence. In what follows, I elaborate on how this project—one that centers on Philadelphia and its commemorative practices in the fifty years following the 1964 murders of three civil rights activists—came to be, including its conceptual foundations and methodology.

Commemorations as Events

Since the fortieth anniversary commemoration appeared to mark a shift in the long-standing trajectory of memory practices in Philadelphia and across Mississippi, the sociological literature on "events" was particularly instructive.[1] "Events," according to William Sewell's now classic formulation, are sequences of occurrences that transform social structures "in ways that could not be fully predicted from the gradual changes that may have made them possible."[2] From this perspective, events can be understood as "turning points" between more stable and durable trajectories, or what Andrew Abbott has described as the "smooth befores and afters."[3] Yet while historical events are most often understood as large-scale happenings that engender macro structural change (for example, revolutions, royal successions, and religious revivals), recent sociological research suggests that structure-transforming events may occur on a smaller scale, powerfully influencing local or even national dynamics.[4] Drawing on this theoretical insight, I came to conceptualize the 2004 commemoration in Philadelphia as an event that significantly transformed the surrounding social environment.

Identifying the consequences of the fortieth anniversary commemoration, however, posed distinct challenges, for the outcomes of complex social phenomena like commemorations are often multiple, ranging from micro attitudinal shifts to macro structural change. Moreover, such outcomes are rarely independent, making it difficult to distinguish clear causal relationships. I approached the process inductively, asking a variety of informants both inside and outside of Neshoba County whether and how the commemoration had lasting reverberations in the city, county, and/or state, allowing for alternative explanations to emerge and thus enhancing the project's validity. Responses to this open-ended question coalesced around four institutional transformations, three of which appear in this book (the Edgar Ray Killen trial, the civil and human rights education bill, and the Mississippi Truth Project).

The fourth hypothesized outcome—the election of Philadelphia's first black mayor, James Young, in 2009—while plausibly connected to the fortieth anniversary commemoration, did not yield enough concrete data to include in the study, as I could not verify the discrete actions connecting the commemoration and the subsequent election.

Having identified three potential institutional outcomes, I then examined whether and how the fortieth anniversary commemoration facilitated these transformations, a process that required a systematic methodology grounded in counterfactual logic. In recent decades historically oriented social scientists have sought to make counterfactual inquiries both explicit and systematic, differentiating between counterfactuals that are thought provoking but insufficiently rigorous imaginative exercises and those that meet the criteria of social science.[5] In this effort, social scientists have developed formal qualitative methods to address methodological concerns about counterfactuals, path dependency, and configurational causation, including Event Structure Analysis (ESA), which I used in my qualitative historical inquiry.[6]

Event Structure Analysis

Originally developed by David Heise and extended by Larry Griffin for historical analysis, ESA is an iterative, interactive qualitative methodology that is structured by ETHNO, a software program that guides researchers through a series of counterfactual questions based on a chronology of actions. This challenges researchers to consider the relationship between each action in a sequence of actions, helping them discern distinct causal pathways.[7] Often used to illuminate causal processes in single-case or comparative studies, ESA is ideal for identifying causal linkages, mechanisms, and processes that can be more difficult to ascertain through a variable-based comparative historical analysis.[8]

To investigate the processes precipitating the twenty-fifth and fortieth anniversary commemorations—as well the connection between the latter commemoration and the Killen trial, education bill, and truth project—I constructed a detailed chronology of each event, drawing from historical literature in accordance with standard ESA procedure. While these resources provided an important context that informed my analysis, few scholars had written about more recent events in Mississippi, including Neshoba County. To understand this more recent history required additional primary research. Taken together, historical, archival, and interview data enabled me to generate a thorough chronology of actions that constituted each event (the 1989 and 2004 commemorations, Killen trial, education bill, and truth project), a process that required deep knowledge of each case and of possible worlds that are conceptually and analytically close to the real past.[9] ESA thus depends on researchers' interpretive skills, as does any qualitative approach.[10]

After identifying discrete actions in the historical chronology, ESA requires that the researcher assign abbreviated codes and add them to the computer program in chronological order (for an example, see table A.1), with each action representing a separate hypothesis as to the prerequisite character of each action in the narrative

TABLE A.1 Chronology of the 2004 commemoration

Abbreviation	Date	Description of action
Integration	1970	Mississippi public schools integrated
1989Com	June 1989	Commemoration planning committee holds 1989 commemoration
Ret2Silence	June 1989	Philadelphia returns to broad civic silence
Casino	1994	Mississippi Band of Choctaw Indians builds nearby casino
TourCouncil	2000	State grants Philadelphia permission to establish its Tourism Council
WWIRR	Nov 2002	Glisson appointed direction of Winter Institute
HeritageTour	Dec 2002	Mississippi Development Authority (MDA) begins heritage tourism
ClemPrince	Fall 2003	Clemons and Prince discuss need for a citywide commemoration
MSTourism	Feb 2004	Tourism Council seeks assistance from MDA
Brochure	Feb 2004	Tourism Council decides to compile African American heritage brochure
GlissBroch	Mar 2004	Molpus invites WWIRR to assist brochure committee
Lots2Attend	Mar 2004	Molpus receives call indicating thousands could visit town for forthieth anniversary
MolpusCon	Mar 15 2004	Molpus convenes steering committee to discuss commemoration
CoChairs	Mar 15 2004	Clemons and Prince appointed cochairs of task force
Coalition	Mar 22 2004	Clemons and Prince convene task force (that is, the Philadelphia Coalition)
Glisson	Mar 2004	Clemons and Prince invite Glisson to assist Philadelphia Coalition
Compromise	May 2004	Glisson brokers compromise between agents of memory
MtZion	May 2004	Mt. Zion leaders decide to support Philadelphia Coalition
LocalResources	May 2004	Philadelphia Coalition secure resources from city, county, and tribe
2004Com	June 2004	Philadelphia Coalition hosts 2004 citywide commemoration

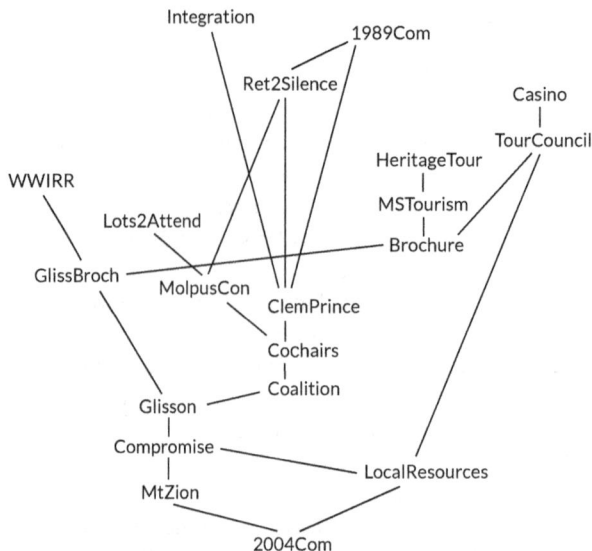

FIGURE A.1 Example of event structure (the 2004 commemoration).

sequence. ETHNO then guides researchers through a series of yes/no questions to the following counterfactual question: Would the subsequent action have occurred if not for the previous action? ETHNO then uses these answers to reconstitute the event, with each line representing an imputed causal link (that is, the event structure; see figure A.1). In effect, this methodology structures the qualitative historical analysis by challenging analysts to consider alternative hypotheses at each stage of the chronology, making visible the causal assumptions that often remain implicit within historical analysis. Thus, ESA does not reveal causality. Rather, it elicits the researcher's understanding of complex causal relationships by scrutinizing whether and how the relationship between two temporally ordered events is, in fact, causal.

This iterative process served as a constant check, helping me identify empirical gaps in the sequence of actions that I might otherwise have missed; challenging me to revisit my data when I was uncertain about the connections between two actions; and enabling me to ask more refined, targeted questions. ESA was therefore a vital tool in my research process, illuminating the causal connections between the fortieth anniversary commemoration and the Killen trial (chapter 3), education bill, (chapter 4), and truth project (chapter 5) and providing a basis for comparisons across commemorative events, which further enhanced the project's theoretical insights (chapters 2, 6, and 7).[11]

Data Collection and Analysis

To construct and interpret the event structures required a deep knowledge of Mississippi and its mnemonic practices over the course of fifty years and in a variety of social spheres (legal, educational, and civil). Consequently, this required different approaches to data collection and a variety of research materials.

Documents

Given the historical orientation of this project and my training in comparative historical methodology, I began my research as most historical sociologists would—in the archives.[12] The official archives—the Mississippi Department of Archives and History (in Jackson), Department of Archives and Special Collections at the University of Mississippi (in Oxford), Moorland-Spingarn Research Center at Howard University (in Washington, D.C.), Special Collections at the University of Southern Mississippi (in Hattiesburg), Wisconsin Historical Society (in Madison), and Schomburg Center for Research in Black Culture (in New York City)—were rich resources for documents related to the Freedom Summer, the 1964 killings, and the Mississippi civil rights movement more generally, subjects that were also well covered by the secondary historical literature. Furthermore, given the long process through which documents come to be archived, many of my archival trips did less to illuminate Mississippi's more recent history than I had hoped, with several notable exceptions.[13] The Mississippi Department of Archives and History's subject files on "Schwerner, Chaney, and Goodman," for instance, included news clippings from hard-to-access publications as well as programs from memorial services and conferences. Likewise, the archives at the University of Southern Mississippi contained a rich collection of oral histories pertaining to the history of Neshoba County. These oral histories, conducted in the 1970s and 1980s, provided rich personal accounts of the civil rights movement in Neshoba County and its aftermath from key informants who were difficult (or impossible) for me to interview because of their advanced age or, in several cases, because they had passed away. Finally, the Andrew Goodman Memorial Collection at the Schomburg Center for Research in Black Culture provided access to a variety of documents related to Goodman's life and death, including a full transcript of the speech his father delivered to the press after the bodies were finally discovered, in which he describes the killings as a cultural trauma.[14]

At times, however, the socially constructed categories of the archives made it difficult to locate material that was relevant to my particular research questions. To locate documents related to Mississippi's more recent mnemonic practices, I had to search elsewhere. Targeted word searches in the Access World News database revealed national coverage of Philadelphia's annual commemorations, the Killen trial, education bill, and truth project, but local and regional news coverage (in the *Neshoba Democrat* and *Meridian Star*) was generally available only on microfilm.[15] When searching these resources, I focused on the two weeks before and after the June 21 anniversary, except in years where major court cases were under way (1964–67 and 2004–5).

In addition to archival documents and newspaper resources, other forms of media informed my analysis, often providing richer details on more contemporary events. In several cases, key informants shared personal papers in the form of journals, meeting notes, emails, and computer files. These were especially illuminating, as they were candid and provided contemporaneous reactions to events as they unfolded. Likewise, the William Winter Institute for Racial Reconciliation posted digital recordings on Vimeo, an online video hosting platform, that included recordings of several Philadelphia Coalition meetings, the Mississippi Truth Project signing ceremony, and interviews with longtime residents of Neshoba County. These videos spoke directly to the events under investigation and provided rich, relevant quotations. Internet resources, however, can be ephemeral, and in some cases, these resources are no longer publicly available.[16] This is true of the Winter Institute Vimeo site, where many of the videos appear to have been removed after the organization cut its ties with the University of Mississippi in 2018.

Interviews

In-depth interviews with sixty-two key informants supplemented and enhanced my archival research, filling in empirical gaps and providing a more holistic view of respondents' experiences as well as the meaning-making systems through which they made sense of those experiences. Given the historical nature of this research, each key informant occupied a unique position and was, to some extent, irreplaceable. Thus, a major part of this research was not about finding patterns across these key informants but about understanding the complexities surrounding mnemonic practices, especially decision-making processes, obstacles to implementation, and roads not taken. As a result, I prepared a semistructured interview schedule for each interview, focusing on the historical events in which each key informant had been most involved.

At first I was surprised by how willing people were to speak with me, a young white woman from a northern university, but this generosity remained constant throughout my years of research and regardless of the individual's social status—whether storekeeper or state senator. Nearly every individual I contacted agreed to be interviewed, often inviting me to meet the same day. This made advance planning challenging and required that I be both flexible and mobile, sometimes driving three or four hours across the state at a moment's notice. Offering to meet "whenever and wherever is most convenient for you" took on new meaning in Mississippi's vast landscape.

Despite this geographical scale, Mississippi was also "a small town," as one of my respondents aptly put it. To say that everyone knew everyone else is only a slight exaggeration. I was often surprised by the density of social networks, which opened up opportunities to interview additional key informants but also made issues of confidentiality paramount. This is why I refrained from attributing quotations to specific individuals, except when quoting from previously published texts or when the individual gave me explicit permission to do so. Most interviews lasted between one and four hours and took place in professional offices, private homes, and public spaces such as libraries, cafes, and in one case a gas station. Whenever possible, interviews were audio-recorded and transcribed in full, yet certain circumstances (particularly loud public spaces) prevented the use of a digital recorder, in which case I took detailed notes, including direct quotations, that I later typed up as field notes.

My focus on "collective" (as opposed to "collected") aspects of memory, to borrow Jeffrey Olick's distinction, led me to begin my interviews with the agents of memory most intimately involved with the Philadelphia commemorations' planning process and aftermath, most of whom were members of the Philadelphia Coalition.[17] While I could not interview every member of the coalition, I interviewed a variety of members who represented the group's major social identities and ideological orientations—with one exception. I was unable to secure interviews with either Choctaw member of the coalition, and instead I had to rely on previously published quotations, online videos, and testimony from others affiliated with the tribe.

In most cases, members of the Philadelphia Coalition had been interviewed on numerous occasions, which led them to have preconceived notions about my research objectives and a general sense of interview fatigue. Many residents of Neshoba County assumed that I, like most of the academics and reporters they had interacted with, was writing a book about the Killen trial, arguably the most sensational news to have come out of Neshoba County in nearly half a century. Some respondents were also concerned that I was engaged in some sort of "gotcha" journalism, planning to publish yet another story about how nothing had changed in Philadelphia—a concern that remained salient throughout my interactions with county residents and undoubtedly was influenced by my outsider status. These reservations emerged only well into interviews, after establishing rapport.

Sharing information about who I was, where I came from, and why I was interested in Mississippi's history of racial violence was central to building trust with key informants. Consequently, I began interviews with a description of my research project as well as a brief sketch of my biography, acknowledging my social identities.[18] This seemed to put people at ease and often prompted later questions about my personal thoughts on race relations in the United States. I answered these questions honestly, while also being careful to maintain a critical distance. This duality—of needing to be inside and outside, a conversational companion and a critical observer—characterized my time in the field. Furthermore, it is important to note that my status as an insider or outsider fluctuated depending on the social circumstance.[19] When interviewing white county residents, for instance, I was a regional outsider but a racial insider. Given this intersectionality, white respondents would sometimes articulate regional folkways in great detail while also making sweeping generalizations that assumed my understanding based on our shared race.

Observations

While most of the events discussed in this book took place before I first visited Mississippi in 2009, observational research still informed my historical analysis. From 2009 to 2014, I attended six consecutive annual commemoration services, attending both the Philadelphia Coalition–affiliated program at Mt. Zion and the "Mississippi Martyrs Memorial" event at the former site of the Longdale community center, now a cinderblock shell of its former structure. After Keith Parker, a Neshoba County native and professional sociologist, initiated the annual National Civil Rights Conference in Meridian in 2010, I attended that yearly event as well. While public, these memory events occurred in sacred places (such as churches and sites of lynching) and involved sacred rituals (including candle lighting and wreath laying), so I kept my note taking to a minimum during such events, returning to the privacy of my car when possible to jot down notes or record voice memos. Most significantly, these annual commemorative events revealed deep structures of meaning underlying the rituals, symbols, and language that each group deployed in its efforts to recognize and reckon with the 1964 murders. Furthermore, showing up year after year helped establish my credibility with key informants who might otherwise have been reluctant to speak to me. By the fiftieth anniversary commemoration in 2014, the event organizers had come to expect my presence, assigning me some minor organizational tasks like setting up chairs and preparing food for visitors.

While these annual visits, which generally lasted 2–3 weeks, provided me with a rich source of observational data, I felt compelled to spend a sustained period of time living in the region to better understand the day-to-day concerns of local residents and how the mnemonic practices that were the focus of my research intersected with the more mundane aspects of everyday life in Neshoba County. In the winter of 2013, I moved to Union, Mississippi, a town of two thousand people just fifteen minutes from downtown Philadelphia, where I lived for nearly six months. A local family with deep Mississippi ties had graciously allowed me to rent their pool house. Over the course of my stay, they became a great source of support as well as cultural knowledge, inviting me to join them for family dinners, Bible study, and programs at the local school, among other local happenings. While attending a local high school musical on one such occasion, I learned that Killen hailed from Union only after I noticed that the lead actor, a fifteen-year-old student, shared his last name. Experiencing these deep family lineages in the region helped me gain a better sense of what was at stake when commemorating historic racial violence in these communities.

After each day in the field, I returned to the pool house to write extensive field notes on my observations, interactions, and conversations, noting descriptive details as well as theoretical insights. I later honed these emerging insights with integrative conceptual memos that informed future questions and observations.[20] In this way, the data collection and analysis were intertwined, with initial observations leading to implicit hypotheses that altered my experience in the field.[21]

Concluding Thoughts

This study has offered a detailed analysis of Philadelphia's mnemonic practices over the course of fifty years, paying particular attention to the causes and consequences of two notable community-wide commemorations in 1989 and 2004 and exploring the conditions that enabled local memory practices to facilitate broader structural transformations. I did not, therefore, set out to complete an ethnography of Philadelphia, Neshoba County, or Mississippi more generally, nor did I provide a comprehensive assessment of all the memory work taking place in Mississippi during this time period. There are countless agents of memory working diligently to transform or defend Mississippi's mnemonic practice who are not featured in this book. Rather, the research and findings presented here are the product of a particular set of sociological tools and concepts.

Undoubtedly, single case studies have their limitations. In general, such studies cannot address factors that are held constant within their boundaries, limiting possibilities for broader generalizations.[22] Yet, as Dietrich Rueschemeyer has convincingly argued, "much of the skepticism about the theoretical value of single historical case studies derives from the mistaken equation of a single case with a single observation."[23] On the contrary, case study research involves multiple observations of a given subject, often using multiple sources of data to enhance a study's validity. Furthermore, researchers may use historical case studies to test and retest emerging theories against multiple points of data throughout the analysis, in addition to generating new theories and hypotheses.[24]

Philadelphia's story is therefore both unique and representative. Like any good story, the particulars—or what historical sociologists call contingencies—illuminate broader social phenomena and speak to a shared human experience. In this way, I hope that this study may serve as a helpful point of reference, illuminating similarities and differences with other cases for scholars and activists interested in memory work and social change.

Appendix B

Archival Collections

Department of Archives and Special Collections at the University of Mississippi, Oxford

Ed King Collection
Race Relations Collection

Mississippi Department of Archives and History, Jackson

Congress of Federated Organization Papers
Dick Molpus Speeches, 1987–1995
Education, 2005–Present (Subject File)
Education Legislation 1984 (Subject File)
Integration 1964 (Subject File)
Mississippi Burning (Subject File)
Neshoba County (Subject File)
Norma Sanders Bourdeax Collection
Office Files—Dick Molpus, 1984–1995
Philadelphia (Subject File)
Schwerner, Chaney, Goodman, undated–1969 (Subject File)
Schwerner, Chaney, Goodman, 1970–1989 (Subject File)
Schwerner, Chaney, Goodman, 1989–1999 (Subject File)
Schwerner, Chaney, Goodman, 2000–2004 (Subject File)
Schwerner, Chaney, Goodman, 2005– (Subject File)
WLBT Newsfilm Collection

Moorland-Spingarn Research Center at Howard University, Washington, DC

Civil Rights Documentation Project

Schomburg Center for Research in Black Culture, New York, NY

Andrew Goodman Memorial Collection

Special Collections at the University of Southern Mississippi, Hattiesburg

Chaney, Schwerner and Goodman (2005–present)
Civil Rights—Chaney, Schwerner and Goodman (1964–2004)
Martin (Josephine D.) Papers
Oral History Collection
Zeman (Zoya) Freedom Summer Collection

Wisconsin Historical Society, Madison, WI

Carolyn Goodman Papers
Citizens for Civil Rights in Mississippi
Congress of Racial Equality Records, 1941–1967
Scholarship, Education and Defense Fund for Racial Equality Records, 1944–1976

Appendix C

List of Interviews

Conducted by the Author

Abadie, Ann, Oxford, MS, June 29, 2009
Austin, Curtis, Hattiesburg, MS, June 30, 2010
Brooks, Owen, Jackson, MS, July 1, 2010
Clark, Fred, Philadelphia, MS, June 18, 2012
Clemons, Leroy, Philadelphia, MS, May 15, 2013
Dearman, Stanley, Philadelphia, MS, March 21, 2013
DeWeese, Fenton, Choctaw, MS, March 22, 2013
Espy, Portia, by phone, October 30, 2018
Evans, George, Jackson, MS, July 10, 2009
Fertig, Ralph, Philadelphia, MS, June 22, 2012
Freelon-Foster, Diane, Grenada, MS, October 15, 2016
Gibson, John, Philadelphia, MS, June 22, 2012
Gibson, Peggy, Philadelphia, MS, June 23, 2014
Glisson, Susan, Oxford, MS, July 1, 2009; Jackson, MS, June 29, 2010; Jackson, MS, June 30, 2013; and by phone, September 18, 2013, and November 14, 2016
Gordon, Von, Jackson, MS, October 24, 2018
Grayson, April, Oxford, MS, October 16, 2016
Grupper, Ira, by phone, May 25, 2010
Harbin, Tomeka, Cleveland, MS, October 16, 2016
Hawthorne, Jennifer, Philadelphia, MS, June 20, 2014
Hayden, Bridget, by phone, October 6, 2016
Hearst, Paul, Jackson, MS, October 26, 2018
Hillegas, Jan, Philadelphia, MS, June 21, 2009
Holden, Matthew and Dorothy, Jackson, MS, July 8, 2009
Horhn, John, Jackson, MS, October 18, 2016
Jordan, Joe, Philadelphia, MS, April 24, 2013
Junior, Pamela, Jackson, MS, October 25, 2018
Kirksey, Elsie, Philadelphia, MS, March 25, 2013
Ladd, Donna, Jackson, MS, June 30, 2010
Magarrell, Lisa, by phone, April 27, 2009
Martin, Jackie, McComb, MS, October 14, 2016
McCullough, Sarah, by phone, June 19, 2013
McDonald, Janis, by phone, June 14, 2014
McDonald, Jewell, Philadelphia, MS, April 10, 2013
Mitchell, Jerry, Jackson, MS, March 13, 2013

Molina, Dave, Oxford, MS, July 13, 2009; and by phone, May 14, 2013
Molpus, Dick, Jackson, MS, July 14, 2009
Owens, Deborah, by phone, April 22, 2013
Perkins, John, Jackson, MS, June 26, 2009
Posey, Deborah, Philadelphia, MS, June 24, 2014
Powell, Barbara and Barry, Jackson, MS, July 11, 2009
Prince, Jim, Philadelphia, MS, April 9, 2013
Rowell, Kaye, Philadelphia, MS, March 12, 2013
Shaffer, Stephen, Starkeville, MS, March 20, 2013
Shannon, Ta'Shia, Philadelphia, MS, April 17, 2013
Spears, Chauncey, Meridian, MS, June 19, 2013
Steele, John, Philadelphia, MS, June 22, 2012
Thomas, Alex, by phone, June 19, 2013
Tisdale, Eva, Philadelphia, MS, April 5, 2013
Tollison, Gray, Oxford, MS, June 23, 2012
Tuberville, Howard, Meridian, MS, October 17, 2016
Tucker, Charles, Jackson, MS, June 29, 2010
Whitfield, Ed, by phone, May 17, 2013
Wilkerson, Steve, Philadelphia, MS, April 3, 2013
Williams, Jill, by phone, December 2, 2016
Williamson, Gloria, Philadelphia, MS, April 17, 2013
Winters, Neddie, Jackson, MS, June 7, 2009
Young, James, Philadelphia, MS, March 28, 2013

In the Oral History Collection, Special Collections at the University of Southern Mississippi, Hattiesburg

Cole, Howard, September 13, 1973
Collier, Clinton, July 28, 1981
Jones, Lille, December 11, 1974
Lee, Clay, July 8, 1980
Mars, Florence, January 5, 1978
Posey, Buford, October 12, 2007
York, Kenneth, October 21, 1998

Notes

Preface

1. Kaufman, "Silicon Valley High School Struggles with Integration."
2. Gibson, "Does Truth Lead to Reconciliation?"; Brahm, "Uncovering the Truth."
3. The Greensboro Truth and Reconciliation Commission is generally recognized as the first U.S.-based truth commission. The Mississippi truth commission, had it come to fruition, would have been the first statewide truth commission in the United States.
4. H-Net is an international online forum for scholars in the humanities and social sciences, which is organized into subject-specific "networks." See H-Net (home page).
5. Vinitzky-Seroussi, "Commemorating a Difficult Past."
6. Quoted in Prince, "Historian Sees Coalition's Efforts as a Model for the State."

Introduction

1. "Philadelphia" (with no state name) in this book refers to Philadelphia, Mississippi. When a Philadelphia in any other state is mentioned, it will be accompanied by the state name (for example, Philadelphia, Pennsylvania).
2. Dittmer, *Local People*, 247.
3. Mars, *Witness in Philadelphia*, 89.
4. Nevin, "A Strange, Tight Little Town."
5. Quoted in Willie Morris, *The Courting of Marcus Dupree*, 16.
6. Prince, "Historian Sees Coalition's Efforts as a Model for the State."
7. Winter, "The Memory Boom in Contemporary Historical Studies"; Blight, "The Memory Boom"; Klein, "On the Emergence of Memory in Historical Discourse."
8. Santayana, *Reason in Common Sense*, 284. Many have speculated about how and why this global cultural transformation occurred. Perhaps, as some have argued, generational change was responsible. Those who came of age after World War II abhorred the misdeeds of their parents and grandparents and, uninhibited by the weight of history, pushed for radical inclusion, a politics of recognition. Or perhaps postmodernism is to blame. As master narratives gave way to multiplicities of meaning, the boundary between history and memory began to fade. Or maybe the end of the Cold War encouraged this turn to the past. The triumph of capitalism over communism's utopian aspirations led to what Francis Fukuyama

famously called the "end of history" (*The End of History and the Last Man*) or what John Torpey described as a gloomy sense of "post-ness" (*Making Whole What Has Been Smashed*, 8). See also Klein, "On the Emergence of Memory in Historical Discourse"; Nora, "Reasons for the Current Upsurge in Memory."

9. Arlie Hochschild's groundbreaking work on emotional labor has popularized the idea of "feeling rules" (the social guidelines that direct feelings), which can be applied to large collectivities such as the nation ("Emotion Work, Feeling Rules, and Social Structure"). This is particularly evident in the title of Elazar Barkan's book on restitution for historical injustices, *The Guilt of Nations*, as well as in Hiro Saito's work on the "structure of feeling" surrounding the Japanese national memory of the bombing of Hiroshima ("Reiterated Commemoration," 369).

10. Olick, *The Politics of Regret*; Jeffrey Alexander, "Cultural Pragmatics"; Jeffrey Alexander, Giesen, and Mast, *Social Performance*.

11. Beitler, *Remaking Transitional Justice*; Inwood, Alderman, and Barron, "Addressing Structural Violence through US Reconciliation Commissions"; Nobles, *The Politics of Official Apologies*.

12. Leslie Harris, Campbell, and Brophy, eds., *Slavery and the University*.

13. Cotter, "A Memorial to the Lingering Horror of Lynching."

14. On August 12, 2017, James Alex Fields Jr. drove his car into a crowd of people protesting a Unite the Right rally in Charlottesville, Virginia, killing thirty-two-year-old Heather Heyer. See York, "Charlottesville Pays Tribute to Heather Heyer."

15. This trend is also variously referred to as "restitution politics," "politics of the past," "politics of apology," and "reconciliation politics." See Olick, *The Politics of Regret*; Torpey, *Politics and the Past*; Michael Cunningham, "Prisoners of the Japanese and the Politics of Apology"; Moon, *Narrating Political Reconciliation*.

16. Barry Schwartz, a sociologist and scholar of collective memory, has described commemorations as operating as both mirrors and lamps: as a mirror, a commemoration reflects past events in terms of the needs, fears, and interests of a community in the present; and as a lamp, it shapes meanings, understandings, aspirations, and agendas for the future (*Abraham Lincoln and the Forge of National Memory*, 7).

17. Eviatar Zerubavel, *Time Maps*.

18. Durkheim, *The Elementary Forms of Religious Life*; Halbwachs, *On Collective Memory*.

19. Simko, *The Politics of Consolation*, 9. As Robin Wagner-Pacifici and Barry Schwartz first noted in their foundational piece on the Vietnam War Memorial, in which they explored the paradox of commemorating an event "without consensus, or without pride" ("The Vietnam Veterans Memorial," 379). In doing so, they helped launch a vibrant literature on commemorations of difficult pasts that spans vast and varied empirical terrain. From this research, we have learned that commemorations of difficult pasts tend to fall into two ideal types: multivocal commemorations that seek to accommodate multiple viewpoints within one commemorative space; and fragmented commemorations, in which multiple commemorative spaces reinforce distinct narratives of the same event, reflecting and reinforcing dis-

sensus. See also Vinitzky-Seroussi, "Commemorating a Difficult Past"; Steidl, "Remembering May 4, 1970."

20. Whigham, "Remembering to Prevent"; Margalit, *The Ethics of Memory*; LaCapra, *Writing History, Writing Trauma*.

21. Ricoeur, *Figuring the Sacred*, 290. See also Margalit, *The Ethics of Memory*; Booth, *Communities of Memory*.

22. LaCapra, *Writing History, Writing Trauma*, 45.

23. Whether these "transitional justice" mechanisms were successful in restoring democracy and a commitment to human rights remains debated within the literature. For example, see Brahm, "Uncovering the Truth." See also Adorno, "What Does Coming to Terms with the Past Mean?"; Teitel, "Transitional Justice Genealogy"; and Misztal, "Memory and Democracy."

24. Rieff, *In Praise of Forgetting*, 122.

25. Rieff, *In Praise of Forgetting*, 40. See also Benedict Anderson, *Imagined Communities*; Hobsbawm and Ranger, *The Invention of Tradition*.

26. Maier, "A Surfeit of Memory?," 136. See also Bruckner, *The Tyranny of Guilt*.

27. Hobbes, *Body, Man, and Citizen*; John Rawls, *Political Liberalism*. Friedrich Nietzsche famously argued that too much history could be "the gravedigger of the present" (*Untimely Meditations*, 62).

28. Scholars often point to the Athenian amnesty of 403 B.C.E. as a quintessential example, as it brought the civil war to an end and cemented the democratic reconciliation following the bloody oligarchy of the Thirty Tyrants. See Elster, *Closing the Books*; Loraux, *The Divided City*.

29. Schudson, "Dynamic Distortion of Collective Memory," 348. Elizabeth Jelin makes a similar point in *State Repression and the Labors of Memory*.

30. My definition of "memory movements" differs slightly from those of others who focus solely on efforts to change representations of the past or seek redress. For example, Raj Ghoshal defines memory movements as "sustained collective efforts to bring increased attention to, seek redress for, and/or commemorate incidents or individuals from the past, or to transform the prevailing way that such incidents are understood.... That is, memory movements seek to upend general inattention or attention to some aspect of the past, or to transform how some aspect of the past is understood" (*Racial Violence*, 11). Likewise, Bin Xu and Gary Alan Fine describe memory movements as "movements that are aimed at creating or reconstructing narratives of the distant past and, based on the new narrative, demand redress for past sufferings" ("Memory Movement," 168).

31. Melucci, "The New Social Movements."

32. Zamponi, "Collective Memory and Social Movements"; Kubal and Beccera, "Social Movements and Collective Memory"; Eyerman, "Social Movements and Memory."

33. Griffin, "Generations and Collective Memory Revisited." See also Griffin and Bollen, "What Do These Memories Do?"; Fredrick Harris, "It Takes a Tragedy to Arouse Them."

34. Dawson, *Behind the Mule*, 51. See also Isaac, "The Movement of Movements."

35. Fine, *Difficult Reputations*; Christopher Parker and Barreto, *Change They Can't Believe In*. See also Jansen, "Resurrection and Appropriation."

36. Kubal and Becerra, "Social Movements and Collective Memory." On repertoires of contention, see Tilly, *Regimes and Repertoires*; Tarrow, *Power in Movement*.

37. Eyerman, "Social Movements and Memory," 83.

38. Jelin makes this point in *State Repression and the Labors of Memory*. On "moral entrepreneurs," see Becker, *Outsiders*, 147.

39. Kubal and Becerra, "Social Movements and Collective Memory."

40. My understanding of political opportunities is captured by Sidney Tarrow's definition of political opportunities as "consistent—but not necessarily formal, permanent, or national—sets of clues that encourage people to engage in contentious politics" (*Power in Movement*, 32). On resource mobilization, see McCarthy and Zald, "Resource Mobilization and Social Movements." On framing, see Benford and Snow, "Framing Processes and Social Movements."

41. David Meyer, "Protest and Political Opportunities"; McCarthy and Zald, "Resource Mobilization and Social Movements"; Snow and Benford, "Ideology, Frame Resonance, and Participant Mobilization."

42. Kubal, *Cultural Movements and Collective Memory*.

43. Ghoshal, "Transforming Collective Memory," 336.

44. Elizabeth Armstrong and Crage, "Movements and Memory."

45. Elizabeth Armstrong and Crage, "Movements and Memory," 726.

46. DeGloma, "The Strategies of Mnemonic Battle."

47. Irwin-Zarecka, *Frames of Remembrance*, 47.

48. It would also be reasonable to ask why we should presume that commemorations can be consequential. Process-oriented approaches to collective memory, which examine the malleability of memory over the longue durée, offer some insights into the causal nature of commemoration by highlighting its path dependency. This suggests that previous commemorations influence subsequent commemorations in both form and content through what Jeffrey Olick calls "genre memory," the way in which commemorations are affected explicitly or implicitly by generic models of commemoration ("Genre Memories and Memory Genres"). Likewise, others have detected how previous memory struggles shape subsequent use of historical figures and events in campaigns of public interest.

While these examples touch upon consequences of commemoration, they do not explicitly theorize the consequences of commemoration, nor do they explore consequences beyond the realm of memory. See Jansen, "Resurrection and Appropriation"; Saito, "Reiterated Commemoration."

49. While I investigated educational outcomes, my research initially focused on a Teaching American History grant that was awarded to Neshoba County schools, but the research revealed that this initiative had been set in motion before the commemoration.

50. Weber, "Objective Possibility and Adequate Causation in Historical Explanation"; Abbott, "On the Concept of Turning Point."

51. Gould, *A Wonderful Life*.

52. Bulhof, "What If?"; Bunzl, "Counterfactual History: A User's Guide."

53. Bulhof, "What If?," 147. For several decades, social scientists have highlighted the important role of well-constructed counterfactuals, differentiating between counterfactuals as thought-provoking but insufficiently rigorous imaginative exercises and counterfactuals that meet the criteria of rigorous social science. The latter, which are based on indirect evidence and are what I hope to present in this book, must fulfill a number of criteria. For example, they must clearly specify antecedents (that is, the hypothesized independent variables) and consequences (the dependent variables), generate plausible hypotheses that require minimal rewriting of history, and articulate mechanisms or connecting principles that are consistent with well-established theory and statistics. The legitimacy of counterfactual claims also depends on one's understanding of causality. Counterfactuals, according to James Fearon, search for "conceivable causes" based on "factors that could actually have been different according to the best of our knowledge about how the social and physical worlds work" ("Causes and Counterfactuals in Social Science," 41). This is similar to what Margaret Somers has described as "causal narrativity": "a reclaimed notion of causality based on narrativity, sequence, and contingency rather than universality and predictive law" ("Where Is Sociology after the Historic Turn?," 68). In this sense, causality is not a covering law but a historically intelligible explanation (Stinchcombe, *Theoretical Methods in Social History*). See Elster, *Logic and Society*; Hawthorn, *Plausible Worlds*; Tetlock and Belkin, "Counterfactual Thought Experiments in World Politics"; Mahoney, "Path Dependence in Historical Sociology"; Capoccia and Keleman, "The Study of Critical Junctures."

54. Griffin, "Narrative, Event-Structure Analysis, and Causal Interpretation in Historical Sociology."

55. Mill, *A System of Logic*. See also Lewis-Beck, Bryman, and Liao, "Negative Case"; Sewell, "Historical Events as Transformations of Structures" and "Three Temporalities."

56. The archives I consulted were the Mississippi Department of Archives and History (in Jackson), the Department of Archives and Special Collections at the University of Mississippi (in Oxford), the Moorland-Spingarn Research Center at Howard University (in Washington, D.C.), the Special Collections at the University of Southern Mississippi (in Hattiesburg), Wisconsin Historical Society (in Madison), and the Schomburg Center for Research in Black Culture (in New York City). For information about the specific archival material I consulted, see appendix B.

57. NewsBank, Access World News.

58. Ball, *Justice in Mississippi*.

59. Allport, *The Nature of Prejudice*.

60. Ganucheau, "Ballot Petition Aims to Protect Confederate Heritage." Ultimately, the 107,216 signatures required were not submitted by the deadline and the initiative expired.

61. Ladd, "Mississippi Governor Declares April 'Confederate Heritage Month.'"

Chapter One

1. Kundera, *The Book of Laughter and Forgetting*, 4.
2. While often attributed to Winston Churchill, this quotation may be an abbreviation of Jawaharlal Nehru's assertion: "History is almost always written by the victors and conquerors and gives their view. Or, at any rate, the victors' version is given prominence and holds the field" (*The Discovery of India*, 196).
3. Orwell, *1984*, 33.
4. Ball, *Justice in Mississippi*, 31.
5. Fitzhugh Brundage, a historian at the University of North Carolina, makes this point in *The Southern Past: A Clash of Race and Memory*, in which he explores how southerners have come to define themselves since 1964 and who has done the defining. The power held by whites, Brundage argues (especially the control of public space, where he suggests that memory is sustained), enabled white southerners and white-dominated institutions to marginalize and ignore blacks' view of the past and their role as southerners.
6. Mars, *Witness in Philadelphia*, 12 (emphasis added).
7. Of course, the prominence of privileged social groups in national and regional histories is not specific to the American South. See Zinn, *A People's History of the United States*; Loewen, *Lies My Teacher Told Me*.
8. Mars, *Witness in Philadelphia*, 1.
9. Cagin and Dray, *We Are Not Afraid*, 14; Satz, "The Mississippi Choctaw."
10. Oral history with Clay Lee, July 8, 1980, 17, Oral History Collection, University of Southern Mississippi, Hattiesburg.
11. Mars, *Witness in Philadelphia*, 35.
12. Cagin and Dray, *We Are Not Afraid*, 15.
13. Cagin and Dray, *We Are Not Afraid*, 15.
14. Quoted in Mars, *Witness in Philadelphia*, 2; See also Willie Morris, *The Courting of Marcus Dupree*, 62.
15. Willie Morris, *The Courting of Marcus Dupree*, 61.
16. Cagin and Dray, *We Are Not Afraid*, 16.
17. Mars, *Witness in Philadelphia*.
18. Newton, *The Ku Klux Klan in Mississippi*; David Cunningham, *Klansville, U.S.A.*
19. Willie Morris, *The Courting of Marcus Dupree*, 69.
20. Quoted in Willie Morris, *The Courting of Marcus Dupree*, 72.
21. Rand, *Ink on My Hands*, 318.
22. Quoted in Huie, *Three Lives for Mississippi*, 125.
23. Brown v. Board of Education.
24. See Newton, *The Ku Klux Klan in Mississippi*, 109.
25. Payne, *I've Got the Light of Freedom*, 34–35; Dittmer, *Local People*, 45.
26. Mississippi Department of Archives and History, "Sovereignty Commission Online."
27. Irons, *Reconstituting Whiteness*.

28. Quoted in Dittmer, *Local People*, 60. See also Irons, *Reconstituting Whiteness*.

29. Quoted in Dittmer, *Local People*, 6. See also Bermanzohn, *Violence, Nonviolence, and the U.S. Civil Rights Movement*.

30. Watson, *Freedom Summer*, 52.

31. Quoted in Watson, *Freedom Summer*, 143.

32. Dittmer, *Local People*, 217.

33. Whitehead, *Attack on Terror*, 26.

34. "Burning Crosses."

35. Quoted in Mars, *Witness in Philadelphia*, 81.

36. Quoted in Watson, *Freedom Summer*, 24.

37. Quoted in Hendrickson, *Sons of Mississippi*, 47.

38. Hendrickson, *Sons of Mississippi*, 174.

39. Dittmer, *Local People*, 199.

40. McAdam, *Freedom Summer*, 33.

41. On the debate over white involvement in Freedom Summer, see Dittmer, *Local People*, 208–11.

42. On the early history of Longdale, see Yates and Ridout, *Red Clay Hills of Neshoba*, 36.

43. Mars, *Witness in Philadelphia*, 76.

44. Mars, *Witness in Philadelphia*, 76.

45. Cagin and Dray, *We Are Not Afraid*, 318.

46. Kotz, *Judgment Days*, 174. On the failure of the media to cover the disappearance of African American civil rights workers during the summer of 1964—in particular, Moore and Dee—see McDonald, "Heroes and Spoilers."

47. Cagin and Dray, *We Are Not Afraid*, 372.

48. Mars, *Witness in Philadelphia*.

49. On how perpetrator communities manage collective guilt, see Smelser, "Psychological Trauma and Cultural Trauma"; Giesen, "Triumph and Trauma"; and Tsutsui, "The Trajectory of Perpetrators' Trauma."

50. Huie, *Three Lives for Mississippi*, 38.

51. Oral history with Howard Cole, Oral History Collection, University of Southern Mississippi, Hattiesburg.

52. Quoted in Willie Morris, *The Courting of Marcus Dupree*, 18.

53. Oral history with Clay Lee, 16.

54. Cagin and Dray, *We Are Not Afraid*, 344.

55. Quoted in Cagin and Dray, *We Are Not Afraid*, 344.

56. Nevin, "A Strange, Tight Little Town," 39.

57. Quoted in Ball, *Murder in Mississippi*, 7.

58. Quoted in Ball, *Murder in Mississippi*, 80.

59. The grand jury's statement is quoted at length in Mars, *Witness in Philadelphia*, 130–31.

60. Quoted in Mars, *Witness in Philadelphia*, 131.

61. Quoted in Mars, *Witness in Philadelphia*, 265.

62. Mars, *Witness in Philadelphia*, 143.
63. Silver, *Mississippi*, 6.
64. Hendrickson, *Sons of Mississippi*, 47.
65. Oral history with Buford Posey, October 12, 2007, Oral History Collection, University of Southern Mississippi, Hattiesburg. See also Newton, *The Ku Klux Klan in Mississippi*.
66. Mars, *Witness in Philadelphia*.
67. Quoted in oral history with Clay Lee, 49.
68. Oral history with Clay Lee, 49.
69. Winter Institute, "Neshoba County—Clay Lee," n.p.
70. Ball, *Justice in Mississippi*, 218.
71. Quoted in Mars, *Witness in Philadelphia*, 263.
72. Eviatar Zerubavel, *The Elephant in the Room*, 2.
73. Morgan, "Oral history with Howard Cole," n.p.
74. Quoted in Cagin and Dray, *We Are Not Afraid*, 454.
75. Quoted in Willie Morris, *The Courting of Marcus Dupree*, 188.
76. Quoted in Lelyveld, "Turning Point," 94–95.
77. Wheeler, "They Gathered and the Fire Still Flickered."
78. On "carrier groups," see Weber, Roth, and Wittich, *Economy and Society*; Jeffrey Alexander, "Towards a Theory of Cultural Trauma."
79. Yael Zerubavel, *Recovered Roots*. The concept of countermemory can be traced back to Michel Foucault's 1971 essay, "Nietzsche, Genealogy, History" where the idea was mentioned in passing. Others have since used the concept in multiple ways, focusing on countermemory as both additive and oppositional. See, for example, Wegner, "Rethinking Countermemory."
80. Fine, *Difficult Reputations*, 21.
81. Quoted in Cagin and Dray, *We Are Not Afraid*, 408. See also Goodman, Robert. "Final Press Conference Before National T.V.," August, 5, 1964, folder 4, box 2, Andrew Goodman Memorial Collection, Schomburg Center for Research in Black Culture, New York.
82. Quoted in Sitton, "Tragedy in Mississippi," E6.
83. Quoted in Williams, *Eyes on the Prize*, 242.
84. Jeffrey Alexander, *Cultural Trauma and Collective Identity*, 1.
85. Jeffrey Alexander, *Cultural Trauma and Collective Identity*, 62.
86. Quoted in "Small Crowd Turns out for CR Trio Memorial."
87. Quoted in "Small Crowd Turns out for CR Trio Memorial."
88. Quoted in Roberts, "Motorcade in Mississippi," 15.
89. "Philadelphia March." June 21, 1966, Reel D46, LCN 180, WLBT Newsfilm Collection, Mississippi Department of Archives and History, Jackson.
90. Quoted in Burrow, *Martin Luther King, Jr., and the Theology of Resistance*, 83.
91. Mars, *Witness in Philadelphia*, 207–10; Reed, "Philadelphia, Miss., Whites and Negroes Trade Shots," 1. On King, see Willie Morris, *The Courting of Marcus Dupree*, 16.
92. Quoted in Willie Morris, *The Courting of Marcus Dupree*, 207.
93. Kirksey interview with author, March 25, 2013.
94. Mars, *Witness in Philadelphia*, 281.

Chapter Two

1. "Roots of Struggle: Rewards of Sacrifice." See also Myers, "MDA, Tourism Council Unveil Civil Rights Brochure"; Charles E. Cobb, "On the Road to Freedom," 279.

2. Halbwachs, *On Collective Memory*; Olick and Robbins, "Social Memory Studies"; Zelizer, "Reading the Past against the Grain"; Irwin-Zarecka, *Frames of Remembrance*.

3. Vinitzky-Seroussi, "Commemorating a Difficult Past"; Wagner-Pacifici and Schwartz, "The Vietnam Veterans Memorial."

4. Cohen, *States of Denial*; Rivera, "Managing 'Spoiled' National Identity"; Vinitzky-Seroussi and Teeger, "Unpacking the Unspoken"; Eviatar Zerubavel, *The Elephant in the Room*.

5. Eviatar Zerubavel clarifies and articulates a number of concepts related to collective memory more broadly in *Social Mindscapes* (93–99). These include mnemonic communities, socialization, and battles.

6. Here, I join other cultural scholars who highlight the competitive nature of discursive fields. Social movement scholars influenced by organizational ecology also highlight how social movement organizations must compete for scarce resources (including cultural resources). See Wuthnow, *Communities of Discourse*; DeGloma, *Seeing the Light*; and Stern, "The Evolution of Social-Movement Organizations."

7. Wagner-Pacifici and Schwartz, "The Vietnam Veterans Memorial."

8. In her book-length study of Yitzhak Rabin's assassination, Vinitzky-Seroussi notes that fragmented commemoration does not always enhance conflict. In some cases, fragmented commemoration "may enhance tranquility as it constructs a type of mnemonic zone in which specific narratives can be heard and survive until they can be continued in more generalized commemorative practices when the broader social milieu becomes less tense" (*Yitzhak Rabin's Assassination*, 149).

9. Steidl, "Remembering May 4, 1970," 750. See also Wagner-Pacifici and Schwartz, "The Vietnam Veterans Memorial"; Vinitzky-Seroussi, "Commemorating a Difficult Past."

10. Eviatar Zerubavel, *The Elephant in the Room*, 1.

11. Eviatar Zerubavel, *The Elephant in the Room*, 2. Several book-length studies on silence and denial as a social (as opposed to a psychological) phenomenon identify how conspiracies of silence are created and maintained. These studies suggest that the concept of mutual denial is key for understanding "how one can actually be aware and (at least publicly) unaware of something at the same time" (*The Elephant in the Room*, 3). Collective denial, like its individual psychological variant, is the result of pain, fear, shame, and embarrassment—all emotions surrounding difficult pasts. It is not surprising, then, that perpetrators of past violence, as well as their families and communities, would suppress these violent pasts both consciously and unconsciously. See Cohen, *States of Denial*; Giesen, "The Trauma of Perpetrators"; Smelser, "Psychological Trauma and Cultural Trauma"; and Tsutsui, "The Trajectory of Perpetrators' Trauma."

12. Eviatar Zerubavel, *The Elephant in the Room*, 85. For works on democratic political culture, see Jeffrey Alexander and Smith, "The Discourse of American Civil Society"; Berezin, "Politics and Culture"; and Somers, "What's Political or Cultural about Political Culture and the Public Sphere?"

13. Thomas DeGloma makes this distinction between different types of memory battles—those over the existence, nature, or relevance of the past ("The Strategies of Mnemonic Battle").

14. Gocek, *Denial of Violence*.

15. Bodnar, *Remaking America*; Boyarin, *Remapping Memory*.

16. Berrey, *The Jim Crow Routine*; Blight, *Race and Reunion*; Bodnar, *Remaking America*; Brundage, *The Southern Past*; McLaurin, "Commemorating Wilmington's Racial Violence of 1898."

17. Eviatar Zerubavel, *The Elephant in the Room*, 61.

18. Irwin-Zareka, *Frames of Remembrance*. See also Olick and Robbins, "Social Memory Studies," 127.

19. Bodnar, *Remaking America*; Eviatar Zerubavel, "Social Memories."

20. Ewick and Silbey, "Subversive Stories and Hegemonic Tales."

21. This is what sociologists refer to as "commemorability." See Yael Zerubavel, *Recovered Roots*.

22. Pennebaker and Banasik, "On the Creation and Maintenance of Collective Memories"; Oliver and Myers, "How Events Enter the Public Sphere"; Schudson, "How Culture Works"; Wagner-Pacifici, "Memories in the Making"; Spillman, "When Do Collective Memories Last?"

23. Elizabeth Armstrong and Crage, "Movements and Memory," 726.

24. Alan Parker, *Mississippi Burning*.

25. Toplin, "Mississippi Burning"; Hoerl, "Burning Mississippi into Memory?"; Scruggs, Afi-Odelia E.,"Is 'Burning' History or Fiction?," January 11, 1989. Mississippi Burning (Subject File), Mississippi Department of Archives and History, Jackson.

26. Quoted in Toplin, "Mississippi Burning," 42.

27. Quoted in Toplin, "Mississippi Burning," 42.

28. For example, see Canby, "'Mississippi Burning.'"

29. Interview with author, March 21, 2013. On the periodic nature of commemorations, see Olick, "Genre Memories and Memory Genres"; Eviatar Zerubavel, "Calendars and History."

30. Quoted in "Mississippi Town Won't Get Film," A15.

31. The *New York Times* data is advantageous for several reasons, including the facts that the data cover the entire research period (1964–2009) and each article reflects original content. Other databases, such as Access World News, aggregates data from hundreds of U.S.-based publications (not including the *New York Times*), many of which reprint articles from the Associated Press. In this sense, the *New York Times* data captures the depth of coverage whereas the Access World News data reflects the breadth of national coverage. In a search that used the terms Chaney AND Goodman AND Schwerner OR "Mississippi Burning," the *New York Times* and Access World News reflected similar patterns for 1980–2009: coverage of the mur-

ders spiked in the winter of 1989 and again in 2004 and 2005. The spike in 1989 — and to a smaller extent in 1988 — is largely due to the release of the film *Mississippi Burning*. When "Mississippi Burning" is removed as a search term, the number of *New York Times* articles drops from 170 to 19, still significantly more than in 1988 (10 articles) or 1987 (1 article).

32. Quoted in Minor, "Image in Film Worries Mississippians," 16.
33. "Civil Rights Caravan to Mark Deaths."
34. McDonald interview with author, April 10, 2013.
35. For more on the social construction of victims and villains and other familiar types of protagonists, see Jasper, Young, and Zuern, "Character Work in Social Movements."
36. Interview with author, March 21, 2013.
37. Mitchell, "Journalism Legend Stanley Dearman Died Saturday"; "Klan Marches without Incident Here Sunday."
38. Mitchell, "Journalism Legend Stanley Dearman Died Saturday."
39. Quoted in Goldstein, "Stanley Dearman."
40. Garfrerick, "The Community Weekly Newspaper."
41. Interview with author, April 9, 2013.
42. Molpus Woodlands Group, "Our Beginnings."
43. Molpus, "Philadelphia, Mississippi."
44. Dearman interview with author, March 21, 2013.
45. In the governor's race six years later, Molpus (a Democrat) was defeated by Kirk Fordice (a Republican), who won the election with 55.4 percent of the vote — and even carried Molpus's home county (Nash and Taggert, *Mississippi Politics*, 254). Some have speculated that Molpus's involvement in the 1989 commemoration played a role in his defeat. See Sokol, *There Goes My Everything*, 328.
46. This is a good example of where the project's methodology, Event Structure Analysis (ESA), was particularly useful. ESA's counterfactual logic challenged me to clarify the precursors of the Pennsylvanians' actions. After reviewing several dozen newspaper articles that describe the Philadelphia to Philadelphia project, one article illuminated the proximate cause: the film, *Mississippi Burning*. The film, then, precipitated local leaders (for example, Dearman) to act and provided access to organizational resources (those of the Pennsylvanians) that would have otherwise been absent. See Blake, "Mississippi Yearning."
47. The 1989 Philadelphia-to-Philadelphia project was not the first. In 1964, a church group in the northern Philadelphia initiated a cross-city collaboration — also called Philadelphia-to-Philadelphia — to help improve race relations in the southern Philadelphia. See Mars, *Witness in Philadelphia*, 200–204.
48. The thirteen charted buses were organized by the Chaney, Goodman, and Schwerner Memorial Coalition, which had been founded by family members of the slain civil rights workers. See Hannaford, "1,000 Turn Out to Honor Slain Rights Workers."
49. "Plans Progressing for June Observance," 1A.
50. Quoted in Rejebian, "'We Wish We Could Bring Them Back,' Molpus Says."
51. Molpus, "Dick Molpus."

52. Molpus, "Dick Molpus." Molpus's remarks epitomize what some scholars refer to as conversion narratives—telling stories that reflect changes in perception or worldview. For works on conversion narratives, see Somers and Block, "From Poverty to Perversity"; Eviatar Zerubavel, *Time Maps*, 19. On southern conversation narratives, see Hobson, *But Now I See*.

53. Dick Molpus, interview with author, July 14, 2009.
54. Dearman interview with author, March 21, 2013.
55. Interview with author, July 14, 2009.
56. Nash and Taggert, *Mississippi Politics*.

57. Pair, "Memorial Service Marks 30th Anniversary of 1964 Murders"; "The Chaney Goodman Schwerner Memorial Coalition," folder 2, box 3, Andrew Goodman Memorial Collection, Schomburg Center for Research in Black Culture, New York.

58. Dearman, "June 21, 1964."
59. Olick, "Genre Memories and Memory Genres."
60. Gill, "Mississippi Justice at Last"; Romano, "Narratives of Redemption."
61. Ball, *Justice in Mississippi*.
62. Interview with author, May 15, 2013.
63. Interview with author, April 9, 2013.
64. Dearman, "Dr. Carolyn Goodman."
65. Prince interview with author, April 9, 2013.
66. Interview with author, May 15, 2013.

67. These individual awakenings represent the first stage of silence breaking outlined by Ken Plummer in his sociology of storytelling (*Telling Sexual Stories*).

68. Again, ESA encouraged me to consider the proximate causes of the collaboration between Clemons and Prince (that is, their meeting in front of City Hall) as well as more deeply rooted structural factors such as school desegregation.

69. Interview with author, May 15, 2013.
70. Interview with author, May 15, 2013 (emphasis added).
71. Interview with author, April 9, 2013.
72. Prince, "Task Force Sets Theme for 40th Anniversary."
73. Lawson, *One America in the Twenty-First Century*.
74. Nash and Taggert, *Mississippi Politics*, 144.
75. Interview with author, June 19, 2013.
76. Steve Wilkerson, interview with author, April 3, 2013.
77. Interview with author, March 22, 2013.
78. Prince, "Why Stir Up the Past?"
79. Prince, "Why Stir Up the Past?"
80. Quoted in Ladd, "I Felt the Earth Move."
81. Olick, "Genre Memories and Memory Genres."
82. Bell, "Brown v. Board of Education."
83. Carrier, *A Traveler's Guide to the Civil Rights Movement*; Dwyer and Alderman, *Civil Rights Memorials and the Geography of Memory*.

84. The city of Greensboro, North Carolina, enacted the first truth commission in 2004, but Mississippi's truth commission initiative, being statewide, would have

been substantially broader in scope had it come to fruition. After launching the public phase of the project, during which several hundred Mississippi citizens signed a declaration of intent, Winter Institute staff members put the South African–style commission on hold in favor of a moral localized oral history initiative. On the Greensboro Truth Commission, see Magarrell and Wesley, *Learning from Greensboro*; Cunningham, Nugent, and Slodden, "The Durability of Collective Memory"; Jovanovic, *Democracy, Dialogue, and Community Action*; Beitler, *Remaking Transitional Justice*; Inwood, "The Politics of Being Sorry"; and Ghoshal, "What Does Remembering Racial Violence Do?"

Chapter Three

1. On precursors to the Killen trial, see Romano, *Racial Reckoning*; Vollers, *Ghosts of Mississippi*.
2. Ball, *Murder in Mississippi*, 133.
3. Quoted in Ball, *Murder in Mississippi*, 136.
4. Minor, "Neshoba Event 'Nothing Short of a Miracle.'"
5. Mitchell, "Crimes of the Past."
6. Quoted in Mitchell, "Crimes of the Past."
7. Quoted in Mitchell, "Crimes of the Past."
8. Mary Winstead, author of *Back to Mississippi: A Personal Journey Through the Events That Changed America in 1964*, quoted in Ball, *Murder in Mississippi*, 37.
9. Cagin and Dray, *We Are Not Afraid*, xiii.
10. Mitchell, "44 Days."
11. Quoted in Mitchell, "'64 Killings Probe Nears End."
12. Quoted in Stout, "Cecil Price."
13. Tusa and Tusa, *The Nuremberg Trial*; Rosen, "The Influence of the Nuremberg Trial on International Criminal Law."
14. Noack, "U.S. Deports 95-Year-Old Nazi Guard Jakiw Palij"; Gray and Shuster, "How the Last Surviving Nazis Could Be Brought to Justice."
15. Gray and Shuster, "How the Last Surviving Nazis Could Be Brought to Justice."
16. Govan, "Spanish Civil War Crimes Investigation Launched"; Agence France-Presse, "Spanish Doctor Stands Trial Over Franco-Era 'Stolen Babies.'"
17. Madeleine Davis, "Is Spain Recovering Its Memory?"
18. Mitchell, "Congress Opens Doors for More Civil Rights Cold Cases."
19. See Romano, *Racial Reckoning*.
20. Romano's *Racial Reckoning* is an important exception.
21. Gill, "Mississippi Justice at Last," 26.
22. For instance, Mitchell persuaded Klansman Billy Roy Pitts to testify against Bowers, who had orchestrated the 1966 firebombing of civil rights leader Vernon Dahmer. This time, Bowers was convicted and died behind bars at the age of eighty-two. In another example, Myrlie Evers, the widow of Medgar Evers, had the only surviving copy of the 1964 trial transcript. This was ultimately used in the 1998 Beckwith trial, which resulted in his conviction for the murder. See Gill, "Mississippi Justice at Last."

23. Treen, "Southern Man."
24. Romano, *Racial Reckoning*, 98–100.
25. Shaffer, "From Exclusion to Inclusion," 15.
26. "Mississippians Divided on Most Public Issues."
27. Romano, *Racial Reckoning*, 231.
28. Mitchell, "Almost Half in Neshoba Survey Favored Trial in '64 Killings."
29. Cobb, *The Selling of the South*, 122. See also Fleischmann, "Urbanization of the South."
30. Dearman interview with author, March 21, 2013.
31. Schuman, Steeh, and Bobo, *Racial Attitudes in America*; Griffin and Hargis, "The Past in Black and White"; Harris, "Collective Memory, Collective Action."
32. Interview with author, September 18, 2013.
33. Glisson interview with author, September 18, 2013.
34. Philadelphia Coalition member journal, May 3, 2004.
35. Tsutsui, "The Trajectory of Perpetrators' Trauma."
36. Philadelphia Coalition member journal, May 25, 2004.
37. Philadelphia Coalition member journal, May 11, 2004.
38. For video of coalition members reading the resolution, see "The Philadelphia Coalition."
39. Ladd, "Haley's Choice."
40. Ladd, "Haley's Choice."
41. Interview with author, April 10, 2013.
42. Distilling the "event structure" of this particular historical sequence required me to research the legal prerequisites for initiating such a case in Mississippi. In doing so, I learned that the Neshoba County district attorney had to be involved as well as the attorney general, which helped explain why the Philadelphia Coalition cochairs reached out to both the district attorney and attorney general and further clarified the event structure analysis of the Killen trial.
43. Quoted in Salter, "Sunday Morning with Mark Duncan."
44. Quoted in Salter, "Sunday Morning with Mark Duncan."
45. Winter Institute, "Neshoba County."
46. Winter Institute, "Neshoba County."
47. Dearman, "June 21, 1964: It's Time for an Accounting."
48. Prince interview with author, April 9, 2013.
49. Interview with author, June 30, 2013.
50. "The Philadelphia Coalition."
51. Vinitzky-Seroussi, "Commemorating a Difficult Past"; Somers, "What's Political or Cultural about Political Culture and the Public Sphere?"
52. *United States v. Price*, 383 U.S. 787 (1966).
53. Olick, "Genre Memories and Memory Genres," 383.
54. Eviatar Zerubavel, *Time Maps*, 326.
55. Olick, "Genre Memories and Memory Genres," 393.
56. On mnemonic capacity, see Elizabeth Armstrong and Crage, "Movements and Memory."

57. Romano, *Racial Reckoning*, 2–3. David Cunningham makes a similar argument in *Klansville, U.S.A.*, 226–31.

Chapter Four

1. Silver, "History Changes More Slowly than State." Six months before Silver's 1975 review of Richard McLemore's two-volume *A History of Mississippi*, the Harvard historian David Herbert Donald, reviewing the McLemore text in the *American Historical Review*, described it as having been written for white Mississippians, containing little material on the experience of black Mississippians, and having no index entry for "lynching." See Eagles, *Civil Rights, Culture Wars*.
2. Silver, *Mississippi*.
3. Quoted in Epstein, "Two Southern Liberals," 64.
4. Pinar, "Notes on Understanding Curriculum as a Racial Text," 60. On the concept of the "hidden curriculum" in schools, see Jackson, *Life in Classrooms*; and Giroux and Purpel, *The Hidden Curriculum and Moral Education*.
5. Bolton, *The Hardest Deal of All*; Eagles, *Civil Rights, Culture Wars*.
6. At the time of this writing, Mississippi remains the only state to have done so.
7. SB 2718, article 1.
8. Bolton, *The Hardest Deal of All*, 7.
9. Bolton, *The Hardest Deal of All*, 34.
10. Bolton, *The Hardest Deal of All*, xvii.
11. Bolton, *The Hardest Deal of All*, 61.
12. Some private academies were established by the councils and required that teachers sign a contract that included the statement that "forced congregation of persons in social situations solely because they are of different races is a moral wrong, and . . . the proven educational results of such forced interracial congregation are disastrous for children of both the white and black races" (quoted in Bolton, *The Hardest Deal of All*, 175).
13. Cannon, "Black Monday."
14. Bolton, "The Last Stand of Massive Resistance."
15. Frankenberg and Lee, "Race in American Public Schools."
16. Rebecca Miller Davis, "The Three R's," 6. See also Eagles, *Civil Rights, Culture Wars*, 53.
17. Eagles, *Civil Rights, Culture Wars*, 6.
18. Rebecca Miller Davis, "The Three R's," 9. In one notable example, the 1975 version of the Bettersworth text ignored the contemporary historiography on slavery, arguing that slavery was so expensive that "planters often neglected their own families to care for their costly slaves" (Bettersworth, *Your Mississippi*, 184). Such distortions were not uncommon in textbooks across the Deep South. The sociologist, historian, and Mississippi textbook author James Loewen contends that southern states continued to write "white history" despite changes in historiography. "For years," argued Loewen, "any textbook sold in Dixie had to call the Civil War 'the War Between the States'" or even the more pro-Confederate term "'the War for

Southern Independence'" (*Lies My Teacher Told Me*, 280). This terminology persisted not only as a result of prevailing ideological positions, but also because of the calculus of textbook publishers that were convinced that changing this terminology would render their products unmarketable.

19. Quoted in Rebecca Miller Davis, "The Three R's," 9.
20. Eagles, *Civil Rights, Culture Wars*.
21. Eagles, *Civil Rights, Culture Wars*. See also Loewen and Sallis, *Mississippi: Conflict and Change*.
22. Eagles notes that twenty of the state's seventy-two school districts adopted the text, but eleven of those also adopted at least one other book, and the text had the strongest appeal in black counties of the Mississippi Delta and nearby towns (*Civil Rights, Culture Wars*, 229). See also Wendell Rawls, "Court Bars Rejection of Textbooks for Racial Reasons."
23. Eagles, *Civil Rights, Culture Wars*, 229.
24. Rebecca Miller Davis, "The Three R's," 33–34.
25. Since the mid-1990s, Holocaust education programs have become more common across the United States, including state-legislated programs like that in Mississippi. See Brabham, "Holocaust Education"; Fallace, "The Origins of Holocaust Education in American Public Schools."
26. HB 1269, 1.
27. Associated Press, "Creation of Holocaust Commission Stirs Debate on Miss. Racial Past." See also Julie Goodman, "Holocaust Bill Challenged, Passed in House."
28. Interview with author, October 18, 2016.
29. Fallace, "The Origins of Holocaust Education in American Public Schools," 81.
30. States that had passed laws requiring or encouraging the education of the Holocaust in the curriculum as of 2005 include Alabama, California, Connecticut, Georgia, Florida, Illinois, Massachusetts, Mississippi, Nevada, New Jersey, New York, North Carolina, Rhode Island, South Carolina, Tennessee, Washington, and West Virginia. See Weeden, "State Policies Concerning Holocaust Education"; Butterfly Project, "New Campaign Seeks to Mandate Holocaust Education in All 50 States."
31. There are very few Jewish organizations in Mississippi. In 2001, only 1,500 of the 2,849,000 Mississippi residents were Jewish. See Nussbaum and Rockoff, "Mississippi."
32. Kucia, "The Europeanization of Holocaust Memory and Eastern Europe"; Misco, "Holocaust Curriculum Development for Latvian Schools."
33. Carlson, "Constructing the Margins," 414.
34. Ghoshal, "Transforming Collective Memory," 333.
35. Interview with author, June 30, 2013.
36. Quoted in Byrd, "Facing Neshoba's Dark Past." DS9.
37. Quoted in Byrd, "Facing Neshoba's Dark Past." DS9.
38. Interview with author, April 22, 2013.
39. Interview with author, April 22, 2013.
40. Interview with author, April 22, 2013.

41. Clemons interview with author, May 15, 2013.
42. Prince, "Cracks in the Coalition."
43. Menkart, Murray, and View, *Putting the Movement Back into Civil Rights Teaching*.
44. Vogler, "Comparing the Impact of Accountability Examinations."
45. Interview with author, April 22, 2013.
46. Hollowell, "Mississippi Learning."
47. Ladd, "Civil Rights Education Summit in Neshoba County."
48. Hampton, "David Hampton."
49. Hampton, "David Hampton" (emphasis added), G1.
50. Glisson interview with author, June 30, 2013.
51. Clemons interview with author, May 15, 2013.
52. SB 2718, Article 1.
53. Tollison interview with author, June 23, 2013. Tollison's support for the bill is somewhat puzzling, since he switched to the Republican party shortly after the bill's passage and tends to be cautious of programs that, in his own words, get "stuck in the past." Tollison's uncharacteristic support for the education bill thus further demonstrates the unique political opening generated by the Killen trial.
54. Pinney and Serra, "A Voice for Black Interests."
55. Shaffer and Menifield, "Representation of African Americans."
56. Vinitzky-Seroussi and Teeger, "Unpacking the Unspoken," quoted in Schudson, "Dynamic Distortion of Collective Memory," 354–55.
57. Southern Poverty Law Center, "Teaching the Movement," 13.
58. David Cunningham and Rondini, "Legacies of Racial Contention."
59. See David Cunningham and Rondini, "Legacies of Racial Contention."
60. Benavot and Resh, "Educational Governance, School Autonomy, and Curriculum Implementation"; Rodríguez-Gómez, Foulds, and Sayed, "Representations of Violence in Social Science Textbooks"; Chisholm, "The Making of South Africa's National Curriculum Statement"; Freedman, Weinstein, Murphy, and Longman, "Teaching History after Identity-Based Conflicts."
61. Mississippi Department of Education, *Mississippi Subject Area Testing Program*.

Chapter Five

1. Hayner, *Unspeakable Truths*; Bakiner, *Truth Commissions*.
2. Sara Parker, "All Aboard the Truth Bandwagon."
3. Organizers used the terms "Mississippi Truth Commission" and "Mississippi Truth Project" interchangeably until 2009, after which the Mississippi Truth Project encompassed a trio of truth-seeking initiatives that included civil rights curricular development, the Welcome Table community retreats (discussed below), and an oral history project that was the outgrowth of the aborted truth commission. So while no Mississippi truth commission ultimately came to fruition, a range of truth-seeking initiatives did occur under the "Mississippi Truth Project" umbrella.
4. Interview with author, October 18, 2016.

5. Hayner, *Unspeakable Truths*, 11.

6. Bickford, "Unofficial Truth Projects."

7. Grandin, "The Instruction of Great Catastrophe," 46. Which truth commission ought to receive the distinction of being the first remains a subject of debate. Some scholars and transitional justice practitioners cite a commission in Uganda established by President Idi Amin in 1974 as the first truth commission. While this commission included many elements common to more contemporary truth commissions, such as operating under the same government under investigation, gathering victims' testimony in public, documenting human rights abuses, and publishing a final report, some argue that it was not a genuine effort to improve the country's human rights climate. See Hayner, *Unspeakable Truths*; Carver, "Called to Account." For comprehensive lists of truth commissions, see Bakiner, *Truth Commissions*, 27–29.

8. The TRC received a critical reception from domestic audiences but was largely lauded by the international community. See Mamdani, "Amnesty or Impunity?"

9. Bakiner, *Truth Commissions*, 53.

10. Hayner, *Unspeakable Truths*; Bakiner, *Truth Commissions*; Buckley-Zistel, "Narrative Truths."

11. Gibson, "Overcoming Apartheid"; Hirsch, MacKenzie, and Sesay, "Measuring the Impacts of Truth and Reconciliation Commissions"; Brahm, "Uncovering the Truth"; Tanya Goodman, *Staging Solidarity*.

12. In addition to Canada and South Korea, truth commissions have appeared in such consolidated democracies as Brazil, Canada, Ghana, Grenada, Mauritius, Panama, Paraguay, the Solomon Islands, and South Korea.

13. Nagy, "The Scope and Bounds of Transitional Justice."

14. Kim, "Local, National, and International Determinants of Truth Commissions."

15. Wells, *The Red Record*. Thanks to Geoff Ward for bringing this to my attention.

16. Olick, *The Politics of Regret*.

17. Miller, "Wartime Internment of Japanese"; Yamamoto, *Interracial Justice*, 53.

18. Magarrell and Gutierrez, "Lessons in Truth-Seeking."

19. Schreiner, "Senate Expresses Regret for 1898 Riot."

20. See Bickford, "Unofficial Truth Projects"; Bakiner, *Truth Commissions*.

21. Magarrell and Wesley, *Learning from Greensboro*.

22. Inwood, "Dealing with Hate."

23. Bermanzohn, *Through Survivors' Eyes*; Magarrell and Wesley, *Learning from Greensboro*; Beitler, *Remaking Transitional Justice*; David Cunningham, Nugent, and Slodden, "The Durability of Collective Memory"; Ghoshal, "What Does Remembering Racial Violence Do?"; Jovanovic, *Democracy, Dialogue, and Community Action*.

24. For video of coalition members reading the resolution, see "The Philadelphia Coalition."

25. Quoted in Glisson, "The Sum of Its Parts," 194.

26. Quoted in Ladd, "After Killen."

27. Bender, "Open Letter to Haley Barbour."

28. Taylor, "Social Movement Continuity."

29. Glisson, "The Sum of Its Parts"; "Mississippi Coalition Calls for New Vision for the State."

30. Bullard, *Race, Place, and Environmental Justice After Hurricane Katrina*; Levitt and Whitaker, *Hurricane Katrina*; Somers, "Genealogies of Katrina."

31. Molina interview with author, May 14, 2013.

32. "Mississippi Coalition Calls for New Vision for the State."

33. Glisson, "The Sum of Its Parts."

34. Quoted in Straight, "West Point Leaders Seek to Improve Race Relations through Dialogue."

35. Martin interview with author, October 14, 2016.

36. Glisson, "The Sum of Its Parts," 195.

37. Weems, "Institute Helps Kick Off Year of Dialogue on Race."

38. Exploratory meetings were held in Jackson in December, February, and April; in Philadelphia in March; and in Greenville in April.

39. Weems, "Mississippi Truth Project Leads the Charge in Confronting the Past."

40. For information on the final report, see Magarrell and Wesley, *Learning from Greensboro*.

41. Julie Armstrong, "Regional Alliance Formed to Repair Legacy of Racial Violence"; Magarrell and Wesley, *Learning from Greensboro*, 142. See also Regional Alliance for Truth and Racial Reconciliation, "ATRR Organization."

42. Quoted in Lex Alexander, "TRC's Effects on City Praised," B1.

43. David Cunningham, Nugent, and Slodden, "The Durability of Collective Memory"; Inwood, "The Politics of Being Sorry."

44. Androff, "Can Civil Society Reclaim Truth?"

45. Ghoshal, "What Does Remembering Racial Violence Do?"

46. Glisson, "The Sum of Its Parts," 195–96.

47. Quoted in Younge, "New Generation of Americans Tries Truth and Reconciliation."

48. Magarrell and Gutierrez, "Lessons in Truth-Seeking."

49. Since its inception, members of the Mississippi Truth Project have met in Lima, Peru; Bellagio, Italy; Freetown, Sierra Leone; Rabat, Morocco; Asuncion, Paraguay; Jakarta, Indonesia; New Haven, Connecticut; and Monrovia, Liberia, to discuss best practices for truth commissions. See Magarrell and Gutierrez, "Lessons in Truth-Seeking."

50. Interview with author, October 17, 2016.

51. Interview with author, October 16, 2016.

52. Interview with author, October 16, 2016.

53. Interview with author, October 17, 2016.

54. Snow and Benford, "Ideology, Frame Resonance, and Participant Mobilization," 198.

55. "Draft of Declaration," in possession of author. See also Winter Institute, "Declaration of Intent Meeting."

56. Snow and Benford, "Ideology, Frame Resonance, and Participant Mobilization."

57. Winter Institute, "Declaration of Intent Meeting."
58. Winter Institute, "Declaration of Intent Meeting."
59. Winter Institute, "Declaration of Intent Meeting."
60. Somers, "The Narrative Constitution of Identity."
61. Winter Institute, "Declaration of Intent Meeting" (emphasis added).
62. Winter Institute, "Declaration of Intent Meeting."
63. Interview with author, October 16, 2016.
64. Tucker, "Mississippi Truth Project Enters New Phase."
65. Harbin interview with author, October 16, 2016.
66. Tucker, "Mississippi Truth Project Enters New Phase."
67. Molina interview with author May 14, 2013.
68. I attended that conference with support from the Weiser Center for Emerging Democracies and a Bodine Grant from the Department of Sociology at the University of Michigan. The conference was the same year as the United Nations' International Year of Reconciliation in 2009.
69. Glisson, "The Sum of Its Parts," 5; see also Tucker, "Mississippi Truth Project Enters New Phase."
70. Grayson interview with author, October 16, 2016.
71. Grayson interview with author, October 16, 2016.
72. Martin interview with author, October 14, 2016.
73. Brandeis University's collaboration with the Mississippi Truth Project included students in David Cunningham's Applied Research Methods class in 2009 and a "Justice Brandeis Semester," in which Brandeis students worked with community members to conduct archival research in Mississippi during the summer of 2011. See David Cunningham, "Method of Truth and Reconciliation."
74. Glisson, "The Sum of Its Parts," 192.
75. Glisson, "The Sum of Its Parts," 201.
76. Here, I draw on the ideas of Onur Bakiner on incomplete truth commissions (*Truth Commissions*, 30).
77. Tucker interview with author, June 29, 2010.
78. Ignatieff, "Articles of Faith," 113.
79. Labuda, "Racial Reconciliation in Mississippi," 21.
80. Glisson, "The Sum of Its Parts," 194.
81. Elster, "Coming to Terms with the Past"; Dancy and Poe, "What Comes before Truth?"
82. Meyer, "World Society, Institutional Theories, and the Actor."

Chapter Six

1. Winter Institute, "Neshoba County: Philadelphia Coalition After Party—Ta'shia."
2. Winter Institute, "Neshoba County: Philadelphia Coalition After Party—Deborah."
3. Waddell, "Philadelphia Coalition After Party."
4. Prince, "Historian Sees Coalition's Efforts as a Model for the State."

5. Wilkerson, "Steve Wilkerson," 14.

6. In this respect, the 1989 commemoration serves as a negative case. Given the remarkable similarities between the 1989 and 2004 commemorations, it is reasonable to assume that the 1989 commemoration could have facilitated racially significant institutional transformations but did not.

7. For helpful reviews on the intersection between memory and movements, see Zamponi, "Collective Memory and Social Movements"; Kubal and Becerra, "Social Movements and Collective Memory"; and Eyerman, "Social Movements and Memory." See also Gongaware, "Collective Memory Anchors."

8. Gongaware, "Collective Memory Anchors"; Daphi, *Becoming a Movement.*

9. In addition to research by Elizabeth Armstrong and Suzanna Crage that includes the concept of "mnemonic capacity" ("Movements and Memory," 726) and Raj Ghoshal ("Transforming Collective Memory"), Timothy Kubal examines the success of memory mobilization by studying four types of movements—patriotic, religious, ethnic, and anticolonial—as they attempt to shape memories of Christopher Columbus. He adopts a political process frame suggesting that memory movements are more successful when political opportunities are advantageous, resources are ample, and communication is effective—factors that are largely encompassed by Armstrong and Crage's "mnemonic capacity." See Kubal, *Cultural Movements and Collective Memory.*

10. Irwin-Zarecka, *Frames of Remembrance.*

11. Armstrong and Crage, "Movements and Memory," 725.

12. Ghoshal, "Transforming Collective Memory," 332.

13. Ghoshal, "Transforming Collective Memory," 341. See also Jansen, "Resurrection and Appropriation."

14. Ghoshal, "Transforming Collective Memory," 336.

15. Ghoshal, "Transforming Collective Memory."

16. Mill, *A System of Logic.*

17. Olick, "Genre Memories and Memory Genres."

18. Simon and Garfunkel, "He Was My Brother."

19. Mars, *Witness in Philadelphia,* 84.

20. Interview with author, April 3, 2013.

21. Harter, Stephens, and Japp, "President Clinton's Apology for the Tuskegee Syphilis Experiment"; Lawson, *One America in the Twenty-First Century*; Pickett, "'We Were All Prisoners of the System.'"

22. Kubal and Becerra, "Social Movements and Collective Memory"; Kubal, *Cultural Movements and Collective Memory.*

23. Key, *Southern Politics in State and Nation.*

24. Interview with author, April 3, 2013.

25. Interview with author, April 3, 2013.

26. Boyer, "The Yuppies of Mississippi."

27. Boyer, "The Yuppies of Mississippi."

28. Quoted in Boyer, "The Yuppies of Mississippi," SM8.

29. Mabus, "Ray Mabus." See also Gammage, "Freedom Summer: Two Montco Remembers Mississippi."

30. Ladd, "Haley's Choice."
31. Associated Press, "Bush Declares Three Killed in State Are 'Heroes.'"
32. Lauter, "Rights Martyrs' Relatives Speak Bluntly to Bush."
33. Associated Press, "Bush Declares Three Killed in State Are 'Heroes.'"
34. "Cochran and Lott: Sign on Now."
35. Snow and Benford, "Ideology, Frame Resonance, and Participant Mobilization."
36. Kubal, *Cultural Movements and Collective Memory*.
37. Naqvi, "The Right to the Truth in International Law." See also Savelsberg and King, *American Memories*; Curtis, *Mass Atrocity, Collective Memory, and the Law*.
38. Jeffrey Alexander et al., *Cultural Trauma and Collective Identity*; Till, "Wounded Cities"; DeGloma, "Expanding Trauma through Space and Time."
39. Rotberg and Thompson, *Truth v. Justice*; Shore, *Religion and Conflict Resolution*. See also Klein, "On the Emergence of Memory in Historical Discourse," 145.
40. McCammon, "Resonance, Frame," 1092.
41. Interview with author, April 13, 2013.
42. Quoted in Blake, "From Philly to Philly," 05.
43. Quoted in Barrientos, "Caravan of Buses Going to Miss. to Honor 3 Slain in '64," A05.
44. Similar accusations of tokenism were made in 2004, but they came largely from individuals who lived outside Philadelphia.
45. Winter Institute, "Neshoba County—Interview with Nettie Ann Cox."
46. Interview with author, April 9, 2013.
47. Pedriana, "From Protective to Equal Treatment."
48. McIntyre, *Law in the Sociological Enterprise*, 118.
49. Conway, *Commemoration and Bloody Sunday*, 149.
50. Spillman, "When Do Collective Memories Last?"
51. Wagner-Pacifici and Schwartz, "The Vietnam Veterans Memorial."
52. Prince interview with author, April 9, 2013.
53. Clemons interview with author, May 15, 2013.
54. Barkan, *The Guilt of Nations*, ix. See also Nobles, *The Politics of Official Apologies*; Dancy, Kim, and Wiebelhaus-Brahm, "The Turn to Truth"; Hayner, *Unspeakable Truths*; Naqvi, "The Right to the Truth in International Law."
55. Teitel, "Transitional Justice Globalized."
56. Teitel, "Transitional Justice Globalized," 1. See also Hirsch, "And the Truth Shall Make You Free"; Krüger, "From Truth to Reconciliation."
57. Ryle, "A Sorry Apology from Clinton."
58. Henry, *Long Overdue*.
59. Mannheim, "The Problems of Generations"; Corning and Schuman, *Generations and Collective Memory*.
60. Corning and Schuman, *Generations and Collective Memory*; Schuman and Scott, "Generations and Collective Memory"; Griffin, "Generations and Collective Memory Revisited."
61. Schuman, Steeh, and Bobo, *Racial Attitudes in America*; Gibson, "Does Truth Lead to Reconciliation?"; Griffin and Bollen, "What Do These Memories Do?"

62. Fredrick Harris, "Collective Memory, Collective Action" and "It Takes a Tragedy to Arouse Them."

63. Schuman, Steeh, and Bobo, *Racial Attitudes in America*; Firebaugh and Davis, "Trends in Antiblack Prejudice."

64. Griffin and Hargis, "Still Distinctive after All These Years," 118.

65. "A Different Neshoba County."

66. Quoted in Salter, "Sunday Morning with Sid Salter."

67. Boyer, "The Yuppies of Mississippi."

68. Quoted in Boyer, "The Yuppies of Mississippi," SM8.

69. Andrews, *Freedom Is a Constant Struggle*.

70. Taylor, "Social Movement Continuity"; Klandermans, *The Social Psychology of Protest*.

71. Interview with author, May 15, 2013.

72. Klandermans, *The Social Psychology of Protest*.

73. Interview with author, March 25, 2013.

74. Interview with author, April 3, 2013.

75. Interview with author, June 24, 2014.

76. Interview with author, April 15, 2013.

77. Kirskey interview with author, March 25, 2013.

78. Klandermans, *The Social Psychology of Protest*. See also Jasper, "Emotions and Social Movements."

79. Taylor, "Social Movement Continuity"; Nepstad, "Persistent Resistance."

80. Taylor, "Social Movement Continuity."

81. Interview with author, March 25, 2013.

82. Interview with author, June 24, 2014.

83. Winter Institute, "Neshoba County: Philadelphia Coalition after Party—Susan Glisson" (emphasis added). The quotation is from Berry, *The Wild Birds*, 136.

84. Barkan, *The Guilt of Nations*; Torpey, *Politics and the Past*; Olick, *The Politics of Regret*.

Chapter Seven

1. Sue, *Race Talk and the Conspiracy of Silence*; DiAngelo, "White Fragility"; Oluo, "So You Want to Talk about Race."

2. Massey and Denton, *American Apartheid*; Charles, "The Dynamics of Racial Residential Segregation."

3. See May, "Race Talk and Local Collective Memory."

4. Griffin and Hargis, "The Past in Black and White."

5. Griffin and Hargis, "The Past in Black and White."

6. Griffin and Bollen, "What Do These Memories Do?"

7. Schuman and Rieger, "Historical Analogies."

8. Goodwin, Jasper, and Polletta, "The Return of the Repressed," 65.

9. Jasper, *The Emotions of Protest*, 87.

10. Fredrick Harris, "It Takes a Tragedy to Arouse Them."

11. Hochschild, "Emotion Work, Feeling Rules, and Social Structure," 551.

12. Goodwin and Pfaff, "Emotion Work in High-Risk Social Movements"; Taylor, "Social Movement Continuity."

13. Wright and Baray, "Models of Social Change in Social Psychology"; Subašić, Reynolds, and Turner, "The Political Solidarity Model of Social Change."

14. Allport, *The Nature of Prejudice*. See also Pettigrew and Tropp, "A Meta-Analytic Test of Intergroup Contact Theory."

15. Pettigrew, "Intergroup Contact Theory," 76. See also Allport, *The Nature of Prejudice*. In Allport's initial formulation, "cooperation" and "common goals" are listed as two separate conditions. For the sake of simplicity, I have combined those two factors.

16. Crisp, Stathi, Turner, and Husnu, "Imagined Intergroup Contact"; Pettigrew and Tropp, "A Meta-Analytic Test of Intergroup Contact Theory."

17. Jeffries and Ransford, "Interracial Social Contact."

18. However, others note the limitations of out-group learning, suggesting that learning only alters stereotypes if "(a) the outgroup's behavior is starkly inconsistent with their stereotype and strongly associated with their label, (b) occurs often and in many situations, and (c) the outgroup members are seen as typical" (Pettigrew, "Intergroup Contact Theory," 71). So while out-group learning is significant, it is probably insufficient to transform attitudes in isolation from other processes.

19. Kenworthy, Turner, Hewstone, and Voci, "Intergroup Contact," 287.

20. Kenworthy, Turner, Hewstone, and Voci, "Intergroup Contact," 287.

21. See Gibson and Claassen, "Racial Reconciliation in South Africa."

22. In some cases, in-group reappraisal can cause individuals to distance themselves from their own social group. A 2010 survey of native Dutch people found that contact with members of ethnic minority groups generated critical self-awareness of in-group values, beliefs, and customs and a more pluralist, rather than in-group-centric, perspective. See Verkuyten, Thijs, and Bekhuis, "Intergroup Contact and Ingroup Reappraisal."

23. Taylor and Whittier, "Collective Identity in Social Movement Communities"; Klandermans, *The Social Psychology of Protest*; Snow and McAdam, "Identity Work Processes in the Context of Social Movements"; Polletta and Jasper, "Collective Identity and Social Movements"; Hunt and Benford, "Collective Identity, Solidarity, and Commitment."

24. Taylor and Whittier, "Collective Identity in Social Movement Communities"; Downton and Wehr, "Persistent Pacifism"; Nepstad, "Persistent Resistance."

25. Taylor and Whittier, "Collective Identity in Social Movement Communities"; Hunt, Benford, and Snow, "Identity Fields"; Mansbridge, "The Making of Oppositional Consciousness."

26. Klandermans, *The Social Psychology of Protest*; Hunt and Benford, "Collective Identity, Solidarity, and Commitment."

27. Nepstad, "Creating Transnational Solidarity"; Jacobs, "The Narrative Integration of Personal and Collective Identity in Social Movements"; Polletta, *It Was Like a Fever*; Daphi, *Becoming a Movement*; Fernades, *Curated Stories*.

28. Polletta, *It Was Like a Fever*, 12.
29. Hunt and Benford, "Collective Identity, Solidarity, and Commitment"; Nepstad, "Commitment."
30. Jasper, *The Emotions of Protest*, 105.
31. DeGloma, "The Strategies of Mnemonic Battle."
32. Pettigrew and Tropp, "A Meta-Analytic Test of Intergroup Contact Theory."
33. Interview with author, June 20, 2014.
34. Demby, "I'm from Philly."
35. Interview with author, May 15, 2013.
36. Interview with author, May 15, 2013.
37. Glisson, "The Sum of Its Parts"; Pickett, "We Were All Prisoners of the System."
38. Interview with author, April 3, 2013.
39. Interview with author, April 9, 2013.
40. Interview with author, April 10, 2013.
41. Winter Institute, "Neshoba County: Philadelphia Coalition After Party—Elsie and Stan."
42. Interview with author, March 22, 2013.
43. Interview with author, April 3, 2013.
44. Interview with author, April 3, 2013.
45. Interview with author, April 10, 2013.
46. Quoted in Prince, "Community Leaders to Issue a Call for Justice in 1964 Civil Rights Slayings."
47. Interview with author, June 24, 2014.
48. Interview with author, May 15, 2013.
49. McCarthy and Zald, "Resource Mobilization and Social Movements"; Cress and Snow, "Mobilization at the Margins."
50. Pettigrew, "Intergroup Contact Theory."
51. Quoted in Boyer, "The Yuppies of Mississippi," SM8.
52. Ladd, "Haley's Choice."
53. Interview with author, May 15, 2013.
54. Interview with author, May 15, 2013.
55. Interview with author, March 22, 2013.
56. Sue, *Race Talk and the Conspiracy of Silence*. On rhetorical incoherence, see Bonilla-Silva, *Racism without Racists*.
57. Glisson, "Telling the Truth," 34.
58. Glisson, "Telling the Truth," 34.
59. Quoted in Glisson, "Telling the Truth," 35.
60. Glisson, "Telling the Truth," 36.
61. Interview with author, April 9, 2013.
62. Interview with author, June 24, 2014.
63. Interview with author, March 25, 2013.
64. Glisson, "Telling the Truth," 36.
65. Elizabeth Armstrong and Crage, "Movements and Memory," 726.
66. Andrews, *Freedom Is a Constant Struggle*.

67. Taylor, "Social Movement Continuity"; Taylor and Whittier, "Collective Identity in Social Movement Communities"; Klandermans, *The Social Psychology of Protest.*

68. Pettigrew, "Intergroup Contact Theory."

Chapter Eight

1. Raspberry, "A 'Sorry' Excuse from Cochran."
2. Raspberry, "A 'Sorry' Excuse from Cochran."
3. Ward, *Hanging Bridge.*
4. McCord, *Mississippi*; Morris, *Origins of the Civil Rights Movement*; Payne, *I've Got the Light of Freedom*; Andrews, *Freedom Is a Constant Struggle.*
5. Quoted in *Oxford Eagle* Staff, "David Crews' Book Quotes Famous Mississippians."
6. Ball, *Justice in Mississippi,* 31.
7. Morris, *Origins of the Civil Rights Movement.*
8. Bell, "Brown v. Board of Education." For a more recent reassessment and critique of the interest-convergence theory, see also Driver, "Rethinking the Interest-Convergence Thesis."
9. Eviatar Zerubavel, *Time Maps,* 26.
10. Raj Ghoshal develops the idea that mnemonic capacity is a feature of environments in "Transforming Collective Memory."
11. Bainbridge, "In 2005, MLK Day Finally Recognized in Greenville County."
12. Quoted in Jacoby, "A Mosque at Ground Zero?"
13. Vinitzky-Seroussi, *Yitzhak Rabin's Assassination,* 152. See also Vinizky-Seroussi's more recent work, "Banal Commemoration."
14. Harris, "It Takes a Tragedy to Arouse Them"; Jansen, "Resurrection and Appropriation."
15. Similarly, Kenneth Andrews's movement infrastructure model finds that the impacts of social movements are cumulative ("Social Movements and Policy Implementation").
16. Schudson, "The Present in the Past Versus the Past in the Present," 108.
17. Olick, "Genre Memories and Memory Genres," 383.
18. Ghoshal, "Transforming Collective Memory," 332. Here, I focus on the first of three components of Ghoshal's mnemonic opportunity structure: an environment's present commemorative capacity. The remaining two factors are a past incident's ascribed significance and moral valence at the time the event occurred.
19. Elizabeth Armstrong and Crage, "Movements and Memory," 727. See also Bourdieu, *Distinction*; Berezin, "Cultural Form and Political Meaning"; Jacobs, "Civil Society and Crisis."
20. To some extent, this reflects the distinction between "official" and "vernacular" memory that John Bodnar observes (*Remaking America,* 15). However, vernacular practices of public remembrance, which tend to have more ephemeral forms (such as parades and performances) and other temporary interventions are

beginning to resemble official practices of remembrance by taking on more permanent forms. As Ekaterina Haskins notes, "the line between official and vernacular memory practices . . . is becoming blurry, as designers, museum professionals and art critics begin to ponder how 'permanent' memorials might engage their popular audiences instead of imposing on them the ossified values of political and cultural elites" ("Between Archive and Participation," 403–4).

21. Durkheim, *The Elementary Forms of Religious Life*.

22. Challenging the Durkheimian connection between commemoration and unity inspired the seminal work of Robin Wagner-Pacifici and Barry Schwartz, "The Vietnam Veterans Memorial."

23. This insight comes from recent work on cultural pragmatics. See Jeffrey Alexander, Giesen, and Mast, *Social Performance*, 32; Jeffrey Alexander, "Cultural Pragmatics."

24. Vinitzky-Seroussi, "Commemorating a Difficult Past."

25. See Dessel and Rogge, "Evaluation of Intergroup Dialogue."

26. Winter Institute, "The Welcome Table."

27. Interview with author, April 9, 2013.

28. Interview with author, November 14, 2016.

29. Tell, *Remembering Emmett Till*.

30. Huie, "The Shocking Story of Approved Killing in Mississippi"; Devery Anderson, *Emmett Till*.

31. Tell, "Protecting the Memory of Emmett Till from the Scourge of Vandals."

32. Tell, "Protecting the Memory of Emmett Till from the Scourge of Vandals."

33. Tell, *Remembering Emmett Till*, back cover.

34. Tell, *Remembering Emmett Till*.

35. Gibson, "Does Truth Lead to Reconciliation?," 215. Gibson employed surveys to measure South Africans' attitudes about a variety of measures related to interracial reconciliation, support of human rights, political tolerance, and institutional legitimacy.

36. David Cunningham, Nugent, and Slodden, "The Durability of Collective Memory."

37. See, for example, Giugni, "Was It Worth the Effort?"; Guigni, McAdam, and Tilly, *How Social Movements Matter*; Andrews, "Social Movements and Policy Implementation"; Earl, "The Cultural Consequences of Social Movements."

38. On the labor of memory, see Jelin, *State Repression and the Labors of Memory*.

39. Eviatar Zerubavel, *Time Maps*, 25.

40. The Mississippi Civil Rights Museum and the Mississippi History Museum are parts of a two-museum collaboration called Two Mississippi Museums. Both museums opened on the same day—the state's bicentennial.

41. Ishee, "Civil Rights Leaders, President Trump Celebrate Opening of Two Mississippi Museums."

42. Mitchell, "Civil Rights, History Museums May Surpass Expected Attendance."

43. Interview with author, October 25, 2018.

44. Wolf, "Voting Rights Act."

Epilogue

1. Myers, "Vandals Hit Civil Rights Marker."
2. Amy, "Justice Quest Goes On after 'Freedom Summer' Court Cases End."
3. Brown, "First Black Mayor in City Known for Klan Killings"; McGreal, "Mississippi Town Breaks With Its Past to Elect First Black Mayor."
4. Field notes, June 14, 2014.
5. Field notes, June 14, 2014.
6. Hirschman, *The Rhetoric of Reaction*.
7. Myers, "Killen Ordered back to Prison."
8. Mohr, "High Court Rejects Appeal in 'Miss. Burning' Case."
9. Mohr, "High Court Rejects Appeal in 'Miss. Burning' Case."
10. Quoted in Mohr, "High Court Rejects Appeal in 'Miss. Burning' Case."
11. Elliott, "Elderly Convict Remains Right-lipped Slaying of Three-civil-rights Workers Sparked National Outrage in '60s"; Mitchell, "Klansman Who Orchestrated Mississippi Burning Killings Dies in Prison."
12. Quoted in Lantigua-Williams, "What Closing the 'Mississippi Burning' Case Means for Civil Rights."
13. Quoted in Reeves, "Seeking Justice, Backers Aim to Expand Emmett Till Act," 6A.
14. Romano, "Small Steps towards Truth."
15. Romano, "Small Steps towards Truth."
16. Quoted in Byrd, "Civil Rights Curriculum," A1.
17. David Cunningham and Rondini, "Legacies of Racial Contention."
18. David Cunningham and Rondini, "Legacies of Racial Contention," 329.
19. According to the Southern Poverty Law Center's 2011 report on civil rights education in the United States, only a dozen states—referred to as "local control" states—leave districts to set required content and frameworks ("Teaching the Movement").
20. Spears interview with author, June 19, 2013.
21. Mader, "Have Lessons about Mississippi's Violent Past Become Optional?"
22. Mannie, "Miss. Students Ignorant about Civil Rights Movement."
23. Field notes, June 16, 2014.
24. Quoted in Mader, "Have Lessons about Mississippi's Violent Past Become Optional?"
25. Southern Poverty Law Center, "Teaching the Movement 2014." The first report, published in 2011, was Southern Poverty Law Center, "Teaching the Movement."
26. Southern Poverty Law Center, "Teaching the Movement 2014," 9–10. Of the states in the South, three received an A (South Carolina, Louisiana, and Georgia, in order of their scores); four received a B (North Carolina, Alabama, Virginia, and Florida); and four received a C (Tennessee, Mississippi, Arkansas, and West Virginia). The remaining states earned a D or F, and Mississippi ranked ninth out of the twelve southern states.
27. Gates, "What Was the Civil Rights Movement?"

28. Southern Poverty Law Center, "Teaching the Movement 2014."
29. Interview with author, October 16, 2016.
30. Tucker, "Mississippi Truth Project Enters New Phase."
31. Ladd, "Love Thy Neighbor."
32. April Grayson, interview with author, October 16, 2016.
33. Straight, "West Point Leaders Seek to Improve Race Relations Through Dialogue."
34. Quoted in Straight, "West Point Leaders Seek to Improve Race Relations Through Dialogue."
35. Molina interview with author, May 14, 2013.
36. Molina interview with author, May 14, 2013.
37. McClendon, "Mitch Landrieu Launches Racial Reconciliation Dialogue with $1.2 Million Grant."
38. In the period April 2014–May 2015, the Winter Institute helped launch the Welcome Table New Orleans, facilitating dialogue circles across the city in which more than two hundred residents participated. A year later, Mitch Landrieu, the city's mayor, announced that the city would remove all four of its Confederate monuments, and while the Winter Institute maintains that it does not support any particular ideas or outcomes, in a *Washington Post* opinion piece, Landrieu attributed his decision to remove the monuments to the Welcome Table process ("Why I'm Taking down Confederate Monuments in New Orleans)". See also Ganucheau, "Winter Institute Helped New Orleans Address Confederate Monuments."
39. Borden, "South Carolina Debuts a New Model for Bridging Racial Divides"; Sexton, "A Journey toward Understanding."
40. Sexton, "A Journey toward Understanding."
41. Quoted in Sexton, "A Journey toward Understanding" (emphasis added).
42. Glisson, "The Sum of Its Parts."
43. Glisson interview with author, November 14, 2016.
44. Inwood, "Dealing with Hate."
45. Bialik, "5 Facts About Blacks in the U.S."
46. Quoted in Inwood, "Dealing with Hate."
47. Landsman, *Crimes of the Holocaust*.
48. Quoted in International Center for Transitional Justice, "Is the United States Ready for a Truth-Telling Process?"
49. International Center for Transitional Justice, "Is the United States Ready for a Truth-Telling Process?" Such organizations include the Black Women's Truth and Reconciliation Commission; Bridging the Divide; Universities Studying Slavery; the work at Georgetown, Harvardm and Brown Universities; Ferguson's Truth-Telling Project; Northeastern University Law School's Civil Rights and Restorative Justice Institute; Coming to the Table; the Equal Justice Initiative; Richmond's Initiatives of Change; the Kellogg Foundation's Truth, Racial Healing, Transformation Enterprise; and the Mass Slavery Apology. On Kellogg's initiative, see W. G. Kellogg Foundation, "Truth, Racial Healing, and Transformation."
50. "Neshoba Acknowledges '64 Murders."
51. Quoted in "Economic Impact of Commemoration Noted."

52. Loewe, "Civil Rights Tourism in Mississippi," 90.
53. Quoted in McBride, "Cry for Justice in Neshoba Driving Historic Cause."
54. Quoted in McBride, "Cry for Justice in Neshoba Driving Historic Cause."
55. Field notes, June 18, 2011.
56. Field notes, June 17, 2014.

Appendix A

1. Abbott, "From Causes to Events"; Sewell, "Historical Events as Transformations of Structures"; Mahoney, "Path Dependence in Historical Sociology"; Hess and Martin, "Repression, Backfire, and the Theory of Transformative Events"; Haydu, "Reversals of Fortune"; Wagner-Pacifici, "Theorizing the Restlessness of Events"; Berezin, "Events as Templates of Possibility"; Meyer and Kimeldorf, "Eventful Subjectivity."

2. Sewell, "Historical Events as Transformations of Structures," 843.

3. Abbott, *Time Matters*, 247. Eviatar Zerubavel also discusses such turning points in *Time Maps*.

4. Wagner-Pacifici, "Theorizing the Restlessness of Events"; Berezin, "Events as Templates of Possibility"; Meyer and Kimeldorf, "Eventful Subjectivity."

5. The legitimacy of counterfactual claims also depends on one's understanding of causality. Counterfactuals, according to James Fearon, search for "conceivable causes" based on "factors that could actually have been different according to the best of our knowledge about how the social and physical worlds work" ("Causes and Counterfactuals in Social Science," 41). This is similar to what other social scientists have described as causal narrativity, "a reclaimed notion of causality based on narrativity, sequence, and contingency rather than universality and predictive law." In this sense, causality is not a covering law, but a "historically intelligible explanation." Somers, "Where Is Sociology after the Historic Turn?," 68).

6. Amenta, "Making the Most of a Historical Case Study."

7. See Heise, "Event Structure Analysis," for more information, including the software's default conditions. The software presumes that each action is "used up" by another action when the second action occurs. I chose to override this condition, considering that the murders had multiple direct and indirect results. See also Heise, "Modeling Event Structures"; Griffin, "Narrative, Event-Structure Analysis, and Causal Interpretation in Historical Sociology."

8. Isaac, Street, and Knapp, "Analyzing Historical Contingency with Formal Methods," 118.

9. Elster, *Logic and Society*.

10. Griffin, "Narrative, Event-Structure Analysis, and Causal Interpretation in Historical Sociology," 1102.

11. For the sake of readability, the event structure diagrams have been excluded from the primary text. For additional examples of my use of ESA, see Whitlinger, "From Countermemory to Collective Memory" and "From Commemoration to Conviction."

12. Mahoney and Rueschemeyer, "Comparative Historical Analysis."

13. Potter and Romano, *Doing Recent History*.
14. Alexander, "Towards a Theory of Cultural Trauma."
15. NewsBank, Access World News.
16. Jensen, "New Media, Old Methods."
17. Olick, "Collective Memory."
18. Alford Young, for instance, notes that biases and shortcomings associated with a researcher's outsider status can be overcome or managed "by the researcher's explicit acknowledgment of the existence of social distance or categorical dissimilarities between him or her and the individuals under study" ("Experiences in Ethnographic Interviewing about Race," 98). Young also challenges the prevailing notion that occupying an outsider position necessarily hinders a researcher from acquiring rich qualitative data.
19. Reinharz, "Who Am I? The Need for a Variety of Selves in the Field."
20. Emerson, Fretz, and Shaw, *Writing Ethnographic Fieldnotes*.
21. Fine, "The When of Theory," 82.
22. Rueschemeyer, "Can One or a Few Cases Yield Theoretical Gains?"
23. Rueschemeyer, "Can One or a Few Cases Yield Theoretical Gains?," 322.
24. Rueschemeyer, "Can One or a Few Cases Yield Theoretical Gains?" See also Gerring, "The Case Study."

Bibliography

Abbott, Andrew. "From Causes to Events: Notes on Narrative Positivism." *Sociological Methods and Research* 20, no. 4 (1992): 428–55.

———. "On the Concept of Turning Point." *Comparative Social Research* 16 (1997): 85–105.

———. *Time Matters: On Theory and Method*. Chicago: University of Chicago Press, 2001.

Adorno, Theodore. "What Does Coming to Terms with the Past Mean?" In *Bitburg in Moral and Political Perspective*, edited by Geoffrey H. Hartman, 114–29. Bloomington: Indiana University Press, 1986.

Agence France-Presse. "Spanish Doctor Stands Trial over Franco-Era 'Stolen Babies.'" *Guardian*, June 26, 2018. https://www.theguardian.com/world/2018/jun/26/spanish-doctor-eduardo-vela-trial-franco-era-stolen-babies.

Alexander, Jeffrey C., and Philip Smith. "The Discourse of American Civil Society: A New Proposal for Cultural Studies." *Theory and Society* 22, no. 2 (1993): 151–207.

Alexander, Jeffrey C., Ron Eyerman, Bernard Giesen, Neil Smelser, and Piotr Sztompka. *Cultural Trauma and Collective Identity*. Berkeley: University of California Press, 2004.

Alexander, Jeffrey C. "Cultural Pragmatics: Social Performance between Ritual and Strategy." *Sociological Theory* 22, no. 4 (2004): 527–73.

———. "Towards a Theory of Cultural Trauma." In *Cultural Trauma and Collective Identity*, edited by Jeffrey C. Alexander, Ron Eyerman, Bernard Giesen, Neil Smelser, and Piotr Sztompka, 1–30. Berkeley: University of California Press, 2004.

Alexander, Jeffrey C., Bernard Giesen, and Jason L. Mast. *Social Performance: Symbolic Action, Cultural Pragmatics, and Ritual*. New York: Cambridge University Press, 2006.

Alexander, Lex. "TRC's Effects on City Praised." *News and Record*, July 7, 2006. https://www.greensboro.com/news/general_assignment/trc-s-effects-on-city-praised/article_e7009b47-2d08-5c50-968d-1152f453d3f1.html.

Allport, Gordon Willard. *The Nature of Prejudice*. Boston: Addison-Wesley, 1979.

Amy, Jeff. "Justice Quest Goes On after 'Freedom Summer' Court Cases End." *Associated Press News Service*, June 28, 2016. https://apnews.com/81d0f17dd8094e3b8f1816ba394ed2a4.

Anderson, Benedict. *Imagined Communities: Reflections on the Origin and Spread of Nationalism*. London: Verso, 1983.

Anderson, Devery. *Emmett Till: The Murder That Shocked the World and Propelled the Civil Rights Movement*. Oxford: University of Mississippi Press, 2015.

Andrews, Kenneth T. *Freedom Is a Constant Struggle: The Mississippi Civil Rights Movement and Its Legacy*. Chicago: University of Chicago Press, 2004.

———. "Social Movements and Policy Implementation: The Mississippi Civil Rights Movement and the War on Poverty, 1965–1971." *American Sociological Review* 66, no. 1 (2001): 71–95.

Androff, David. "Can Civil Society Reclaim Truth? Results from a Community-Based Truth and Reconciliation Commission." *International Journal of Transitional Justice* 6, no. 2 (2012): 296–317.

Armstrong, Elizabeth, and Suzanna Crage. "Movements and Memory: The Making of the Stonewall Myth." *American Sociological Review* 71, no. 5 (2006): 724–51.

Armstrong, Julie. "Regional Alliance Formed to Repair Legacy of Racial Violence." *Wellspring* 3, no 1 (2006): 1–8.

Associated Press. "Bush Declares Three Killed in State Are 'Heroes.'" *Greenwood Commonwealth*, June 25, 1989.

———. "Creation of Holocaust Commission Stirs Debate on Miss. Racial Past." WLOX, April 14, 2004. http://www.wlox.com/story/1786148/creation-of-holocaust-commission-stirs-debate-on-miss-racial-past?clienttype=printable.

Bainbridge, Judith. "In 2005, MLK Day Finally Recognized in Greenville County." *Greenville News*, March 11, 2017. https://www.greenvilleonline.com/story/news/local/greenville-roots/2017/03/11/martin-luther-king-jr-greenville/98792992/.

Bakiner, Onur. *Truth Commissions: Memory, Power, and Legitimacy*. Philadelphia: University of Pennsylvania Press, 2015.

Ball, Howard. *Justice in Mississippi: The Murder Trial of Edgar Ray Killen*. Lawrence: University Press of Kansas, 2006.

———. *Murder in Mississippi: United States v. Price and the Struggle for Civil Rights*. Lawrence: University Press of Kansas, 2004.

Barkan, Elazar. *The Guilt of Nations: Restitution and Negotiating Historical Injustices*. Baltimore, MD: Johns Hopkins University Press, 2001.

Barrientos, Tanya. "Caravan of Buses Going to Miss. to Honor 3 Slain in '64." *Philadelphia Inquirer*, June 18, 1989.

Becker, Howard. *Outsiders: Studies in the Sociology of Deviance*. New York: Free Press, 1963.

Beitler, James Edward, III. *Remaking Transitional Justice: The Rhetorical Authorization of the Greensboro Truth and Reconciliation Commission*. New York: Springer, 2013.

Bell, Derrick A., Jr. "Brown v. Board of Education and the Interest-Convergence Dilemma." *Harvard Law Review* 93, no. 3 (1980): 518–33.

Benavot, Aaron, and Nura Resh. "Educational Governance, School Autonomy, and Curriculum Implementation: A Comparative Study of Arab and Jewish Schools in Israel." *Journal of Curriculum Studies* 35, no. 2 (2003): 171–96.

Bender, Rita Schwerner. "Open Letter to Haley Barbour." *Clarion-Ledger,* July 17, 2005.

Benford, Robert D., and David A. Snow. "Framing Processes and Social Movements: An Overview and Assessment." *Annual Review of Sociology* 26 (2000): 611–39.

Berezin, Mabel. "Cultural Form and Political Meaning: State-Subsidized Theater, Ideology, and the Language of Style in Fascist Italy." *American Journal of Sociology* 99, no. 5 (1994): 1237–86.

———. "Events as Templates of Possibility: An Analytic Typology of Political Facts." In *The Oxford Handbook of Cultural Sociology*, edited by Jeffrey C. Alexander, Ronald Jacobs, and Philip Smith, 613–35. New York: Oxford University Press, 2012.

———. "Politics and Culture: A Less Fissured Terrain." *Annual Review of Sociology* 23 (1997): 361–83.

Bermanzohn, Sally A. *Through Survivors' Eyes: From the Sixties to the Greensboro Massacre*. Nashville, TN: Vanderbilt University Press, 2003.

———. "Violence, Nonviolence, and the U.S. Civil Rights Movement." In *Violence and Politics: Globalization's Paradox*, edited by Kenton Worcester, Sally A. Bermanzohn, and Mark Unger, 146–64. New York: Routledge, 2002.

Berrey, Stephen A. *The Jim Crow Routine: Everyday Performances of Race, Civil Rights, and Segregation in Mississippi*. Chapel Hill: University of North Carolina Press, 2015.

Berry, Wendell. *The Wild Birds: Six Stories of the Port William Membership*. San Francisco: North Point Press, 1986.

Bettersworth, John K. *Your Mississippi*. Austin, TX: The Steck Company Publishers, 1975.

Bialik, Kristen. "5 Facts About Blacks in the U.S." *Pew Research Center*. Accessed November 22, 1019. https://www.pewresearch.org/fact-tank/2018/02/22/5-facts-about-blacks-in-the-u-s/.

Bickford, Louis. "Unofficial Truth Projects." *Human Rights Quarterly* 29, no. 4 (2007): 994–1035.

Blake, Joseph P. "From Philly to Philly, with Love: Visit to Miss. Honored Murdered Trio." *Philadelphia Daily News*, June 20, 1989.

———. "Mississippi Yearning: Marking 25th Anniversary of Murdered Civil Rights Workers." *Philadelphia Daily News*, June 5, 1989.

Blight, David W. *Race and Reunion: The Civil War in American Memory*. Cambridge, MA: Harvard University Press, 2001.

Blight, David W. "The Memory Boom: Why and Why Now?" In *Memory in Mind and Culture*, edited by Pascal Boyer and James V. Wertsch, 238–51. New York: Cambridge University Press, 2009.

Bodnar, John E. *Remaking America: Public Memory, Commemoration, and Patriotism in the Twentieth Century*. Princeton, NJ: Princeton University Press, 1992.

Bolton, Charles C. *The Hardest Deal of All: The Battle over School Integration in Mississippi, 1870–1980*. Oxford: University Press of Mississippi, 2007.

———. "The Last Stand of Massive Resistance: Mississippi Public School Integration, 1970. *Mississippi History Now*. Accessed December 1, 2019. http://www.mshistorynow.mdah.ms.gov/articles/305/the-last-stand-of-massive-resistance-1970.

Bonilla-Silva, Eduardo. *Racism without Racists: Colorblind Racism and the Persistence of Racial Inequality in the United States.* Lanham, MD: Rowan and Littlefield, 2006.

Booth, William James. *Communities of Memory: On Witness, Identity, and Justice.* Ithaca, NY: Cornell University Press, 2006.

Borden, Jeremy. "South Carolina Debuts a New Model for Bridging Racial Divides." *Christian Science Monitor,* July 18, 2017. https://www.csmonitor.com/USA/Justice/2017/0718/South-Carolina-debuts-a-new-model-for-bridging-racial-divides.

Bourdieu, Pierre. *Distinction: A Social Critique of the Judgement of Taste.* New York: Routledge, 2013.

Boyarin, Jonathan. *Remapping Memory: The Politics of Timespace.* Minneapolis: University of Minnesota Press, 1994.

Boyer, Peter. "The Yuppies of Mississippi: How They Took Over the Statehouse." *New York Times Magazine,* February 28, 1988.

Brabham, Edna Greene. "Holocaust Education: Legislation, Practices, and Literature for Middle-School Students." *Social Studies* 88, no. 3 (1997): 139–43.

Brahm, Eric. "Uncovering the Truth: Examining Truth Commission Success and Impact." *International Studies Perspectives* 8, no. 1 (2007): 16–35.

Brown, Robbie. "First Black Mayor in City Known for Klan Killings." *New York Times,* May 21, 2009. http://www.nytimes.com/2009/05/22/us/22mayor.html.

Brown v. Board of Education, 347 U.S. 483 (1954).

Bruckner, Pascal. *The Tyranny of Guilt: An Essay on Western Masochism.* Princeton, NJ: Princeton University Press, 2010.

Brundage, W. Fitzhugh. *The Southern Past: A Clash of Race and Memory.* Cambridge, MA: Belknap Press of Harvard University Press, 2005.

Buckley-Zistel, Susanne. "Narrative Truths: On the Construction of the Past in Truth Commissions." In *Transitional Justice Theories,* edited by Susanne Buckley-Zistel, Teresa Koloma Beck, Christian Braun, and Friederike Mieth, 144–62. New York: Routledge, 2014.

Bulhof, Johannes. "What If? Modality and History." *History and Theory* 38, no. 2 (1999): 145–68.

Bullard, Robert D. *Race, Place, and Environmental Justice after Hurricane Katrina: Struggles to Reclaim, Rebuild, and Revitalize New Orleans and the Gulf Coast.* New York: Routledge, 2018.

"Burning Crosses." *Neshoba Democrat,* April 9, 1964.

Bunzl, Martin. "Counterfactual History: A User's Guide." *American Historical Review* 109, no. 3 (2004): 845–58.

Burrow, Rufus, Jr. *Martin Luther King, Jr., and the Theology of Resistance.* Jefferson, NC: McFarland, 2014.

Butterfly Project. "New Campaign Seeks to Mandate Holocaust Education in All 50 States." 2017. https://www.notthelastbutterfly.com/50-state-initiative.html.

Byrd, Sheila. "Civil Rights Curriculum." *Mississippi Press,* December 28, 2010.

———. "Facing Neshoba's Dark Past—Memorializing Civil Rights Victims Was Just the Start." *Commercial Appeal,* August 22, 2004.

Cagin, Seth, and Philip Dray. *We Are Not Afraid: The Story of Goodman, Schwerner, and Chaney, and the Civil Rights Campaign for Mississippi*. New York: Nation Books, 2006.

Canby, Vincent. "'Mississippi Burning': Generating Heat or Light? Taking Risks to Illuminate a Painful Time in America: Film Review." *New York Times*, January 8, 1989.

Cannon, Carole. "Black Monday: Mississippi's Ugly Response to 'Brown v. Board' Decision." *Jackson Free Press*, May 12, 2004. http://www.jacksonfreepress.com/news/2004/may/12/black-monday/.

Capoccia, Giovanni, and R. Daniel Kelemen. "The Study of Critical Junctures: Theory, Narrative, and Counterfactuals in Historical Institutionalism." *World Politics* 59 (2007): 341–69.

Carlson, Dennis L. "Constructing the Margins: Of Multicultural Education and Curriculum Settlements." *Curriculum Inquiry* 25, no. 4 (1995): 407–31.

Carrier, Jim. *A Traveler's Guide to the Civil Rights Movement*. Orlando, FL: Harcourt, 2004.

Carver, Richard. "Called to Account: How African Governments Investigate Human Rights Violations." *African Affairs* 89, no. 356 (1990): 391–415.

Charles, Camille Zubrinsky. "The Dynamics of Racial Residential Segregation." *Annual Review of Sociology* 29, no. 1 (2003): 167–207.

Chisholm, Linda. "The Making of South Africa's National Curriculum Statement." *Journal of Curriculum Studies* 37, no. 2 (March 2005): 193–208.

"Civil Rights Caravan to Mark Deaths." *New York Times*, March 8, 1989.

Cobb, Charles E. *On the Road to Freedom: A Guided Tour of the Civil Rights Trail*. Chapel Hill, NC: Algonquin Books of Chapel Hill, 2008.

Cobb, James C. *The Selling of the South: The Southern Crusade for Industrial Development, 1936–1990*. Champaign: University of Illinois Press, 1993.

"Cochran and Lott: Sign on Now." Editorial. *Jackson Free Press*, June 22, 2005. http://www.jacksonfreepress.com/news/2005/jun/22/cochran-and-lott-sign-on-now/.

Cohen, Stanley. *States of Denial: Knowing about Atrocities and Suffering of Others*. Malden, MA: Blackwell, 2001.

Conway, Brian. *Commemoration and Bloody Sunday: Pathways of Memory*. New York: Palgrave Macmillan, 2010.

Corning, Amy, and Howard Schuman. *Generations and Collective Memory*. Chicago: University of Chicago Press, 2015.

Cotter, Holland. "A Memorial to the Lingering Horror of Lynching." *New York Times*, June 1, 2018. https://www.nytimes.com/2018/06/01/arts/design/national-memorial-for-peace-and-justice-montgomery-alabama.html.

Cress, Daniel M., and David A. Snow. "Mobilization at the Margins: Resources, Benefactors, and the Viability of Homeless Social Movement Organizations." *American Sociological Review* 61, no. 6 (1996): 1089–109.

Crisp, Richard J., Sofia Stathi, Rhiannon N. Turner, and Senel Husnu. "Imagined Intergroup Contact: Theory, Paradigm and Practice." *Social and Personality Psychology Compass* 3, no. 1 (2009): 1–18.

Cunningham, David. *Klansville, U.S.A.: The Rise and Fall of the Civil Rights–Era Ku Klux Klan.* New York: Oxford University Press, 2013.

———. "Method of Truth and Reconciliation." In *Sociologists in Action: Sociology, Social Change, and Social Justice,* edited by Kathleen Odell Korgen, Jonathan M. White, and Shelly White, 163–68. Thousand Oaks, CA: Pine Force Press, 2011.

Cunningham, David, Colleen Nugent, and Caitlin Slodden. "The Durability of Collective Memory: Reconciling the 'Greensboro Massacre.'" *Social Forces* 88, no. 4 (2010): 1517–42.

Cunningham, David, and Ashley Rondini. "Legacies of Racial Contention: Implementing Mississippi's Civil Rights/Human Rights Curriculum, 2006–2011." *Du Bois Review* 14, no. 1 (2017): 325–48.

Cunningham, Michael. "Prisoners of the Japanese and the Politics of Apology: A Battle over History and Memory." *Journal of Contemporary History* 39, no. 4 (2004): 561–74.

Curtis, Michael. *Mass Atrocity, Collective Memory, and the Law.* New York: Routledge, 2017.

Dancy, Geoff, Hunjoon Kim, and Eric Wiebelhaus-Brahm. "The Turn to Truth: Trends in Truth Commission Experimentation." *Journal of Human Rights* 9, no. 1 (2010): 45–64.

Dancy, Geoff, and Steven C. Poe. "What Comes before Truth? The Political Determinants of Truth Commission Onset." Paper presented at the Annual Convention of the International Studies Association, San Diego, CA, 2006.

Daphi, Priska. *Becoming a Movement: Identity, Narrative and Memory in the European Global Justice Movement.* New York: Rowman and Littlefield International, 2017.

Davis, Madeleine. "Is Spain Recovering Its Memory? Breaking the Pacto Del Olvido." *Human Rights Quarterly* 27, no. 3 (2005): 858–80.

Davis, Rebecca Miller. "The Three R's—Reading, 'Riting, and Race: The Evolution of Race in Mississippi History Textbooks, 1900–1995." *Journal of Mississippi History* (2010): 1–45.

Dawson, Michael C. *Behind the Mule: Race and Class in African-American Politics.* Princeton, NJ: Princeton University Press, 1995.

Dearman, Stanley. "Dr. Carolyn Goodman, Mother of Andrew Goodman, Interviewed." *Neshoba Democrat,* April 24, 1989.

———. "June 21, 1964: It's Time for an Accounting." Editorial. *Neshoba Democrat,* May 3, 2000.

DeGloma, Thomas. "Expanding Trauma through Space and Time: Mapping the Rhetorical Strategies of Trauma Carrier Groups." *Social Psychology Quarterly* 72, no. 2 (2009): 105–22.

———. *Seeing the Light: The Social Logic of Personal Discovery.* Chicago: University of Chicago Press, 2014.

———. "The Strategies of Mnemonic Battle: On the Alignment of Autobiographical and Collective Memories in Conflicts over the Past." *American Journal of Cultural Sociology* 3, no. 1 (2015): 156–90.

Demby, Gene. "I'm From Philly. 30 Years Later, I'm Still Trying to Make Sense of the MOVE Bombing." NPR, May 13, 2015. https://www.npr.org/sections/codeswitch/2015/05/13/406243272/im-from-philly-30-years-later-im-still-trying-to-make-sense-of-the-move-bombing.

Dessel, Adrienne, and Mary E. Rogge. "Evaluation of Intergroup Dialogue: A Review of the Empirical Research." *Conflict Resolution Quarterly* 26, no. 2 (2008): 199–238.

DiAngelo, Robin J. *White Fragility: Why It's So Hard for White People to Talk about Racism*. Boston: Beacon Press, 2018.

"A Different Neshoba County." *Neshoba Democrat*, June 30, 2004. http://neshobademocrat.com/print.asp?ArticleID=8290&SectionID=2&SubSectionID=297.

Dittmer, John. *Local People: The Struggle for Civil Rights in Mississippi*. Champaign: University of Illinois Press, 1995.

Downton, James, Jr., and Paul Wehr. "Persistent Pacifism: How Activist Commitment Is Developed and Sustained." *Journal of Peace Research* 35, no. 5 (1998): 531–50.

Driver, Justin. "Rethinking the Interest-Convergence Thesis." *Northwestern University Law Review* 105, no. 1 (2011): 149–98.

Durkheim, Emile. *The Elementary Forms of Religious Life*. Glencoe, IL: Free Press, 1995.

Dwyer, Owen J., and Derek H. Alderman. *Civil Rights Memorials and the Geography of Memory*. Athens: University of Georgia Press, 2008.

Eagles, Charles W. *Civil Rights, Culture Wars: The Fight over a Mississippi Textbook*. Chapel Hill: University of North Carolina Press, 2017.

Earl, Jennifer. "The Cultural Consequences of Social Movements." In *The Blackwell Companion to Social Movements*, edited by David A. Snow, Sarah A. Soule, and Hanspeter Kriesi, 508–30. Malden, MA: Wiley-Blackwell, 2013.

"Economic Impact of Commemoration Noted." *Neshoba Democrat*, June 10, 2004.

Elliott, Jack. "Elderly Convict Remains Tight-Lipped about Slaying of Three Civil Rights Workers Sparked National Outrage in '60s." *Charleston Daily Mail*, December 23, 2014, P7A.

Elster, Jon. *Closing the Books: Transitional Justice in Historical Perspective*. New York: Cambridge University Press, 2004.

———. "Coming to Terms with the Past: A Framework for the Study of Justice in the Transition to Democracy." *European Journal of Social Theory* 39, no. 1 (1998): 7–48.

———. *Logic and Society: Contradictions and Possible Worlds*. New York: John Wiley and Sons, 1978.

Emerson, Robert M., Rachel I. Fretz, and Linda L. Shaw. *Writing Ethnographic Fieldnotes*. Chicago: University of Chicago Press, 2011.

Epstein, Joseph. "Two Southern Liberals: Review of Mississippi: The Closed Society by James Silver." *Commentary* 38, no. 6 (December 1964): 73.

Ewick, Patricia, and Susan S. Silbey. "Subversive Stories and Hegemonic Tales: Toward a Sociology of Narrative." *Law and Society Review* 29, no. 2 (1995): 197–226.

Eyerman, Ron. "Social Movements and Memory." In *The Routledge International Handbook of Memory Studies*, edited by Anna Lisa Tota and Trever Hagen, 79–83. New York: Routledge, 2016.

Fallace, Thomas. D. "The Origins of Holocaust Education in American Public Schools." *Holocaust and Genocide Studies* 20, no. 1 (2006): 80–102.

Fearon, James D. "Causes and Counterfactuals in Social Science: Exploring an Analogy between Cellular Automata and Historical Processes." In *Counterfactual Thought Experiments in World Politics: Logical, Methodological, and Psychological Perspectives*, edited by Philip E. Tetlock and Aaron Belkin, 39–67. Princeton, NJ: Princeton University Press, 1996.

Fernandes, Sujatha. *Curated Stories: The Uses and Misuses of Storytelling*. New York: Oxford University Press, 2017.

Fine, Gary Alan. *Difficult Reputations: Collective Memories of the Evil, Inept, and Controversial*. Chicago: University of Chicago Press, 2001.

———. "The When of Theory." In *Workshop on Scientific Foundations of Qualitative Research*, edited by Charles Ragin, Joane Nagel, and Patricia White, 81–82. Washington: National Science Foundation, 2004.

Firebaugh, Glenn, and Kenneth Davis. "Trends in Antiblack Prejudice, 1972–1984: Region and Cohort Effects." *American Journal of Sociology* 94, no. 2 (1988): 251–72.

Fleischmann, Arnold. "Urbanization of the South." In *The Oxford Handbook of Southern Politics*, edited by Charles S. Bullock III and Mark J. Rozell, 80–102. New York: Oxford University Press, 2012.

Foucault, Michel. *Nietzsche, Genealogy, Morality: Essays on Nietzsche's On the Genealogy of Morals*. Edited by Richard Schacht. Berkeley: University of California Press, 1994.

Frankenberg, Erica, and Chungmei Lee. "Race in American Public Schools: Rapidly Resegregating School Districts." Harvard University Civil Rights Project, August 2002. https://files.eric.ed.gov/fulltext/ED468063.pdf.

Freedman, Sarah Warshauer, Harvey M. Weinstein, Karen Murphy, and Timothy Longman. "Teaching History after Identity-Based Conflicts: The Rwanda Experience." *Comparative Education Review* 52, no. 4 (2008): 663–90.

Fukuyama, Francis. *The End of History and the Last Man*. New York: Free Press, 2006.

Gammage, Jeff. "Freedom Summer: Two Montco Remembers Mississippi." *Philadelphia Inquirer*, June 18, 1989.

Ganucheau, Adam. "Ballot Petition Aims to Protect Confederate Heritage." *Clarion-Ledger*, November 5, 2004.

———. "Winter Institute Helped New Orleans Address Confederate Monuments." *Mississippi Today*, May 17, 2017. https://mississippitoday.org/2017/05/17/winter-institute-helped-new-orleans-address-confederate-monuments/.

Garfrerick, Beth H. "The Community Weekly Newspaper: Telling America's Stories." *American Journalism* 27, no. 3 (2010): 151–57.

Gates, Henry Louis, Jr. "What Was the Civil Rights Movement?" *Root*, August 12, 2013. https://www.theroot.com/what-was-the-civil-rights-movement-1790897669.

Geisen, Bernhard. "The Trauma of Perpetrators: The Holocaust as the Traumatic Reference of German National Identity." In *Cultural Trauma and Collective Identity*, edited by Jeffrey C. Alexander, Ron Eyerman, Bernhard Giesen, Neil J. Smelser, and Piotr Sztompka, 112–54. Berkeley: University of California Press, 2004.

———. *Triumph and Trauma*. Boulder, CO: Paradigm, 2004.

Gerring, John. "The Case Study: What It Is and What It Does." In *The Oxford Handbook of Political Science*, edited by Robert E. Goodin. Oxford: Oxford University Press, 2011.

Ghoshal, Raj. "Remembering Racial Violence: Memory Movements and the Resurgence of Traumatic Pasts." PhD diss., University of North Carolina at Chapel Hill, 2010.

———. "Transforming Collective Memory: Mnemonic Opportunity Structures and the Outcomes of Racial Violence Memory Movements." *Theory and Society* 42, no. 4 (2013): 329–50.

———. "What Does Remembering Racial Violence Do? Greensboro's Truth Commission, Mnemonic Overlap, and Attitudes toward Racial Redress." *Race and Justice* 5, no. 2 (2015): 168–91.

Gibson, James L. "Does Truth Lead to Reconciliation? Testing the Causal Assumptions of the South African Truth and Reconciliation Process." *American Journal of Political Science* 48, no. 2 (2004): 201–17.

———. "Overcoming Apartheid: Can Truth Reconcile a Divided Nation?" *Politikon* 31, no. 2 (2004): 129–55.

Gibson, James L., and Christopher Claassen. "Racial Reconciliation in South Africa: Interracial Contact and Changes over Time." *Journal of Social Issues* 66, no. 2 (2010): 255–72.

Gill, Joseph W. "Mississippi Justice at Last: The Trials and Convictions of Beckwith, Bowers and Killen." *Prosecutor* 41, no. 4 (2007): 26.

Giroux, Henry A., and David E. Purpel. *The Hidden Curriculum and Moral Education: Deception or Discovery?* San Pablo, CA: Mccutchan, 1983.

Glisson, Susan M. "The Sum of Its Parts: The Importance of Deconstructing Truth Commissions." *Race and Justice* 5, no. 2 (2015): 192–202.

———. "Telling the Truth: How Breaking Silence Brought Redemption to One Mississippi Town." In *Telling Stories to Change the World: Global Voices on the Power of Narrative to Build Community and Make Social Justice Claims*, edited by Rickie Solinger, Madeline Fox, and Kayhan Irani, 31–38. New York: Routledge, 2008.

Gocek, Fatma Muge. *Denial of Violence: Ottoman Past, Turkish Present, and Collective Violence against the Armenians, 1789–2009*. New York: Oxford University Press, 2014.

Goldstein, Richard. "Stanley Dearman, Editor Who Sought Justice in 1964 Murders, Dies at 84." *New York Times*, March 1, 2017.

Gongaware, Timothy B. "Collective Memory Anchors: Collective Identity and Continuity in Social Movements." *Social Forces* 43, no. 3 (2010): 214–39.

Goodman, Julie. "Holocaust Bill Challenged, Passed in House." *Clarion-Ledger*, April 15, 2004.

Goodman, Tanya. *Staging Solidarity: Truth and Reconciliation in a New South Africa*. Boulder, CO: Paradigm, 2009.

Goodwin, Jeff, James Jasper, and Francesca Polletta. "The Return of the Repressed: The Fall and Rise of Emotions in Social Movement Theory." *Mobilization* 5, no. 1 (2000): 65–83.

Goodwin, Jeff, and Steven Pfaff. "Emotion Work in High-Risk Social Movements: Managing Fear in the US and East German Civil Rights Movements." In *Passionate Politics: Emotions and Social Movements,* edited by Jeff Goodwin, James Jasper, and Francesca Polletta, 282–302. Chicago: University of Chicago Press, 2001.

Gould, Stephen J. *A Wonderful Life: The Burgess Shale and the Nature of History*. New York: W. W. Norton, 1989.

Govan, Fiona. "Spanish Civil War Crimes Investigation Launched." *Telegraph*, October 16, 2008. https://www.telegraph.co.uk/news/worldnews/europe/spain/3212605/Spanish-Civil-War-crimes-investigation-launched.html.

Grandin, Greg. "The Instruction of Great Catastrophe: Truth Commissions, National History, and State Formation in Argentina, Chile, and Guatemala." *American Historical Review* 110, no. 1 (2005): 46–67.

Gray, Eliza, and Simon Shuster. "How the Last Surviving Nazis Could Be Brought to Justice." *Time*, January 20, 2016. http://time.com/4186602/prosecute-last-surviving-nazis/.

Griffin, Larry J. "Generations and Collective Memory Revisited: Race, Region, and Memory of Civil Rights." *American Sociological Review* 69, no. 4 (2004): 544–57.

———. "Narrative, Event-Structure Analysis, and Causal Interpretation in Historical Sociology." *American Journal of Sociology* 98, no. 5 (1993): 1094–133.

Griffin, Larry J., and Kenneth A. Bollen. "What Do These Memories Do? Civil Rights Remembrance and Racial Attitudes." *American Sociological Review* 74, no. 4 (2009): 594–614.

Griffin, Larry J., and Peggy G. Hargis. "The Past in Black and White." *Southern Literary Journal* 40, no. 2 (2008): 42–69.

———. "Still Distinctive after All These Years: Trends in Racial Attitudes in and out of the South." *Southern Cultures* 14, no. 3 (2008): 117–41.

Guigni, Marco G. "Was It Worth the Effort? The Outcomes and Consequences of Social Movements." *Annual Review of Sociology* 24, no. 1 (1998): 371–93.

Guigni, Marco, Doug McAdam, and Charles Tilly. *How Social Movements Matter*. Minneapolis: University of Minnesota Press, 1999.

Halbwachs, Maurice. *On Collective Memory*. Chicago: University of Chicago Press, 1925.

Hampton, David. "David Hampton." *Clarion-Ledger*, June 26, 2005.

Hannaford, Jim. "1,000 Turn Out to Honor Slain Rights Workers." *Meridian Star*, June 22, 1989.

Harris, Fredrick C. "Collective Memory, Collective Action, and Black Activism in the 1960s." In *Breaking the Cycles of Hatred: Memory, Law, and Repair*, edited by Martha Minow, 154–69. Princeton, NJ: Princeton University Press, 2002.

———. "It Takes a Tragedy to Arouse Them: Collective Memory and Collective Action during the Civil Rights Movement." *Social Movement Studies* 5, no. 1 (2007): 19–43.

Harris, Leslie, James Campbell, and Alfred Brophy, eds. *Slavery and the University: Histories and Legacies*. Athens: University of Georgia Press, 2019.

Harter, Lynn M., Ronald J. Stephens, and Phyllis M. Japp. "President Clinton's Apology for the Tuskegee Syphilis Experiment: A Narrative of Remembrance, Redefinition, and Reconciliation." *Howard Journal of Communications* 11, no. 1 (2000): 19–34.

Haskins, Ekaterina. "Between Archive and Participation: Public Memory in a Digital Age." *Rhetoric Society Quarterly* 37, no. 4 (2007): 401–22.

Hawthorn, Geoffrey. *Plausible Worlds: Possibility and Understanding in History and the Social Sciences*. New York: Cambridge University Press, 1991.

Haydu, Jeffrey. "Reversals of Fortune: Path Dependency, Problem Solving, and Temporal Cases." *Theory and Society* 39, no. 1 (2010): 25–48.

Hayner, Priscilla B. *Unspeakable Truths: Transitional Justice and the Challenge of Truth Commissions*. New York: Routledge, 2011.

HB 1269, Regular Session (Mississippi 2004). Accessed November 29, 2019. http://billstatus.ls.state.ms.us/documents/2004/pdf/HB/1200-1299/HB1269SG.pdf.

Heise, David. "Event Structure Analysis." June 5, 2014. http://www.indiana.edu/~socpsy/ESA/Tutorial.html.

———. "Modeling Event Structures." *Journal of Mathematical Sociology* 14 (1989): 139–68.

Hendrickson, Paul. *Sons of Mississippi: A Story of Race and Its Legacy*. New York: Vintage, 2004.

Henry, Charles P. *Long Overdue: The Politics of Racial Reparations*. New York: New York University Press, 2009.

Hess, David, and Brian Martin. "Repression, Backfire, and the Theory of Transformative Events." *Mobilization* 11, no. 2 (2006): 249–67.

Hirsch, Michael Ben-Josef. "And the Truth Shall Make You Free: The International Norm of Truth-Seeking." PhD diss., Massachusetts Institute of Technology, 2009.

Hirsch, Michal Ben-Josef, Megan MacKenzie, and Mohamed Sesay. "Measuring the Impacts of Truth and Reconciliation Commissions: Placing the Global 'Success' of TRCs in Local Perspective." *Cooperation and Conflict* 47, no. 3 (2012): 386–403.

Hirschman, Albert O. *The Rhetoric of Reaction*. Cambridge, MA: Harvard University Press, 1991.

H-Net: Humanities and Social Sciences Online (home page). Accessed October 30, 2019. https://networks.h-net.org/.

Hobbes, Thomas. *Body, Man, and Citizen*. Edited by Richard S. Peters. New York: Collier, 1967.

Hobsbawm, Eric J., and Terrence O. Ranger. *The Invention of Tradition*. New York: Cambridge University Press, 1983.

Hobson, Fred. *But Now I See: The White Southern Racial Conversion Narrative*. Baton Rouge: Louisiana State University Press, 1999.

Hochschild, Arlie Russell. "Emotion Work, Feeling Rules, and Social Structure." *American Journal of Sociology* 85, no. 3 (1979): 551–75.

Hoerl, Kristen. "Burning Mississippi into Memory? Cinematic Amnesia as a Resource for Remembering Civil Rights." *Critical Studies in Media Communication* 26, no. 1 (2009): 54–79.

Hollowell, Annette. "Mississippi Learning." *Wellspring* 2, no. 2 (2006): 4.

Huie, William Bradford. "The Shocking Story of Approved Killing in Mississippi." *Look*, January 24, 1956, 46–48.

———. *Three Lives for Mississippi*. New York: WCC Books, 1965.

Hunt, Scott A., and Robert D. Benford. "Collective Identity, Solidarity, and Commitment." In *The Blackwell Companion to Social Movements*, edited by David A. Snow, Sarah A. Soule, and Hanspeter Kriesi, 433–57. Malden, MA: Blackwell, 2004.

Hunt, Scott A., Robert D. Benford, and David A. Snow. "Identity Fields: Framing Processes and the Social Construction of Movement Identities." In *New Social Movements: From Ideology to Identity*, edited by Enrique Laraña, Hank Johnston, and Joseph R. Gusfield, 185–208. Philadelphia, PA: Temple University Press, 1994.

Ignatieff, Michael. "Articles of Faith." *Index on Censorship* 25, no. 5 (1996): 110–22.

International Center for Transitional Justice. "Is the United States Ready for a Truth-Telling Process?" August 9, 2017. https://www.ictj.org/news/united-states-ready-truth-telling-process.

Inwood, Joshua. "The Politics of Being Sorry: The Greensboro Truth Process and Efforts at Restorative Justice." *Social and Cultural Geography* 13, no. 6 (2012): 607–24.

Inwood, Joshua, Derek Alderman, and Melanie Barron. "Addressing Structural Violence through US Reconciliation Commissions: The Case Study of Greensboro, NC and Detroit, MI." *Political Geography* 52 (2016): 57–64.

Inwood, Joshua. "Dealing with Hate: Can America's Truth and Reconciliation Commissions Help?" *Conversation*, February 28, 2017. http://theconversation.com/dealing-with-hate-can-americas-truth-and-reconciliation-commissions-help-73170.

Irons, Jenny. *Reconstituting Whiteness: The Mississippi State Sovereignty Commission*. Nashville, TN: Vanderbilt University Press, 2010.

Irwin-Zarecka, Iwona. *Frames of Remembrance: The Dynamics of Collective Memory*. New Brunswick, NJ: Transaction, 1994.

Isaac, Larry. "The Movement of Movements: Culture Moves in the Long Civil Rights Struggle." *Social Forces* 87, no. 1 (2009): 33–64.

Isaac, Larry, Debra A. Street, and Stan J. Knapp. "Analyzing Historical Contingency with Formal Methods." *Sociological Methods and Research* 23, no. 1 (1994): 114–41.

Ishee, Rachel. "Civil Rights Leaders, President Trump Celebrate Opening of Two Mississippi Museums." *Daily Mississippian*, December 9, 2017. http://thedmonline.com/civil-rights-leaders-president-trump-celebrate-opening-two-mississippi-museums/.
Jackson, Philip Wesley. *Life in Classrooms*. New York: Teachers College Press, 1990.
Jacobs, Ronald N. "Civil Society and Crisis: Culture, Discourse, and the Rodney King Beating." *American Journal of Sociology* 101, no. 5 (1996): 1238–72.
———. "The Narrative Integration of Personal and Collective Identity in Social Movements." In *Narrative Impact: Social and Cognitive Foundations*, edited by Melanie C. Green, Jeffrey J. Strange, and Timothy C. Brock, 205–28. Mahwah, NJ: Lawrence Erlbaum, 2002.
Jacoby, Jeff. "A Mosque at Ground Zero?" Boston.com, June 6, 2010. http://archive.boston.com/bostonglobe/editorial_opinion/oped/articles/2010/06/06/a_mosque_at_ground_zero/.
Jansen, Robert S. "Resurrection and Appropriation: Reputational Trajectories, Memory Work, and the Political Use of Historical Figures." *American Journal of Sociology* 112, no. 4 (2007): 953–1007.
Jasper, James M. "Emotions and Social Movements: Twenty Years of Theory and Research." *Annual Review of Sociology* 37 (2011): 285–303.
———. *The Emotions of Protest*. Chicago: University of Chicago Press, 2018.
Jasper, James M., Michael Young, and Elke Zuern. "Character Work in Social Movements." *Theory and Society* 47, no. 1 (2018): 113–31.
Jeffries, Vincent, and H. Edward Ransford. "Interracial Social Contact and Middle-Class White Reactions to the Watts Riot." *Social Problems* 16, no. 3 (1969): 312–24.
Jelin, Elizabeth. *State Repression and the Labors of Memory*. Minneapolis: University of Minnesota Press, 2003.
Jensen, Klaus Bruhn. "New Media, Old Methods—Internet Methodologies and the Online/Offline Divide." In *The Handbook of Internet Studies*, edited by Mia Consalvo and Charles Ess, 43–58. Malden, MA: Wiley-Blackwell, 2011.
Jovanovic, Spoma. *Democracy, Dialogue, and Community Action: Truth and Reconciliation in Greensboro*. Fayetteville: University of Arkansas Press, 2012.
Kaufman, Jonathan. "Silicon Valley High School Struggles with Integration." *Washington Post*, March 31, 2000.
Kenworthy, Jared B., Rhiannon N. Turner, Miles Hewstone, and Alberto Voci. "Intergroup Contact: When Does It Work, and Why?" In *On the Nature of Prejudice: Fifty Years after Allport*, 278–92. London: Blackwell, 2005.
Key, V. O., Jr. *Southern Politics in State and Nation*. Knoxville: University of Tennessee Press, 1996.
Kim, Hunjoon. "Local, National, and International Determinants of Truth Commissions: The South Korean Experience." *Human Rights Quarterly* 34 (2012): 726–50.
"Klan Marches without Incident Here Sunday." *Neshoba Democrat*, March 8, 1989.
Klandermans, Bert. *The Social Psychology of Protest*. Cambridge, MA: Blackwell, 1997.

Klein, Kerwin Lee. "On the Emergence of Memory in Historical Discourse." *Representations* 69, no. SI (2000): 125–50.

Kotz, Nick. *Judgment Days: Lyndon Baines Johnson, Martin Luther King, Jr., and the Laws That Changed America*. Boston: Houghton Mifflin, 2005.

Krüger, Anne K. "From Truth to Reconciliation: The Global Diffusion of Truth Commissions." In *Reconciliation, Civil Society, and the Politics of Memory: Transitional Initiatives in the 20th and 21st Century*, edited by Birgit Schwelling. Bielefeld, Germany: Transcript Verlag, 2012.

Kubal, Timothy. *Cultural Movements and Collective Memory: Christopher Columbus and the Rewriting of the National Origin Myth*. New York: Palgrave Macmillan, 2008.

Kubal, Timothy, and Rene Becerra. "Social Movements and Collective Memory." *Sociology Compass* 8, no. 6 (2014): 865–75.

Kucia, Marek. "The Europeanization of Holocaust Memory and Eastern Europe." *East European Politics and Societies* 30, no. 1 (February 1, 2016): 97–119.

Kundera, Milan. *The Book of Laughter and Forgetting*. New York: HarperCollins, 1996.

Labuda, Patryk. "Racial Reconciliation in Mississippi: An Evaluation of the Proposal to Establish a Mississippi Truth and Reconciliation Commission." *Harvard Journal on Racial and Ethnic Justice* 27 (2011): 1–48.

LaCapra, Dominick. *Writing History, Writing Trauma*. Baltimore, MD: Johns Hopkins University Press, 2014.

Ladd, Donna. "After Killen: What's Next for Mississippi?" *Jackson Free Press*, June 22, 2005. http://www.jacksonfreepress.com/news/2005/jun/22/after-killen-whats-next-for-mississippi/.

———. "Civil Rights Education Summit in Neshoba County." *Jackson Free Press*, June 22, 2005. http://www.jacksonfreepress.com/news/2005/jun/22/civil-rights-education-summit-in-neshoba-county/.

———. "Haley's Choice: Native Son Barbour Comes Home." *Jackson Free Press*, October 29, 2003.

———. "I Felt the Earth Move." *Jackson Free Press*, June 24, 2004.

———. "Love Thy Neighbor: How to Connect in Divided Times. *Jackson Free Press*, December 21, 2016.

———. "Mississippi Governor Declares April 'Confederate Heritage Month,' No Slavery Mention." *Jackson Free Press*, February 24, 2016.

Landrieu, Mitch. "Why I'm Taking down Confederate Monuments in New Orleans." *Washington Post*, May 14, 2017.

Landsman, Stephan. *Crimes of the Holocaust: The Law Confronts Hard Cases*. Philadelphia: University of Pennsylvania Press, 2005.

Lantigua-Williams, Juleyka. "What Closing the 'Mississippi Burning' Case Means for Civil Rights." *Atlantic*, June 21, 2016. https://www.theatlantic.com/politics/archive/2016/06/mississippi-civil-rights-killings-goodman-chaney-schwerner/487907/.

Lauter, David. "Rights Martyrs' Relatives Speak Bluntly to Bush." *Los Angeles Times*, June 24, 1989.

Lawson, Steven, ed. *One America in the Twenty-First Century*. New Haven, CT: Yale University Press, 2009.
Lelyveld, Joseph. "Turning Point." *New York Times Magazine*, April 10, 1977, 94–95.
Levitt, Jeremy I., and Matthew C. Whitaker. *Hurricane Katrina: America's Unnatural Disaster*. Lincoln: University of Nebraska Press, 2009.
Lewis-Beck, Michael S., Alan Bryman, and Tim Futing Liao. "Negative Case." In *The SAGE Encyclopedia of Social Science Research Methods*, edited by Michael S. Lewis-Beck, Alan Bryman, and Tim Futing Liao. Thousand Oaks, CA: Sage Publications, 2004. https://dx.doi.org/10.4135/9781412950589.n618.
Loewe, Ronald. "Civil Rights Tourism in Mississippi: Openings, Closures, Redemption and Remuneration." *Sociology Mind* 4, no. 1 (2014): 84–92.
Loewen, James W. *Lies My Teacher Told Me: Everything Your American History Textbook Got Wrong*. New York: Touchstone, 1996.
Loewen, James W., and Charles Sallis. *Mississippi: Conflict and Change*. New York: Pantheon, 1974.
Loraux, Nicole. *The Divided City: On Memory and Forgetting in Ancient Athens*. Translated by Corinne Pache and Jeff Fort. New York: Zone Books, 2002.
Mabus, Ray. "Ray Mabus." *Neshoba Democrat*, July 5, 1989.
Mader, Jackie. "Have Lessons about Mississippi's Violent Past Become Optional?" *Hechinger Report*, June 22, 2014. https://hechingerreport.org/lessons-mississippis-violent-past-become-optional/.
Magarrell, Lisa, and Blaz Gutierrez. "Lessons in Truth-Seeking: International Experiences Informing United States Initiatives." International Center for Transitional Justice, New York, NY, 2006.
Magarrell, Lisa, and Joya Wesley. *Learning from Greensboro: Truth and Reconciliation in the United States*. Philadelphia: University of Pennsylvania Press, 2010.
Mahoney, James. "Path Dependence in Historical Sociology." *Theory and Society* 29, no. 4 (2000): 507–48.
Mahoney, James, and Dietrich Rueschemeyer. "Comparative Historical Analysis." In *Comparative Historical Analysis in the Social Sciences*, edited by James Mahoney and Dietrich Rueschemeyer, 3–38. New York: Cambridge University Press, 2003.
Maier, Charles S. "A Surfeit of Memory? Reflections on History, Melancholy and Denial." *History and Memory* 5, no. 2 (1993): 136–52.
Mamdani, Mahmood. "Amnesty or Impunity? A Preliminary Critique of the Report of the Truth and Reconciliation Commission of South Africa." *Diacritics* 32, nos. 3–4 (2002): 32–59.
Mannheim, Karl. "The Problems of Generations." In *Essays in the Sociology of Knowledge*, edited by Karl Mannheim, 276–322. London: Routledge, 1952.
Mannie, Sierra. "Miss. Students Ignorant about Civil Rights Movement." Mississippi Public Broadcasting, October 2, 2017. http://www.mpbonline.org/blogs/news/2017/10/01/miss-students-ignorant-about-civil-rights-movement/.
Mansbridge, Jane. "The Making of Oppositional Consciousness." In *Oppositional Consciousness: The Subjective Roots of Social Protest*, edited by Jane Mansbridge and Aldon Morris, 1–19 Chicago: University of Chicago Press, 2001.

Margalit, Avishai. *The Ethics of Memory*. Cambridge, MA: Harvard University Press, 2002.

Mars, Florence. *Witness in Philadelphia*. Baton Rouge: Louisiana State University Press, 1977.

Massey, Douglas S., and Nancy A. Denton. *American Apartheid: Segregation and the Making of the Underclass*. Cambridge, MA: Harvard University Press, 1993.

May, Reuben A. Buford. "Race Talk and Local Collective Memory among African American Men in a Neighborhood Tavern." *Qualitative Sociology* 23, no. 2 (2000): 201–14.

McAdam, Doug. *Freedom Summer*. New York: Oxford University Press, 1990.

McBride, Ernest. "Cry for Justice in Neshoba Driving Historic Cause." *Jackson Advocate*, July 7, 2011.

McCammon, Holly. "Resonance, Frame." In *The Wiley-Blackwell Encyclopedia of Social and Political Movements*, edited by David A. Snow, Donatella della Porta, Bert Klandermans, and Doug McAdam, 1092–96. Malden, MA: Wiley-Blackwell, 2013.

McCarthy, John D., and Mayer N. Zald. "Resource Mobilization and Social Movements: A Partial Theory." *American Journal of Sociology* 82, no. 6 (1977): 1212–41.

McClendon, Robert. "Mitch Landrieu Launches Racial Reconciliation Dialogue with $1.2 Million Grant. *Times-Picayune*, April 23, 2014. https://www.nola.com/politics/index.ssf/2014/04/mitch_landrieu_launches_racial.html.

McCord, William. *Mississippi: The Long, Hot Summer*. With an introduction by Françoise N. Hamlin. Jackson: University Press of Mississippi, 2016.

McDonald, Janis L. "Heroes and Spoilers: The Role of the Media in the Prosecutions of Unsolved Civil Rights Era Murders." *Ohio Northern University Law Review* 34 (2008): 797–826.

McGreal, Chris. "Mississippi Town Breaks with Its Past to Elect First Black Mayor." *Guardian*, May 22, 2009. http://www.guardian.co.uk/world/2009/may/22/philadelphia-mississippi-race-segregation-mayor.

McIntyre, Lisa J. *Law in the Sociological Enterprise: A Reconstruction*. Boulder, CO: Westview Press, 1994.

McLaurin, Melton Alonza. "Commemorating Wilmington's Racial Violence of 1898: From Individual to Collective Memory." *Southern Cultures* 6, no. 4 (2000): 35–57.

Melucci, Alberto. "The New Social Movements: A Theoretical Approach." *Social Science Information* 19, no. 2 (1980): 199–226.

Menkart, Deborah, Alana D. Murray, and Jenice View, eds. *Putting the Movement Back into Civil Rights Teaching: A Resource Guide for K–12 Classrooms*. Washington: Teaching for Change, 2004.

Meyer, David. "Protest and Political Opportunities." *Annual Review of Sociology* 30 (2004): 125–45.

Meyer, John W. "World Society, Institutional Theories, and the Actor." *Annual Review of Sociology* 36 (2010): 1–20.

Meyer, Rachel, and Howard Kimeldorf. "Eventful Subjectivity: The Experiential Sources of Solidarity." *Journal of Historical Sociology* 28, no. 4 (2015): 429–57.

Mill, John Stuart. *A System of Logic, Ratiocinative and Inductive: Being a Connected View of the Principles of Evidence, and the Methods of Scientific Investigation*. New York: Cambridge University Press, 2012.

Miller, Judith. "Wartime Internment of Japanese Was 'Grave Injustice,' Panel Says." *New York Times*, February 25, 1983.

Minor, Bill. "Image in Film Worries Mississippians." *New York Times*, January 15, 1989.

———. "Neshoba Event 'Nothing Short of a Miracle.'" *Sun Herald*, July 1, 2004.

Misco, Thomas. "Holocaust Curriculum Development for Latvian Schools: Arriving at Purposes, Aims, and Goals through Curriculum Deliberation." *Theory and Research in Social Education* 35, no. 3 (2012): 393–426.

"Mississippi Coalition Calls for New Vision for the State." *Wellspring* 2, no. 2 (2006): 1.

Mississippi Department of Archives and History. "Sovereignty Commission Online." Accessed Novemer 26, 2019. https://www.mdah.ms.gov/arrec/digital_archives/sovcom/scagencycasehistory.php.

Mississippi Department of Education. *Mississippi Subject Area Testing Program*. 2nd ed. Jackson: Mississippi Department of Education, 2011.

"Mississippi Town Won't Get Film." *New York Times*, January 9, 1989.

"Mississippians Divided on Most Public Issues." Mississippi State University. Accessed November 3, 2019. http://sds17.pspa.msstate.edu/poll/PressRelease94.html.

Misztal, Barbara A. "Memory and Democracy." *American Behavioral Scientist* 48, no. 10 (2005): 1320–38.

Mitchell, Jerry. "44 Days: State Considers Pursuing Murder Charges in Case." *Clarion-Ledger*, May 7, 2000.

———. "'64 Killings Probe Nears End." *Clarion-Ledger*, May 3, 2001.

———. "Almost Half in Neshoba Survey Favored Trial in '64 Killings." *Clarion-Ledger*, July 5, 2005.

———. "Civil Rights, History Museums May Surpass Expected Attendance." *Clarion-Ledger*, February 22, 2018.

———. "Congress Opens Door for More Civil Rights Cold Cases." *Clarion-Ledger*, December 13, 2016.

———. "Crimes of the Past." *Clarion-Ledger*, December 28, 1998.

———. "Journalism Legend Stanley Dearman Died Saturday." *Clarion-Ledger*, February 25, 2017.

———. "Klansman Who Orchestrated Mississippi Burning Killings Dies in Prison." *Clarion-Ledger*, January 12, 2018.

Mohr, Holbrook. "High Court Rejects Appeal in 'Miss. Burning' Case." *Associated Press*, November 4, 2013.

Molpus, Dick. "Dick Molpus." *Neshoba Democrat*, July 5, 1989.

———. "Philadelphia, Mississippi: A Story of Racial Reconciliation." *Mississippi History Now*, December 2014. http://www.mshistorynow.mdah.ms.gov/articles/389/philadelphia-mississippi-a-story-of-racial-reconciliation.

Molpus Woodlands Group. "Our Beginnings." Accessed November 16, 2018. https://www.molpus.com/about-us/our-beginnings.html.

Moon, Claire. *Narrating Political Reconciliation: South Africa's Truth and Reconciliation Commission*. Plymouth, UK: Lexington Books, 2008.

Morris, Aldon. *Origins of the Civil Rights Movement*. New York: Free Press, 1984.

Morris, Willie. *The Courting of Marcus Dupree*. Jackson: University Press of Mississippi, 1992.

Myers, Debbie. "Killen Ordered back to Prison." *Neshoba Democrat*, September 9, 2005.

———. "MDA, Tourism Council Unveil Civil Rights Brochure." *Neshoba Democrat*, June 7, 2004. Accessed November 28, 2019. http://www.neshobademocrat.com/Content/40th-ANNIVERSARY/40th-Anniversary/Article/MDA-Tourism-Council-unveil-civil-rights-brochure/20/330/8093.

———. "Vandals Hit Civil Rights Marker." *Neshoba Democrat*, April 17, 2013.

Nagy, Rosemary L. "The Scope and Bounds of Transitional Justice and the Canadian Truth and Reconciliation Commission." *International Journal of Transitional Justice* 7, no. 1 (2013): 52–73.

Naqvi, Yasmin. "The Right to the Truth in International Law: Fact or Fiction?" *International Review of the Red Cross* 88, no. 862 (2006): 245–73.

Nash, Jere, and Andy Taggert. *Mississippi Politics: The Struggle for Power, 1976–2008*. Jackson: University Press of Mississippi, 2009.

Nehru, Jawaharlal. *The Discovery of India*. New York: Oxford University Press, 2015.

Nepstad, Sharon Erickson. "Commitment." In *The Wiley-Blackwell Encyclopedia of Social and Political Movements*, edited by David A. Snow, Donatella della Porta, Bert Klandermans, and Doug McAdam. Malden, MA: Wiley-Blackwell, 2013.

———. "Creating Transnational Solidarity: The Use of Narrative in the U.S.–Central America Peace Movement." *Mobilization* 6, no. (2001): 21–36.

———. "Persistent Resistance: Commitment and Community in the Plowshares Movement." *Social Problems* 51, no. 1 (2004): 43–60.

"Neshoba Acknowledges '64 Murders." *Neshoba Democrat*, June 24, 2004.

Nevin, David. "A Strange, Tight Little Town, Loath to Admit Complicity." *Life*, December 18, 1964, 34–39.

NewsBank. Access World News. Accessed October 30, 2019. https://www.newsbank.com/libraries/public/solutions/us-international/access-world-news.

Newton, Michael. *The Ku Klux Klan in Mississippi: A History*. Jefferson, NC: McFarland, 2010.

Nietzsche, Friedrich. *Untimely Meditations*. Edited by Daniel Breazeale. Translated by R. J. Hollingdale. Cambridge: Cambridge University Press, 1997.

Noack, Rick. "U.S. Deports 95-Year-Old Nazi Guard Jakiw Palij to Germany as Prosecutions for Holocaust Crimes Surge." *Washington Post*, August 21, 2018.

https://www.washingtonpost.com/world/2018/08/21/us-deports-former-nazi-guard-germany-says-many-more-are-under-investigation/?utm_term=.0bfe37793f1a.

Nobles, Melissa. *The Politics of Official Apologies*. New York: Cambridge University Press, 2008.

Nora, Pierre. "Reasons for the Current Upsurge in Memory." *Eurozine*, April 19, 2002, 1–6.

Nussbaum, Perry E., and Stuart Rockoff. "Mississippi." In *Encyclopedia Judaica*, edited by Michael Berenbaum and Fred Skolnik, 364–66. New York: Macmillan, 2006.

Olick, Jeffrey K. "Collective Memory: The Two Cultures." *Sociological Theory* 17, no. 3 (1999): 333–48.

———. "Genre Memories and Memory Genres: A Dialogical Analysis of May 8, 1945 Commemorations in the Federal Republic of Germany." *American Sociological Review* 64, no. 3 (1999): 381–402.

———. *The Politics of Regret: On Collective Memory and Historical Responsibility*. New York: Routledge, 2007.

Olick, Jeffrey K., and Joyce Robbins. "Social Memory Studies: From 'Collective Memory' to the Historical Sociology of Mnemonic Practices." *Annual Review of Sociology* 24, no. 1 (1998): 105–40.

Oliver, Pamela E., and Daniel J. Myers. "How Events Enter the Public Sphere: Conflict, Location, and Sponsorship in Local Newspaper Coverage of Public Events." *American Journal of Sociology* 105, no. 1 (1999): 38–87.

Oluo, Ijeoma. *So You Want to Talk about Race*. Cambridge, MA: Da Capo Press, 2018.

Orwell, George. *1984*. Boston: Houghton Mifflin Harcourt, 1983.

Oxford Eagle Staff. "David Crews' Book Quotes Famous Mississippians." *Oxford Eagle*, October 20, 2016. https://www.oxfordeagle.com/2016/10/20/crews-book-quotes-famous-mississippians/.

Pair, Dann. "Memorial Service Marks 30th Anniversary of 1964 Murders." *Neshoba Democrat*, June 29, 1994.

Parker, Alan. *Mississippi Burning*. United States: Orion Pictures, 1988.

Parker, Christopher S., and Matt A. Barreto. *Change They Can't Believe In: The Tea Party and Reactionary Politics in America*. Updated ed. Princeton, NJ: Princeton University Press, 2014.

Parker, Sara. "All Aboard the Truth Bandwagon: An Examination of Our Fascination with Truth Commissions." *Antipoda* 4 (2007): 207–24.

Payne, Charles M. *I've Got the Light of Freedom: The Organizing Tradition and the Mississippi Freedom Struggle*. 2nd ed. Berkeley: University of California Press, 2007.

Pedriana, Nicholas. "From Protective to Equal Treatment: Legal Framing Processes and Transformation of the Women's Movement in the 1960s." *American Journal of Sociology* 111, no. 6 (2006): 1718–61.

Pennebaker, James W., and Becky L. Banasik. "On the Creation and Maintenance of Collective Memories: History as Social Psychology." In *Collective Memory of Political Events: Social Psychological Perspectives*, edited by James W. Pennebaker, Dario Paez, and Bernard Rime, 3-20. Mahwah, NJ: Lawrence Erlbaum Associates, 1997.

Pettigrew, Thomas F. "Intergroup Contact Theory." *Annual Review of Psychology* 49, no. 1 (1998): 65-85.

Pettigrew, Thomas F., and Linda R. Tropp. "A Meta-Analytic Test of Intergroup Contact Theory." *Journal of Personality and Social Psychology* 90, no. 5 (2006): 751-783.

Pickett, Otis. "'We Were All Prisoners of the System': William Winter, Susan Glisson, and the Founding of the William Winter Institute for Racial Reconciliation." *The Southern Quarterly* 54, no. 1 (2016): 151-69.

Pinar, William F. "Notes on Understanding Curriculum as a Racial Text." In *Race, Identity, and Representation in Education*, edited by Cameron McCarthy, 60-70. New York: Routledge, 1993.

Pinney, Neil, and George Serra. "A Voice for Black Interests: Congressional Black Caucus Cohesion and Bill Cosponsorship." *Congress and the Presidency* 29, no. 1 (2002): 69-86.

"Plans Progressing for June Observance." *Neshoba Democrat*, May 24, 1989.

Plummer, Ken. *Telling Sexual Stories: Power, Change and Social Worlds*. New York: Routledge, 2002.

Polletta, Francesca. *It Was Like a Fever: Storytelling in Protest and Politics*. Chicago: University of Chicago Press, 2009.

Polletta, Francesca, and James M. Jasper. "Collective Identity and Social Movements." *Annual Review of Sociology* 27, no. 1 (2001): 283-305.

Potter, Claire Bond, and Renee C. Romano. *Doing Recent History: On Privacy, Copyright, Video Games, Institutional Review Boards, Activist Scholarship, and History That Talks Back*. Athens: University of Georgia Press, 2012.

Prince, Jim. "Cracks in the Coalition." *Neshoba Democrat*, April 20, 2015.

———. "Historian Sees Coalition's Efforts as a Model for the State." *Neshoba Democrat*, June 24, 2004.

———. "Task Force Sets Theme for 40th Anniversary." *Neshoba Democrat*, April 28, 2004.

———. "Why Stir up the Past?" Editorial. *Neshoba Democrat*, June 30, 2004.

Rand, Clayton. *Ink on My Hands*. Carrick and Evans, 1940.

Raspberry, William. "A 'Sorry' Excuse from Cochran." *Sun Herald*, June 21, 2005.

Rawls, John. *Political Liberalism*. New York: Columbia University Press, 1993.

Rawls, Wendell, Jr. "Court Bars Rejection of Textbooks for Racial Reasons." *New York Times*, April 5, 1980.

Reed, Roy. "Philadelphia, Miss., Whites and Negroes Trade Shots." *New York Times*, June 22, 1966.

Reeves, Jay. "Seeking Justice, Backers Aim to Expand Emmett Till Act." *Charleston Gazette*, September 22, 2014.

Regional Alliance for Truth and Racial Reconciliation. "ATRR Organization." Accessed November 6, 2019. http://www.atrr.org/.

Reinharz, Shulamit. "Who Am I? The Need for a Variety of Selves in the Field." In *Reflexivity and Voice*, edited by Rosanna Hertz, 3–20. Thousand Oaks, CA: Sage, 1997.

Rejebian, Michael. "'We Wish We Could Bring Them Back,' Molpus Says." *Clarion-Ledger*, June 22, 1989.

Ricoeur, Paul. *Figuring the Sacred: Religion, Narrative and Imagination*. Minneapolis, MN: Fortress, 1995.

Rieff, David. *In Praise of Forgetting: Historical Memory and Its Ironies*. New Haven, CT: Yale University Press, 2017.

Rivera, Lauren A. "Managing 'Spoiled' National Identity: War, Tourism, and Memory in Croatia." *American Sociological Review* 73, no. 4 (2008): 613–34.

Roberts, Gene. "Motorcade in Mississippi." *New York Times*, June 21, 1965.

Rodríguez-Gómez, Diana, Kim Foulds, and Yusuf Sayed. "Representations of Violence in Social Science Textbooks: Rethinking Opportunities for Peacebuilding in the Colombian and South African Post-Conflict Scenarios." *Education as Change* 20, no. 3 (2016): 76–97.

Rolph, Stephanie R. *Resisting Inequality: The Citizens' Council, 1954–1989*. Baton Rouge: Louisiana State University Press, 2018.

Romano, Renee. "Narratives of Redemption: The Birmingham Church Bombing Trials and the Construction of Civil Rights Memory." In *The Civil Rights Movement in American Memory*, edited by Renee Romano and Leigh Raiford, 96–134. Athens: University of Georgia Press, 2006.

———. *Racial Reckoning: Prosecuting America's Civil Rights Murders*. Cambridge, MA: Harvard University Press, 2014.

———. "Small Steps towards Truth." Harvard University Press Blog, January 18, 2017. http://harvardpress.typepad.com/hup_publicity/2017/01/small-steps-towards-truth-renee-romano.html.

"Roots of Struggle: Rewards of Sacrifice." *African American Heritage Driving Tour*, Philadelphia-Neshoba County Tourism Council, 2004.

Rosen, Tove, ed. "The Influence of the Nuremberg Trial on International Criminal Law." Robert H. Jackson Center. Accessed November 3, 2019. https://www.robertjackson.org/speech-and-writing/the-influence-of-the-nuremberg-trial-on-international-criminal-law/.

Rotberg, Robert I., and Dennis Thompson. *Truth v. Justice: The Morality of Truth Commissions*. Princeton, NJ: Princeton University Press, 2010.

Rueschemeyer, Dietrich. "Can One or a Few Cases Yield Theoretical Gains?" In *Comparative Historical Analysis in the Social Sciences*, edited by James Mahoney and Dietrich Rueschemeyer, 305–36. New York: Cambridge University Press, 2003.

Ryle, John. "A Sorry Apology from Clinton." *Guardian*, April 13, 1998. https://www.theguardian.com/Columnists/Column/0,5673,234216,00.html.

Saito, Hiro. "Reiterated Commemoration: Hiroshima as National Trauma." *Sociological Theory* 24, no. 4 (2006): 353–76.

Salter, Sid. "Sunday Morning with Mark Duncan." *Clarion-Ledger*, July 3, 2003.

———. "Sunday Morning with Sid Salter." *Clarion-Ledger*, June 20, 2004.

Santayana, George. *Reason in Common Sense*. London: Constable, 1910.
Satz, Ronald N. "The Mississippi Choctaw: From the Removal Treaty to the Federal Agency." In *After Removal: The Choctaw in Mississippi*, edited by Samuel J. Wells and Roseanna Tubby, 3–32. Oxford: University Press of Mississippi, 1986.
Savelsberg, Joachim J., and Ryan D. King. *American Memories: Atrocities and the Law*. New York: Russell Sage Foundation, 2011.
SB 2718, Regular Session (Mississippi 2006). Accessed November 29, 2019. http://billstatus.ls.state.ms.us/documents/2006/html/SB/2700-2799/SB2718SG.htm.
Schreiner, Mark. "Senate Expresses Regret for 1898 Riot." *Wilmington Star News*, August 2, 2007.
Schudson, Michael. "Dynamic Distortion of Collective Memory." In *Memory Distortion: How Minds, Brains, and Societies Reconstruct the Past*, edited by Daniel L. Schacter, 346–64. Cambridge, MA: Harvard University Press, 1997.
———. "How Culture Works: Perspectives from Media Studies on the Efficacy of Symbols." *Theory and Society* 18, no. 2 (1989): 153–80.
———. "The Present in the Past Versus the Past in the Present." *Communications* 11, no. 2 (1989): 105–13.
Schuman, Howard, and Cheryl Rieger. "Historical Analogies, Generational Effects, and Attitudes toward War." *American Sociological Review* 57, no. 3 (1992): 315–26.
Schuman, Howard, and Jaqueline Scott. "Generations and Collective Memories." *American Sociological Review* 54, no. 3 (1989): 359–81.
Schuman, Howard, Charlotte Steeh, and Lawrence Bobo. *Racial Attitudes in America: Trends and Interpretations*. Cambridge, MA: Harvard University Press, 1985.
Schwartz, Barry. *Abraham Lincoln and the Forge of National Memory*. Chicago: University of Chicago Press, 2000.
Schwartz, Barry, and Howard Schuman. "The Two Meanings of Collective Memory." *Newsletter of Sociology of Culture* 14, no. 2 (2000): 1–3.
Sewell, William. "Historical Events as Transformations of Structures: Inventing Revolution at the Bastille." *Theory and Society* 25, no. 6 (1996): 841–81.
———. "Three Temporalities: Toward an Eventful Sociology." In *The Historic Turn in the Human Sciences*, edited by Terrence J. McDonald, 245–80. Ann Arbor: University of Michigan Press, 1996.
Sexton, Megan. "A Journey toward Understanding." University of South Carolina. August 29, 2017. http://www.sc.edu/uofsc/posts/2017/08/welcome_table.php.
Shaffer, Stephen D. "From Exclusion to Inclusion: The Evolution of Racial Politics in the Party Systems in the South." Paper presented at the Annual Meeting of the American Political Science Association, San Francisco, CA, August 29–September 1, 1996.
Shore, Megan. *Religion and Conflict Resolution: Christianity and South Africa's Truth and Reconciliation Commission*. New York: Routledge, 2016.

Silver, James. "History Changes More Slowly Than State." *Delta Democrat,* August 3, 1975.
———. *Mississippi: The Closed Society.* New York: Harcourt, 1964.
Simko, Christina. *The Politics of Consolation: Memory and the Meaning of September 11.* New York: Oxford University Press, 2015.
Simon, Paul, and Art Garfunkel. "He Was My Brother." In *Simon and Garfunkel: Complete Albums Collection.* New York: Sony Legacy, 2014.
Sitton, Claude. "Tragedy in Mississippi: Deep-Seated Feelings of Negroes Are Reflected in Funeral for Slain Civil Rights Worker." *New York Times,* August 9, 1964.
Smelser, Neil. "Psychological Trauma and Cultural Trauma." In *Cultural Trauma and Collective Identity,* edited by Jeffrey C. Alexander, Ron Eyerman, Bernard Giesen, Neil Smelster, and Piotr Sztompka, 31–59. Berkeley: University of California Press, 2004.
Snow, David A., and Robert D. Benford. "Ideology, Frame Resonance, and Participant Mobilization." *International Social Movement Research* 1, no. 1 (1988): 197–217.
Snow, David A., and Doug McAdam. "Identity Work Processes in the Context of Social Movements: Clarifying the Identity/Movement Nexus." In *Self, Identity, and Social Movements,* edited by Sheldon Stryker, Timothy Joseph Owens, and Robert W. White, 13:41–67. Minneapolis: University of Minnesota Press, 2000.
Sokol, Jason. *There Goes My Everything: White Southerners in the Age of Civil Rights, 1945–1975.* New York: Vintage Books, 2006.
Somers, Margaret R. "Genealogies of Katrina: The Unnatural Disasters of Market Fundamentalism, Racial Exclusion, and Statelessness." In *Genealogies of Citizenship: Markets, Statelessness, and the Right to Have Rights,* 63–117. New York: Cambridge University Press, 2008.
———. "The Narrative Constitution of Identity: A Relational and Network Approach." *Theory and Society* 23, no. 5 (1994): 605–49.
———. "What's Political or Cultural about Political Culture and the Public Sphere? Toward an Historical Sociology of Concept Formation." *Sociological Theory* 13, no. 2 (1995): 113–44.
———. "Where Is Sociology after the Historic Turn? Knowledge Cultures, Narrativity, and Historical Epistemologies." In *The Historic Turn in the Human Sciences,* edited by Terrence J. McDonald, 53–89. Ann Arbor: University of Michigan Press, 1996.
Somers, Margaret R., and Fred Block. "From Poverty to Perversity: Ideas, Markets, and Institutions over 200 Years of Welfare Debate." *American Sociological Review* 70 (2005): 260–87.
Southern Poverty Law Center. "Teaching the Movement: The State of Civil Rights Education in the United States 2011." September 2011. https://www.splcenter.org/sites/default/files/d6_legacy_files/downloads/publication/TeachingtheMovement.pdf.
———. "Teaching the Movement 2014: The State of Civil Rights Education in the United States." March 2014. http://www.tolerance.org/sites/default/files/general/Teaching%20the%20Movement%202014_final_web_0.pdf.

Spillman, Lyn. "When Do Collective Memories Last? Founding Moments in the United States and Australia." *Social Science History* 22, no. 4 (1998): 445–77.

Steidl, Christina R. "Remembering May 4, 1970: Integrating the Commemorative Field at Kent State." *American Sociological Review* 78, no. 5 (2013): 749–72.

Stepler, Renee. "5 Key Takeaways about Views of Race and Inequality in America." Pew Research Center. June 27, 2016. http://www.pewresearch.org/fact-tank/2016/06/27/key-takeaways-race-and-inequality/.

Stern, Charlotte. "The Evolution of Social-Movement Organizations: Niche Competition in Social Space." *European Sociological Review* 15, no. 1 (1999): 91–105.

Stinchcombe, Arthur L. *Theoretical Methods in Social History*. New York: Academic Press, 1978.

Stout, David. "Cecil Price, 63, Deputy Guilty in Killing of 3 Rights Workers." *New York Times*, May 9, 2001.

Straight, June C. "West Point Leaders Seek to Improve Race Relations through Dialogue." *Commercial Dispatch*, August 14, 2007.

Subašić, Emina, Katherine J. Reynolds, and John C. Turner. "The Political Solidarity Model of Social Change: Dynamics of Self-Categorization in Intergroup Power Relations." *Personality and Social Psychology Review* 12, no. 4 (2008): 330–52.

Sue, Derald Wing. *Race Talk and the Conspiracy of Silence: Understanding and Facilitating Difficult Dialogues on Race*. Malden, MA: Wiley, 2016.

Tarrow, Sidney G. *Power in Movement: Collective Action, Social Movements and Politics*. Cambridge: Cambridge University Press, 1998.

Taylor, Verta. "Social Movement Continuity: The Women's Movement in Abeyance." *American Sociological Review* 54, no. 5 (1989): 761–75.

Taylor, Verta, and Nancy Whittier. "Collective Identity in Social Movement Communities: Lesbian Feminist Mobilization." In *Frontiers in Social Movement Theory*, edited by Aldon D. Morris and Carol McClurg Mueller, 104–30. New Haven, CT: Yale University Press, 1992.

Teitel, Ruti. "Transitional Justice Genealogy." *Harvard Human Rights Journal* 16 (2003): 69–94.

———. "Transitional Justice Globalized." *International Journal of Transitional Justice* 2, no. 1 (2008): 1–4.

Tell, Dave. "Protecting the Memory of Emmett Till from the Scourge of Vandals." *Chicago Tribune*, July 26, 2019.

———. *Remembering Emmett Till*. Chicago: University of Chicago Press, 2019.

Tetlock, Philip E., and Aaron Belkin. "Counterfactual Thought Experiments in World Politics: Logical, Methodological, and Psychological Perspectives." In *Counterfactual Thought Experiments in World Politics: Logical, Methodological, and Psychological Perspectives*, edited by Philip E. Tetlock and Aaron Belkin. Princeton, NJ: Princeton University Press, 1996.

"The Philadelphia Coalition." *Mississippi Civil Rights Project*. Accessed November 27, 2019. https://mscivilrightsproject.org/neshoba/organization-neshoba/the-philadelphia-coalition/.

Till, Karen E. "Wounded Cities: Memory-Work and a Place-Based Ethics of Care." *Political Geography* 31, no. 1 (2012): 3–14.
Tilly, Charles. *Regimes and Repertoires*. Chicago: University of Chicago Press, 2010.
Toplin, Robert Brent. "Mississippi Burning: 'A Standard to Which We Couldn't Live Up.'" In *History by Hollywood: The Use and Abuse of the American Past*, edited by Robert Brent Toplin. Urbana: University of Illinois Press, 1996.
Torpey, John. *Making Whole What Has Been Smashed: On Reparations Politics*. Cambridge, MA: Harvard University Press, 2006.
———. *Politics and the Past: On Repairing Historical Injustices*. Lanham, MD: Rowman and Littlefield, 2003.
Treen, Joe. "Southern Man: Klan-Busting Journalist Jerry Mitchell." *Mother Jones*, January 4, 2007. https://www.motherjones.com/politics/2007/01/klan-busting-journalist-jerry-mitchell-beckwith-case/2/.
Tsutsui, Kiyoteru. "The Trajectory of Perpetrators' Trauma: Mnemonic Politics around the Asia-Pacific War in Japan." *Social Forces* 87, no. 3 (2009): 1389–422.
Tucker, Charles H. "Mississippi Truth Project Enters New Phase." *Wellspring* 6, no. 1 (2010): 7.
Tusa, Ann, and John Tusa. *The Nuremberg Trial*. New York: Skyhorse, 2010.
Verkuyten, Maykel, Jochem Thijs, and Hidde Bekhuis. "Intergroup Contact and Ingroup Reappraisal: Examining the Deprovincialization Thesis." *Social Psychology Quarterly* 73, no. 4 (2010): 398–416.
Vinitzky-Seroussi, Vered. "Banal Commemoration." In *The Routledge International Handbook of Memory Studies*, edited by Anna Lisa Tota and Trever Hagen, 84–92. New York: Routledge, 2016.
———. "Commemorating a Difficult Past: Yitzhak Rabin's Memorials." *American Sociological Review* 67, no. 1 (2002): 30–51.
———. *Yitzhak Rabin's Assassination and the Dilemmas of Commemoration*. Albany: State University of New York Press, 2009.
Vinitzky-Seroussi, Vered, and Chana Teeger. "Unpacking the Unspoken: Silence in Collective Memory and Forgetting." *Social Forces* 88, no. 3 (2010): 1103–22.
Vogler, Kenneth E. "Comparing the Impact of Accountability Examinations on Mississippi and Tennessee Social Studies Teachers' Instructional Practices." *Educational Assessment* 13, no. 1 (2008): 1–32.
Vollers, Maryanne. *Ghosts of Mississippi: The Murder of Medgar Evers, the Trials of Byron De La Beckwith, and the Haunting of the New South*. New York: Back Bay Books, 1995.
Wagner, Ulrich, and Miles Hewstone. "Intergroup Contact." In *The Oxford Handbook of Intergroup Conflict*, edited by Linda Tropp, 193–209. New York: Oxford University Press, 2012.
Wagner-Pacifici, Robin. "Memories in the Making: The Shapes of Things That Went." *Qualitative Sociology* 19, no. 3 (1996): 301–21.
———. "Theorizing the Restlessness of Events." *American Journal of Sociology* 115, no. 5 (2010): 1351–86.

Wagner-Pacifici, Robin, and Barry Schwartz. "The Vietnam Veterans Memorial: Commemorating a Difficult Past." *American Journal of Sociology* 87, no. 2 (1991): 376–420.

Ward, Jason Morgan. *Hanging Bridge: Racial Violence and America's Civil Rights Century*. New York: Oxford University Press, 2016.

Watson, Bruce. *Freedom Summer: The Savage Season That Made Mississippi Burn and Made America a Democracy*. New York: Viking, 2010.

Weber, Max. "Objective Possibility and Adequate Causation in Historical Explanation." In *The Methodology of the Social Sciences*, 164–88. New York: Free Press, 1949.

Weber, Max, Guenther Roth, and Claus Wittich. *Economy and Society: An Outline of Interpretive Sociology*. Berkeley: University of California Press, 1978.

Weeden, Dustin D. "State Policies Concerning Holocaust Education." *State Notes*, June 2005. http://www.ecs.org/clearinghouse/62/34/6234.pdf.

Weems, Patrick. "Institute Helps Kick Off Year of Dialogue on Race." *Wellspring* 4, no. 1 (September 2007): 4.

———. "Mississippi Truth Project Leads the Charge in Confronting the Past." *Wellspring* 4, no. 3 (December 2008): 4.

Wegner, Jarula. "Rethinking Countermemory: Black-Jewish Negotiations in Rap Music." *Memory Studies*, August. 2018. doi:10.1177/1750698018794801.

Wells, Ida B. *The Red Record*. New York: Open Road Media, 2015.

W. G. Kellogg Foundation. "Truth, Racial Healing, and Transformation." Accessed November 22, 2019. https://healourcommunities.org/.

Wheeler, Lonnie. "They Gathered and the Fire Still Flickered." *Clarion-Ledger*, December 13, 1976.

Whigham, Kerry. "Remembering to Prevent: The Preventive Capacity of Public Memory." *Genocide Studies and Prevention* 11, no. 2 (2017): 53–71.

Whitehead, Don. *Attack on Terror: The FBI against the Ku Klux Klan in Mississippi*. New York: Funk and Wagnalls, 1970.

Whitlinger, Claire. "From Commemoration to Conviction: Prosecuting Edgar Ray Killen for the 'Mississippi Burning' Murders." *Race and Justice* 5, no. 2 (2015): 144–67.

———. "From Countermemory to Collective Memory: Acknowledging the 'Mississippi Burning' Murders." *Sociological Forum* 30, no. S1 (2015): 648–70.

Wilkerson, Steve. "Steve Wilkerson." *Neshoba Democrat*, July 5, 1989.

Williams, Juan. *Eyes on the Prize: America's Civil Rights Years, 1954–1965*. New York: Penguin, 2013.

Winstead, Mary. *Back to Mississippi: A Personal Journey Through the Events That Changed America in 1964*. New York: Hyperion, 2002.

Winter Institute. "Declaration of Intent Meeting." Accessed December 3, 2019. https://vimeo.com/8959346.

———. "Neshoba County—Interview with Clay Lee." Accessed August 11, 2011. http://vimeo.com/album/1668458.

———. "Neshoba County—Interview with Nettie Ann Cox." Accessed August 11, 2011. http://vimeo.com/album/1665694.

———. "Neshoba County: Interview with Sally Beam 01." Accessed October 16, 2017. https://vimeo.com/27503190.

———. "Neshoba County: Philadelphia Coalition After Party—Deborah." Accessed November 7, 2019. https://vimeo.com/showcase/1669695/video/27775269.

———. "Neshoba County: Philadelphia Coalition After Party—Elsie and Stan." Winter Institute. Accessed November 9, 2019. http://vimeo.com/album/1669695/video/27775299.

———. "Neshoba County: Philadelphia Coalition After Party—Nettie Ann Cox." Accessed November 11, 2019. https://vimeo.com/showcase/1669695/video/27776440.

———. "Neshoba County: Philadelphia Coalition After Party—Rayburn Waddell." Accessed November 9, 2019. https://vimeo.com/showcase/1669695/video/27776508.

———. "Neshoba County: Philadelphia Coalition After Party—Susan Glisson." Accessed November 9, 2019. http://vimeo.com/album/1669695/video/27776478.

———. "Neshoba County: Philadelphia Coalition After Party—Ta'shia." Accessed November 7, 2019. http://vimeo.com/album/1669695/video/27776488.

———. "Neshoba County—Sally Beam." Winter Institute Vimeo. Accessed November 11, 2019. https://vimeo.com/album/1663724.

———. "The Welcome Table." *Youtube*, July 26, 2012. https://www.youtube.com/watch?v=X4cCz9oUvOA.

Winter, Jay. "The Memory Boom in Contemporary Historical Studies." *Raritan* 21, no. 1 (2001): 52–66.

Wolf, Richard. "Voting Rights Act: Do We Still Need It?—High Court Must Gauge Just How Much the South Has Changed." *USA Today*, February 20, 2013.

Wright, Stephen C., and Gamze Baray. "Models of Social Change in Social Psychology: Collective Action or Prejudice Reduction? Conflict or Harmony?" In *Beyond Prejudice: Extending the Social Psychology of Conflict, Inequality and Social Change*, edited by John Dixon, 225–47. New York: Cambridge University Press, 2012.

Wuthnow, Robert. *Communities of Discourse: Ideology and Social Structure in the Reformation, the Enlightenment, and European Socialism*. Cambridge, MA: Harvard University Press, 2009.

Xu, Bin, and Gary Alan Fine. "Memory Movement and State-Society Relationship in Chinese World War II Victims' Reparations Movement against Japan." In *Northeast Asia's Difficult Past: Essays in Collective Memory*, edited by Minkyoung Kim and Barry Schwartz, 166–89. New York: Palgrave, 2010.

Yamamoto, Eric K. *Interracial Justice: Conflict and Reconciliation in Post–Civil Rights America*. New York: New York University Press, 1999.

Yates, Jenelle B., and Theresa T. Ridout. *Red Clay Hills of Neshoba: Roots-Reflections-Ramblings: The Early History of Neshoba County, Mississippi*. Neshoba County Historical Society, 1992.

York, Andrew Buncombe. "Charlottesville Pays Tribute to Heather Heyer, Killed by White Supremacist in Riots." *Independent*, December 25, 2017.

Young, Alford A., Jr. "Experiences in Ethnographic Interviewing about Race: The Inside and Outside of It." In *Researching Race and Racism*, edited by Martin Bulmer and John Solomos, 97–103. New York: Routledge, 2004.

Younge, Gary. "New Generation of Americans Tries Truth and Reconciliation to Heal Old Racial Wounds." *Guardian*, June 14, 2004.

Zamponi, Lorenzo. "Collective Memory and Social Movements." In *The Wiley-Blackwell Encyclopedia of Social and Political Movements*, edited by David A. Snow, Donatella della Porta, Bert Klandermans, and Doug McAdam, 225–29. Malden, MA: Wiley-Blackwell, 2013.

Zamponi, Lorenzo, and Priska Daphi. "Breaks and Continuities in and between Cycles of Protest: Memories and Legacies of the Global Justice Movement in the Context of Anti-Austerity Mobilisations." In *Spreading Protest: Social Movements in Times of Crisis*, edited by Donatella della Porta and Alice Mattoni, 193–226. Colchester, UK: European Consortium for Political Research Press, 2014.

Zelizer, Barbie. "Reading the Past against the Grain: The Shape of Memory Studies." *Review and Criticism* 12, no. 2 (1995): 214–39.

Zerubavel, Eviatar. "Calendars and History: A Comparative Study of the Social Organization of National Memory." In *States of Memory: Continuities, Conflicts, and Transformations in National Retrospection*, edited by Jeffrey K. Olick, 315–38. Durham, NC: Duke University Press, 2003.

———. *The Elephant in the Room: Silence and Denial in Everyday Life*. New York: Oxford University Press, 2006.

———. "Social Memories: Steps to a Sociology of the Past." *Qualitative Sociology* 19, no. 3 (1996): 283–99.

———. *Social Mindscapes: An Invitation to Cognitive Sociology*. Cambridge, MA: Harvard University Press, 1997.

———. *Time Maps: Collective Memory and the Social Shape of the Past*. Chicago: University of Chicago Press, 2003.

Zerubavel, Yael. *Recovered Roots: Collective Memory and the Making of Israeli National Tradition*. Chicago: University of Chicago Press, 1995.

Zinn, Howard. *A People's History of the United States*. New York: Harper Perennial Modern Classics, 2005.

Index

Abbott, Andrew, 197
Access World News database, 12, 201, 220–21n31
African American community, 22–23, 82–83, 85–86, 113; annual commemorations and, 13–14, 30, 33–35, 48, 51–52, 68, 102, 105, 107, 133, 170, 171, 175; civil rights education and, 86, 88, 89, 226n22; commemorations and, 7, 16, 17; fortieth anniversary commemoration and, 52, 66, 68, 144, 158, 160, 164, 165, 232n44; history and, 50, 80, 152–53, 159, 225n1; Independence Quarters and, 19, 30, 33, 34, 102, 170; political office and, 11, 50, 65, 85, 91, 93, 110, 140, 141, 185, 194, 198; tourism and, 36, 52, 53, 55, 58, 139, 159, 166; twenty-fifth anniversary commemoration and, 46, 143–44, 157, 158. *See also* civil rights movement; desegregation; Mississippi Burning murders; Mississippi Truth Project (MTP); Mt. Nebo Baptist Church; Mt. Zion United Methodist Church; racial violence
Alexander, Jeffrey, 32
Alexander v. Holmes County Board of Education, 83, 146
Alliance for Truth and Racial Reconciliation, 119
Allport, Gordon, 15, 155
American Nazi Party, 114
Andrew Goodman Foundation, 48, 186
Andrew Goodman Memorial Collection, 201
Andrus Family Fund, 118, 121, 130
Arlington National Cemetery, 173

Armenian genocide, 38
Armstrong, Elizabeth, 9, 40, 134, 135, 151, 177
Associated Press, 54–55

Baker, Ella, 31–32
Bakiner, Onur, 111
Barbour, Haley, 12, 195; civil rights education and, 81, 93, 187; fortieth anniversary commemoration and, 55, 71–73, 77, 104, 142, 162–63, 183; Holocaust education bill and, 85, 92; Killen conviction and, 115–16, 118, 124
Barnett, Ross, 83–84
Beam, Sally, 74
Becker, Howard, 8
Beckwith, Byron De La, Jr., 48, 64, 65, 223n22
Bell, Derrick, 172
Bender, Rita, 105, 115–16, 130, 142–43. *See also* Schwerner, Rita
Benford, Robert, 123
Berry, Wendell, 150
Bettersworth, John K., 84, 225–26n18
"Beyond Reconciliation: Dealing with the Aftermath of Mass Trauma and Political Violence" (conference), 126, 230n68
Bickford, Louis, 111
Black Lives Matter, 192
Bloody Sunday (Northern Ireland), 145
Bolton, Charles, 82
Bowers, Sam, 21, 61, 62, 63, 223n22
Brandeis University, 127, 230n73
Brazil, 113
Brown v. Board of Education, 20, 30, 80, 82, 83, 172, 189

Bryant, Phil, 15
Bryant, Roy, 180
Bulhof, Johannes, 11
Bush, George H. W., 142

Canada, 112
casino tourism, 36, 52–53, 199
Catledge, Turner, 25
Center for Investigative Reporting, 188–89
Center for Oral History and Cultural Heritage (University of Southern Mississippi), 92, 94, 128, 190
Central United Methodist Church, 125
Chaney, Ben, 33, 54, 193, 194
Chaney, Fannie Lee, 24, 60
"Chaney, Goodman and Schwerner Day," 143
Chaney, James Earl (J. E.): civil rights education and, 89–90, 91, 92, 95; commemorating death of and, xii, 16, 30–32, 33, 34, 36, 48, 101, 108; fortieth anniversary commemoration of death and, 1, 54, 104, 132, 137, 147, 193–94; Killen conviction and, 60, 76, 79, 129; marble memorial for and, 30, 35, 102; missing posters and, 32–33, 99, 100, 137–38; Mississippi Summer Project and, 23, 24; murder and, 1–2, 23, 24–26, 28, 61, 76, 101, 164, 201; reopening murders case and, 61, 75; twenty-fifth anniversary of death and, 137, 142, 143, 221n48. *See also* fortieth anniversary commemoration; Mississippi Burning murders; twenty-fifth anniversary commemoration
"Chaney, Schwerner, and Goodman Living Memorial Civil Rights Education Summit," 89–90, 91, 92, 95
Christianity, 149
civil and human rights education bill. *See* civil rights education; Mississippi Senate Bill 2718

Civil Rights Act of 1964, 21, 82
Civil Rights Cold Case Project, 64
civil rights cold cases, 60, 61, 63–65, 76, 79, 133, 187, 223n22
civil rights education, 85–86, 172, 191, 225n6, 238n19, 238n26; African American community and, 86, 88, 89, 226n22; fortieth anniversary commemoration and, 11, 14, 87–90, 91–92, 96–97, 131, 133, 134, 198, 200; Mississippi civil rights education commission and, 81, 94–95; Mississippi Legislature and, 2, 14, 59, 90, 92–95, 96, 169, 187–88, 227n53; Mississippi State Board of Education and, 81, 84, 86, 87–88, 90, 91, 92–96, 97–98; Mississippi Truth Project (MTP) and, 191, 227n3; William Winter Institute for Racial Reconciliation and, 89–90, 91, 92, 93, 94, 95, 96, 108, 189. *See also* curriculum; Holocaust education program; human rights education; Mississippi Senate Bill 2718
civil rights movement, 3, 106, 142, 147, 166; commemorations and, 7, 53, 57, 159, 183–84, 195; historical importance and, 81, 152–53, 183–84; in Mississippi and, xii, 20–23, 68, 81, 99, 127, 170–71, 201; Mississippi Burning murders and, 23, 32–33, 99, 100, 137–38; Mississippi Summer Project and, 12, 20–23, 34, 99, 201; white community and, 20–22, 35, 152–53. *See also* Mississippi Burning murders
Civil Rights Restorative Justice Project 64
Civil War, 18, 39, 225–26n18
Claasen, Christopher, 156
Clarion-Ledger (Jackson), 12, 30, 33, 61, 91, 116
Clark, Robert, 91
Clemons, Leroy, 49–52, 55, 185; fortieth anniversary commemoration and, 53,

70, 73, 92, 103, 148, 158, 159, 161, 163, 193–94, 199, 222n68
Clinton, Bill, 49, 52, 139, 146, 159
Cochran, Thad, 143, 168, 180
Cohen, Richard, 187
Cold Case Justice Initiative, 64, 187
Cole, Howard, 25, 29
collective memory, 3, 219n5; commemorations and, 37, 39, 79, 170, 177, 214n48; countermemories and, 14, 40, 171; Philadelphia and, 14, 39, 40; social movements and, 7–10, 77–78, 134, 136, 182
Collier, Clinton, 33, 143–44
commemorations: banal / bland and, 94, 175; civil rights milestones and, 7, 53, 57, 159, 183–84, 195; commemorability and, 40, 56, 134, 135, 220n21; commemorative capacity and, 87, 136, 138, 176; commemorative resonance and, 136, 138, 143, 144–45, 151, 177–78, 236–37n20; commitment and, 148, 151, 167; countermemories and, 14, 31, 39, 40, 58; difficult pasts and, 6, 8, 9, 37, 38–39, 40, 56, 151, 170, 175, 181, 212–13n19; emotion and, 178, 237n22; financial and political support and, 8–9, 179; forgetting and, 5–6, 37, 63, 213n27, 213n28; fragmented commemoration and, xiii, 37–38, 219n8; historical markers and, 177, 180, 185; intergroup contact and, 9, 15, 152, 153, 155–56, 157, 179, 234n15, 234n18, 234n22, 237n23; libraries and archives and, 136, 176–77; memory movements and, 8–10, 78, 79, 143, 148, 166, 174–75, 176, 214n48; mnemonic capacity and, 9, 40, 135, 151, 157, 166, 172; mobilizing target audiences and, 135–36, 138, 146–47, 151; outcomes and, 9–10, 77, 78, 151, 172, 181–83, 198, 214n48, 215n53, 240n5; planning process and, 152, 167, 176, 178–80,

183; political opportunities and, 8–9, 214n40; power of and, 173–74, 177; of racial violence and, xiii, 2, 3, 15, 135, 136, 152, 167, 169, 173, 174, 178–79, 180, 184; silence-breaking and, 40, 182, 222n67; silenced pasts and, 14, 31, 38–39, 50–51, 58, 171, 219n11, 220n13; social change and, 136, 169, 172; social function and, 4–6, 212n16; storytelling and, 156, 167, 222n67; success of and, 9, 134–36, 151, 174, 231n9; white communities and, 14, 16–17, 33, 35, 39. *See also* fortieth anniversary commemoration; Mississippi Burning murders; Philadelphia, Miss.; Press coverage of commemorations; Truth commissions; twenty-fifth anniversary commemoration
Commission on Wartime Relocation and Internment of Civilians, 112–13
Community Development Partnership (CDP), 1, 36, 52, 53, 55, 58, 139, 159
Confederate iconography, 4, 5, 15, 72, 162, 174, 212n14, 215n60, 239n38
Congress of Racial Equality (CORE), 20, 23, 25
Conway, Brian, 145
Corning, Amy, 146
Council of Conservative Citizens, 72, 163
Council of Europe, 86
Council of Federated Organizations (COFO), 20, 21, 22–23, 24, 25, 28, 30, 33
counterfactual analysis, 11, 170, 182, 198, 200, 215n53, 240n5
countermemories, 14, 31, 36, 39, 40, 58, 171, 218n79
Cox, Nettie, 68, 144
Crage, Suzanna, 9, 40, 134, 135, 151, 177
Crew, David, 169

Cunningham, David, 97, 188
curriculum, 80, 83–87, 226n25, 226n30, 227n3; in Mississippi and, 83–86, 87, 95, 97, 188–89, 225–26n18, 226n22. *See also* civil rights education; Holocaust education program; human rights education

Dahmer, Vernon, 63, 223n22
Davis, Fania, 192
Davis, Rebecca, 83
Dawson, Michael, 7
Dearman, Stanley, 184; fortieth anniversary commemoration and, 66, 147, 158, 159–60; *Neshoba Democrat* and, 41, 44, 48–49, 50, 51, 75, 77, 105; twenty-fifth anniversary commemoration and, 42, 43, 44, 45–46, 52, 157
Dee, Henry Hezekiah, 25
Demjanjuk, John, 63
desegregation, 53, 159, 170; education system and, 20, 30, 51, 80–81, 82–83, 87, 146, 199, 222n68, 225n12; resegregation and, 83; segregated education and, 81–84
DeWeese, Ab, 19
DeWeese, Fenton, 88, 160, 164
Dittmer, John, 22–23
Dozier, John, 191
Duncan, Mark, 62, 73–75
Dupree, Marcus, 30
Durkheim, Emile, 4, 178

Ellis, Lulu, 41
Emmett Till Memorial Commission of Tallahatchie County, 180
Emmett Till Unsolved Civil Rights Crime Act of 2008, 64, 66, 187
Equal Justice Initiative, 4
Espy, Mike, 143
ETHNO (software program), 198, 200, 240n7
European Parliament, 86

Event Structure Analysis (ESA), 11, 198–200, 221n46, 222n68, 224n42, 240n7, 240n11
Evers, Medgar, 22, 48, 57, 63, 64, 223n22
Eyerman, Ron, 8

Federal Bureau of Investigation (FBI), 1, 26, 40, 61, 99, 187
feminist movement, 150
Fine, Gary Alan, 31
First United Methodist Church, 164
Florida, 113
fortieth anniversaryl commemoration, 199; aftermath of and, 59, 132–34, 140, 148, 150, 159–60, 168–69, 172; civil rights education and, 11, 14, 87–90, 91–92, 93, 95, 96–97, 131, 133, 134, 198, 200; commemoration program and, 1, 54–55, 72–73, 104; commemorative resonance and, 144–45, 146, 172–73; commitment and, 148–49, 150, 160–62, 173; compared with twenty-fifth anniversary commemoration and, 11–12, 14–15, 49, 133–34, 136, 137, 138–39, 144, 150–51, 172, 231n6; environmental capacity and, 138–39, 172; financial and political support and, 56, 138, 162–63, 167, 176, 183; impetus for and, 56, 57; intergroup contact and, 153, 157, 159, 164, 166–67, 173; interracial collaboration and, 52–53, 66–67, 153, 158–59, 160, 164, 167, 168, 171, 173; justice resolution and, 69–71, 75, 76, 77, 103, 144, 145, 151, 159; Killen conviction and, 59, 62, 76–77, 87, 114, 133; Killen trial and, 11, 14, 66, 131, 134, 145, 198, 200; Mississippi Band of Choctaw Indians and, 1, 52–53, 69–70, 160; mnemonic capacity and, 157, 166, 172; mobilizing target audiences and, 144–45, 172–73; outcomes and, xiii, 10, 11, 14, 59, 131, 133, 169, 172, 186,

274 Index

193, 197–98, 200, 214n49; outside group commemoration and, xiii, 54, 55, 67–68, 193–94; planning process and, 53–54, 56, 66–68, 71–72, 77, 87–88, 114, 148–49, 150, 158, 161, 164; reopening murders case and, 73–74, 75–76, 224n42; silence-breaking and, 14, 36–37, 55–56, 58–59, 87, 170, 171; social justice and, 66–67, 68, 69–71, 72–73; story-telling and, 67, 164–65, 166, 167, 173; success of and, 7, 91–92, 104, 132, 136, 153, 159–60; task force formation and, 49–52, 158, 222n68; truth project and, 11, 14, 110, 114, 117, 129–30, 131, 133, 134, 169, 198, 200. *See also* African American community; Mt. Zion United Methodist Church; Neshoba County; *particular people involved*; Philadelphia Coalition; press coverage of commemorations; Press coverage of Mississippi Burning murders; twenty-fifth anniversary commemoration; white community; William Winter Institute for Racial Reconciliation

framing theory, 123, 143
Frankenberg, Erica, 83
Freedom Rides, 20, 57, 195
Freedom Summer. *See* Mississippi Summer Project
Freedom Summer '94, 48
Freeman, Morgan, 180
Fulton, Lee Ann, 189

Gates, Henry Louis, Jr., 189
gay rights, 9, 135, 177
Ghoshal, Raj, 9, 87, 135–36, 138, 176
Gibson, James, 156, 181–82, 237n35
Gill, Joseph, 64
Glisson, Susan, 108, 179–80, 191; civil rights education and, 93; fortieth anniversary commemoration and, 52, 53, 54, 56, 67, 68, 70, 78, 150, 159, 164, 199; justice resolution and, 75–76, 87; truth project and, 116, 120, 128, 129. *See also* William Winter Institute for Racial Reconciliation

Goode, Wilson, 46, 157, 158, 162
Goodman, Andrew: civil rights education and, 89–90, 91, 92, 95; commemorating death of and, xii, 16, 30–32, 33, 34, 36, 101, 108; fortieth anniversary commemoration of death and, 1, 104, 132, 137, 147, 163, 193–94; Killen conviction and, 60, 76, 79, 129; marble memorial for and, 30, 35, 102; missing posters and, 32–33, 99, 100, 137–38; Mississippi Summer Project and, 24; murder and, 1–2, 23, 24–26, 28, 61, 76, 101, 164, 186, 201; reopening murders case and, 61, 73, 75; twenty-fifth anniversary of death and, 48, 137, 142, 143, 221n48. *See also* fortieth anniversary commemoration; Mississippi Burning murders; twenty-fifth anniversary commemoration

Goodman, Carolyn, 50, 73, 75, 104, 163
Goodman, David, 48, 186
Goodman, Robert, 31, 32, 201
Goodwin, Jeff, 153
Gould, Stephen, 11
Grandin, Greg, 111
Grayson, April, 190
Greensboro Massacre, 114, 120
Greensboro Truth and Reconciliation Commission, 114, 118, 119, 120–21, 123, 130, 182, 211n3 [1], 222–23n84
Griffin, Larry, 147, 198

Halbwachs, Maurice, 4
Harbin, Tomeka, 121–22, 126
Hargis, Peggy, 147
Harris, Fredrick, 7
Hawthorne, Jennifer, 157
Hayner, Priscilla, 110
Hechinger Report, 188–89
Heise, David, 198

Hendrickson, Paul, 27
historical markers, 48, 108, 133, 177, 180, 185
H-net listserve, xii, 211n4
Holocaust Education Commission, 92
Holocaust education program, 84–86, 92, 96, 226n25, 226n30
Hood, Jim, 62, 71, 73, 74–75, 186
Horhn, John, 85, 109–10, 113
Howard University, 201
Huie, William Bradford, 25
human rights commissions, 111
human rights education, 86, 93–94, 95, 96, 97–98, 133, 188. *See also* Civil rights education
human rights violations, 62–63, 111, 113, 120, 145, 228n7
Hurricane Katrina, 109, 116, 117, 189

Ignatieff, Michael, 129
In Praise of Forgetting (Rieff), 5
International Center for Transitional Justice (ICTJ), xi–xii, 119, 120–21, 130, 146, 150–51
Inwood, Joshua, 192
Irwin-Zarecka, Iwona, 39

Jackson, Miss., 18, 23, 42, 53, 129; *Clarion-Ledger* and, 12, 19, 30, 33, 61, 91, 116; desegregation and, 82, 83; Medgar Evers murder and, 22, 57; Mississippi Truth Project (MTP) and, 109, 110, 117, 119, 121, 125
Jackson Free Press, 72, 91
Jackson State University, 92, 94–95
Japan, 63
Japanese Americans, 112–13
Jasper, James, 153, 154, 156–57
Jeffries, Vincent, 155
Jet magazine, 154
Johnson, Earl, Jr., 21
Johnson, Lyndon B., 24
Jones, Lillian, 30
Junior, Pamela, 183–84

Kennedy, Robert F., 24
Kilgore, Don, 66
Killen, Edgar Ray "Preacher," 13, 68, 204; conviction and, 2, 59, 60, 62, 76–78, 87, 91, 96, 114–16, 118, 124, 129, 130, 133, 186; death and, 186, 187; earlier trial and, 29, 60, 61; legal challenges and, 186; trial and, 15, 74, 75, 78, 79, 90–91, 130, 172, 179, 194, 201, 203, 224n42, 227n53. *See also* fortieth anniversary commemoration; Mississippi Burning murders; Neshoba County; Philadelphia, Miss.
King, Martin Luther, Jr., 2, 7, 32–33, 34, 100, 149, 170, 174
Kirksey, Elsie, 148–49, 150, 165
Klandermans, Bert, 148, 149, 150
Kolberg, Lawrence, 85
Kubal, Timothy, 8
Ku Klux Klan, 19, 20, 64, 166; Greensboro Massacre and, 114, 120; Mississippi Burning murders and, 1, 25, 26, 28–29, 30, 33, 39, 129; Mississippi Summer Project and, 21–22, 23, 24, 34; Mt. Zion United Methodist Church firebombing and, 24, 33, 47, 101, 164, 193; Philadelphia and, 22, 26, 42–43, 48, 69; reopening murders case and, 61, 62, 74

Labuda, Patryk, 129
Ladd, Donna, 72, 91
Lauderdale County, 41, 60
Lee, Chungmei, 83
Lee, Clay, 25, 28
Lewis, John, 55, 72–73, 77, 104, 163, 185–86
Life magazine, 26
"Lift Every Voice and Sing" (ballad), 125, 142
Loewe, Ronald, 194
Loewen, James, 84, 94
Longdale community, 24, 106, 170, 193, 194, 203. *See also* Mt. Zion United Methodist Church

Los Angeles, 155
Lott, Trent, 143, 168
lynching, 4, 112, 135, 154, 168, 180

Mabus, Ray, 142, 147, 162
MacArthur Foundation, 64
Managing Truth Commissions affinity group, 121
Mannheim, Karl, 146
Mars, Florence, 17, 18, 28, 29, 35
McAdam, Doug, 23
McCammon, Holly, 143
McClain, Charles, 29
McDonald, Janis, 187
McDonald, Jewel Rush, 164
"memory boom," 3, 211–12n8
Memory movements, 130–31, 213n30, 231n9; commemorations and, 8–10, 78, 79, 143, 148, 166, 174–75, 176, 214n48; difficult pasts and, 37–39, 174–75; as social movements and, 6–10, 134, 136, 139, 166, 176, 182
Meredith, James, 53
Meridian, Miss., 18, 23, 24, 27, 28–29, 41, 115, 195, 203
Meridian Naval Air Station, 24–25
Milam, J. W., 180
Mill, John Stuart, 12, 137
Millsaps College, 84, 117
Minor, Bill, 42
Minor, Wilson F., 21
Mississippi: A History (Bettersworth), 84, 225–26n18
Mississippi Band of Choctaw Indians, 17–18, 88, 199, 203; fortieth anniversary commemoration and, 1, 52–53, 69–70, 160
Mississippi bicentennial, 183, 237n40
Mississippi Burning (movie, 1988), xii, 1, 60, 144, 160; twenty-fifth anniversary commemoration impetus and, 40–44, 46, 56, 57–58, 171, 221n46
Mississippi Burning murders, 26–27, 132; apology for and, 47, 55, 140, 143, 222n52; case closure and, 186–87; commemorability and, 40, 55–56; earlier commemorations and, 2, 13–14, 16, 30, 33–35, 41, 57, 102, 170, 177; earlier trial and, 29, 60, 61, 62, 76; early memorial march and, 2, 16, 34, 170; events of and, 1–2, 24–29, 61, 99; events of commemorations of and, 198–200, 240n11; fiftieth anniversary and, 106, 107, 108, 185–86, 204; Killen conviction and, 2, 60, 62, 76–78, 114–16, 118, 129, 186; Killen trial and, 63, 65, 66, 79, 90–91, 92, 131, 168; later commemorations and, 13, 89–91, 118, 194–95, 203–4; libraries and archives and, 12, 201, 215n56; many-years' silence and, 13, 14, 16, 29, 33, 36–37, 39, 47, 49–50, 55, 57, 58, 60, 76, 151, 169, 170; murder site and, 1, 26, 61, 185; reopening case and, 60–62, 65–66, 68, 71, 73–74, 76, 224n42. *See also* African American community; Chaney, James Earl (J. E.); Civil rights movement; fortieth anniversary commemoration; Goodman, Andrew; Ku Klux Klan; *Mississippi Burning* (movie, 1988); Mt. Zion United Methodist Church; Neshoba County; Philadelphia, Miss.; press coverage of Mississippi Burning murders; Schwerner, Michael H.; twenty-fifth anniversary commemoration; White community
Mississippi civil rights education commission, 81, 94–95
Mississippi Civil Rights Museum, 183–84, 237n40
Mississippi Coalition for Racial Justice (McRJ), 116–17, 119, 120, 121, 125, 130
Mississippi: Conflict and Change (Loewen and Sallis), 84, 94
Mississippi constitution, 142
Mississippi Department of Archives and History, 180, 201

Mississippi Department of Education, 12, 94, 187–88
Mississippi Development Authority, 53, 58, 199
Mississippi Freedom Democratic Party, 31, 32, 33, 100
Mississippi History Museum, 183, 237n40
Mississippi Legislature, 21, 163; African Americans and, 65, 85, 91, 93, 110; civil rights education and, 2, 14, 59, 90, 92–95, 96, 169, 187–88, 227n53; Holocaust education and, 84–86, 92, 96, 226n25, 226n30; Killen conviction and, 91, 96; public education and, 81, 82, 83–84; truth commission and, 85, 110, 113
Mississippi Martyrs Memorial xii, xiii, 106, 203
Mississippi Senate Bill 2718, 11, 14, 81, 84, 85, 92–95, 96, 187, 191, 227n53
Mississippi State Board of Education: civil rights education and, 81, 84, 86, 87–88, 90, 91, 92–96, 97–98; curriculum and, 83–84, 87, 95, 97, 225–26n18, 226n22; desegregation and, 80–81, 82–83, 87
Mississippi State Sovereignty Commission, 21, 114, 116
Mississippi State University, 65
Mississippi Summer Project, 12, 20–23, 34, 99, 115, 201
Mississippi: The Closed Society (Silver), 80
Mississippi Truth Project (MTP), 2, 172, 211n3 [1]; beginnings and, xii, 59, 85, 109, 118–20, 121–22, 229n38; challenges to and, 126–28, 189; civil rights education and, 191, 227n3; declaration of intent and, 121, 122–25, 128; declaration of intent signing and, 109, 125–26, 202, 222–23n84; fortieth anniversary commemoration and, 11, 14, 110, 114, 117, 129–30, 131, 133, 134, 169, 198, 200; Hurricane Katrina and, 109, 117, 189; mandate and, 122, 127, 128; oral histories and, 127–29, 190, 222–23n84, 227n3; origins of and, 109–10, 129–30, 227n3; outcomes and, 128–31, 189–92, 227n3, 229n49, 230n73; story-telling and, 122, 127. *See also* Jackson, Miss.; Truth and Reconciliation Commission (South Africa) (TRC); truth commissions; William Winter Institute for Racial Reconciliation
Mitchell, Jerry, 44, 61, 64, 223n22
mnemonic capacity, 9, 40, 135, 138–39, 151, 157, 166, 172, 231n9
"mnemonic opportunity structure," 176–77, 236n18
Mohammed, Curtis, 193
Molpus, Dick, 52, 147; fortieth anniversary commemoration and, 49, 53, 55, 158, 199; twenty-fifth anniversary commemoration and, 42, 45–46, 47–48, 49, 55, 140, 143, 157, 221n45
moonshine, 24
Moore, Charles Eddie, 25
Moore, John, 188
Moore, Mike, 60–62, 71
Moore, Nettie Cox. *See* Cox, Nettie
Morris, Willie, 19
Mt. Nebo Baptist Church, 30, 35, 102, 170, 177
Mt. Zion United Methodist Church: annual commemorations and, 13, 33, 34–35, 51–52, 68, 101, 158, 170, 185, 194, 203; fiftieth anniversary and, 105, 108, 185–86; fortieth anniversary commemoration and, 54, 55, 68, 137, 158, 161, 193, 199; historical marker and, 48, 108, 133; Ku Klux Klan firebombing and, 24, 33, 47, 101, 164, 193; Mississippi Burning murders and, 13, 24; twenty-fifth anniversary commemoration and, 46, 47, 48, 133, 137, 157

Nash, Diane, 106, 193, 195
National Association for the Advancement of Colored People (NAACP), 20, 22, 27–28, 46, 49, 57, 64, 144, 157, 158

National Civil Rights Conference, 194, 195, 203
National Memorial for Peace and Justice, 4
National Portrait Gallery, 173
Nature of Prejudice (Allport), 155
Neshoba County: commemorations and, 3, 7, 16–17, 146–47, 170, 195; earlier commemorations and, 13, 33–35, 101; fortieth anniversary commemoration and, 67, 70, 114, 132, 133, 151, 159, 160, 164, 165, 169, 183, 214n49; historical markers and, 48, 108, 133, 185; history and, 17–20; interviews and, 12–13, 169, 197, 202–3, 241n18; Killen conviction and, 2, 60, 76, 91; Killen trial and, 65, 76, 115, 116, 203; Ku Klux Klan and, 19, 20, 21–22, 24; later commemorations and, xii–xiii, 13, 105, 106, 107, 108; *Mississippi Burning* (movie, 1988) and, 42–43; Mississippi Burning murders and, 1–2, 13, 24–30, 60, 129, 132, 137, 138, 187; recent race relations and, xiii, 2, 34; reopening murders case and, 61–62, 65, 73–75, 224n42; twenty-fifth anniversary commemoration and, 44, 45–46, 133, 148, 160, 169, 221n45. *See also* African American community; Mt. Zion United Methodist Church; white community
Neshoba County Coliseum, 1, 54–55, 68, 140, 161
Neshoba County Fair, 24
Neshoba Democrat, 12, 18, 19, 22, 66, 149, 179; fortieth anniversary commemoration and, 52, 54, 69, 147, 193; later commemorations and, xii–xiii, 185; Mississippi Burning murders coverage over the years and, 41, 43, 45, 48–49, 50, 75, 77; Stanley Dearman and, 41, 44, 48–49, 50, 51, 75, 77, 105
Neshoba Education Foundation, 89
Neshoba Youth Coalition, 185

Nevin, David, 26
New Orleans, 191, 239n38
New York City, 24, 31, 47, 48, 135, 146, 221n48
New York Times, 25, 33, 41–42, 43, 44, 62, 71, 220–21n31
New York Times Magazine, 142
North Carolina, 113–14, 120, 182
Northeastern University, 64
Northern Ireland, 145
Nuremberg trials, 62–63

Oklahoma, 17, 113
Olick, Jeffrey, 77–78, 112, 176, 202
One America Initiative, 49, 52, 139, 146, 159
oral histories, 92, 94, 127–29, 190, 201, 222–23n84, 227n3
Owens, Deborah, 88–89, 90

pacto del olvido, 6, 63
Palij, Jakiw, 63
Paraguay, 113
Parker, Alan, xii, 40–41
Parker, Keith, 194, 203
Patterson, Robert, 20
Pearl River Resort and Casino, 36, 52–53
Pearson, Betty, 180
Pennsylvania State University, 192
Peru, 121
Pettigrew, Thomas, 155
Pew Research Center, 192
Philadelphia, Miss., 132, 211n1; civil rights education and, 97, 189; collective memory and, 14, 39, 40; commemorations and, 3, 11, 58, 180, 181, 182, 197, 204–5; commemorative capacity and, 87, 95, 139, 175; Community Development Partnership (CDP) and, 1, 36, 52, 53, 55, 58, 139, 159; earlier commemorations and, 2, 13–14, 16, 30, 33, 34–35, 41, 57, 102, 170; fiftieth anniversary and, 105, 106, 107, 185–86; forty-first

Index   279

Philadelphia, Miss. (cont.)
anniversary and, 89–91, 129; Independence Quarters and, 19, 30, 33, 34, 102, 170; Killen conviction and, 60, 91, 124, 129, 130; Killen trial and, 90–91, 92, 93, 96, 115, 116, 130, 131, 169, 179, 227n53; Ku Klux Klan and, 22, 26, 42–43, 48, 69; later commemorations and, xii–xiii, 13, 105–7, 118, 185–86, 194–95, 203–4; *Mississippi Burning* (movie, 1988) and, 40, 41–42, 44, 57–58, 171; Mississippi Burning murders and, 1–2, 13, 25–26, 27–28, 29, 39, 40, 48–49, 103; political environment from 1964–2004 and, 139–42; recent race relations and, 2, 11, 15, 59, 147, 168, 184, 185–86, 194, 198; reopening murders case and, 74–75, 76; tourism and, 36, 43–44, 52–53, 55, 58, 139, 159, 166. *See also* African American community; fortieth anniversary commemoration; Mississippi Burning murders; Mississippi Truth Project (MTP); Neshoba County; Press coverage of commemorations; Press coverage of Mississippi Burning murders; twenty-fifth anniversary commemoration; White community

Philadelphia, Pa., 46, 47, 56, 138, 157, 211n1 [2], 221n46, 221n47. *See also* twenty-fifth anniversary commemoration

Philadelphia Coalition, 12, 175, 179, 203; civil rights education and, 87–90, 91–92; commitment and, 15, 148–49, 150, 151, 157, 165–66, 167, 173; financial and political support and, 163, 199; fortieth anniversary commemoration aftermath and, 10, 185, 194; fortieth anniversary commemoration and, 1, 7, 72–73, 77, 95, 132, 140, 142, 144, 147, 199; intergroup contact and, 157, 164, 165, 167; interracial collaboration and, 53, 54, 56, 72, 78, 117–18, 167, 168, 193–94; justice resolution and, 62, 68, 69, 70, 71, 73, 75, 76, 87, 91, 103, 163, 190; Killen conviction and, 62, 91, 114–15, 116, 124; Killen trial and, 194, 224n42; outside group commemoration and, 67–68, 193–94; storytelling and, 87–89, 167, 173; truth project and, 118, 127, 130. *See also* William Winter Institute for Racial Reconciliation

Philadelphia-Neshoba Tourism Board, 36

Philadelphia-to-Philadelphia project, 46, 138, 157–58, 162, 221n46, 221n47. *See also* twenty-fifth anniversary commemoration

Polletta, Francesca, 153, 156

Posey, Burford, 27–28

Posey, Deborah, 132, 149, 150, 161, 164, 165

press coverage of commemorations, 12, 201; earlier commemorations and, 30, 33, 170; fortieth anniversary commemoration and, 52, 72, 77, 147, 193–94; fortieth anniversary commemoration justice resolution and, 70–71, 103, 163; fortieth anniversary commemoration local and national and, 2, 54–55, 132, 163; Killen trial and, 91, 114–15, 179; later commemorations and, xii–xiii, 185; twenty-fifth anniversary commemoration and, 45, 50, 176. *See also* Clarion-Ledger (Jackson); *Neshoba Democrat*

press coverage of Mississippi Burning murders: fortieth anniversary commemoration and, 75–76, 77; local and national at the time and, 2, 25–26, 220–21n31; remembering over the years and, 41–42, 43, 48–49, 57, 75, 201, 220–21n31; twenty-fifth anniversary commemoration and, 50, 56–57

Price, Cecil, 24, 33, 34, 62, 74

Price, Cecil, Jr., 30

280 Index

Prince, Jim, 45, 49–52, 179, 184, 185; fortieth anniversary commemoration aftermath and, 89, 149; fortieth anniversary commemoration and, 53, 54, 55, 75, 77, 144, 158, 159, 160, 165, 193, 194, 199, 222n68; fortieth anniversary commemoration justice resolution and, 66, 70, 73, 103

Rabin, Yitzhak, 37, 38, 175, 219n8
Racial Reckoning (Romano), 187
racial violence, 19, 113–14, 122, 155; commemorations of and, xiii, 2, 3, 15, 135, 136, 152, 167, 169, 173, 174, 178–79, 180, 184; lynching and, 4, 112, 135, 154, 168, 180; Mt. Zion United Methodist Church firebombing and, 24, 33, 47, 101, 164, 193; political regret and, 3–4, 64, 146, 187. *See also* Mississippi Burning murders; Mississippi Truth Project (MTP); truth commissions
racism, xi, 96, 168, 184, 192
Rainey, Lawrence, 24, 26, 33
Rand, Clayton, 19
Ransford, Edward, 155
Raspberry, William, 168
Reconstruction, 19, 29, 50, 91
Recovered Roots (Y. Zerubavel), 31
Red Record, The (Wells), 112
Remembering Emmett Till (Tell), 180
Restorative Justice for Oakland Youth, 192
Ricoeur, Paul, 5
Rieff, David, 5
Roberts, George, 193
Romano, Renee, 79, 187
Rondini, Ashley, 97, 188
Roof, Dylann, 4
Rosewood Compensation Bill, 113
Rosewood race riot, 113
Rowell, Kaye, 53
Rueschemeyer, Dietrich, 205
Rush, Georgia, 164

Rush, John Thomas, 164
Rushdie, Salman, 61

"Saladin Project," 61
Sallis, Charles, 84, 94
Santayana, George, 3
Satanic Verses, The (Rushdie), 61
Schomburg Center for Research in Black Culture, 201
Schudson, Michael, 6, 176
Schuman, Howard, 146
Schwartz, Barry, 37, 145
Schwerner, Michael H.: civil rights education and, 89–90, 91, 92, 95; commemorating death of and, xii, 16, 30–32, 33, 34, 36, 48, 101, 105, 108; fortieth anniversary commemoration of death and, 1, 104, 132, 137, 147, 193–94; Killen conviction and, 60, 76, 79, 129; marble memorial for and, 30, 35, 102; missing posters and, 32–33, 99, 100, 137–38; Mississippi Summer Project and, 23, 24, 115; murder and, 1–2, 23, 24–26, 28, 61, 76, 101, 164, 201; reopening murders case and, 61, 75; twenty-fifth anniversary of death and, 47, 137, 142, 143, 221n48. *See also* fortieth anniversary commemoration; Mississippi Burning murders; twenty-fifth anniversary commemoration
Schwerner, Rita, 23, 32, 47. *See also* Bender, Rita
segregation. *See* desegregation
September 11, 2001, 174
Sewell, William, 197
Shannon, Ta'Shia, 132, 133
Silver, James, 27, 80
slavery, 4, 84, 96, 122, 146, 225–26n18
Smith, Hazel Brannon, 29
Snow, David, 123
social justice: civil rights cold cases and, 60, 61, 63–65, 76, 79, 133, 187, 223n22; commemorations and, 4–6, 212n16; fortieth anniversary

social justice (cont.)
commemoration and, 66–67, 68, 69–71, 72–73; human rights violations and, 62–63, 111, 113, 120, 145, 228n7; political regret and, 146, 212n9; victims' families' memories and, 60, 63–64, 73, 77, 223n22. *See also* press coverage of Mississippi Burning murders; truth commissions

social movements, 96, 116, 174, 214n40, 236n15; collective action outcomes and, 182; commitment and, 148, 150, 156; emotion and, 153–54, 155–56; intergroup contact and, 154, 155–57, 234n15, 234n18, 234n22memory activists and, 77–78, 134; memory movements and, 6–10, 136, 139, 166, 176, 182; mobilizing target audiences and, 122–24; shared resources and, 161–62, 219n6

Society of the Daughters of the American Revolution, 83

Sons of Mississippi (Hendrickson), 27

South Africa, 130, 156, 237n35. *See also* Truth and Reconciliation Commission (South Africa) (TRC)

South Carolina, 4, 191

South Carolina Collaborative on Race and Reconciliation, 191

Southeast Tourism Society Professional Marketing Institute, 53

"Southern Exposure: A Regional Summit on Racial Violence and Reconciliation" (conference), 119

Southern Poverty Law Center, 94, 187, 189, 192, 238n19, 238n26

South Korea, 63, 112

Spain, 6, 63

Springfield race riots (1908), 136

Steele, Cornelius, 24

Steele, John, 54, 193, 194

Steele, Mabel, 34, 193

Steidl, Christina, 38

Stonewall Riots, 9, 134–35, 177

Storey, Peter, 126, 190

story-telling, 67, 87–89, 109, 122, 127, 156, 164–65, 166, 167, 173, 222n67

Stringer, Bob, 62

Student Nonviolent Coordinating Committee (SNCC), 20, 22, 23, 31, 137

Subject Area Testing Program (SATP), 90

Sullivan, Joseph, 26

Sustainable Equity, 191

Syracuse University Law School, 64, 187

systematic comparison, 11, 170

Tallahatchie County, 180

Talley, Pete, 46, 157

Tannehill, Jack, 45

Taylor, Verta, 116, 150

Teeger, Chana, 94

Tell, Dave, 180

Tell John (radio show), 110

Thanksgiving holiday, 37

Thomas, Alex, 53, 139

Thompson, Bennie, 180

Till, Emmett, 7, 64, 66, 154, 180, 187

Till Bill. *See* Emmett Till Unsolved Civil Rights Crime Act of 2008

Tisdale, Eva, 68

Tollison, Gary, 93, 227n53

Tougaloo College, 84, 92, 94

tourism, 43–44, 195; African American community and, 36, 52, 53, 55, 58, 139, 159, 166; casino tourism and, 36, 52–53, 199

Trail of Tears, 69–70

transitional justice, xi–xii, 96, 111, 114, 119, 120–21, 126, 130, 133, 145–46, 213n23

Treaty of Dancing Rabbit Creek of 1831, 17

Trump, Donald, 183

Truth, Racial Healing, and Transformation initiative, 192, 239n49

Truth and Reconciliation Commission (South Africa) (TRC), 146, 181–82, 228n8, 237n35; Mississippi Truth Project (MTP) and, 2, 14, 59, 85, 109,

110, 118, 126, 189, 190, 192, 222–23n84; other truth commissions and, xi, 111, 114, 120, 126
truth commissions, xi, 5, 109, 110–14, 126, 228n7, 228n12, 229n49, 230n76; political regret and, 112, 113, 145; in the United States, xii, 112–14, 118, 119, 120–21, 123, 130, 182, 192, 211n3 [1], 222–23n84. *See also* Greensboro Truth and Reconciliation Commission; Mississippi Truth Project (MTP); Truth and Reconciliation Commission (South Africa) (TRC)
Truth Telling Project, 192
Tucker, Charles, 129, 191
Tulsa Race Riot Reconciliation Act, 113
Turberville, Howard, 121, 122
Turner, Ken, 61–62
Tuskeegee syphilis experiments, 146
Tutu, Desmond, 109, 110
Twain, Mark, 183
twenty-fifth anniversary commemoration, 147, 199; African American community and, 46, 143–44, 157, 158; aftermath of and, 57, 58–59, 138–39, 140, 148, 172, 175–76, 221n45; commemoration program and, 45, 47–48, 55, 140, 142, 222n52; compared with fortieth anniversary commemoration and, 11–12, 14–15, 49, 133–34, 136, 137, 138–39, 144, 150–51, 172, 231n6; financial and political support and, 142–43, 162–63; impetus for and, 40–44, 46, 56–58, 171, 198, 221n46; intergroup contact and, 153, 157, 160, 166–67; interracial collaboration and, 35, 133, 153, 157, 160, 164, 169, 171; outside support and, 46, 47, 56, 138, 157–58, 162, 221n47, 221n48; planning process and, 45–46, 49, 52, 157, 158–59, 160; silence-breaking and, 14, 36–37, 40, 58, 143, 144, 170, 171; white community and, 44, 46, 58–59, 142–43. *See also* fortieth anniversary commemoration; Mt. Zion United Methodist Church; press coverage of commemorations; press coverage of Mississippi Burning murders

Union, Miss., 13, 204
United Nations Decade for Human Rights Education, 86
United Nations Educational, Scientific, and Cultural Organization, 90
U.S. Department of Education, curriculum and, 86–87
U.S. Department of Justice, 1, 70, 71, 187
U.S. House of Representatives, 143, 185
U.S. Senate, 143, 168
U.S. Supreme Court, 20, 51, 80, 82, 83, 143, 146, 172, 184, 186
University of Mississippi, 27, 41, 44, 45, 49, 54, 80, 92, 119, 201, 202; desegregation commemoration and, 53, 159; One America Initiative and, 52, 139, 159. *See also* William Winter Institute for Racial Reconciliation
University of South Carolina (USC), 191
University of Southern Mississippi, 92, 94, 128, 190, 201
Uruguay, 113

Van Zyl, Paul, 120
Vietnam Veterans Memorial, 145, 212–13n19
Vietnam War, 37, 38
Vinitzky-Seroussi, Vered, 37, 94, 175, 219n8
Vivian, C. T., 193
voter registration, 22, 23, 142–43
Voting Rights Act of 1965, 137, 184

Waddell, Rayburn, 70–71, 103, 132
Wagner-Pacifici, Robin, 37, 145
Ward, Hope Morgan, 125
Watts race riot, 155
Weber, Max, 11
Weems, Patrick, 117–18, 190

Welcome Table program, 89, 117–18, 127, 128, 129, 190, 192, 227n3; New Orleans and, 191, 239n38
Welcome Table SC, 191
Wells, Ida B., 112
Wells Memorial United Methodist Church, 119
Wellspring, 117
Welty, Eudora, 142
Wheeler, Lonnie, 30
White, Malcolm, 195
White Citizens' Council, 20–21, 69, 72, 82, 114, 163
white community, 18–19, 140–43, 216n2, 216n5, 216n7; civil rights education and, 89, 97; civil rights movement and, 20–22, 35, 152–53; commemorations and, 14, 16–17, 33, 35, 39; desegregation and, 82–83, 170, 225n12; fortieth anniversary commemoration and, 52, 66, 69, 70–71, 72, 114–15, 132, 144, 160–61, 163, 165; history textbooks and, 80, 83–84, 225n1, 225–26n18; Mississippi Burning murders and, 14, 16, 25, 27–29, 33, 35, 89, 114–15, 132, 138, 170; segregated education and, 81–84; twenty-fifth anniversary commemoration and, 44, 46, 58–59, 142–43. *See also* Ku Klux Klan
Wild Birds, The (Berry), 150
Wilkerson, Steve, 88, 138–39, 140, 149, 159, 160

Wilkins, Roy, 22
Williamson, Gloria, 93
William Winter Institute for Racial Reconciliation, 12, 179, 185, 201–2, 239n38; civil rights education and, 89–90, 91, 92, 93, 94, 95, 96, 108, 189; fortieth anniversary commemoration and, 54, 56, 67, 77, 78, 93, 130, 159, 172, 199; fortieth anniversary commemoration justice resolution and, 70, 71; founding of and, 52, 139; truth project and, 116, 117–19, 120, 121, 125, 126, 127–28, 130, 190, 191–92, 222–23n84. *See also* Glisson, Susan; Philadelphia Coalition; Welcome Table program
Wilmington Race Riots, 113
Winter, William, 45, 52, 116, 130, 139. *See also* William Winter Institute for Racial Reconciliation
Wisconsin Historical Society, 201
Witness in Philadelphia (Mars), 17
W. K. Kellogg Foundation, 191, 192
Wonderful Life (Gould), 11
World War II, 63, 112

Young, James, 11, 66, 69, 185, 194, 198
"Yuppies of Mississippi, The" (Boyer), 142

Zerubavel, Eviatar, 29, 38, 78, 183
Zerubavel, Yael, 31

www.ingramcontent.com/pod-product-compliance
Lightning Source LLC
Chambersburg PA
CBHW021933081225
36429CB00050B/438